iOS 7 Programming Fundamentals

Objective-C, Xcode, and Cocoa Basics

Matt Neuburg

Beijing · Cambridge · Farnham · Köln · Sebastopol · Tokyo

iOS 7 Programming Fundamentals

by Matt Neuburg

Copyright © 2014 Matt Neuburg. All rights reserved.

Printed in the United States of America.

Published by O'Reilly Media, Inc., 1005 Gravenstein Highway North, Sebastopol, CA 95472.

O'Reilly books may be purchased for educational, business, or sales promotional use. Online editions are also available for most titles (*http://my.safaribooksonline.com*). For more information, contact our corporate/institutional sales department: 800-998-9938 or *corporate@oreilly.com*.

Editor: Rachel Roumeliotis	**Cover Designer:** Karen Montgomery
Production Editor: Kristen Brown	**Interior Designer:** David Futato
Proofreader: O'Reilly Production Services	**Illustrator:** Matt Neuburg
Indexer: Matt Neuburg	

October 2013:   First Edition

Revision History for the First Edition:

2013-10-10:   First release

See *http://oreilly.com/catalog/errata.csp?isbn=9781491945575* for release details.

ISBN: 978-1-491-94557-5

[LSI]

Table of Contents

Part III.   Cocoa

Preface

After three editions of my book on programming iOS — *Programming iOS 4* (May 2011), *Programming iOS 5* (March 2012), and *Programming iOS 6* (March 2013) — it is as if a friendly but powerful giant had ripped the book in two, just after the end of Part III (Chapter 13). There are now *two* books:

- This book, *iOS 7 Programming Fundamentals*, comprising chapters 1–13 of the earlier books.
- The other book, *Programming iOS 7*, comprising chapters 14–40 of the earlier books.

The giant was friendly, because it was high time. *Programming iOS 6* had grown to an unwieldy and forbidding 1150 pages. In fact, I had been begging for this giant even before *Programming iOS 4* was published — indeed, before it was even conceived of. My original proposal to O'Reilly Media, back in early 2010, had been for a book to be called *Fundamentals of Cocoa Programming*, intended to cover very much the same material as the present book, *iOS 7 Programming Fundamentals*. But the proposal was accepted only on condition that it be extended to cover much more of Cocoa Touch (iOS) programming; so I complied and set to work on this longer project, and later, despite my impassioned pleas in the autumn of 2010, I was unable to persuade the publisher to break up the lengthy manuscript into two: by that time, all the king's horses and all the king's men could no longer crack Humpty Dumpty apart.

The new situation, therefore, is just what I always wanted in the first place — but not quite, because what I most desired was a single book in two volumes. My idea was that the books would have the same title, distinguished as Volume I and Volume II, with successive numbering of pages and chapters: if Volume I ended, say, with Chapter 13 and page 400, then Volume II would start with Chapter 14 and page 401. To this delightfully Victorian extreme, I'm sorry to say, O'Reilly Media were implacably opposed.

Thus, *Programming iOS 7*, though it starts with its own Chapter 1 and page 1, nevertheless still picks up exactly where *iOS 7 Programming Fundamentals* leaves off. They complement and supplement one another. Those who desire a complete grounding in the knowledge needed to begin writing iOS apps with a solid and rigorous understanding of what they are doing and where they are heading will, I hope, obtain both books. At the same time, the two-book architecture should, I believe, render the size and scope of each book individually more acceptable and attractive to more readers.

Those who feel that they know already all there is to know about C, Objective-C, Xcode, and the linguistic and architectural basis of the Cocoa framework, or who are content to pick up such underpinnings as they go along, need no longer (as some in the past have done) complain that the book is occupied with 13 preliminary chapters before the reader starts really writing any significant iOS code, because those 13 chapters have now been abstracted into a separate volume, *iOS 7 Programming Fundamentals*, and the other book, *Programming iOS 7*, now begins, like Homer's *Iliad*, in the middle of the story, with the reader jumping with all four feet into views and view controllers, and with a knowledge of the language and the Xcode IDE already presupposed. And if such a reader subsequently changes his or her mind and decides that a thorough grounding in those underpinnings might in fact be desirable, *iOS 7 Programming Fundamentals* will still be available and awaiting study.

As for this book, *iOS 7 Programming Fundamentals* itself, it is the prodigal child, the book I originally wanted to write but which was then subsumed during three editions into the larger world of *Programming iOS 4*, *Programming iOS 5*, and *Programming iOS 6*. Now it is home again, where it belongs, in a volume of its own. Its three parts teach the underlying basis of all iOS programming:

- Part I introduces the Objective-C language, starting with C (which constitutes much more of practical Objective-C than many beginners realize) and then building up to the object-oriented concepts and mechanics of classes and instances.

- Part II takes a break from language and turns to Xcode, the world in which all iOS programming ultimately takes place. It explains what an Xcode project is and how it is transformed into an app, and how to work comfortably and nimbly with Xcode to consult the documentation and to write, navigate, and debug code, as well as how to bring your app through the subsequent stages of running on a device and submission to the App Store. There is also a very important chapter on nibs and the nib editor (Interface Builder), including outlets and actions as well as the mechanics of nib loading; however, such specialized topics as autolayout constraints in the nib are postponed to the other book.

- Part III returns to Objective-C, this time from the point of view of the Cocoa Touch framework. Cocoa provides important foundational classes and adds linguistic and architectural devices such as categories, protocols, delegation, and notifications, as well as the pervasive responsibilities of memory management. Key–value coding and key–value observing are also discussed here.

The reader of this book will thus get a thorough grounding in the fundamental knowledge and techniques that any good iOS programmer needs. The book itself doesn't show how to write any particularly interesting iOS apps (though it is backed by dozens of example projects that you can download from my GitHub site, *http://github.com/matt neub/Programming-iOS-Book-Examples*), but it does constantly use my own real apps and real programming situations to illustrate and motivate its explanations. And then you'll be ready for *Programming iOS 7*, of course!

Versions

This book is geared to iOS 7 and Xcode 5. In general, only very minimal attention is given to earlier versions of iOS and Xcode. It is not my intention to embrace in this book any detailed knowledge about earlier versions of the software, which is, after all, readily and compendiously available in my earlier books. There are, nevertheless, a few words of advice about backwards compatibility, and now and then I will call out a particularly noteworthy change from earlier versions. For example, it has been hard to refrain from pointing out the confusing accretions of interface and terminology caused by the changes in how the status bar works and in the sizes of icons and launch images.

Xcode 5 no longer offers the user, creating a new app project from one of the project templates, an option as to whether or not to use Automatic Reference Counting (ARC), the compiler-based manual memory management technology that has made life so much easier for iOS programmers in recent years. ARC is simply turned on by default. Therefore, this book assumes from the outset that you are using ARC. I do still quite often distinguish the ARC compiler behavior from the non-ARC compiler behavior, but I no longer describe what the non-ARC behavior is, except in Chapter 12 where I still explain what ARC does by describing what you would have to do if you weren't using it.

Xcode also no longer provides a template-based option as to whether or not to use a storyboard. All projects (except the Empty Application template) come with a main storyboard, and there is no option to use a main *.xib* file instead. Taking my cue from this, I have adapted my teaching style to assume that storyboards are primary and that you'll usually be using one. I do also show how to construct a project whose nibs come entirely from *.xib* files; this is more work than in the past, because you can't do it simply by unchecking a checkbox in the template-creation dialog.

I have also embraced, often without much fanfare, the various other iOS 7 and Xcode 5 innovations. Apple has clearly set out, with this generation of their software, to make iOS programming easier and more pleasant than ever; and by and large they have succeeded. Such innovations as modules and autolinking, asset catalogs, the Accounts preference pane, and the Test navigator contrive to make your life far more comfortable, and I simply assume as a matter of course that you will want to use them.

Acknowledgments

My thanks go first and foremost to the people at O'Reilly Media who have made writing a book so delightfully easy: Rachel Roumeliotis, Sarah Schneider, Kristen Brown, and Adam Witwer come particularly to mind. And let's not forget my first and long-standing editor, Brian Jepson, who had nothing whatever to do with this edition, but whose influence is present throughout.

I have been saved from many embarrassing errors by the sharp and dedicated eyes of Peter Olsen, a long-time reader who faithfully posts notes to the book's online Errata page, apparently just because that's the kind of amazing and dedicated person he is.

As in the past, I have been greatly aided by some fantastic software, whose excellences I have appreciated at every moment of the process of writing this book. I should like to mention, in particular:

- git (*http://git-scm.com*)
- SourceTree (*http://www.sourcetreeapp.com*)
- TextMate (*http://macromates.com*)
- AsciiDoc (*http://www.methods.co.nz/asciidoc*)
- BBEdit (*http://barebones.com/products/bbedit/*)
- Snapz Pro X (*http://www.ambrosiasw.com*)
- GraphicConverter (*http://www.lemkesoft.com*)
- OmniGraffle (*http://www.omnigroup.com*)

The book was typed and edited entirely on my faithful Unicomp Model M keyboard (*http://pckeyboard.com*), without which I could never have done so much writing over so long a period so painlessly. For more about my physical work environment, see *http://matt.neuburg.usesthis.com*.

From the Programming iOS 4 Preface

The popularity of the iPhone, with its largely free or very inexpensive apps, and the subsequent popularity of the iPad, have brought and will continue to bring into the fold many new programmers who see programming for these devices as worthwhile and doable, even though they may not have felt the same way about OS X. Apple's own annual WWDC developer conventions have reflected this trend, with their emphasis shifted from OS X to iOS instruction.

The widespread eagerness to program iOS, however, though delightful on the one hand, has also fostered a certain tendency to try to run without first learning to walk. iOS gives the programmer mighty powers that can seem as limitless as imagination itself, but it also has fundamentals. I often see questions online from programmers who are evidently deep into the creation of some interesting app, but who are stymied in a way that reveals quite clearly that they are unfamiliar with the basics of the very world in which they are so happily cavorting.

It is this state of affairs that has motivated me to write this book, which is intended to ground the reader in the fundamentals of iOS. I love Cocoa and have long wished to write about it, but it is iOS and its popularity that has given me a proximate excuse to do so. Here I have attempted to marshal and expound, in what I hope is a pedagogically helpful and instructive yet ruthlessly Euclidean and logical order, the principles on which sound iOS programming rests, including a good basic knowledge of Objective-C (starting with C itself) and the nature of object-oriented programming, advice on the use of the tools, the full story on how Cocoa objects are instantiated, referred to, put in communication with one another, and managed over their lifetimes, and a survey of the primary interface widgets and other common tasks. My hope, as with my previous books, is that you will both read this book cover to cover (learning something new often enough to keep you turning the pages) and keep it by you as a handy reference.

This book is not intended to disparage Apple's own documentation and example projects. They are wonderful resources and have become more wonderful as time goes on. I have depended heavily on them in the preparation of this book. But I also find that they don't fulfill the same function as a reasoned, ordered presentation of the facts. The online documentation must make assumptions as to how much you already know; it can't guarantee that you'll approach it in a given order. And online documentation is more suitable to reference than to instruction. A fully written example, no matter how well commented, is difficult to follow; it demonstrates, but it does not teach.

A book, on the other hand, has numbered chapters and sequential pages; I can assume you know C before you know Objective-C for the simple reason that Chapter 1 precedes Chapter 2. And along with facts, I also bring to the table a degree of experience, which I try to communicate to you. Throughout this book you'll see me referring to "common beginner mistakes"; in most cases, these are mistakes that I have made myself, in addition to seeing others make them. I try to tell you what the pitfalls are because I assume that, in the course of things, you will otherwise fall into them just as naturally as I did as I was learning. You'll also see me construct many examples piece by piece or extract and explain just one tiny portion of a larger app. It is not a massive finished program that teaches programming, but an exposition of the thought process that developed that program. It is this thought process, more than anything else, that I hope you will gain from reading this book.

Conventions Used in This Book

The following typographical conventions are used in this book:

Italic
> Indicates new terms, URLs, email addresses, filenames, and file extensions.

Constant width

Used for program listings, as well as within paragraphs to refer to program elements such as variable or function names, databases, data types, environment variables, statements, and keywords.

Constant width bold

Shows commands or other text that should be typed literally by the user.

Constant width italic

Shows text that should be replaced with user-supplied values or by values determined by context.

 This icon signifies a tip, suggestion, or general note.

 This icon indicates a warning or caution.

Using Code Examples

Supplemental material (code examples, exercises, etc.) is available for download at *https://github.com/mattneub/Programming-iOS-Book-Examples*.

This book is here to help you get your job done. In general, if example code is offered with this book, you may use it in your programs and documentation. You do not need to contact us for permission unless you're reproducing a significant portion of the code. For example, writing a program that uses several chunks of code from this book does not require permission. Selling or distributing a CD-ROM of examples from O'Reilly books does require permission. Answering a question by citing this book and quoting example code does not require permission. Incorporating a significant amount of example code from this book into your product's documentation does require permission.

We appreciate, but do not require, attribution. An attribution usually includes the title, author, publisher, and ISBN. For example: "*iOS 7 Programming Fundamentals* by Matt Neuburg (O'Reilly). Copyright 2014 Matt Neuburg, 978-1-491-94557-5."

If you feel your use of code examples falls outside fair use or the permission given above, feel free to contact us at *permissions@oreilly.com*.

Safari® Books Online

 *Safari Books Online* is an on-demand digital library that delivers expert content in both book and video form from the world's leading authors in technology and business.

Technology professionals, software developers, web designers, and business and creative professionals use Safari Books Online as their primary resource for research, problem solving, learning, and certification training.

Safari Books Online offers a range of product mixes and pricing programs for organizations, government agencies, and individuals. Subscribers have access to thousands of books, training videos, and prepublication manuscripts in one fully searchable database from publishers like O'Reilly Media, Prentice Hall Professional, Addison-Wesley Professional, Microsoft Press, Sams, Que, Peachpit Press, Focal Press, Cisco Press, John Wiley & Sons, Syngress, Morgan Kaufmann, IBM Redbooks, Packt, Adobe Press, FT Press, Apress, Manning, New Riders, McGraw-Hill, Jones & Bartlett, Course Technology, and dozens more. For more information about Safari Books Online, please visit us online.

How to Contact Us

Please address comments and questions concerning this book to the publisher:

O'Reilly Media, Inc.
1005 Gravenstein Highway North
Sebastopol, CA 95472
800-998-9938 (in the United States or Canada)
707-829-0515 (international or local)
707-829-0104 (fax)

We have a web page for this book, where we list errata, examples, and any additional information. You can access this page at *http://oreil.ly/ios7_programming_fundamentals*.

To comment or ask technical questions about this book, send email to *bookquestions@oreilly.com*.

For more information about our books, courses, conferences, and news, see our website at *http://www.oreilly.com*.

Find us on Facebook: *http://facebook.com/oreilly*

Follow us on Twitter: *http://twitter.com/oreillymedia*

Watch us on YouTube: *http://www.youtube.com/oreillymedia*

PART I
Language

Apple has provided a vast toolbox for programming iOS to make an app come to life and behave the way you want it to. That toolbox is the *API* (application programming interface). To use the API, you must speak the API's language. That language, for the most part, is Objective-C, which itself is built on top of C; some pieces of the API use C itself. This part of the book instructs you in the basics of these languages:

- Chapter 1 explains C. In general, you will probably not need to know all the ins and outs of C, so this chapter restricts itself to those aspects of C that you need to know in order to use both Objective-C and the C-based areas of the API.

- Chapter 2 prepares the ground for Objective-C, by discussing object-based programming in general architectural terms. It also explains some extremely important words that will be used throughout the book, along with the concepts that lie behind them.

- Chapter 3 introduces the basic syntax of Objective-C.

- Chapter 4 continues the explanation of Objective-C, discussing the nature of Objective-C classes, with emphasis on how to create a class in code.

- Chapter 5 completes the introduction to Objective-C, discussing how instances are created and initialized, along with an explanation of such related topics as polymorphism, instance variables, accessors, `self` and `super`, key–value coding, and properties.

We'll return in Part III to a description of further aspects of the Objective-C language — those that are particularly bound up with the Cocoa frameworks.

CHAPTER 1

Just Enough C

Do you believe in C? Do you believe in anything
that has to do with me?

—Leonard Bernstein and Stephen Schwartz,
Mass

To program for iOS, you need to speak to iOS. Everything you say to iOS will be in accordance with the iOS API. (An API, for *application programming interface*, is a list or specification of things you are allowed to say when communicating.) Therefore, you will need some knowledge of the C programming language, for two reasons:

- Most of the iOS API involves the Objective-C language, and most of your iOS programming will be in the Objective-C language. Objective-C is a superset of C. This means that Objective-C presupposes C; everything that is true of C trickles up to Objective-C. A common mistake is to forget that "Objective-C is C" and to neglect a basic understanding of C.

- Some of the iOS API involves C rather than Objective-C. Even in Objective-C code, you often need to use C data structures and C function calls. For example, a rectangle is represented as a CGRect, which is a C struct, and to create a CGRect from four numbers you call `CGRectMake`, which is a C function. The iOS API documentation will very often show you C expressions and expect you to understand them.

The best way to learn C is to read *The C Programming Language* (PTR Prentice Hall, 1988) by Brian W. Kernighan and Dennis M. Ritchie, commonly called K&R (Ritchie was the creator of C). It is one of the best computer books ever written: brief, dense, and stunningly precise and clear. K&R is so important for effective iOS programming that I keep a physical copy beside me at all times while coding, and I recommend that you do the same. Another useful manual is *The C Book*, by Mike Banahan, Declan Brady, and Mark Doran, available online at *http://publications.gbdirect.co.uk/c_book/*.

It would be impossible for me to describe all of C in a single chapter. C is not a large or difficult language, but it has some tricky corners and can be extremely subtle, powerful, and low-level. Moreover, since C is described fully and correctly in the manuals I've just mentioned, it would be a mistake for me to repeat what they can tell you better than I. So this chapter is *not* a technical manual of C.

You don't have to know *all* about C, though, in order to use Objective-C effectively; so my purpose in this chapter is to outline those aspects of C that are important for you to understand at the outset, before you start using Objective-C for iOS programming. This chapter is "Just Enough C" to start you off comfortably and safely.

If you know no C at all, I suggest that, as an accompaniment to this chapter, you also read select parts of K&R (think of this as "C: The Good Parts Version"). Here's my proposed K&R syllabus:

- Quickly skim K&R Chapter 1, the tutorial.
- Carefully read K&R Chapters 2 through 4.
- Read the first three sections of K&R Chapter 5 on pointers and arrays. You don't need to read the rest of Chapter 5 because you won't typically be doing any pointer arithmetic, but you do need to understand clearly what a pointer is, as Objective-C is all about objects, and every reference to an object is a pointer; you'll be seeing and using that * character constantly.
- Read also the first section of K&R Chapter 6, on structures (structs); as a beginner, you probably won't define any structs, but you will use them quite a lot, so you'll need to know the notation (for example, as I've already said, a CGRect is a struct).
- Glance over K&R Appendix B, which covers the standard library, because you may find yourself making certain standard library calls, such as the mathematical functions; forgetting that the library exists is a typical beginner mistake.

 The C defined in K&R is not precisely the C that forms the basis of Objective-C. Developments subsequent to K&R have resulted in further C standards (ANSI C, C89, C99), and the Xcode compiler extends the C language in its own ways. By default, Xcode projects are treated as GNU99, which is itself an extension of C99 (though you could specify another C standard if you really wanted to). Fortunately, the most important differences between K&R's C and Xcode's C are small, convenient improvements that are easily remembered, so K&R remains the best and most reliable C reference.

Compilation, Statements, and Comments

C is a compiled language. You write your program as text; to run the program, things proceed in two stages. First your text is compiled into machine instructions; then those machine instructions are executed. Thus, as with any compiled language, you can make two kinds of mistake:

- Any purely syntactic errors (meaning that you spoke the C language incorrectly) will be caught by the compiler, and the program won't even begin to run.

- If your program gets past the compiler, then it will run, but there is no guarantee that you haven't made some other sort of mistake, which can be detected only by noticing that the program doesn't behave as intended.

The C compiler is fussy, but you should accept its interference with good grace. The compiler is your friend: learn to love it. It may emit what looks like an irrelevant or incomprehensible error message, but when it does, the fact is that you've done something wrong and the compiler has helpfully caught it for you. Also, the compiler can warn you if something seems like a possible mistake, even though it isn't strictly illegal; these warnings, which differ from outright errors, are also helpful and should not be ignored.

I have said that running a program requires a preceding stage: compilation. But in fact there is another stage that precedes compilation: preprocessing. Preprocessing modifies your text, so when your text is handed to the compiler, it is not identical to the text you wrote. Preprocessing might sound tricky and intrusive, but in fact it proceeds only according to your instructions and is helpful for making your code clearer and more compact.

Xcode allows you to view the effects of preprocessing on your program text (choose Product → Perform Action → Preprocess [Filename]), so if you think you've made a mistake in instructing the preprocessor, you can track it down. I'll talk more later about some of the things you're likely to say to the preprocessor.

C is a statement-based language; every statement ends in a semicolon. (Forgetting the semicolon is a common beginner's mistake.) For readability, programs are mostly written with one statement per line, but this is by no means a hard and fast rule: long statements (which, unfortunately, arise very often because of Objective-C's verbosity) are commonly split over multiple lines, and extremely short statements are sometimes written two or three to a line. You cannot split a line just anywhere, however; for example, a literal string can't contain a return character. Indentation is linguistically meaningless and is purely a matter of convention (and C programmers argue over those conventions with near-religious fervor); Xcode helps "intelligently" by indenting automatically, and you can use its automatic indentation both to keep your code readable and to confirm that you're not making any basic syntactic mistakes.

Compiler History

Originally, Xcode's compiler was the free open source GCC (*http://gcc.gnu.org*). Eventually, Apple introduced its own free open source compiler, LLVM (*http://llvm.org*), also referred to as Clang, thus allowing for improvements that were impossible with GCC. Changing compilers is scary, so Apple proceeded in stages:

- In Xcode 3, along with both LLVM and GCC, Apple supplied a hybrid compiler, LLVM-GCC, which provided the advantages of LLVM compilation while parsing code with GCC for maximum backward compatibility, without making it the default compiler.

- In Xcode 4, LLVM-GCC became the default compiler, but GCC remained available.

- In Xcode 4.2, LLVM 3.0 became the default compiler, and pure GCC was withdrawn.

- In Xcode 4.6, LLVM advanced to version 4.2.

- In Xcode 5, LLVM-GCC has been withdrawn; the compiler is now LLVM 5.0, and the transition from GCC to LLVM is complete.

Comments are delimited in K&R C by /* ... */; the material between the delimiters can consist of multiple lines (K&R 1.2). In modern versions of C, a comment also can be denoted by two slashes (//); the rule is that if two slashes appear, they and everything after them on the same line are ignored:

```
int lower = 0; // lower limit of temperature table
```

These are sometimes called C++-style comments and are much more convenient for brief comments than the K&R comment syntax.

Throughout the C language (and therefore, throughout Objective-C as well), capitalization matters. All names are case-sensitive. There is no such data type as Int; it's lowercase "int." If you declare an int called lower and then try to speak of the same variable as Lower, the compiler will complain. By convention, variable names tend to start with a lowercase letter.

Variable Declaration, Initialization, and Data Types

C is a strongly typed language. Every variable must be declared, indicating its data type, before it can be used. Declaration can also involve explicit initialization, giving the variable a value; a variable that is declared but not explicitly initialized is of uncertain value (and should be regarded as dangerous until it *is* initialized). In K&R C, declarations must precede all other statements, but in modern versions of C, this rule is relaxed so that you don't have to declare a variable until just before you start using it:

```
int height = 2;
int width = height * 2;
height = height + 1;
int area = height * width;
```

The basic built-in C data types are all numeric: char (one byte), int (four bytes), float and double (floating-point numbers), and varieties such as short (short integer), long (long integer), unsigned short, and so on. A numeric literal may optionally express its type through a suffixed letter or letters: for example, 4 is an int, but 4UL is an unsigned long; 4.0 is a double, but 4.0f is a float. Objective-C makes use of some further numeric types derived from the C numeric types (by way of the `typedef` statement, K&R 6.7) designed to respond to the question of whether the processor is 64-bit; the most important of these are NSInteger (along with NSUInteger) and CGFloat. You don't need to use them explicitly unless an API tells you to, and even when you do, just think of NSInteger as int and CGFloat as float, and you'll be fine.

To *cast* (or *typecast*) a variable's value explicitly to another type, precede the variable's name with the other type's name in parentheses:

```
int height = 2;
float fheight = (float)height;
```

In that particular example, the explicit cast is unnecessary because the integer value will be cast to a float implicitly as it is assigned to a float variable, but it illustrates the notation. You'll find yourself typecasting quite a bit in Objective-C, mostly to subdue the worries of the compiler (examples appear in Chapter 3).

Another form of numeric initialization is the enumeration, or enum (K&R 2.3). It's a way of assigning names to a sequence of numeric values and is useful when a value represents one of several possible options. The Cocoa API uses this device a lot. For example, the three possible types of status bar animation might be defined like this:

```
typedef enum {
    UIStatusBarAnimationNone,
    UIStatusBarAnimationFade,
    UIStatusBarAnimationSlide,
} UIStatusBarAnimation;
```

That definition assigns the value 0 to the name `UIStatusBarAnimationNone`, the value 1 to the name `UIStatusBarAnimationFade`, and the value 2 to the name `UIStatusBar-AnimationSlide`. The upshot is that you can use the suggestively meaningful names without caring about, or even knowing, the arbitrary numeric values they represent. It's a useful idiom, and you may well have reason to define enumerations in your own code.

That definition also assigns the name UIStatusBarAnimation to this enumeration as a whole. A named enumeration is not a data type, but you can pretend that it is, and the compiler can warn you if you mix enumeration types. For example, suppose you were to write this code:

```
UIStatusBarAnimation anim = UIInterfaceOrientationPortrait;
```

That isn't illegal; `UIInterfaceOrientationPortrait` is another name for 0, just as if you had said `UIStatusBarAnimationNone`. However, it comes from a different named enumeration, namely UIInterfaceOrientation. The compiler detects this, and warns you. Just as with a real data type, you can even squelch that warning by typecasting.

In iOS 7, the status bar animation types are defined like this:

```
typedef NS_ENUM(NSInteger, UIStatusBarAnimation) {
    UIStatusBarAnimationNone,
    UIStatusBarAnimationFade,
    UIStatusBarAnimationSlide,
};
```

That notation was introduced in LLVM compiler version 4.0, which made its debut in Xcode 4.4. NS_ENUM is a macro, a form of preprocessor text substitution discussed at the end of this chapter; when the text substitution is performed, that code turns out to be shorthand for this:

```
typedef enum UIStatusBarAnimation : NSInteger UIStatusBarAnimation;
enum UIStatusBarAnimation : NSInteger {
    UIStatusBarAnimationNone,
    UIStatusBarAnimationFade,
    UIStatusBarAnimationSlide,
};
```

That looks almost exactly like the old way of expressing the same enumeration, but the new way involves some notation that isn't part of standard C, telling the compiler what variety of integer value is being used here (it's an NSInteger). This makes UIStatusBar-Animation even more like a genuine data type; in addition, the new enum notation lets Xcode help you more intelligently when performing code completion, as discussed in Chapter 9. Another macro, NS_OPTIONS, evaluates in Objective-C as a synonym of NS_ENUM (they are distinct only in C++ code, which is not discussed in this book).

There appears to be a native text type (a string) in C, but this is something of an illusion; behind the scenes, it is a null-terminated array of char. For example, in C you can write a string literal like this:

```
"string"
```

But in fact this is stored as 7 bytes, the numeric (ASCII) equivalents of each letter followed by a byte consisting of 0 to signal the end of the string. This data structure, called a C string, is rarely encountered while programming iOS. In general, when working with strings, you'll use an Objective-C object type called NSString. An NSString is totally different from a C string; it happens, however, that Objective-C lets you write a literal NSString in a way that looks very like a C string:

```
@"string"
```

Notice the at-sign! This expression is actually a directive to the Objective-C compiler to form an NSString object. A common mistake is forgetting the at-sign, thus causing your expression to be interpreted as a C string, which is a completely different animal.

Because the notation for literal NSStrings is modeled on the notation for C strings, it is worth knowing something about C strings, even though you won't generally encounter them. For example, K&R lists a number of escaped characters (K&R 2.3), which you can also use in a literal NSString, including the following:

\n

> A Unix newline character

\t

> A tab character

\"

> A quotation mark (escaped to show that this is not the end of the string literal)

\\

> A backslash

 NSStrings are natively Unicode-based, and it is perfectly legal to type a non-ASCII character directly into an NSString literal; warnings to the contrary are outdated, and you should ignore them. The \x and \u escape sequences are nice to know about, but you are unlikely to need them.

K&R also mention a notation for concatenating string literals, in which multiple string literals separated only by white space are automatically concatenated and treated as a single string literal. This notation is useful for splitting a long string into multiple lines for legibility, and Objective-C copies this convention for literal NSStrings as well, except that you have to remember the at-sign:

```
@"This is a big long literal string "
@"which I have broken over two lines of code.";
```

Structs

C offers few simple native data types, so how are more complex data types made? There are three ways: structures, pointers, and arrays. Both structures and pointers are going to be crucial when you're programming iOS. C arrays are needed less often, because Objective-C has its own NSArray object type.

A C structure, usually called a struct (K&R 6.1), is a compound data type: it combines multiple data types into a single type, which can be passed around as a single entity.

Moreover, the elements constituting the compound entity have names and can be accessed by those names through the compound entity, using dot-notation. The iOS API has many commonly used structs, typically accompanied by convenience functions for working with them.

For example, the iOS documentation tells you that a CGPoint is defined as follows:

```
struct CGPoint {
    CGFloat x;
    CGFloat y;
};
typedef struct CGPoint CGPoint;
```

Recall that a CGFloat is basically a float, so this is a compound data type made up of two simple native data types; in effect, a CGPoint has two CGFloat parts, and their names are x and y. (The rather odd-looking last line merely asserts that one can use the term CGPoint instead of the more verbose `struct CGPoint`.) So we can write:

```
CGPoint myPoint;
myPoint.x = 4.3;
myPoint.y = 7.1;
```

Just as we can assign to `myPoint.x` to *set* this part of the struct, we can say `myPoint.x` to *get* this part of the struct. It's as if `myPoint.x` were the name of a variable. Moreover, an element of a struct can itself be a struct, and the dot-notation can be chained. To illustrate, first note the existence of another iOS struct, CGSize:

```
struct CGSize {
    CGFloat width;
    CGFloat height;
};
typedef struct CGSize CGSize;
```

Put a CGPoint and a CGSize together and you've got a CGRect:

```
struct CGRect {
    CGPoint origin;
    CGSize size;
};
typedef struct CGRect CGRect;
```

So suppose we've got a CGRect variable called `myRect`, already initialized. Then `myRect.origin` is a CGPoint, and `myRect.origin.x` is a CGFloat. Similarly, `myRect.size` is a CGSize, and `myRect.size.width` is a CGFloat. You could change just the width part of our CGRect directly, like this:

```
myRect.size.width = 8.6;
```

Instead of initializing a struct by assigning to each of its elements, you can initialize it at declaration time by assigning values for all its elements at once, in curly braces and separated by commas, like this:

```
CGPoint myPoint = { 4.3, 7.1 };
CGRect myRect = { myPoint, {10, 20} };
```

You don't have to be assigning to a struct-typed variable to use a struct initializer; you can use an initializer anywhere the given struct type is expected, but you might also have to cast to that struct type in order to explain to the compiler what your curly braces mean, like this:

```
CGContextFillRect(con, (CGRect){myPoint, {10, 20}});
```

In that example, `CGContextFillRect` is a function. I'll talk about functions later in this chapter, but the upshot of the example is that what comes after the first comma has to be a CGRect, and can therefore be a CGRect initializer provided it is accompanied by a CGRect cast.

Pointers

The other big way that C extends its range of data types is by means of pointers (K&R 5.1). A pointer is an integer (of some size or other) designating the location in memory where the real data is to be found. Knowing the structure of that real data and how to work with it, as well as allocating a block of memory of the required size beforehand and disposing of that block of memory when it's no longer needed, is a very complicated business. Luckily, this is exactly the sort of complicated business that Objective-C is going to take care of for us. So all you really have to know to use pointers is what they are and what notation is used to refer to them.

Let's start with a simple declaration. If we wanted to declare an integer in C, we could say:

```
int i;
```

That line says, "`i` is an integer." Now let's instead declare a *pointer* to an integer:

```
int* intPtr;
```

That line says, "`intPtr` is a pointer to an integer." Never mind how we know there really is going to be an integer at the address designated by this pointer; here, I'm concerned only with the notation. It is permitted to place the asterisk in the declaration before the name rather than after the type:

```
int *intPtr;
```

You could even put a space on both sides of the asterisk (though this is rarely done):

```
int * intPtr;
```

I prefer the first form, but I do occasionally use the second form, and Apple quite often uses it, so be sure you understand that these are all ways of saying the same thing. No matter how the spaces are inserted, the name of the type is still `int*`. If you are asked what type `intPtr` is, the answer is `int*` (a pointer to an int); the asterisk is part of the name of the type of this variable. If you needed to cast a variable p to this type, you'd cast like this: `(int*)p`. Once again, it is possible that you'll see code where there's a space before the asterisk, like this: `(int *)p`.

The most general type of pointer is *pointer-to-void* (`void*`), the *generic pointer*. It is legal to use a generic pointer wherever a specific type of pointer is expected. In effect, pointer-to-void casts away type checking as to what's at the far end of the pointer. Thus, the following is legal:

```
int* p1; // and pretend p1 has a value
void* p2;
p2 = p1;
p1 = p2;
```

Pointers are very important in Objective-C, because Objective-C is all about objects (Chapter 2), and every variable referring to an object is itself a pointer. In effect, Objective-C takes advantage of the fact that a C pointer can designate real data whose nature and bookkeeping are arbitrary. In this case, that real data is an Objective-C object. Objective-C knows what this means, but you generally won't worry about it — you'll just work with the C pointer and let Objective-C take care of the details. For example, I've already mentioned that the Objective-C string type is called NSString. So the way to declare an NSString variable is as a pointer to an NSString:

```
NSString* s;
```

An NSString literal is an NSString value, so we can even declare and initialize this NSString object, thus writing a seriously useful line of Objective-C code:

```
NSString* s = @"Hello, world!";
```

In pure C, having declared a pointer-to-integer called `intPtr`, you are liable to speak later in your code of `*intPtr`. This notation, outside of a declaration, means "the thing pointed to by the pointer `intPtr`." You speak of `*intPtr` because you wish to access the integer at the far end of the pointer; this is called *dereferencing* the pointer.

But in Objective-C, this is generally *not* the case. In your code, you'll be treating the pointer to an object as the object; you'll never dereference it. So, for example, having declared s as a pointer to an NSString, you will *not* then proceed to speak of `*s`; rather, you will speak simply of s, as if it *were* the string. All the Objective-C stuff you'll want to do with an object will expect the pointer, not the object at the far end of the pointer; behind the scenes, Objective-C itself will take care of the messy business of following the pointer to its block of memory and doing whatever needs to be done in that block of memory. This fact is extremely convenient for you as a programmer, but it does cause Objective-C users to speak a little loosely; we tend to say that "s is an NSString," when of course it is actually a pointer to an NSString.

The logic of how pointers work, both in C and in Objective-C, is different from the logic of how simple data types work. The difference is particularly evident with assignment.

Assignment to a simple data type changes the data value. Assignment to a pointer re-points the pointer. Suppose ptr1 and ptr2 are both pointers, and you say:

```
ptr1 = ptr2;
```

Now ptr1 and ptr2 are pointing at the same thing. Any change to the thing pointed to by ptr1 will also change the thing pointed to by ptr2, because they are the same thing (Figure 1-1). Meanwhile, whatever ptr1 was pointing to before the assignment is now not being pointed to by ptr1; it might, indeed, be pointed to by nothing (which could be bad). A firm understanding of these facts is crucial when working in Objective-C, and I'll return to this topic in Chapter 3.

Arrays

A C array (K&R 5.3) consists of multiple elements of the same data type. An array declaration states the data type of the elements, followed by the name of the array, along with square brackets containing the number of elements:

```
int arr[3]; // means: arr is an array consisting of 3 ints
```

To refer to an element of an array, use the array's name followed by the element number in square brackets. The first element of an array is numbered 0. So we can initialize an array by assigning values to each element in turn:

```
int arr[3];
arr[0] = 123;
arr[1] = 456;
arr[2] = 789;
```

Alternatively, you can initialize an array at declaration time by assigning a list of values in curly braces, just as with a struct. In this case, the size of the array can be omitted from the declaration, because it is implicit in the initialization (K&R 4.9):

```
int arr[] = {123, 456, 789};
```

Curiously, the name of an array is the name of a pointer (to the first element of the array). Thus, for example, having declared arr as in the preceding examples, you can use arr wherever a value of type int* (a pointer to an int) is expected. This fact is the basis of some highly sophisticated C idioms that you almost certainly won't need to know about (which is why I don't recommend that you read any of K&R Chapter 5 beyond section 3).

Here's an example where a C array might be useful when programming iOS. The function CGContextStrokeLineSegments is declared like this:

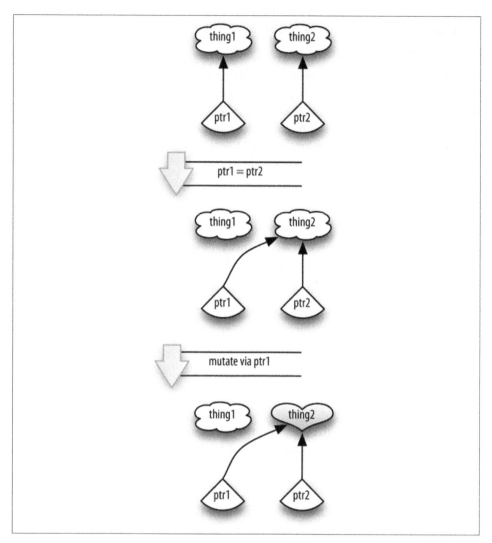

Figure 1-1. Pointers and assignment

```
void CGContextStrokeLineSegments (
    CGContextRef c,
    const CGPoint points[],
    size_t count
);
```

The second parameter is a C array of CGPoints. That's what the square brackets tell you. So to call this function, you'd need to know at least how to make an array of CGPoints. You might do it like this:

```
CGPoint arr[] = {{4,5}, {6,7}, {8,9}, {10,11}};
```

Having done that, you can pass `arr` as the second argument in a call to `CGContextStroke-`
`LineSegments`.

Also, a C string, as I've already mentioned, is actually an array. For example, the NSString
method `stringWithUTF8String:` takes (according to the documentation) "a NULL-
terminated C array of bytes in UTF8 encoding;" but the parameter is declared not as an
array, but as a `char*`. Those are the same thing, and are both ways of saying that this
method takes a C string.

(The colon at the end of the method name `stringWithUTF8String:` is not a misprint;
many Objective-C method names end with a colon. I'll explain why in Chapter 3.)

Operators

Arithmetic operators are straightforward (K&R 2.5), but watch out for the rule that
"integer division truncates any fractional part." This rule is the cause of much novice
error in C. If you have two integers and you want to divide them in such a way as to get
a fractional result, you must represent at least one of them as a float:

```
int i = 3;
float f = i/2; // beware! not 1.5
```

To get 1.5, you should have written `i/2.0` or `(float)i/2`.

The integer increment and decrement operators (K&R 2.8), `++` and `--`, work differently
depending on whether they precede or follow their variable. The expression `++i` replaces
the value of `i` by 1 more than its current value and then uses the resulting value; the
expression `i++` uses the current value of `i` and then replaces it with 1 more than its
current value. This is one of C's coolest features.

C also provides bitwise operators (K&R 2.9), such as bitwise-and (`&`) and bitwise-or (`|`);
they operate on the individual binary bits that constitute integers. You are most likely
to need bitwise-or, because the Cocoa API often uses bits as switches when multiple
options are to be specified simultaneously. For example, when specifying how a UIView
is to be animated, you are allowed to pass an `options` argument whose value comes
from the UIViewAnimationOptions enumeration, whose definition begins as follows:

```
typedef NS_OPTIONS(NSUInteger, UIViewAnimationOptions) {
    UIViewAnimationOptionLayoutSubviews         = 1 << 0,
    UIViewAnimationOptionAllowUserInteraction   = 1 << 1,
    UIViewAnimationOptionBeginFromCurrentState  = 1 << 2,
    UIViewAnimationOptionRepeat                 = 1 << 3,
    UIViewAnimationOptionAutoreverse            = 1 << 4,
    // ...
};
```

The << symbol is the left shift operator; the right operand says how many bits to shift the left operand. So pretend that an NSUInteger is 8 bits (it isn't, but let's keep things simple and short). Then this enumeration means that the following name–value pairs are defined (using binary notation for the values):

UIViewAnimationOptionLayoutSubviews
    00000001

UIViewAnimationOptionAllowUserInteraction
    00000010

UIViewAnimationOptionBeginFromCurrentState
    00000100

UIViewAnimationOptionRepeat
    00001000

UIViewAnimationOptionAutoreverse
    00010000

The reason for this bit-based representation is that these values can be combined into a single value (a *bitmask*) that you pass to set the options for this animation. All Cocoa has to do to understand your intentions is to look to see which bits in the value that you pass are set to 1. So, for example, 00011000 would mean that UIViewAnimationOption-Repeat and UIViewAnimationOptionAutoreverse are both true (and that the others, by implication, are all false).

The question is how to form the value 00011000 in order to pass it. You could just do the math, figure out that binary 00011000 is decimal 24, and set the options argument to 24, but that's not what you're supposed to do, and it's not a very good idea, because it's error-prone and makes your code incomprehensible. Instead, use the bitwise-or operator to combine the desired options:

    (UIViewAnimationOptionRepeat | UIViewAnimationOptionAutoreverse)

This notation works because the bitwise-or operator combines its operands by setting in the result any bits that are set in either of the operands, so 00001000 | 00010000 is 00011000, which is just the value we're trying to convey. (And how does the runtime parse the bitmask to discover whether a given bit is set? With the bitwise-and operator.)

Simple assignment (K&R 2.10) is by the equal sign. But there are also compound assignment operators that combine assignment with some other operation. For example:

    height *= 2; // same as saying: height = height * 2;

The ternary operator (?:) is a way of specifying one of two values depending on a condition (K&R 2.11). The scheme is as follows:

    (condition) ? exp1 : exp2

If the condition is true (see the next section for what that means), the expression *exp1* is evaluated and the result is used; otherwise, the expression *exp2* is evaluated and the result is used. For example, you might use the ternary operator while performing an assignment, using this schema:

```
myVariable = (condition) ? exp1 : exp2;
```

What gets assigned to myVariable depends on the truth value of the condition. There's nothing happening here that couldn't be accomplished more verbosely with flow control, but the ternary operator can greatly improve clarity, and I use it a lot.

Flow Control and Conditions

Basic flow control is fairly simple and usually involves a condition in parentheses and a block of conditionally executed code in curly braces. These curly braces constitute a new scope, into which new variables can be introduced. So, for example:

```
if (x == 7) {
    int i = 0;
    i += 1;
}
```

After the closing curly brace in the fourth line, the i introduced in the second line has ceased to exist, because its scope is the inside of the curly braces. If the contents of the curly braces consist of a single statement, the curly braces can be omitted, but I would advise beginners against this shorthand, as you can confuse yourself. A common beginner mistake (which will be caught by the compiler) is forgetting the parentheses around the condition. The full set of flow control statements is given in K&R Chapter 3, and I'll just summarize them schematically here (Example 1-1).

Example 1-1. The C flow control constructs

```
if (condition) {
    statements;
}

if (condition) {
    statements;
} else {
    statements;
}

if (condition) {
    statements;
} else if (condition) {
    statements;
} else {
    statements;
}
```

```
while (condition) {
    statements;
}

do {
    statements;
} while (condition);

for (before-all; condition; after-each) {
    statements;
}
```

The if...else if...else structure can have as many else if blocks as needed, and the else block is optional. Instead of an extended if...else if...else if...else structure, when the conditions would consist of comparing various values against a single value, you can use the switch statement; be careful, though, as it is rather confusing and can easily go wrong (see K&R 3.4 for full details). The main trick is to remember to end every case with a break statement, unless you want it to "fall through" to the next case (Example 1-2).

Example 1-2. A switch statement

```
NSString* key;
switch (tag) {
    case 1: { // i.e., if tag is 1
        key = @"lesson";
        break;
    }
    case 2: { // i.e., if tag is 2
        key = @"lessonSection";
        break;
    }
    case 3: { // i.e., if tag is 3
        key = @"lessonSectionPartFirstWord";
        break;
    }
}
```

The C for loop needs some elaboration for beginners (Example 1-1). The *before-all* statement is executed once as the for loop is first encountered and is usually used for initialization of the counter. The condition is then tested, and if true, the block is executed; the condition is usually used to test whether the counter has reached its limit. The *after-each* statement is then executed, and is usually used to increment or decrement the counter; the condition is then immediately tested again. Thus, to execute a block using integer values 1, 2, 3, 4, and 5 for i, the notation is:

```
int i;
for (i = 1; i < 6; i++) {
    // ... statements ...
}
```

The need for a counter intended to exist solely within the for loop is so common that C99 permits the declaration of the counter as part of the *before-all* statement; the declared variable's scope is then inside the curly braces:

```
for (int i = 1; i < 6; i++) {
    // ... statements ...
}
```

The for loop is one of the few areas in which Objective-C extends C's flow-control syntax. Certain Objective-C objects, such as NSArray, represent enumerable collections of other objects; "enumerable" basically means that you can cycle through the collection, and cycling through a collection is called *enumerating* the collection. (I'll discuss the main enumerable collection types in Chapter 10.) To make enumerating easy, Objective-C provides a for...in operator, which works like a for loop:

```
SomeType* oneItem;
for (oneItem in myCollection) {
    // ... statements ....
}
```

On each pass through the loop, the variable oneItem (or whatever you call it) takes on the next value from within the collection. As with the C99 for loop, oneItem can be declared in the for statement, limiting its scope to the curly braces:

```
for (SomeType* oneItem in myCollection) {
    // ... statements ....
}
```

To abort a loop from inside the curly braces, use the break statement. To abort the current iteration from within the curly braces and proceed to the next iteration, use the continue statement. In the case of while and do, continue means to perform immediately the conditional test; in the case of a for loop, continue means to perform immediately the *after-each* statement and then the conditional test.

C also has a goto statement that allows you to jump to a named (labeled) line in your code (K&R 3.8); even though goto is notoriously "considered harmful," there are situations in which it is pretty much necessary, especially because C's flow control is otherwise so primitive.

 It is permissible for a C statement to be compounded of multiple statements, separated by commas, to be executed sequentially. The last of the multiple statements is the value of the compound statement as a whole. This construct, for instance, lets you perform some secondary action before each test of a condition or perform more than one *after-each* action.

We can now turn to the question of what a condition consists of. C has no separate boolean type; a condition either evaluates to 0, in which case it is considered false, or it doesn't, in which case it is true. Comparisons are performed using the equality and relational operators (K&R 2.6); for example, == compares for equality, and < compares for whether the first operand is less than the second. Logical expressions can be combined using the logical-and operator (&&) and the logical-or operator (||); using these along with parentheses and the not operator (!) you can form complex conditions. Evaluation of logical-and and logical-or expressions is short-circuited, meaning that if the left condition settles the question, the right condition is never even evaluated.

 Don't confuse the logical-and operator (&&) and the logical-or operator (||) with the bitwise-and operator (&) and the bitwise-or operator (|) discussed earlier. Writing & when you mean && (or *vice versa*) can result in surprising behavior.

The operator for testing basic equality, ==, is not a simple equal sign; forgetting the difference is a common novice mistake. The problem is that such code is legal: simple assignment, which is what the equal sign means, has a value, and any value is legal in a condition. So consider this piece of (nonsense) code:

```
int i = 0;
while (i = 1) {
    i = 0;
}
```

You might think that the while condition tests whether i is 1. You might then think: i is 0, so the while body will never be performed. Right? Wrong. The while condition does not test whether i is 1; it assigns 1 to i. The value of that assignment is also 1, so the condition evaluates to 1, which means true. So the while body *is* performed. Moreover, even though the while body assigns 0 to i, the condition is then evaluated again and assigns 1 to i a second time, which means true yet again. And so on, forever; we've written an endless loop, and the program will hang.

C programmers revel in the fact that testing for zero and testing for false are the same thing and use it to create compact conditional expressions, which are considered elegant and idiomatic. Such idioms can be confusing, but one of them is commonly used in Objective-C, namely, in order to test an object reference to see whether it is nil. Since nil is a form of zero (as discussed further in Chapter 3), one can ask whether an object s is nil like this:

```
if (!s) {
    // ...
}
```

Objective-C introduces a BOOL type, which you should use if you need to capture or maintain a condition's value as a variable, along with constants YES and NO (representing 1 and 0), which you should use when setting a boolean value. Don't compare anything against a BOOL, not even YES or NO, because a value like 2 is true in a condition but is not equal to YES or NO. (Getting this wrong is a common beginner mistake, and can lead to unintended results.) Just use the BOOL directly as a condition, or as part of a complex condition, and all will be well. For example:

```
BOOL isnil = (nil == s);
if (isnil) { // not: if (isnil == YES)
    // ...
}
```

Functions

C is a function-based language (K&R 4.1). A *function* is a block of code defining what should happen; when other code *calls* (invokes) that function, the function's code does happen. A function returns a value, which is substituted for the call to that function.

Here's a definition of a function that accepts an integer and returns its square:

```
int square(int i) {
    return i * i;
}
```

Now I'll call that function:

```
int i = square(3);
```

Because of the way square is defined, that is exactly like saying:

```
int i = 9;
```

That example is extremely simple, but it illustrates many key aspects of functions.

Let's analyze how a function is defined:

```
int❶ square❷(❸int i) {❹
    return i * i;
}
```

❶   We start with the type of value that the function returns; here, it returns an int.

❷   Then we have the name of the function, which is square.

❸   Then we have parentheses, and here we place the data type and name of any values that this function expects to receive. Here, `square` expects to receive one value, an int, which we are calling `i`. The name `i` (along with its expected data type) is a *parameter*; when the function is called, its value will be supplied as an *argument*. If a function expects to receive more than one value, multiple parameters in its definition are separated by a comma (and when the function is called, the arguments supplied are likewise separated by a comma).

❹   Finally, we have curly braces containing the statements that are to be executed when the function is called.

Those curly braces constitute a scope; variables declared within them are local to the function. The names used for the parameters in the function definition are also local to the function; in other words, the `i` in the first line of the function definition is the same as the `i` in the second line of the function definition, but it has nothing to do with any `i` used outside the function definition (as when the result of the function call is assigned to a variable called `i`). The value of the `i` parameter in the function definition is assigned from the corresponding argument when the function is called; in the previous example, it is 3, which is why the function result is 9. Supplying a function call with arguments is thus a form of assignment. Suppose a function is defined like this:

```
int myfunction(int i, int j) { // ...
```

And suppose we call that function:

```
int result = myfunction(3, 4);
```

That function call effectively assigns 3 to the function's `i` parameter and 4 to the function's `j` parameter.

When a `return` statement is encountered, the value accompanying it is handed back as the result of the function call, and the function terminates. It is legal for a function to return no value; in such a case, the `return` statement has no accompanying value, and the definition states the type of value returned by the function as `void`. It is also legal to call a function and ignore its return value even if it has one. For example, we could say:

```
square(3);
```

That would be a somewhat silly thing to say, because we have gone to all the trouble of calling the function and having it generate the square of 3 — namely 9 — but we have done nothing to *capture* that 9. It is exactly as if we had said:

```
9;
```

You're allowed to say that, but it doesn't seem to serve much purpose. On the other hand, the point of a function might be not so much the value it returns as other things it does as it is executing, so then it might make perfect sense to ignore its result.

The parentheses in a function's syntax are crucial. Parentheses are how C knows there's a function. Parentheses after the function name in the function *definition* are how C knows this is a function definition, and they are needed even if this function takes no parameters. Parentheses after the function name in the function *call* are how C knows this is a function call, and they are needed even if this function call supplies no arguments. Using the bare name of a function is possible, because the name is the name of something, but it doesn't call the function. (I'll talk later about something it does do.)

Let's return to the simple C function definition and call that I used as my example earlier. Suppose we combine that function definition and the call to that function into a single program:

```
int square(int i) {
    return i * i;
}
int i = square(3);
```

That is a legal program, but only because the definition of the square function precedes the call to that function. If we wanted to place the definition of the square function elsewhere, such as after the call to it, we would need at least to precede the call with a declaration of the square function (Example 1-3). The declaration looks just like the first line of the definition, but it is a statement, ending with a semicolon rather than a left curly brace.

Example 1-3. Declaring, calling, and defining a function

```
int square(int i);
int i = square(3);
int square(int i) {
    return i * i;
}
```

The parameter names in the declaration do not have to match the parameter names in the definition, but all the types (and, of course, the name of the function) must match. The types constitute the *signature* of this function. In other words, it does not matter if the first line, the declaration, is rewritten thus:

```
int square(int j);
```

What does matter is that, both in the declaration and in the definition, square is a function taking one int parameter and returning an int. (In a modern Objective-C program, though, the function declaration usually won't be necessary, even if the function call precedes its definition; see "Modern Objective-C Function and Method Declarations" on page 29.)

In Objective-C, when you're sending a message to an object (Chapter 2), you won't use a function call; you'll use a method call (Chapter 3). But you will most definitely use plenty of C function calls as well. For example, earlier we initialized a CGPoint by setting its x element and its y element, but what you'll usually do to make a new CGPoint is to call `CGPointMake`, which is declared like this:

```
CGPoint CGPointMake (
    CGFloat x,
    CGFloat y
);
```

Despite its multiple lines and its indentations, this is indeed a C function declaration, just like the declaration for our simple `square` function. It says that `CGPointMake` is a C function that takes two CGFloat parameters and returns a CGPoint. So now you know (I hope) that it would be legal (and typical) to write this sort of thing:

```
CGPoint myPoint = CGPointMake(4.3, 7.1);
```

Pointer Parameters and the Address Operator

Objective-C is chock-a-block with pointers (and asterisks), because that's how Objective-C refers to an object. Objective-C methods typically work with objects, so they typically expect pointer parameters and return a pointer value. But this doesn't make things more complicated. Pointers are what Objective-C expects, but pointers are also what Objective-C gives you. Pointers are exactly what you've got, so there's no problem.

For example, one way to concatenate two NSStrings is to call the NSString method `stringByAppendingString:`, which the documentation tells you is declared as follows:

```
- (NSString *)stringByAppendingString:(NSString *)aString
```

This declaration is telling you (after you allow for the Objective-C syntax) that this method expects one `NSString*` parameter and returns an `NSString*`. That sounds messy, but it isn't, because *every* NSString is really an `NSString*`. So nothing could be simpler than to obtain a new NSString consisting of two concatenated NSStrings:

```
NSString* s1 = @"Hello, ";
NSString* s2 = @"World!";
NSString* s3 = [s1 stringByAppendingString: s2];
```

Sometimes, however, a function or method expects as a parameter a pointer to a thing, but what you've got is not that pointer but the thing itself. Thus, you need a way to create a pointer to that thing. The solution is the address operator (K&R 5.1), which is an ampersand before the name of the thing.

For example, there's an NSString method for reading from a file into an NSString, which is declared like this:

```
+ (id)stringWithContentsOfFile:(NSString *)path
                    encoding:(NSStringEncoding)enc
                       error:(NSError **)error
```

Never mind for now what an id is, and don't worry about the Objective-C method declaration syntax. Just consider the types of the parameters. The first one is an NSString*; that's no problem, as every reference to an NSString is actually a pointer to an NSString. An NSStringEncoding turns out to be merely an alias to a primitive data type, an NSUInteger, so that's no problem either. But what on earth is an NSError**?

By all logic, it looks like an NSError** should be a pointer to a pointer to an NSError. And that's exactly what it is. This method is asking to be passed a pointer to a pointer to an NSError. Well, it's easy to declare a pointer to an NSError:

```
NSError* err;
```

But how can we obtain a pointer to that? With the address operator! So our code might look, schematically, like this:

```
NSString* path = // something or other
NSStringEncoding enc = // something or other
NSError* err = nil;
NSString* result =
    [NSString stringWithContentsOfFile: path encoding: enc error: &err];
```

The important thing to notice is the ampersand. Because err is a pointer to an NSError, &err is a pointer to a pointer to an NSError, which is just what we're expected to provide. Thus, everything goes swimmingly. I'll discuss in Chapter 3 how you're supposed to use result and err after such a method call.

You can use the address operator to create a pointer to any named variable. A C function is technically a kind of named variable, so you can even create a pointer to a function! This is an example of when you'd use the name of the function without the parentheses: you aren't calling the function, you're talking about it. For example, &square is a pointer to the square function. Moreover, just as the bare name of an array is implicitly a pointer to its first element, the bare name of a function is implicitly a pointer to the function; the address operator is optional. In Chapter 3, I describe a situation in which specifying a pointer to a function is a useful thing to do.

Files

As your program grows, you can divide and organize it into multiple files. This kind of organization can make a large program much more maintainable — easier to read, easier to understand, easier to change without accidentally breaking things. A large C program therefore usually consists of two kinds of file: code files, whose filename extension is .c, and header files, whose filename extension is .h. The build system will automatically "see" all the files and will know that together they constitute a single program, but there is also a rule in C that code inside one file cannot "see" another file unless it is explicitly told to do so. Thus, a file itself constitutes a scope; this is a deliberate and valuable feature of C, because it helps you keep things nicely pigeonholed.

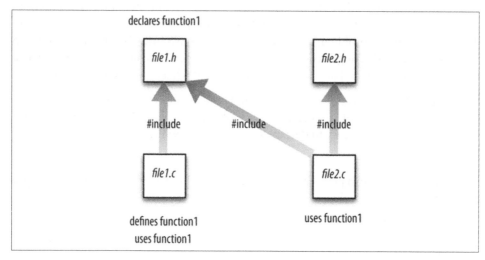

Figure 1-2. How a large C program is divided into files

The way you tell a C file to "see" another file is with the #include directive. The hash sign in the term #include is a signal that this line is an instruction to the preprocessor. In this case, the word #include is followed by the name of another file, and the directive means that the preprocessor should simply replace the directive by the entire contents of the file that's named.

So the strategy for constructing a large C program is something like this:

- In each *.c* file, put the code that only this file needs to know about; typically, each file's code consists of related functionality.

- In each *.h* file, put the function declarations that multiple *.c* files might need to know about.

- Have each *.c* file include those *.h* files containing the declarations it needs to know about.

So, for example, if function1 is defined in *file1.c*, but *file2.c* might need to call function1, the declaration for function1 can go in *file1.h*. Now *file1.c* can include *file1.h*, so all of its functions, regardless of order, can call function1, and *file2.c* can also include *file1.h*, so all of *its* functions can call function1 (Figure 1-2). In short, header files are a way of letting code files share knowledge about one another without actually sharing code (because, if they did share code, that would violate the entire point of keeping the code in separate files).

But how does the compiler know where, among all these multiple *.c* files, to begin execution? Every real C program contains, somewhere, exactly one function called main, and this is always the entry point for the program as a whole: the compiler sets things up so that when the program executes, `main` is called.

The organization for large C programs that I've just described will also be, in effect, the organization for your iOS programs. The chief difference will be that instead of *.c* files, you'll use *.m* files, because *.m* is the conventional filename extension for telling Xcode that your files are written in Objective-C, not pure C. Moreover, if you look at any iOS Xcode project, you'll discover that it contains a file called *main.m*; and if you look at that file, you'll find that it contains a function called `main`. That's the entry point to your application's code when it runs.

The big difference between your Objective-C code files and the C code files I've been discussing is that instead of saying `#include`, your files will say `#import`. The `#import` preprocessor directive is not mentioned in K&R. It's an Objective-C addition to the language. It's based on `#include`, but it is used instead of `#include` because it (`#import`) contains some logic for making sure that the same material is not included more than once. Such repeated inclusion is a danger whenever there are many cross-dependent header files; use of `#import` solves the problem neatly.

Furthermore, your iOS programs consist not only of *your* code files and their corresponding *.h* files, but also of Apple's code files and *their* corresponding *.h* files. The difference is that Apple's code files (which are what constitutes Cocoa, see Part III) have already been compiled. But your code must still `#import` Apple's *.h* files so as to be able to see Apple's declarations. If you look at an iOS Xcode project, you'll find that any *.h* files it contains by default, as well as its *main.m* file, contain a line of this form:

```
#import <UIKit/UIKit.h>
```

That line is essentially a single massive `#import` that copies into your program the declarations for the entire basic iOS API. Moreover, each of your *.m* files imports its corresponding *.h* file, including whatever the *.h* file imports. For example, if you have a file *AppDelegate.m*, it contains this line:

```
#import "AppDelegate.h"
```

But *AppDelegate.h* imports `<UIKit/UIKit.h>`. Thus, *all* your code files include the basic iOS declarations.

As those examples demonstrate, the `#import` directive, like the `#include` directive (K&R 4.11), can specify a file in angle brackets or in quotation marks. The different delimiters have different meanings to the compiler:

Quotation marks
> Look for the named file in the same folder as this file (the *.m* file in which the `#import` line occurs).

Angle brackets

Look for the named file among the various header search paths supplied in the build settings. (These search paths are set for you automatically, and you normally won't need to modify them.)

In general, you'll use angle brackets to refer to a header file owned by the Cocoa API and quotation marks to refer to a header file that you wrote. If you're curious as to what an #import directive imports, Command-click the imported file's name to view the header file directly.

In iOS 7 and Xcode 5, an additional import mechanism is provided, namely *modules*. Modules are used implicitly, behind the scenes, as part of the build process for any new iOS project (and can be turned on through a build setting for old projects); you'll never come into direct contact with a module. The chief purpose of modules is to make your projects compile faster.

Without modules, the compilation process must start by quite literally including the headers for UIKit and the iOS API in every one of your files. For example, earlier I said that CGPoint was defined like this:

```
struct CGPoint {
  CGFloat x;
  CGFloat y;
};
typedef struct CGPoint CGPoint;
```

After the preprocessor operates on all your files, your *.m* files literally *contain* that definition of CGPoint — which is why your code is able to use a CGPoint. The definition of CGPoint and all the other imported material temporarily adds to every one of your files over 30,000 lines of code that the compiler then has to deal with. Modules avoid this overhead. Instead, the material imported from Apple's code files is compiled once, automatically (typically when your project is created or opened), and cached in a separate location; that cached code constitutes the modules. At build time, the preprocessor inserts into your code only a few lines such as these:

```
@import UIKit;
@import Foundation;
```

(You can choose Product → Perform Action → Preprocess [Filename] to confirm this.) The @import compiler directive, with an at-sign instead of a hash sign, is new in Xcode 5, and refers to a module by name. Since the module is already compiled, there's no further work for the compiler to do. I'll talk more about @import and modules when I discuss frameworks and linking in Chapter 6.

Modern Objective-C Function and Method Declarations

Starting with LLVM compiler version 3.1, which made its debut in Xcode 4.3, Objective-C no longer requires that a function declaration precede the use of that function, provided that the definition of that function follows in the same file. This applies to both C functions and Objective-C methods. In other words, code inside an Objective-C class can call a C function or an Objective-C method even if that call *precedes* the definition of that function or method, and even if there is no separate declaration of that function or method. Thus, in modern Objective-C, the order of functions and methods within a *.m* file doesn't matter, and it is not necessary to declare functions or methods within a *.m* file at all! The only place you'll ever need to declare a function or method will be in a *.h* file, and only so that some *.m* file *other* than the one that defines that function or method can import that *.h* file and call the function or method.

This convenience is a feature of Objective-C, not of C. I'm talking about *.m* files, not *.c* files. I'll describe more precisely in Chapter 4 the region of a *.m* file in which this convenience applies — namely, a class's implementation section.

The Standard Library

You have at your disposal a large collection of built-in C library files. A library file is a centrally located collection of C functions, along with a *.h* file that you can include so as to make those functions available to your code.

For example, suppose you want to round a float up to the next highest integer. The way to do this is to call some variety of the `ceil` function. You can read the `ceil` man page by typing `man ceil` in the Terminal. The documentation tells you what `#include` to use to incorporate the correct header and also shows you the function declarations and tells you what those functions do. A small pure C program might thus look like this:

```
#include <math.h>
float f = 4.5;
int i = ceilf(f); // now i is 5
```

In your iOS programs, *math.h* is included for you as part of UIKit, so there's no need to include it again. But some library functions might require an explicit `#import`.

The standard library is discussed in K&R Appendix B. But the modern standard library has evolved since K&R; it is a superset of K&R's library. The `ceil` function, for example, is listed in K&R appendix B, but the `ceilf` function is not. Similarly, if you wanted to generate a random number (which is likely if you're writing a game program that needs to incorporate some unpredictable behavior), you probably wouldn't use the `rand` function listed in K&R; you might use some function that supersedes it, such as the `random` function, or even the `arc4random_uniform` function.

Forgetting that Objective-C is C and that the C library functions are available to your code is a common beginner mistake.

More Preprocessor Directives

Of the many other available preprocessor directives, the one you'll use most often is `#define`. It is followed by a name and a value; at preprocess time, the value is substituted for the name down through this code file. As K&R very well explain (K&R 1.4), this is a good way to prevent "magic numbers" from being hidden and hard-coded into your program in a way that makes the program difficult to understand and maintain.

For example, in an iOS app that lays out some text fields vertically, I might want them all to have the same space between them. Let's say this space is 3.0. I shouldn't write 3.0 repeatedly throughout my code as I calculate the layout; instead, I write:

```
#define MIDSPACE 3.0
```

Now instead of the "magic number" 3.0, my code uses a meaningful name, `MIDSPACE`; the preprocessor sees to it that the text `MIDSPACE` is replaced with the text `3.0`. As a bonus, if I later decide to change this value and try a different one, all I have to change is the `#define` line, not every occurrence of the number 3.0.

A `#define` simply performs text substitution, so any expression can be used as the value. Sometimes you'll want that expression to be an NSString literal. Here's why. In Cocoa, NSString literals can be used as a key to a dictionary or the name of a notification. (Never mind for now what a dictionary or a notification is.) This situation is an invitation to error. If you have a dictionary containing a key `@"mykey"` and you mistype this elsewhere in your code as `@"myKey"` or `@"mikey"`, the compiler won't complain, but your program will misbehave. An elegant solution is to define a name for this literal string:

```
#define MYKEY @"mykey"
```

Now use `MYKEY` throughout your code instead of `@"mykey"`, and if you mistype it (as `MYKKEY` or what have you), the preprocessor won't perform any substitution and the compiler *will* complain, catching the mistake for you.

The `#define` directive can also be used to create a macro (K&R 4.11.2), a more elaborate form of text substitution. You'll encounter a few Cocoa macros when programming iOS, but they will appear indistinguishable from functions; their secret identity as macros usually won't concern you.

The `#warning` directive deliberately triggers a warning in Xcode at compile time; this can be a way to remind yourself of some impending task or requirement:

```
#warning Don't forget to fix this bit of code
```

There is also a `#pragma mark` directive that's useful with Xcode; I talk about it when discussing the Xcode programming environment (Chapter 9).

Data Type Qualifiers

A variable's data type can be declared with a qualifier before the name of the type, modifying something about how that variable is to be used. For example, the declaration can be preceded by the term `const`, which means (K&R 2.4) that it is illegal to change the variable's value; the variable must be initialized in the same line as the declaration, and that's the only value it can ever have.

You can use a `const` variable as an alternative way (instead of `#define`) to prevent "magic numbers" and similar expressions. For example:

```
NSString* const MYKEY = @"Howdy";
```

The Cocoa API itself makes heavy use of this device. For example, in some circumstances Cocoa will pass a dictionary of information to your code. The documentation tells you what keys this dictionary contains. But instead of telling you a key as a literal string value, the documentation tells you the key as a `const` NSString variable name:

```
UIKIT_EXTERN NSString *const UIApplicationStatusBarOrientationUserInfoKey;
```

(Never mind what `UIKIT_EXTERN` means.) This declaration tells you that `UIApplication-StatusBarOrientationUserInfoKey` is the name of an NSString, and you are to trust that its value is set for you. You are to go ahead and use this name whenever you want to speak of this particular key, secure in the knowledge that the actual string value will be substituted — even though you don't know or care what that string value is. In this way, if you make a mistake in typing the variable name, the compiler will catch the mistake because you'll be using the name of an undefined variable.

Another commonly used qualifier is `static`. This term is unfortunately used in two rather different ways in C; the way I commonly use it is inside a function or method. Here, `static` indicates that the memory set aside for a variable should not be released after the function or method returns; rather, the variable remains and maintains its value for the next time the function or method is called. A static variable is useful, for example, when you want to call a function many times without the overhead of calculating the result each time (after the first time). First test to see whether the static value has already been calculated: if it hasn't, this must be the first time the function is being called, so you calculate it; if it has, you just return it. Here's a schematic version:

```
int myfunction() {
    static int result = 0; // 0 means we haven't done the calculation yet
    if (result == 0) {
        // calculate result and set it
    }
    return result;
}
```

A very common use of a static variable in Objective-C is to implement a singleton instance returned by a class factory method. If that sounds complicated, don't worry; it isn't. Here's an example from my own code, which you can grasp even though we haven't discussed Objective-C yet:

```
+ (CardPainter*) sharedPainter {
    static CardPainter* sp = nil;
    if (nil == sp)
        sp = [CardPainter new];
    return sp;
}
```

That code says: If the CardPainter instance sp has never been created, create it, and in any case, now return it. Thus, no matter how many times this method is called, the instance will be created just once and that same instance will be returned every time.

Static variables are a C language feature, not an Objective-C language feature. Therefore, a static variable knows nothing of classes and instances; even if it appears inside a function or a method, it is defined at the level of a file, which means, in effect, at the level of your program as a whole. That's fine when you're using it in a class factory method, because a class is unique to your program as a whole. But never use a static variable in an Objective-C instance method, because your program can have multiple such instances, and the value of this one static variable will apply across all of them. In other words, don't use a C static variable as a lazy substitute for an Objective-C instance variable (Chapter 2). I've made that mistake, and trust me, the results are not pretty.

CHAPTER 2

Object-Based Programming

My object all sublime.

—W. S. Gilbert, *The Mikado*

Objective-C, the native language for programming the Cocoa API, is an object-oriented language; to use it, the programmer must have an appreciation of the nature of objects and object-based programming. There's little point in learning the syntax of Objective-C message sending or instantiation without a clear understanding of what a message or an instance is. That is what this chapter is about.

Objects

An object, in programming, is based on the concept of an object in the real world. It's an independent, self-contained thing. These objects, unlike purely inert objects in the real world, have abilities. So an object in programming is more like a clock than a rock; it doesn't just sit there, but actually does something. Perhaps one could compare an object in programming more to the animate objects of the real world, as opposed to the inanimate objects, except that — unlike real-world animate things — a programming object is supposed to be predictable: in particular, it does what you tell it. In the real world, you tell a dog to sit and anything can happen; in the programming world, you tell a dog to sit and it sits. (This is why so many of us prefer programming to dealing with the real world.)

In object-based programming, a program is organized into many discrete objects. This organization can make life much easier for the programmer. Each object has abilities that are specialized for that object. You can think of this as being a little like how an automobile assembly line works. Each worker or station along the line does one thing (screw on the bumpers, or paint the door, or whatever) and does it well. You can see immediately how this organization helps the programmer. If the car is coming off the assembly line with the door badly painted, it is very likely that the blame lies with the door-painting object, so we know where to look for the bug in our code. Or, if we decide to change the color that the door is to be painted, we have but to make a small change in the door-painting object. Meanwhile, other objects just go on doing what they do. They neither know nor care what the door-painting object does or how it works. Objects are concerned with other objects only to the extent that they interact with them. Those interactions take the form of messages.

Messages and Methods

Nothing in a computer program happens unless it is instructed to happen. In a C program, all code belongs to a function and doesn't run unless that function is called. In an object-based program, all code belongs to an object, and doesn't run unless that object is told to run that code. All the action in an object-based program happens because an object was told to act. What does it mean to tell an object something?

An object, in object-based programming, has a well-defined set of abilities — things it knows how to do. For example, imagine an object that is to represent a dog. We can design a highly simplified, schematic dog that knows how to do an extremely limited range of things: eat, come for a walk, bark, sit, lie down, sleep. The purpose of these abilities is so that the object can be told, as appropriate, to exercise them. So, again, we can imagine our schematic dog, rather like some child's toy robot, responding to simple commands: Eat! Come for a walk! Bark!

In object-based programming, a command directed to an object is called a *message*. To make the dog object eat, we send the `eat` message to the dog object. This mechanism of message sending is the basis of all activity in the program. The program consists entirely of objects, so its activity consists entirely of objects sending messages to one another. Messages are so crucial to the activity of an object-based program that it is tempting to propose a (somewhat circular) definition of the notion *object* in terms of messages: *an object is a thing to which a message can be sent*.

A moment ago, I said that in a C program, all code belongs to a function. The object-based analogue to a function is called a *method*. So, for example, a dog object might have an `eat` method. When the dog object is sent the `eat` message, it responds by calling the `eat` method.

It may sound as if I'm not drawing any clear distinction between a message and a method. But there is a difference. A message is what one object says to another. A method is a bundle of code that gets called. The connection between the two is not perfectly direct. You might send a message to an object that corresponds to no method of that object. For example, you might tell the dog to recite the soliloquy from Hamlet. I'm not sure what will happen if you do that; the details are implementation-dependent. (The dog might just sit there silently. Or it might get annoyed and bite you. Or, I suppose, it might nip off, read Hamlet, memorize the soliloquy, and recite it.) But that implementation-dependence is exactly the point of the distinction between message and method.

Nevertheless, in general the distinction between sending a message and calling a method won't usually be important in real life. Most of the time, when you're using Objective-C, your reason for sending a message to an object will be that that object implements the corresponding method and you are expecting to call that method. So sending a message to an object and calling a method of an object will appear to be the same act.

 Objective-C is object-based; C is not. That is why we speak of C functions but of Objective-C methods.

Classes and Instances

We come now to an extremely characteristic and profound feature of object-based programming. Just like in the real world, every object in the object-based programming world is of some type. This type, called a *class*, is the object-based analogy to the data type in C. Just as a simple variable in C might be an int or a float, an object in the object-based programming world might be a Dog or an NSString. In the object-based programming world, the idea of this arrangement is to ensure that more than one individual object can be relied upon to act the same way.

There can, for example, be more than one dog. You might have a dog called Fido and I might have a dog called Rover. But both dogs know how to eat, come for a walk, and bark. In object-based programming, they know this because they both belong to the Dog class. The knowledge of how to eat, come for a walk, and bark is part of the Dog class. Your dog Fido and my dog Rover possess this knowledge solely by virtue of being Dog objects.

From the programmer's point of view, what this means is simple: all the code you write is put into a class. All the methods you write will be part of some class or other. You don't program an individual dog object: you program the Dog class.

But I just got through saying that an object-based program works through the sending of messages to individual objects. So even though the programmer does not write the code for an individual dog object, there still needs to *be* an individual dog object in order for there to be something to send a message to. It is the Dog class that knows how to bark, but it is an individual dog object that is told to bark, and that actually does bark. So the question is: if all Dog code lives in a Dog class, where do individual dogs come from?

The answer is that they have to be created in the course of the program as it runs. When the program starts out, it contains code for a Dog class, but no individual dog objects.

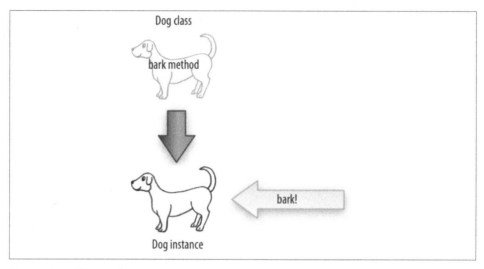

Figure 2-1. Class and instance

If any barking by any dogs is to be done, the program must first create an individual dog object. This object will belong to the Dog class, so it can be sent the bark message. An individual object belonging to the Dog class (or any class) is an *instance* of that class. To manufacture, from a class, an actual individual object that is an instance of that class, is to *instantiate* that class.

Classes, then, exist from the get-go, as part of the fact that the program exists in the first place; they are where the code is. Instances, on the other hand, are manufactured, deliberately and individually, as the program runs. Each instance is manufactured *from* a class, it is an instance *of* that class, and it has methods by virtue of the fact that the class has those methods. The instance can then be sent a message; what it will do in response depends on what code the class contains in its methods. The instance is the individual thing that can be sent messages; the class, with its methods, is the locus of the thing's ability to respond to messages (Figure 2-1).

Because every individual object is an instance of a class, to know what messages you can officially send to that object, you need to know at least what methods its class has endowed it with. The public knowledge of this information is that class's API. (A class may also have methods that you're not really supposed to call from outside that object; these would not be public and other objects couldn't officially send those messages to an instance of that class.) That's why Apple's own Cocoa documentation consists largely of pages listing and describing the methods supplied by some class. For example, to know what messages you can send to an NSString object (instance), you'd start by studying the NSString class documentation. That page is really just a big list of methods,

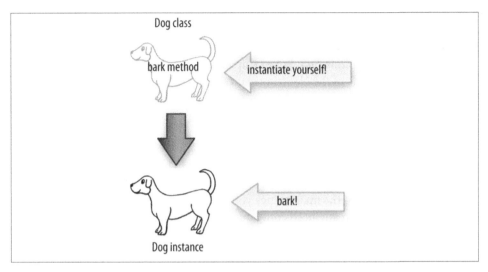

Figure 2-2. Class and instance, take two

so it tells you what an NSString object can do. That isn't everything in the world there is to know about an NSString, but it's a big percentage of it.

Class Methods

I've said that nothing happens in a program unless a message is sent to an object. But I've also said that there are no instances until they are created as the program runs; at the outset, there are only classes. How, then, are these instances to be created? To make an instance as the program runs, it must be possible to send a message to something; otherwise, nothing will happen. But if there are no instances, what is the "make an instance" message to be sent to?

The answer is that classes are themselves objects and can be sent messages. And indeed, one of the most important things you can ask a class to do by sending it a message is to instantiate itself. Thus there is a step missing from our earlier Figure 2-1; it shows a class and an instance, with the code in the class and a message being sent to the instance, but it fails to show how the instance was generated from the class in the first place. A more complete picture would look like Figure 2-2.

It thus begins to look as if there must be two kinds of message: messages that you are allowed to send to a class (such as telling the Dog class to instantiate itself) and messages that you are allowed to send to an instance (such as telling an individual dog to bark). That is exactly true. More precisely, all code lives as a method in a class, but methods are of two kinds: class methods and instance methods. If a method is a class method, you can send that message to the class. If a method is an instance method, you can send that message to an instance of the class.

In Objective-C syntax, class methods and instance methods are distinguished by the use of a plus sign or a minus sign. For example, Apple's NSString class documentation page listing the methods of the NSString class starts out like this:

```
+ string
- init
```

The `string` method is a class method. The `init` method is an instance method.

In general, though not exclusively, class methods tend to be factory methods — that is, methods for generating and vending an instance. This makes sense, because making an instance of itself is one of the main things you're likely to want to ask a class to do. You might think that a class really needs only *one* class method for generating an instance of itself, and that is rigorously true, but classes tend to provide multiple factory methods purely as a convenience to the programmer. For example, here are three NSString class methods:

```
+ string
+ stringWithFormat:
+ stringWithContentsOfFile:encoding:error:
```

They all make instances. The first class method, `string`, generates an empty NSString instance (a string with no text). The second class method, `stringWithFormat:`, generates an NSString instance based on text that you provide, which can include transforming other values into text; for example, you might use it to start with an integer 9 and generate an NSString instance @"9". The third class method reads the contents of a file and generates an NSString instance from those contents. When you come to write your own classes, you too might well create multiple class methods that act as instance factories for your own future programming convenience.

Instance Variables

Now that I've revealed that classes are objects and can be sent messages, you might be wondering why there need to be instances at all. Why doesn't the mere existence of classes as objects suffice for object-based programming? Why would you ever bother to instantiate any of the classes? Why wouldn't you write all your code as class methods, have the program send messages from one class object to another, and be done with it?

The answer is that instances have a feature that classes do not: instance variables. An instance variable is just what the name suggests: it's a variable belonging to an instance. Like instance methods, instance variables are defined as part of the class. But the *value* of an instance variable is set as the program runs and belongs to one instance alone. In other words, different instances can have different values for the same instance variable.

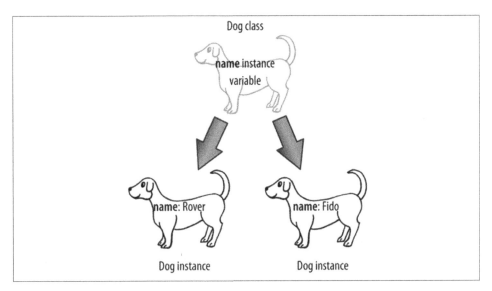

Figure 2-3. Instance variables

For example, suppose we have a Dog class and we decide that it might be a good idea for every dog to have a name. Just as you can learn a real-world dog's name by reading the tag on its collar, we want to be able to assign every dog instance a name and, subsequently, to learn what that name is. So, in designing the Dog class, we declare that this class has an instance variable called name, whose value is a string (probably an NSString, as we're using Objective-C). Now when our program runs we can instantiate Dog and assign the resulting dog instance a name (that is, we can assign its name instance variable a value). We can also instantiate Dog again and assign *that* resulting dog instance a name. Let's say these are two different names: one is @"Rover" and one is @"Fido". Then we've got two instances of Dog, and they are significantly different; they differ in the value of their name instance variables (Figure 2-3).

So an instance is a reflection of the instance methods of its class, but that isn't *all* it is; it's also a collection of instance variables. The class is responsible for what instance variables the instance has, but not for the values of those variables. The values can change as the program runs and apply only to a particular instance. An instance is a cluster of particular instance variable values.

In short, an instance is both code and data. The code it gets from its class and in a sense is shared with all other instances of that class, but the data belong to it alone. The data can persist as long as the instance persists. The instance has, at every moment, a state — the complete collection of its own personal instance variable values. An instance is a device for maintaining state. It's a box for storage of data.

The Object-Based Philosophy

We may summarize the nature of objects in two phrases: encapsulation of functionality, and maintenance of state. (I used this same summary many years ago in my book *REALbasic: The Definitive Guide.*)

Encapsulation of functionality

Each object does its own job, and presents to the rest of the world — to other objects, and indeed in a sense to the programmer — an opaque wall whose only entrances are the methods to which it promises to respond and the actions it promises to perform when the corresponding messages are sent to it. The details of how, behind the scenes, it actually implements those actions are secreted within itself; no other object needs to know them.

Maintenance of state

Each individual instance is a bundle of data that it maintains. Typically that data is private, which means that it's encapsulated as well; no other object knows what that data is or in what form it is kept. The only way to discover from outside what data an object is maintaining is if there's a method that reveals it.

As an example, imagine an object whose job is to implement a stack — it might be an instance of a Stack class. A *stack* is a data structure that maintains a set of data in LIFO order (last in, first out). It responds to just two messages: push and pop. Push means to add a given piece of data to the set. Pop means to remove from the set the piece of data that was most recently pushed and hand it out. It's like a stack of plates: plates are placed onto the top of the stack or removed from the top of the stack one by one, so the first plate to go onto the stack can't be retrieved until all other subsequently added plates have been removed (Figure 2-4).

The stack object illustrates encapsulation of functionality because the outside world knows nothing of how the stack is actually implemented. It might be an array, it might be a linked list, it might be any of a number of other implementations. But a client object — an object that actually sends a push or pop message to the stack object — knows nothing of this and cares less, provided the stack object adheres to its contract of behaving like a stack. This is also good for the programmer, who can, as the program develops, safely substitute one implementation for another without harming the vast machinery of the program as a whole. And just the other way round, the stack object knows nothing and cares less about who is telling it to push or to pop, and why. It just hums along and does its job in its reliable little way.

The stack object illustrates maintenance of state because it isn't just the gateway to the stack data — it *is* the stack data. Other objects can get access to that data, but only by virtue of having access to the stack object itself, and only in the manner that the stack object permits. The stack data is effectively inside the stack object; no one else can see it. All that another object can do is push or pop. If a certain object is at the top of our

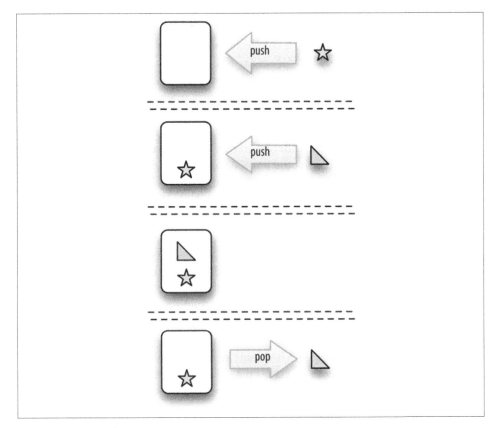

Figure 2-4. A stack

stack object's stack right now, then whatever object sends the pop message to this stack object will receive that object in return. If no object sends the pop message to this stack object, then the object at the top of the stack will just sit there, waiting.

As a second example of the philosophy and nature of object-based programming at work, I'll revert to another imaginary scenario I used in my REALbasic book. Pretend we're writing an arcade game where the user is to "shoot" at moving "targets," and the score increases every time a target is hit. We immediately have a sense of how we might organize our code using object-based programming and can see how object-based programming will fulfill its nature and purpose:

- There will be a Target class. Every target object will be an instance of this class. This decision makes sense because we want every target to behave the same way. A target will need to know how to draw itself; that knowledge will be part of the Target class, which makes sense because all targets will draw themselves in the same way. Thus we have the relationship between class and instance.

- Targets may draw themselves the same way, but they may also differ in appearance. Perhaps some targets are blue, others are red, and so on. This difference between individual targets can be expressed as an instance variable. Call it `color`. Every time we instantiate a target, we'll assign it a color. The Target class's code for drawing an individual target will look at that target's `color` instance variable and use it when filling in the target's shape. Clearly, we could extend this individualization as much as we like: targets could have different sizes, different shapes, and so on, and all of these parametric distinctions could be made on an individual basis through the use of instance variables. Thus we have both encapsulation of functionality and maintenance of state. A target has a state, the parameters that describe how it should look, and also has the ability to draw itself, expressing that state visually.

- When a target is hit by the user, it will explode. So perhaps the Target class will have an `explode` instance method; thus, every target knows how to explode. One thing that should happen whenever a target explodes is that the user's score should increase. So let's imagine a score object — an instance of the Score class. When a target explodes, one of the things its `explode` instance method will do is send an `increase` message to the score object. Thus we have both encapsulation of functionality and maintenance of state. The score object responds indifferently to any object that sends it the `increase` message; it doesn't need to know why it's being sent that message. Nor does the score object even need to know that targets exist, or indeed that it's part of a game. It just sits there maintaining the score, and when it receives the `increase` message, it increases it.

As we imagine constructing an object-based program for performing a particular task, we bear in mind the nature of objects, as sketched in this chapter. There are classes and instances. A class is a set of functionality (methods) describing what all instances of that class can do (encapsulation of functionality). Instances of the same class differ only in the value of their instance variables (maintenance of state). We plan accordingly. Objects are an organizational tool, a set of boxes for encapsulating the code that accomplishes a particular task. They are also a conceptual tool. The programmer, being forced to think in terms of discrete objects, must divide the goals and behaviors of the program into discrete tasks, each task being assigned to an appropriate object.

But no object is an island. Objects can cooperate with one another, namely by communicating with one another — that is, by sending messages to one another. The ways in which appropriate lines of communication can be arranged are innumerable. The assembly-line analogy that I used at the start of this chapter illustrates one such arrangement — first, object 1 operates upon the end-product; then it hands it off to object 2, and object 2 operates upon the end-product, and so on. But that arrangement won't be appropriate to most tasks. Coming up with an appropriate arrangement — an *ar-*

chitecture — for the cooperative and orderly relationship between objects is one of the most challenging aspects of object-based programming.

Using object-based programming effectively to make a program do what you want it to do while keeping it clear and maintainable is something of an art; your abilities will improve with experience. Eventually, you may want to do some further reading on effective planning and construction of the architecture of an object-based program. I recommend in particular two classic, favorite books. *Refactoring*, by Martin Fowler (Addison-Wesley, 1999), describes how you can get a sense that you might need to rearrange what methods belong to what classes (and how to conquer your fear of doing so). *Design Patterns*, by Erich Gamma, Richard Helm, Ralph Johnson, and John Vlissides (also known as "the Gang of Four"), is the bible on architecting object-based programs, listing all the ways you can arrange objects with the right powers and the right knowledge of one another (Addison-Wesley, 1994).

CHAPTER 3

Objective-C Objects and Messages

One of the first object-based programming languages to achieve maturity and widespread dissemination was Smalltalk. It was developed during the 1970s at Xerox PARC under the leadership of Alan Kay and started becoming widely known in 1980. The purpose of Objective-C, created by Brad Cox and Tom Love in 1986, was to build Smalltalk-like syntax and behavior on top of C. Objective-C was licensed by NeXT in 1988 and was the basis for its application framework API, NeXTStep. Eventually, NeXT and Apple merged, and the NeXT application framework evolved into Cocoa, the framework for OS X applications, still revolving around Objective-C. That history explains why Objective-C is the base language for iOS programming. (It also explains why Cocoa class names often begin with "NS" — it stands for "NeXTStep.")

Having learned the basics of C (Chapter 1) and the nature of object-based programming (Chapter 2), you are ready to meet Objective-C. This chapter describes Objective-C structural fundamentals; the next two chapters provide more detail about how Objective-C classes and instances work. (A few additional features of the language are discussed in Chapter 10.) As with the C language, my intention is not to describe the Objective-C language completely, but to provide a practical linguistic grounding, founded on my own experience of those aspects of the language that need to be firmly understood as a basis for iOS programming.

An Object Reference Is a Pointer

A *reference* is just what you think it is: it's a way of picking out some definite individual thing. A particularly good form of reference is to give something a name. If we want to refer to Socrates, it is tedious to have to keep describing him as "that fat bald fellow who keeps asking annoying questions in the marketplace." It's simpler to refer to him by his name, "Socrates." The C equivalent of a name is a variable. Assigning a value to a variable causes that variable (the name) to become a reference to that value.

In C, every variable must be declared to be of some type. The C language includes very few basic data types; it is certainly unprepared for object types. In order to impose objects onto C and turn C into an object-based language, Objective-C takes advantage of the flexibility of C *pointers* (see Chapter 1). A pointer is a C data type, but what is pointed to can be anything at all. Therefore, in Objective-C, every reference to an object is a pointer (and Objective-C itself takes care of dealing with the question of what's being pointed to).

The fact that object references are pointers in Objective-C is particularly evident in the case of a reference to an *instance* (see Chapter 2). In an object-based language such as Objective-C, an instance's type is its class. Thus, we would like to use a class name in Objective-C much as we use any data type name in C. Pointers allow us to do this. Pointers satisfy the requirement of C, on the one hand, that a reference should be of some definite C data type, as well as the requirement of Objective-C, on the other hand, that we should be able to specify any of a vast multiplicity of class types. In Objective-C, if a variable is to refer explicitly to an instance of the class MyClass, that variable is of type `MyClass*` — a pointer to a MyClass. In general, in Objective-C, a reference to an instance is a pointer and the name of the data type of what's at the far end of that pointer is the name of the instance's class.

 Note the convention for capitalization. Variable names tend to start with a lowercase letter; class names tend to start with an uppercase letter.

As I mentioned in Chapter 1, the fact that a reference to an instance is a pointer in Objective-C will generally not cause you any difficulties, because pointers are used consistently throughout the language. For example, a message to an instance is directed at the pointer, so there is no need to dereference the pointer. Indeed, having established that a variable representing an instance is a pointer, you're likely to forget that this variable even *is* a pointer and just work directly with that variable:

```
NSString* s = @"Hello, world!";
NSString* s2 = [s uppercaseString];
```

Having established that s is an `NSString*`, you would never dereference s (that is, you would never speak of `*s`) to access the "real" NSString. So it feels as if the *pointer* is the real NSString. Thus, in the previous example, once the variable s is declared as a pointer to an NSString, the `uppercaseString` message is sent directly to the variable s. (The `uppercaseString` message asks an NSString to generate and return an uppercase version of itself; so, after that code, s2 is `@"HELLO, WORLD!"`)

The tie between a pointer, an instance, and the class of that instance is so close that it is natural to speak of an expression like `MyClass*` as meaning "a MyClass instance," and of a `MyClass*` value as "a MyClass." An Objective-C programmer will say simply that, in the previous example, s *is* an NSString, that `uppercaseString` returns "an NSString," and so forth. It is fine to speak like that, and I do it myself — provided you remember that this is a shorthand. Such an expression means "an NSString instance," and because an instance is represented as a C pointer, it means an `NSString*`, a pointer to an NSString.

Although the fact that instance references in Objective-C are pointers does not cause any special difficulty, you must still be conscious of what pointers are and how they work. As I emphasized in Chapter 1, when you're working with pointers, your actions have a special meaning. So here are some basic facts about pointers that you should keep in mind when working with instance references in Objective-C.

 Forgetting the asterisk in an instance declaration is a common beginner mistake, and will net you a mysterious compiler error message, such as "Interface type cannot be statically allocated."

Instance References, Initialization, and nil

Merely declaring an instance reference's type doesn't bring any instance into existence. For example:

```
NSString* s; // only a declaration; no instance is pointed to
```

After that declaration, s is *typed* as a pointer to an NSString, but it is not *in fact* pointing to an NSString. You have created a pointer, but you haven't supplied an NSString for it to point to. It's just sitting there, waiting for you to point it at an NSString, typically by assignment (as we did with `@"Hello, world!"` earlier). Such assignment *initializes* the variable, giving it, for the first time, an actual meaningful value of the proper type.

You can declare a variable as an instance reference in one line of code and initialize it later, like this:

```
NSString* s;
// ... time passes ...
s = @"Hello, world!";
```

But that is not common. It is much more common, wherever possible, to declare and initialize a variable all in one line of code:

```
NSString* s = @"Hello, world!";
```

Declaration *without* initialization, before the advent of ARC (Chapter 12), created a downright dangerous situation:

```
NSString* s;
```

Without ARC, s could be *anything* after a mere declaration like that. The trouble is, however, that it is *claiming* to be a pointer to an NSString. Fooled by this, you might then proceed to *treat* it as a pointer to an NSString. But it is pointing at garbage. A pointer pointing at garbage is liable to cause serious trouble down the road when you accidentally try to use it as an instance. Sending a message to a garbage pointer, or otherwise treating it as a meaningful instance, can crash your program. Even worse, it might *not* crash your program: it might cause your program to behave very, very oddly instead — and figuring out why can be difficult.

Setting a reference to nil, on the other hand, doesn't point that reference at an actual instance, but at least it ensures that the reference isn't a garbage pointer. To defend against garbage pointers, therefore, it was common, before ARC, if you weren't going to initialize an instance reference pointer at the moment you declared it by assigning it a real value, to assign nil to it:

```
NSString* s = nil;
```

A small but delightful bonus feature of ARC is that this assignment is performed for you, implicitly and invisibly, as soon as you declare a variable without initializing it:

```
NSString* s; // under ARC, s is immediately set to nil for you
```

What is nil? It's a form of zero — the form of zero appropriate to an instance reference. The nil value simply means: "This instance reference isn't pointing to any instance." Indeed, you can test an instance reference against nil as a way of finding out whether it is in fact pointing to a real instance. This is an extremely common thing to do:

```
if (nil == s) // ...
```

As I mentioned in Chapter 1, the explicit comparison with nil isn't strictly necessary; because nil is a form of zero, and because zero means false in a condition, you can perform the same test like this:

```
if (!s) // ...
```

I do in fact write nil tests in that second form all the time, but some programmers would take me to task for bad style. The first form has the advantage that its real meaning is made explicit, rather than relying on a cute implicit feature of C. The first form also deliberately places nil first in the comparison so that if the programmer accidentally omits an equal sign, performing an assignment instead of a comparison, the compiler will catch the error (because assignment to nil is illegal).

Many Cocoa methods use a return value of nil, instead of an expected instance, to signify that something went wrong. You are supposed to capture this return value and test it for nil in order to discover whether something *did* go wrong. For example, the documentation for the NSString class method `stringWithContentsOf-File:encoding:error:` says that it returns "a string created by reading data from the file named by `path` using the encoding, `enc`. If the file can't be opened or there is an

---

encoding error, returns nil." So, as I described in Chapter 1, you call that method like this:

```
NSString* path = // something or other
NSStringEncoding enc = // something or other
NSError* err = nil;
NSString* result =
    [NSString stringWithContentsOfFile: path encoding: enc error: &err];
```

Why is `stringWithContentsOfFile:encoding:error:` structured in this way? In effect, it's so that this method can return *two* results. It returns a real result, which we have captured by assigning it to the NSString pointer we're calling `result`. But if there's an error, it also wants to set the value of another object, an NSError object; the idea is that you can then study that NSError object to find out what went wrong. (Perhaps the file wasn't where you said it was, or it wasn't stored in the encoding you claimed it was.) By passing a pointer to a pointer to an NSError, you give the method free rein to do that. Before the call to `stringWithContentsOfFile:encoding:error:`, `err` was initialized to nil; during the call to `stringWithContentsOfFile:encoding:error:`, if there's an error, the pointer is repointed, thus giving `err` a meaningful NSError value describing that error. (Repointing a pointer in this way is sometimes called *indirection*.)

Thus, your next move after calling this method and capturing the result should be to test that result against nil, just to make sure you've really got an instance now. If the result isn't nil, fine; it's the string you asked for. If the result *is* nil, you then study the NSError that `err` is now pointing to, to learn what went wrong:

```
NSString* path = // something or other
NSStringEncoding enc = // something or other
NSError* err = nil;
NSString* result =
    [NSString stringWithContentsOfFile:path encoding:enc error:&err];
if (nil == result) { // oops! something went wrong...
    // examine err to find out what went wrong
}
```

This pattern is frequently used in Cocoa. *Don't get the pattern wrong.* A very common beginner mistake is to call a method such as `stringWithContentsOf-File:encoding:error:` and then immediately check the value of the error variable (here, `err`). Don't do that! If there was no error, nothing about the value of the error variable is guaranteed. Instead, start by checking the result (here, `result`); if the result indicates (by turning out to be nil) that there was an error, then and only then should you examine the NSError value that was set by indirection.

 In pure C code, you will sometimes see a pointer-to-nothing expressed as NULL. NULL and nil are functionally equivalent nowadays, so feel free to use nil exclusively.

Instance References and Assignment

As I said in Chapter 1, assigning to a pointer does not mutate the value at the far end of the pointer; rather, it repoints the pointer. Moreover, assigning one pointer to another repoints the pointer in such a way that both pointers are now pointing to the very same thing. Failure to keep these simple facts firmly in mind can have results that range from surprising to disastrous.

Pretend that we've implemented the Stack class described in Chapter 2, and consider the following code:

```
Stack* myStack1 = // ... create Stack instance and initialize myStack1 ...
Stack* myStack2 = myStack1;
```

A common misunderstanding is to imagine that the assignment myStack2 = my-Stack1 somehow makes a new, separate instance that duplicates myStack1. That's not at all the case. The assignment doesn't make a new instance; it just points myStack2 at the very same instance that myStack1 is pointing at. It may be possible to make a new instance that duplicates a given instance, but the ability to do so is not a given and it is not going to happen through mere assignment. (For how a separate duplicate instance might be generated, see the NSCopying protocol and the copy method mentioned in Chapter 10.)

Moreover, instances in general are usually mutable: they typically have instance variables that can change. If two references are pointing at one and the same instance, then when the instance is mutated by way of one reference, that mutation also affects the instance as seen through the other reference:

```
Stack* myStack1 = // ... create Stack instance and initialize myStack1 ...
Stack* myStack2 = myStack1;
[myStack1 push: @"Hello"];
[myStack1 push: @"World"];
NSString* s = [myStack2 pop];
```

After we pop myStack2, s is @"World" even though nothing was ever pushed onto myStack2 — and the stack myStack1 contains only @"Hello" even though nothing was ever popped off of myStack1. That's because we did push two strings onto myStack1 and then pop one string off myStack2, and myStack1 *is* myStack2 — in the sense that they are both pointers to the very same stack instance. That's perfectly fine, as long as you understand and intend this behavior.

Sometimes, however, such behavior is not perfectly fine. When your program has more than one reference to the same instance, surprising results can ensue, because (just as in the preceding example) that instance can be mutated by way of one reference at a time when the holder of the other reference is not expecting any such thing to happen. In real life, problems of this kind can arise particularly because instances can have instance variables that point to other objects, and those pointers can persist as long as the

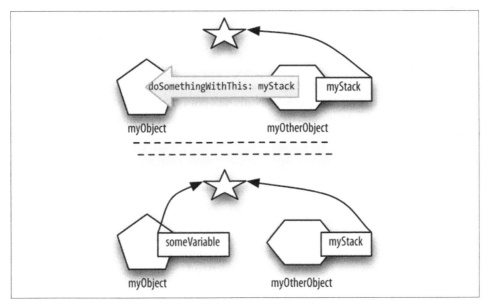

Figure 3-1. Two instances end up with pointers to the same third instance

instances themselves do. Suppose we have an object myObject and we hand it a reference to our stack object:

```
Stack* myStack = // ... create Stack instance and initialize myStack ...
[myObject doSomethingWithThis: myStack]; // pass myStack to myObject
```

After that code, myObject has a pointer to the very same instance we're already pointing to as myStack. So we must be careful and thoughtful. The object myObject might now mutate myStack right under our very noses! Even more, the object myObject might *keep* its reference to the stack instance (by way of an instance variable) and mutate it *later* — possibly much later, in a way that could surprise us. This kind of shared referent situation can be intentional, but it is also something to watch out for and be conscious of (Figure 3-1).

Instance References and Memory Management

The pointer nature of instance references in Objective-C also has implications for management of memory. The scope, and in particular the lifetime, of variables in pure C is typically quite straightforward: if you bring a piece of variable storage into existence by declaring that variable within a certain scope, then when that scope ceases to exist, the variable storage ceases to exist. That sort of variable is called *automatic* (K&R 1.10). So, for example:

```
void myFunction() {
    int i; // storage for an int is set aside
    i = 7; // 7 is placed in that storage
} // the scope ends, so the int storage and its contents vanish
```

But in the case of a pointer, there are two pieces of memory to worry about: the pointer itself, which is an integer signifying an address in memory, and whatever is at that address, at the far end of that pointer. Nothing about the C language causes the destruction of what a pointer points to when the pointer itself is automatically destroyed as it goes out of scope:

```
void myFunction() {
    NSString* s = @"Hello, world!"; // pointer and NSString
    NSString* s2 = [s uppercaseString]; // pointer and NSString
} // the two pointers go out of existence...
// ... but what about the two NSStrings they point to?
```

Some object-based programming languages in which a reference to an instance is a pointer do manage automatically the memory pointed to by instance references (REALbasic and Ruby are examples). But Objective-C is not one of those languages. Because the C language has nothing to say about the automatic destruction of what is pointed to by a reference to an instance, Objective-C implements an explicit mechanism for the management of memory. I'll talk in a later chapter (Chapter 12) about what that mechanism is and what responsibilities for the programmer it entails. Fortunately, under ARC, those responsibilities are fewer than they used to be; but memory must still be managed, and you must still understand how memory management of instances works.

Methods and Messages

An Objective-C method is defined as part of a class. It has three aspects:

Whether it's a class method or an instance method
> If it's a class method, you call it by sending a message to the class itself. If it's an instance method, you call it by sending a message to an instance of the class.

Its parameters and return value
> As with a C function (see Chapter 1), an Objective-C method takes some number of parameters; each parameter is of some specified type. And, as with a C function, it may return a value, which is also of some specified type; if the method returns nothing, its return type is declared as void.

Its name
> An Objective-C method's name must contain exactly as many colons as the method takes parameters, and, if the method takes any parameters, the name must end with a colon.

Calling a Method

To send a message to an object, you use a *message expression*, also referred to, for simplicity and by analogy with C functions, as a *method call*. As you've doubtless gathered, the syntax for sending a message to an object involves square brackets. The first thing in the square brackets is the object to which the message is to be sent; this object is the message's *receiver*. Then follows the message:

```
NSString* s2 = [s uppercaseString]; // send "uppercaseString" message to s ...
// ... (and assign result to s2)
```

If the message is a method that takes parameters, each corresponding argument value comes after a colon:

```
[myStack1 push: @"Hello"]; // send "push:" message to myStack1 ...
// ...with one argument, the NSString @"Hello"
```

To send a message to a class (calling a class method), you can represent the class by the literal name of the class:

```
NSString* s = [NSString string]; // send "string" message to NSString class
```

To send a message to an instance (calling an instance method), you'll need a reference to an instance, which (as you know) is a pointer:

```
NSString* s = @"Hello, world!"; // s is initialized as an NSString instance
NSString* s2 = [s uppercaseString]; // send "uppercaseString" message to s
```

You can send a class method to a class, and an instance method to an instance, no matter how you obtain and represent the class or the instance. For example, @"Hello, world!" is itself an NSString instance, so it's legal to say:

```
NSString* s2 = [@"Hello, world!" uppercaseString];
```

If a method takes no parameters, then its name contains no colons, like the NSString instance method uppercaseString. If a method takes one parameter, then its name contains one colon, which is the final character of the method name, like the hypothetical Stack instance method push:. If a method takes two or more parameters, its name contains that number of colons, and the last colon is the final character of the method name. In the minimal case, the method name ends with *all* its colons. For example, a method taking three parameters might be called hereAreThreeStrings:::. To call it, we split the name after each colon and follow each colon with an argument, which looks like this:

```
[someObject hereAreThreeStrings: @"string1" : @"string2" : @"string3"];
```

That's a legal way to name and call a method, but it isn't very common, mostly because it isn't very informative. Usually the name will have more text; in particular, the part of the name before each colon will describe the parameter that follows that colon.

For example, there's a UIColor class method for generating an instance of a UIColor from four CGFloat numbers representing its red, green, blue, and alpha (transparency) components, and it's called `colorWithRed:green:blue:alpha:`. Notice the clever construction of this name. The `colorWith` part tells something about the method's purpose: it generates a *color*, starting *with* some set of information. All the rest of the name, `Red:green:blue:alpha:`, describes the meaning of each parameter. And you call it like this:

```
UIColor* c = [UIColor colorWithRed: 0.0 green: 0.5 blue: 0.25 alpha: 1.0];
```

Similarly, I've referred several times in this chapter to an NSString class method `string-WithContentsOfFile:encoding:error:`. The name is beautifully descriptive. Even before we learn the exact data types of the parameters, we can guess that the first parameter is a reference to a file, the second parameter describes the file's encoding, and the third parameter is used to return an error by indirection (and that this method returns a string).

The rules for naming an Objective-C method, along with the conventions governing such names (like trying to make the name informative about the method's purpose and the meanings of its parameters), lead to some rather long and unwieldy method names, such as `getBytes:maxLength:usedLength:encoding:options:range:remaining-Range:`. Such verbosity of nomenclature is characteristic of Objective-C. Method calls, and even method declarations, are often split across multiple lines, both for clarity and to prevent a single line of code from becoming so long that it wraps within the editor.

Declaring a Method

A method declaration is the definitive public statement of that method's name, the data type of its return value, and the data types of each of its parameters. For example, the Apple documentation of a class consists chiefly of a list of the declarations of its methods. Thus, it is crucial that you know how to read a method declaration.

The declaration for a method has three parts:

- Either + or -, meaning that the method is a class method or an instance method, respectively.
- The data type of the return value, in parentheses.
- The name of the method, split after each colon. Following each colon is the corresponding parameter, expressed as the data type of the parameter, in parentheses, followed by a placeholder name for the parameter.

So, for example, Apple's documentation tells us that the declaration for the UIColor class method `colorWithRed:green:blue:alpha:` is:

```
+ (UIColor*) colorWithRed: (CGFloat) red green: (CGFloat) green
                    blue: (CGFloat) blue alpha: (CGFloat) alpha
```

(Note that I've split the declaration into two lines, for legibility and to fit onto this page. The documentation puts it all on a single line.)

Make very sure you can read this declaration! You should be able to look at it and say to yourself instantly, "The name of this method is colorWithRed:green:blue:alpha:. It's a class method that takes four CGFloat parameters and returns a UIColor."

The space after each colon in a method call or declaration is optional. Space before a colon is also legal, though in practice one rarely sees this. Space before or after any of the parentheses in a method declaration is also optional.

Nesting Method Calls

Wherever in a method call an object of a certain type is supposed to appear, you can put another method call that returns that type. Thus you can nest method calls. A method call can appear as the receiver in a method call:

```
NSString* s = [[NSString string] uppercaseString]; // silly but legal
```

That's legal because the result of NSString's class method string is an NSString instance (formally, an NSString* value), so we can send an NSString instance method to that result. Similarly, a method call can appear as an argument in a method call:

```
[myStack push: [NSString string]]; // ok if push: expects NSString* parameter
```

However, I must caution you against overdoing that sort of thing. Code with a lot of nested square brackets is very difficult to read (and to write). Furthermore, if one of the nested method calls happens to return an unexpected value, you have no way to detect this fact. It is often better, then, to be even more verbose and declare a temporary variable for each piece of the method call. Just to take an example from my own code, instead of writing this:

```
NSArray* arr = [[MPMediaQuery albumsQuery] collections];
```

I might write this:

```
MPMediaQuery* query = [MPMediaQuery albumsQuery];
NSArray* arr = [query collections];
```

Even though the first version is quite short and legible, and even though in the second version the variable query will never be used again — it exists solely in order to be the receiver of the collections message in the second line — it is worth creating it as a separate variable. For one thing, it makes this code far easier to step through in the debugger later on, when I want to pause after the albumsQuery call and see whether the expected sort of result is being returned (see Chapter 9).

 An incorrect number or pairing of nested square brackets can net you some curious messages from the compiler. For example, too many pairs of square brackets ([[query collections]]) or an unbalanced left square bracket ([[query collections]) is reported as "Expected identifier."

No Overloading

The data type returned by a method, together with the data types of each of its parameters in order, constitute that method's *signature*. It is illegal for two methods of the same type (class method or instance method) to exist in the same class with the same name, even if they have different signatures.

So, for example, you could not have two MyClass instance methods called myMethod, one of which returns void and one of which returns an NSString. Similarly, you could not have two MyClass instance methods called myMethod:, both returning void, one taking a CGFloat parameter and one taking an NSString parameter. An attempt to violate this rule will be stopped dead in its tracks by the compiler, which will announce a "duplicate declaration" error. The reason for this rule is that if two such conflicting methods were allowed to exist, there would be no way to determine from a method call to one of them which method was being called.

You might think that the issue could be decided by looking at the types involved in the call. If one myMethod: takes a CGFloat parameter and the other myMethod: takes an NSString parameter, you might think that when myMethod: is called, Objective-C could look at the actual argument and realize that the former method is meant if the argument is a CGFloat and the latter if the argument is an NSString. But Objective-C doesn't work that way. There are languages that permit this feature, called *overloading*, but Objective-C is not one of them.

Parameter Lists

It isn't uncommon for an Objective-C method to require an unknown number of parameters. A good example is the NSArray class method `arrayWithObjects:`, which looks from the name as if it takes one parameter but in fact takes any number of parameters, separated by comma. The parameters are the objects that are to constitute the elements of the NSArray. The trick here, however, which you must discover by reading the documentation, is that the list must end with nil. The nil is not one of the objects to go into the NSArray (nil isn't an object, so an NSArray can't contain nil); it's to show where the list ends.

So, here's a correct way to call the `arrayWithObjects:` method:

```
NSArray* pep = [NSArray arrayWithObjects:@"Manny", @"Moe", @"Jack", nil];
```

The declaration for `arrayWithObjects:` uses three dots to show that a comma-separated list is legal:

```
+ (id)arrayWithObjects:(id)firstObj, ... ;
```

(I'll explain later in this chapter what `id` means.) Without the nil terminator, the program will not know where the list ends, and bad things will happen when the program runs, as it goes hunting off into the weeds of memory, incorporating all sorts of unintended garbage into the NSArray.

Forgetting the nil terminator used to be a common beginner error, but nowadays the Objective-C compiler notices if you've forgotten the nil, and warns you ("missing sentinel in method dispatch"). Even though it's just a warning, don't run that code! Another way to avoid forgetting the nil terminator in this particular example is to avoid calling `arrayWithObjects:` altogether; this has been possible ever since LLVM compiler version 4.0 (Xcode 4.4 or later), which allows you to form a literal NSArray object directly, using @[...] syntax, like this:

```
NSArray* pep = @[@"Manny", @"Moe", @"Jack"];
```

That's just a notation, a kind of syntactic sugar; behind the scenes, `arrayWith-Objects:` is still being called for you. But it's being called for you correctly, nil terminator and all, so this notation is much more bullet-proof than explicitly calling `arrayWith-Objects:` yourself; plus it's a lot less typing.

Nevertheless, you will still encounter many other Objective-C methods that do have a parameter that's a nil-terminated list of variable length. For example, there's the UIAppearance protocol class method `appearanceWhenContainedIn:`, or UIAlertView's `init-`

WithTitle:message:delegate:cancelButtonTitle:otherButtonTitles:. It's a pity that Apple hasn't somehow tweaked Objective-C or these methods to avoid the use of the nil terminator; for instance, they could have made the variable-length list parameter into an NSArray parameter instead. But until they do, knowing how to call such methods remains important.

The C language has explicit provision for argument lists of unspecified length, which Objective-C methods such as arrayWithObjects: are using behind the scenes. I'm not going to explain the C mechanism, because I don't expect you'll ever write a method or function that requires it; see K&R 7.3 if you need the gory details.

When Message Sending Goes Wrong

The message-sending mechanism is fundamental to Objective-C. For that very reason, it is a major locus of problems. When a message is sent to an object, it is all too easy for things to go wrong. How can things go wrong with such a simple and basic mechanism? Consider the following seemingly trivial expression:

```
[s uppercaseString]
```

In that expression, s is a reference, and uppercaseString is a message. The uppercase-String message is being sent to the reference s. What could possibly go wrong here?

The reference might be to the wrong thing
    An object reference is a pointer. The thing being pointed to is the actual object — supposedly. The reference is only a name. How do you know, from that expression, what s is pointing to? You didn't see me initialize it. It might be nil. It might not be a string. It might be a different string from the one I think it is. A reference might not be a reference to what you think.

The message might be the wrong message
    This possibility goes hand in hand with the previous possibility. If the reference can be to the wrong thing, that thing might not like being sent this message. Or, it might accept being sent this message, but, being the wrong thing, it might produce an outcome different from what you expect.

This isn't mere nit-picking; it's a common and pervasive reality. A vast proportion of the questions I see posed on the Internet about why some code is going wrong turn out to be due to these problems. Programming is deceptive; you can easily fool yourself into making false assumptions. You think you know what a certain reference is, but you don't. The result is that things misbehave mysteriously, or your program crashes. Be conscious of how message sending can go wrong, and when it does go wrong — as I assure you it will — you'll be prepared.

The rest of this section will focus on two particularly insidious ways in which message sending can go wrong: a message is sent to a nil reference, and a message is sent to an object that doesn't like that message.

Messages to nil

It is all too easy for a supposed instance reference to refer accidentally to a noninstance — that is, to nil. I've already said that merely declaring an instance without also initializing it sets that reference to nil (under ARC), and that many Cocoa methods deliberately return nil as a way of indicating that something went wrong. Also, an instance variable declared as an object reference starts out life as nil; if it isn't subsequently set to point to an actual object in the way that you expect, it can go on being nil. (In Chapter 7, I'll discuss an all too common way in which that can happen, namely, when an intended outlet into a nib file hasn't been configured correctly.)

Let's examine the implications of a nil-value pointer for sending a message to a noninstance. You can send a message to an NSString instance like this:

```
NSString* s2 = [s uppercaseString];
```

That code sends the uppercaseString message to s. So s is supposedly an NSString instance. But what if s is nil? With some object-based programming languages, sending a message to nil constitutes a runtime error and will cause your program to terminate prematurely (REALbasic and Ruby are examples). But Objective-C doesn't work like that. In Objective-C, sending a message to nil is legal and does not interrupt execution. Moreover, if you capture the result of the method call, it will be a form of zero — which means that if you assign that result to an instance reference pointer, it too will be nil:

```
NSString* s = nil; // now s is nil
NSString* s2 = [s uppercaseString]; // now s2 is nil
```

Whether this behavior of Objective-C is a good thing is a quasi-religious issue and a subject of vociferous debate among programmers. It is useful, but it is also extremely easy to be tricked by it. The usual scenario is that you accidentally send a message to a nil reference without realizing it, and then later your program doesn't behave as expected. Because the point where the unexpected behavior occurs is later than the moment when the nil pointer arose in the first place, the genesis of the nil pointer can be difficult to track down (indeed, it often fails to occur to the programmer that a nil pointer is the cause of the trouble in the first place).

Short of peppering your code with tests to ascertain that your instance reference pointers are not accidentally nil, there isn't much you can do about this. This behavior is strongly built into the language and is not going to change. So be aware of it! Believing that you have a reference to an instance when in fact you have a reference to nil is a very, very common beginner mistake — and because the runtime doesn't complain when you start using that reference to nil, sending messages to it and possibly generating even more references to nil, nothing happens to disabuse you of this misconception (except that the program doesn't seem to behave quite as expected). If things quietly and mysteriously go wrong, suspect a nil reference, and use debugging techniques (Chapter 9) to investigate.

Certainly, if you know in advance that a particular method call can return nil, don't assume that everything will go well and that it won't return nil. On the contrary, if something can go wrong, it probably will. For example, to omit the nil test after calling `stringWithContentsOfFile:encoding:error:` is just stupid. I don't care if you know perfectly well that the file exists and the encoding is what you say it is — test the result for nil!

Unrecognized Selectors

It is possible to direct a message at an object with no corresponding method. When this happens, the consequences can be fatal: your app can crash. The only guardian against such a contingency is the compiler; but it isn't a very strong guardian. In some cases the compiler will warn you that you might be doing something inadvisable; in other cases the compiler will happily let you proceed.

Here's a situation where the compiler will actually save you from yourself:

```
NSString* s = @"Hello, world!";
[s rockTheCasbah];
```

An NSString has no method `rockTheCasbah`. Before ARC, the compiler would permit that code to compile, but it would warn you that there might be trouble. Under ARC, however, the compiler refuses to compile that code, declaring a fatal error: "No visible @interface for 'NSString' declares the selector 'rockTheCasbah'." (The ARC compiler is strict, because ARC has to do with memory management, and ARC can't manage memory effectively if you are allowed to send messages that make no sense whatever.)

By muddying the waters just a little, however, we can slip past ARC's stringent guardianship. Suppose now that we have a class MyClass which *does* declare a method `rockTheCasbah`. Then we can write this:

```
MyClass* m = @"Hello, world!";
[m rockTheCasbah];
```

We have claimed that m is a MyClass instance, but in fact we have then set it to an NSString instance. That's a strange thing to do, but it isn't strictly illegal. The compiler warns ("incompatible pointer types"), but compilation succeeds, and we are free to laugh recklessly and run that code anyway. What happens?

When the program runs, and when we send an NSString the `rockTheCasbah` message, our program crashes, with a message (in the console log) of this form:

```
-[__NSCFConstantString rockTheCasbah]:
    unrecognized selector sent to instance 0x8650.
```

That console message describes in great detail what happened:

- The phrase *unrecognized selector* is the heart of the matter. The term "selector" is roughly equivalent to "message," so this is a way of saying that a certain object was sent a message it couldn't deal with.

- `-[__NSCFConstantString rockTheCasbah]` describes the message and its receiver, using the shorthand I described earlier: an NSCFConstantString instance was sent an instance message `rockTheCasbah`. (The description of an NSString as an NSCFConstantString is an internal bookkeeping detail.)

- `0x8650` is the value of the instance pointer; it is the address in memory to which m was actually pointing.

 An unrecognized selector situation generates an *exception*, an internal message as the program runs signifying that something bad has happened. It is possible for Objective-C code to "catch" an exception, in which case the program will not crash. The reason the program crashes, technically, is not that a message was sent to an object that couldn't handle it, but that the exception generated in response wasn't caught. That's why the crash log may also say, "Terminating app due to uncaught exception."

In that example, we deliberately got ourselves into trouble, in order to demonstrate what happens when an unrecognized selector situation arises. The example is fanciful; but the consequences are not. I assure you that this kind of thing *will* happen to you, though of course it will come about unintentionally. It will happen because, as I said at the start of this section, your reference is not referring to the thing you think it is. There are many ways in which such a situation can arise; for example, as I'll explain in the next section, you may lie to the compiler accidentally about the class of an object, or the compiler may have no information about the class of an object, so it won't even warn you when you write a method call that will ultimately send an object a message it can't deal with. Watch for that phrase "unrecognized selector" when your program crashes, and know what it means and how to interpret the console message! The details of the console message will help you figure out what went wrong and where.

Typecasting and the id Type

Sometimes, the compiler, attempting to save you from an unrecognized selector situation, will issue a warning or an error when you know very well that what you're trying to do is safe and correct. The problem here is that you know more than the compiler does about what's really going to happen when the program runs. In order to proceed, you need to share your extra knowledge with the compiler. Typically, you'll do this by *typecasting* an object reference (see Chapter 1). Here, a typecast serves as a declaration of what class an object will be when the program runs. The compiler will believe whatever you say in a typecast; thus, typecasting can allay the compiler's worries.

This situation quite often arises in connection with class inheritance. We haven't discussed class inheritance yet (see Chapter 4), but I'll give an example anyway.

Let's take the built-in Cocoa class UINavigationController. Its `topViewController` method is declared to return a UIViewController instance. In real life, though, it is likely to return an instance of some particular UIViewController subclass that you've created. So in order to call a method of the class you've created on the instance returned by `top-ViewController` without upsetting the compiler, you have to reassure the compiler that this instance really will be an instance of the class you've created.

Here's an example from one of my own apps:

```
[[navigationController topViewController] setAlbums: arr];
```

That line of code won't compile; we get the same "no visible @interface" error that I discussed in the previous section. The built-in `topViewController` method returns a UIViewController, and UIViewController has no `setAlbums` method.

I happen to know, however, that in this case the navigation controller's top view controller is an instance of my own RootViewController class. And my RootViewController class *does* have a `setAlbums` method; that's exactly why I'm trying to call that method. What I'm doing is reasonable, legal, and desirable. I need to do it! In order to prevent the compiler from stopping me, I need to assure it that I know what I'm doing, by telling it that the object returned from the `topViewController` method call will in fact be a RootViewController. I do that by typecasting:

```
[(RootViewController*)[navigationController topViewController] setAlbums: arr];
```

That succeeds. There is no error and no warning. The typecast silences the compiler when I propose to send this instance the `setAlbums:` message, because my RootViewController class has a `setAlbums:` instance method and the compiler knows this. And the program, when it runs, doesn't crash, because I'm not lying: this `topView-Controller` method call really *will* return a RootViewController instance.

With great power, however, comes great responsibility. Don't lie to the compiler! Recall this example from the previous section:

```
MyClass* m = @"Hello, world!";
[m rockTheCasbah];
```

The first line caused the compiler to warn us about "incompatible pointer types"; and the compiler was right to be concerned — we were heading for a crash at runtime ("unrecognized selector") when the rockTheCasbah message was sent to an NSString. We can silence the compiler by typecasting:

```
MyClass* m = (MyClass*)@"Hello, world!";
[m rockTheCasbah];
```

Now there's no warning. But we've lied to the compiler, and we're still heading for the very same unrecognized selector crash at runtime (because, just as before, the rockThe-Casbah message is going to be sent to an NSString). The moral is simple: the compiler will believe whatever you say when you typecast, so don't use typecasting to lie to the compiler.

Typecasting does not miraculously change any actual object types. It's just a way of communicating a hint about type information to the compiler. The underlying object being referred to is completely unaffected. The typecast expression (MyClass*)@"Hello, world!" does not magically change the NSString instance @"Hello, world!" into a MyClass instance! Typecasting in the belief that you're actually performing some kind of type conversion is a surprisingly common beginner mistake.

Objective-C also provides a special type designed to silence the compiler's worries about object data types altogether. This is the id type. An id is a pointer, so you don't say id*. It is defined to mean "an object pointer," plain and simple, with no further specification. Thus, every instance reference is also an id.

Use of the id type causes the compiler to stop worrying about the relationship between object types and messages. The compiler can't know anything about what the object will really be, so it throws up its hands and doesn't warn about anything. Moreover, any object value can be assigned or typecast to an id, and a value typed as an id can be assigned where any object type is expected. The notion of assignment includes parameter passing. So you can pass a value typed as an id as an argument where a parameter of some particular object type is expected, and you can pass any object as an argument where a parameter of type id is expected. (I like to think of an id as analogous to both type AB blood and type O blood: it is both a universal recipient and a universal donor.) So, for example:

```
NSString* s = @"Hello, world!";
id unknown = s;
[unknown rockTheCasbah];
```

The second line is legal, because any object value can be assigned to an id. The third line doesn't generate any compiler warning, because any message can be sent to an id.

(Of course the program will *still* crash when it actually runs and unknown turns out to be an NSString — which is incapable of receiving of the rockTheCasbah message!)

Actually, that's an oversimplification. Under ARC, that code might not compile. Instead, you might get an error: "No known instance method for selector 'rockTheCasbah.'" This means that the compiler knows of no rockTheCasbah method in any class. If, however, rockTheCasbah is declared in the header file of any class imported into this one, or if rockTheCasbah is implemented in the current class, that code will compile, with no warning.

If an id's ability to receive any message reminds you of nil, it should. I have already said that nil is a form of zero; I can now specify what form of zero it is. It's zero cast as an id. Of course, it still makes a difference at runtime whether an id is nil or something else; sending a message to nil won't crash the program, but sending an unknown message to an actual object probably will.

Thus, id has the effect of turning off the compiler's type checking altogether. Concerns about what type an object is are postponed until the program is actually running. I do not recommend that you make extensive use of id in this way. The compiler is your friend; you should let its intelligence catch possible mistakes in your code. Thus, I almost never declare a variable or parameter as an id. I want my object types to be specific, so that the compiler can help check my code. On the other hand, the Cocoa API does make frequent use of id — and this is exactly the sort of thing that, as I warned you in the previous section, can result in an unrecognized selector crash down the road.

Consider, for example, the NSArray class, which is the object-based version of an array. In pure C, you have to declare what type of thing lives in an array; for example, you could have "an array of int." In Objective-C, using an NSArray, you can't do that. Every NSArray is an array of id, meaning that each element of the array can be of any object type. You can put a specific type of object into an NSArray because any type of object can be assigned to an id (id is the universal recipient). You can get any specific type of object back out of an NSArray because an id can be assigned to any type of object (id is the universal donor).

NSArray's lastObject method is thus defined as returning an id. Given an NSArray arr, I can fetch its last element like this:

```
id unknown = [arr lastObject];
```

We are now in a potentially dangerous situation. After that code, unknown can be sent any message at all; the compiler won't interfere. Therefore, if I happen to *know* what type of object an array element is, I always assign or cast it to that type as I fetch it from the array. For example, let's say I happen to know that arr contains nothing but NSString instances (because I put them there in the first place). Then I will say:

```
NSString* s = [arr lastObject];
```

The compiler doesn't complain, because an `id` can be assigned to any specific type of object (`id` is the universal donor). Moreover, from here on in, the compiler regards `s` as an NSString, and uses its type checking abilities to make sure I don't send `s` any non-NSString messages, which is just what I wanted. And I didn't lie to the compiler; at runtime, `s` really *is* an NSString, so everything is fine.

There is a further danger, however: this situation is an open invitation for me to lie accidentally to the compiler. Suppose the last element in this NSArray is *not* an NSString. The compiler doesn't know this — it knows nothing of what the NSArray will actually contain at runtime — and `lastObject` returns an `id`, which the compiler will happily allow me to assign to a reference declared as an NSString. We are now courting disaster. Suppose, for example, that in the next line I send the `uppercaseString` message to `s`. The compiler won't bat an eye: after all, I've declared this reference as an NSString, and `uppercaseString` is an NSString method. But if `s` is *not* an NSString, this will probably be an unrecognized selector situation, and we'll crash at runtime.

Another pitfall of using `id` has to do with method name conflicts. Earlier, I said that it is illegal for the same class to define methods of the same type (class method or instance method) with the same name but different signatures. But I did not say what happens when two *different* classes declare a method with the same name but different signatures. If the type of the object receiving the message is specified in your code, there's no problem, because there's no doubt which method is being called: it's the one in that object's class. But if the object receiving the message is an `id`, under ARC, you'll get an error: "Multiple methods named 'rockTheCasbah' found with mismatched result, parameter type or attributes." This is another reason why method names are so verbose: it's in order to make each method name unique, preventing two different classes from declaring conflicting signatures for the same method.

Messages as Data Type

The previous sections revolved around the fact that Objective-C doesn't have to know until runtime what object a message will be sent to. But there's more: Objective-C doesn't have to know until runtime *what message* to send to an object. Certain important methods actually accept both the message and the receiver as parameters; they won't be assembled and used to form an actual message expression until runtime.

For example, consider this method declaration from Cocoa's NSNotificationCenter class:

```
- (void)addObserver:(id)notificationObserver
          selector:(SEL)notificationSelector
              name:(NSString *)notificationName
            object:(id)notificationSender
```

I'll explain later in detail what this method does (in Chapter 11); the important thing to understand here is that it constitutes an instruction to send a certain message to a certain object at some later, appropriate time. For example, our purpose in calling this method might be to arrange to have the message `tickleMeElmo:` sent at some later, appropriate time to the object `myObject`. To do so, we need to supply appropriate arguments to the first two parameters.

Let's consider what arguments we would actually pass for the first two parameters. The object to which the message will be sent, the first parameter (`observer:`), is typed as an `id`, making it possible to specify any type of object to send the message to. So, for the `observer:` argument, we're going to pass `myObject`. The message itself is the `selector:` parameter, which has a special data type, SEL (for "selector," the technical term for a message name). The question now is how to express the message name `tickleMeElmo:`.

You can't just put `tickleMeElmo:` as a bare term; that doesn't work syntactically. You might think you could express it as an NSString, `@"tickleMeElmo:"`, but surprisingly, that doesn't work either. It turns out that the correct way to do it is like this:

```
@selector(tickleMeElmo:)
```

The term `@selector()` is a directive to the compiler, telling it that what's in parentheses is a message name. Notice that what's in parentheses is not an NSString; it's the bare message name. And because it is the name, it must have no spaces and must include any colons that are part of the message name.

So the rule is extremely easy: when a SEL is expected, you'll usually pass a `@selector` expression. Failure to get this syntax right is a common beginner error.

Unfortunately, this syntax is also an invitation to make a typing mistake, with possibly devastating results. If `myObject` implements a `tickleMeElmo:` method and I accidentally type, say, `@selector(tickleMeElmo)`, forgetting the colon, then if the `tickleMeElmo` message without the colon is ever sent to `myObject`, the app will probably crash with an unrecognized selector exception.

Xcode 5, for the first time in the history of Objective-C, introduces a compiler warning in the case where the selector matches no known method ("Undeclared selector 'tickleMeElmo'"). Thus, you might be alerted to the possibility of a future crash — or not. The compiler can't peer into the class of your `observer:` argument and see whether it implements this method; instead, the compiler complains only if no class is already *known* to have such a method. Thus, the converse applies: if the compiler happens to know of *any* `tickleMeElmo` method in *any* class, you'll get no warning, even if the object to which you'll actually be sending the `tickleMeElmo` message at runtime has no such method.

C Functions

Although your code will certainly call many Objective-C methods, it will also probably call quite a few C functions. For example, I mentioned in Chapter 1 that the usual way of describing a CGPoint based on its x and y values is to call CGPointMake, which is declared like this:

```
CGPoint CGPointMake (
    CGFloat x,
    CGFloat y
);
```

Make certain that you can see at a glance that this *is* a C function, not an Objective-C method, and be sure you understand the difference in the calling syntax. To call an Objective-C method, you send a message to an object, in square brackets, with each argument following a colon in the method's name; to call a C function, you use the function's name followed by parentheses containing the arguments.

You might even have reason to write your own C functions as part of a class, instead of writing a method. A C function has lower overhead than a full-fledged method; so even though it lacks the object-oriented abilities of a method, it is sometimes useful to write one, as when some utility calculation must be performed rapidly and frequently.

Also, once in a while you might encounter a Cocoa method or function that requires you to supply a C function as a "callback." An example is the NSArray method `sorted-ArrayUsingFunction:context:`. The first parameter is typed like this:

```
NSInteger (*)(id, id, void *)
```

That expression denotes, in the rather tricky C syntax used for these things, a pointer to a function that takes three parameters and returns an NSInteger. The three parameters of the function are an `id`, an `id`, and a pointer-to-void (which means any C pointer). The bare name of a C function (see Chapter 1) can be used as a pointer to that function. So to call `sortedArrayUsingFunction:context:` you'd need to write a C function that meets this description, and use its name as the first argument.

To illustrate, I'll write a "callback" function to help me sort an NSArray of NSStrings on the last character of each string. (This would be an odd thing to do, but it's only an example!) The NSInteger returned by the function has a special meaning: it indicates whether the first parameter is to be considered less than, equal to, or larger than the second. I'll obtain it by calling the NSString `compare:` method, which returns an NSInteger with that same meaning. Example 3-1 defines the function and shows how we'd call `sortedArrayUsingFunction:context:` with that function as our callback.

Example 3-1. Using a pointer to a callback function

```
NSInteger sortByLastCharacter(id string1, id string2, void* context) {
    NSString* s1 = string1;
    NSString* s2 = string2;
    NSString* string1end = [s1 substringFromIndex:[s1 length] - 1];
    NSString* string2end = [s2 substringFromIndex:[s2 length] - 1];
    return [string1end compare:string2end];
}
// and here's how you'd use it; assume that arr is an NSArray of NSStrings
NSArray* arr2 = [arr sortedArrayUsingFunction:sortByLastCharacter context:nil];
```

CFTypeRefs

Many Objective-C object types have lower-level C counterparts, along with C functions for manipulating them.

For example, besides the Objective-C NSString, there is also something called a CFString; the "CF" stands for "Core Foundation," which is a lower-level C-based API. A CFString is an opaque C struct; "opaque" means that the elements constituting this struct are kept secret, and that you should operate on a CFString only by means of appropriate C functions. As with an NSString or any other object, in your code you'll typically refer to a CFString by way of a C pointer; the pointer to a CFString has a type name, CFStringRef.

You might, on occasion, decide to work with a Core Foundation type even when a corresponding object type exists. For example, you might find that NSString, for all its power, fails to implement a needed piece of functionality, one that is available for a CFString. Luckily, an NSString (a value typed as NSString*) and a CFString (a value typed as CFStringRef) are interchangeable: you can use one where the other is expected, though you may have to typecast in order to quiet the worries of the compiler. The documentation describes this interchangeability by saying that NSString and CFString are *toll-free bridged* to one another.

To illustrate, I'll use a CFString to convert an NSString representing an integer to that integer (this use of CFString is unnecessary, and is just by way of demonstrating the syntax; NSString has an intValue method):

```
NSString* answer = @"42";
int ans = CFStringGetIntValue((CFStringRef)answer);
```

The pointer-to-struct C object types, whose names typically end in "Ref", may be referred to collectively as CFTypeRef, which is actually just the generic pointer-to-void. Thus, crossing the toll-free bridge may usefully be thought of as a cast between an object pointer and a generic pointer — that is, in general terms, from id to void* or from void* to id. Even where there is no toll-free bridging between *specific* types (as there is with NSString and CFString), there is always bridging at the top of the hierarchy, so to speak, between id or NSObject (the base object class, as explained in Chapter 4) and CFTypeRef.

Blocks

A *block* is an extension to the C language, introduced in OS X 10.6 and available in iOS 4.0 and later. It's a way of bundling up some code and handing off that entire bundle as an argument to a C function or Objective-C method. This is similar to what we did in Example 3-1, handing off a pointer to a function as an argument, but instead we're handing off the code *itself*. The latter has some major advantages over the former, which I'll discuss in a moment.

To illustrate, I'll rewrite Example 3-1 to use a block instead of a function pointer. Instead of calling `sortedArrayUsingFunction:context:`, I'll call `sortedArrayUsing-Comparator:`, which takes a block as its parameter. The block is typed like this:

```
NSComparisonResult (^)(id obj1, id obj2)
```

That expression is similar to the syntax for specifying the type of a pointer to a function, but a caret is used instead of an asterisk. It denotes a block that takes two id parameters and returns an NSComparisonResult (which is merely an NSInteger, with just the same meaning as in Example 3-1). We can define the block inline as the argument within our call to `sortedArrayUsingComparator:`, as in Example 3-2.

Example 3-2. Using an inline block instead of a callback function

```
NSArray* arr2 = [arr sortedArrayUsingComparator: ^(id obj1, id obj2) {
    NSString* s1 = obj1;
    NSString* s2 = obj2;
    NSString* string1end = [s1 substringFromIndex:[s1 length] - 1];
    NSString* string2end = [s2 substringFromIndex:[s2 length] - 1];
    return [string1end compare:string2end];
}];
```

The syntax of the inline block definition is:

```
^❶(id obj1, id obj2)❷ {❸
    // ...
}
```

❶   First, the caret.

❷   Then, parentheses containing the parameters, similar to the parameters of a C function definition.

❸   Finally, curly braces containing the block's content. These curly braces constitute a scope.

The return type in an inline block definition is usually omitted. If included, it *follows* the caret, *not* in parentheses. If omitted, you may have to use typecasting in the return line to make the returned type match the expected type.

A block defined inline, as in Example 3-2, isn't reusable; if we had *two* calls to sorted-ArrayUsingComparator: using the same callback, we'd have to write out the callback in full twice. To avoid such repetition, or simply for clarity, a block can be assigned to a variable, which is then passed as an argument to a method that expects a block, as in Example 3-3.

Example 3-3. Assigning a block to a variable

```
NSComparisonResult (^sortByLastCharacter)(id, id) = ^(id obj1, id obj2) {
    NSString* s1 = obj1;
    NSString* s2 = obj2;
    NSString* string1end = [s1 substringFromIndex:[s1 length] - 1];
    NSString* string2end = [s2 substringFromIndex:[s2 length] - 1];
    return [string1end compare:string2end];
};
NSArray* arr2 = [arr sortedArrayUsingComparator: sortByLastCharacter];
NSArray* arr4 = [arr3 sortedArrayUsingComparator: sortByLastCharacter];
```

Perhaps the most remarkable feature of blocks is this: variables in scope at the point where a block is defined keep their value within the block at that moment, even though the block may be executed at some later moment. (Technically, we say that a block is a *closure*, and that variable values outside the block may be *captured* by the block.) This aspect of blocks makes them useful for specifying functionality to be executed at some later time, or even in some other thread.

Here's a real-life example:

```
CGPoint p = [v center];
CGPoint pOrig = p;
p.x += 100;
void (^anim) (void) = ^{
    [v setCenter: p];
};
void (^after) (BOOL) = ^(BOOL f) {
    [v setCenter: pOrig];
};
NSUInteger opts = UIViewAnimationOptionAutoreverse;
[UIView animateWithDuration:1 delay:0 options:opts
                animations:anim completion:after];
```

That code does something quite surprising. The method animateWith-Duration:delay:options:animations:completion: configures a view animation using blocks. But the view animation itself is not performed until later; the animation, and therefore the blocks, will be executed at an indeterminate moment in the future, long after the method call has completed and your code has gone on to other things. Now, there is a UIView object v in scope, along with a CGPoint p and another CGPoint pOrig. The variables p and pOrig are local and automatic; they will go out of scope and cease to exist before the animation starts and the blocks are executed. Nevertheless, the *values* of those variables are being used inside the blocks, as parameters of messages to be sent to v.

Because a block might be executed at some later time, it is not normally legal, inside a block, to assign directly to a local automatic variable defined outside the block; the compiler will stop us ("variable is not assignable"):

```
CGPoint p;
void (^aBlock) (void) = ^{
    p = CGPointMake(1,2); // error
};
```

A local automatic variable can be made to obey special storage rules by declaring the variable using the __block qualifier. This qualifier promotes the variable's storage so that the variable stays alive along with the block that refers to it, and has two chief uses. Here's the first use: If a block will be executed immediately, the __block qualifier permits the block to set a variable outside the block to a value that will be needed after the block has finished.

For example, the NSArray method enumerateObjectsUsingBlock: takes a block and calls it immediately for each element of the array. It is a block-based equivalent of a for...in loop, cycling through the elements of an enumerable collection (Chapter 1). Here, we propose to cycle through the array until we find the value we want; when we find it, we set a variable (dir) to that value. That variable, though, is declared *outside* the block, because we intend to use its value *after* executing the block — we need its scope to extend outside the curly braces of the block. Therefore we qualify the variable's declaration with __block, so that we can assign to it from *inside* the block:

```
CGFloat h = newHeading.magneticHeading;
__block NSString* dir = @"N";
NSArray* cards = @[@"N", @"NE", @"E", @"SE",
                   @"S", @"SW", @"W", @"NW"];
[cards enumerateObjectsUsingBlock:^(id obj, NSUInteger idx, BOOL *stop) {
    if (h < 45.0/2.0 + 45*idx) {
        dir = obj;
        *stop = YES;
    }
}];
// now we can use dir
```

(Note also the assignment to a dereferenced pointer-to-BOOL. This is a way of interrupting the loop prematurely; we have found the value we're looking for, so there's no point looping any further. We can't use a break statement, because this isn't really a for loop. The method `enumerateObjectsUsingBlock:` therefore hands the block a pointer-to-BOOL parameter, which the block can set by indirection to YES as a signal to the method that it's time to stop. This is one of the few situations in iOS programming where it is necessary to dereference a pointer.)

The second chief use of the `__block` qualifier is the converse of the first. It arises when a block will be executed at some time after it is defined, and we want the block to use the value that a variable has at the time the block is executed, rather than capturing the value that it has when the block is defined. Typically this is because the very same method call that accepts the block (for later execution) also sets the value of this variable (now).

For example, the method `beginBackgroundTaskWithExpirationHandler:` takes a block to be executed at some future time (if ever). It also generates and returns a `UIBackgroundTaskIdentifier`, which is really just an integer — and we are going to want to use that integer inside the block, if and when the block is executed. So we're trying to do things in an oddly circular order: the block is handed as an argument to the method, the method is called, the method returns a value, and the block uses that value. The `__block` qualifier makes this possible:

```
__block UIBackgroundTaskIdentifier bti =
    [[UIApplication sharedApplication]
        beginBackgroundTaskWithExpirationHandler: ^{
            [[UIApplication sharedApplication] endBackgroundTask:bti];
        }];
```

At the same time that blocks were introduced into Objective-C, Apple introduced a system library of C functions called Grand Central Dispatch (GCD) that makes heavy use of them. GCD's chief purpose is thread management, but it also comes in handy for expressing neatly and compactly certain notions about when code should be executed. For example, GCD can help us delay execution of our code (*delayed performance*). The following code uses a block to say, "change the bounds of the UIView v1, but not right this moment — wait two seconds and then do it":

```
dispatch_time_t popTime = dispatch_time(DISPATCH_TIME_NOW, 2 * NSEC_PER_SEC);
dispatch_after(popTime, dispatch_get_main_queue(), ^(void){
    CGRect r = [v1 bounds];
    r.size.width += 40;
    r.size.height -= 50;
    [v1 setBounds: r];
});
```

This final example of a block in action rewrites the code from the end of Chapter 1, where a class method vends a singleton object. The GCD function `dispatch_once`, which is very fast and (unlike the Chapter 1 example) thread-safe, promises that its block, here creating the singleton object, will execute only once in the entire life of our program — thus guaranteeing that the singleton *is* a singleton:

```
+ (CardPainter*) sharedPainter {
    static CardPainter* sp = nil;
    static dispatch_once_t onceToken;
    dispatch_once(&onceToken, ^{
        sp = [CardPainter new];
    });
    return sp;
}
```

The block is able to assign to the local variable sp without a __block qualifier because sp has a static qualifier, which has the same effect but even stronger: just as __block promotes the lifetime of its variable to live as long as the block, static promotes the lifetime of its variable to live as long as the program itself. Thus it also has the side-effect of making sp assignable from within the block, just as __block would do.

For further explanation of blocks, see Apple's helpful documentation at *http://develop er.apple.com/library/ios/#documentation/cocoa/Conceptual/Blocks/*, or look up "Blocks Programming Topics" in Xcode's help window. For a complete technical syntax speci- fication for blocks, see *http://clang.llvm.org/docs/BlockLanguageSpec.html*.

CHAPTER 4

Objective-C Classes

This chapter describes some linguistic and structural features of Objective-C having to do with classes; in the next chapter, we'll do the same for instances.

Subclass and Superclass

In Objective-C, as in many other object-oriented languages, a mechanism is provided for specifying a relationship between two classes: they can be *subclass* and *superclass* of one another. For example, we might have a class Quadruped and a class Dog and make Quadruped the superclass of Dog. A class may have many subclasses, but a class can have only one immediate superclass. I say "immediate" because that superclass might itself have a superclass, and so on in a rising chain, until we get to the ultimate superclass, called the *base class*, or *root class*.

Because a class can have many subclasses but only one superclass, there is a hierarchical tree of subclasses, each branching from its superclass, and so on, with a single class, the base class, at the top. Indeed, Cocoa itself consists of just such a tree (a huge tree!) of hierarchically arranged classes, even before you write a single line of code or create any classes of your own. We can imagine diagramming this tree as an outline, with a single ultimate superclass at the top, then all of its immediate subclasses in the next level below that, then each of *their* immediate subclasses in the next level below that, and so on. And in fact Xcode will show you this outline (Figure 4-1): in an iOS project window, choose View → Navigators → Show Symbol Navigator and click Hierarchical, with the first and third icons in the filter bar selected (blue).

The reason for the class–subclass relationship is to allow related classes to share functionality. Suppose, for example, we have a Dog class and a Cat class, and we are considering defining a walk method for both of them. We might reason that both a dog and a cat walk in pretty much the same way, by virtue of both being quadrupeds. So it might make sense to define walk as a method of the Quadruped class, and make both Dog and

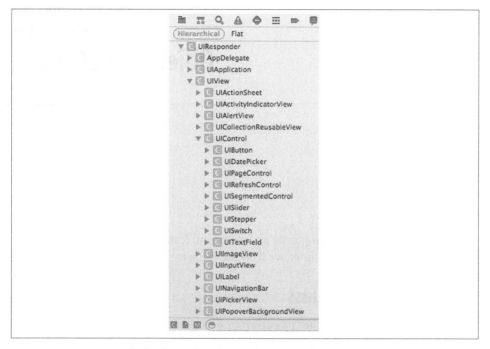

Figure 4-1. Browsing the built-in class hierarchy in Xcode

Cat subclasses of Quadruped. The result is that both Dog and Cat can be sent the `walk` message, even if neither of them has a `walk` method, because each of them has a superclass that *does* have a `walk` method. We say that a subclass *inherits* the methods of its superclass.

The purpose of subclassing is not merely so that a class can inherit another class's methods; it's so that it can define methods of its own. Typically, a subclass consists of the methods inherited from its superclass *and then some*. If Dog has no methods of its own, it's hard to see why it should exist separately from Quadruped. But if a Dog knows how to do something that not every Quadruped knows how to do — let's say, bark — then it makes sense as a separate class. If we define `bark` in the Dog class, and `walk` in the Quadruped class, and make Dog a subclass of Quadruped, then Dog inherits the ability to walk from the Quadruped class and also knows how to bark.

It is also permitted for a subclass to redefine a method inherited from its superclass. For example, perhaps some dogs bark differently from other dogs. We might have a class NoisyDog, for instance, that is a subclass of Dog. Dog defines `bark`, but NoisyDog also defines `bark`, and defines it differently from how Dog defines it. This is called *overriding*. The very natural rule is that if a subclass overrides a method inherited from its superclass, then when the corresponding message is sent to an instance of that subclass, it is the subclass's version of that method that is called.

Along with methods, a subclass also inherits its superclass's instance variables. Naturally, the subclass may also define additional instance variables of its own.

Interface and Implementation

As you know from Chapter 2, all your code is going to go into some class or other. So the first thing we must do is specify what is meant by putting code "into a class" in Objective-C. How does Objective-C say, linguistically and structurally, "This is the code for such-and-such a class"?

To write the code for a class, you must provide two chunks or sections of code, called the *interface* and the *implementation*. Here's the complete minimum code required to define a class called MyClass. This class is so minimal that it doesn't even have any methods of its own:

```
@interface MyClass
@end
@implementation MyClass
@end
```

The `@interface` and `@implementation` compiler directives show the compiler where the interface and implementation sections begin for the class that's being defined, My-Class; the corresponding `@end` lines show where each of those sections end.

In real life, the implementation section is where any methods for MyClass would be defined. So here's a class that's actually defined to do something:

```
@interface MyClass
@end
@implementation MyClass
- (NSString*) sayGoodnightGracie {
    return @"Good night, Gracie!";
}
@end
```

Observe how a method is defined. The first line is just like a method declaration, stating the type of method (class or instance), the type of value returned, and the name of the method along with the types of any parameters and local names for those parameters (see Chapter 3). That's followed by curly braces containing the code to be executed when the method is called, just as with a C function (see Chapter 1).

Our minimal class is still pretty much useless, because it can't be instantiated. In Cocoa, knowledge of how to be instantiated, plus how to do a number of other things that any class should know how to do, resides in the base class, which is the NSObject class. Therefore, all Cocoa classes must be based ultimately on the NSObject class, by declaring as the superclass for your class either NSObject or some other class that inherits from NSObject, as just about any other Cocoa class does. (Indeed, without an explicit superclass, our class declaration won't even compile in Xcode 5: "Class 'MyClass' defined without specifying a base class.")

The syntax for declaring a class's superclass is a colon followed by the superclass name in the `@interface` line, like this:

```
@interface MyClass : NSObject
@end
@implementation MyClass
- (NSString*) sayGoodnightGracie {
    return @"Good night, Gracie!";
}
@end
```

 NSObject is not the only Cocoa base class. It used to be, but there is now another, NSProxy. NSProxy is used only in very special circumstances. If you have no reason for your class to inherit from any other class, make it inherit from NSObject.

In its fullest form, the interface section might contain some more material. In particular, if we want to declare our methods, so that other classes can learn about them and call them, those method declarations go into the interface section. A method declaration in code matches the name and signature for the method definition and ends with a semicolon (required):

```
@interface MyClass : NSObject
- (NSString*) sayGoodnightGracie;
@end
@implementation MyClass
- (NSString*) sayGoodnightGracie {
    return @"Good night, Gracie!";
}
@end
```

(Actually, it's legal for a method definition to have a semicolon as well, before the curly braces. But that notation is rare, and I never use it.)

There are also instance variables to be considered. If our class is to have any instance variables (other than those inherited from its superclass), they must be declared. In modern Objective-C, you will probably declare most of your instance variables implicitly, using a technique that I'll explain in Chapter 5 and Chapter 12. But you might still occasionally declare an instance variable explicitly; and in any case, you certainly need to know how to do so.

Once upon a time, explicit declaration of instance variables had to take place in curly braces at the start of the interface section:

```
@interface MyClass : NSObject {
    // instance variable declarations go here
}
- (NSString*) sayGoodnightGracie;
@end
@implementation MyClass
- (NSString*) sayGoodnightGracie {
    return @"Good night, Gracie!";
}
@end
```

However, starting with LLVM compiler version 3.0 (Xcode 4.2 and later), it is permitted to put instance variable declarations in curly braces at the start of the implementation section instead. This is a more logical place for variable declarations to go, because, as I'll explain in the next section, the interface section can be visible to other classes, while there is usually no reason why instance variables need to be visible to other classes, as they are generally private. Therefore, I prefer the new style:

```
@interface MyClass : NSObject
- (NSString*) sayGoodnightGracie;
@end
@implementation MyClass {
    // instance variable declarations go here
}
- (NSString*) sayGoodnightGracie {
    return @"Good night, Gracie!";
}
@end
```

(If, however, a subclass is to inherit an instance variable from its superclass, there might be reason for the superclass to declare the instance variable in its interface section, so that the subclass can see it and can gain access to that instance variable.)

I'll go into more detail about instance variables in Chapter 5.

Header File and Implementation File

It's perfectly possible for the interface and implementation of a class to appear in the same file, or for multiple classes to be defined in a single file, but that isn't the usual convention. The usual convention is one class, two files: one file containing the interface section, the other file containing the implementation section. The implementation file imports the header file (see Chapter 1 on the #import directive); this effectively unites the full class definition, making the definition legal even though it is split between two files.

For example, let's suppose you are defining a class MyClass. Then you will typically have two files, *MyClass.h* and *MyClass.m*. (Naming a file after the class it defines is not magical or necessary; it's just conventional and convenient.) The interface section goes into *MyClass.h*, which is called the *header file*. The implementation section goes into *MyClass.m*, which is called the *implementation file*. The implementation files imports the header file. The separation into two files is not inconvenient, because Xcode, expecting you to follow this convention, makes it easy to jump from editing a .*h* file to the corresponding .*m* file and *vice versa* (Navigate → Jump to Next Counterpart).

With this arrangement in place, further imports become easy to configure. The header file imports the basic header file for the entire Cocoa framework; in the case of an iOS program, that's *UIKit.h* (again, see Chapter 1). There is no need for the implementation file to import *UIKit.h*, because the header file imports it, and the implementation file imports the header file. If a class needs to know about another class that isn't already imported in this way, it imports that class's header file.

Example 4-1 summarizes this conventional schema; in it, I am also pretending there's another class, MyOtherClass, that MyClass's code needs to be able to refer to.

Example 4-1. Conventional schema for defining a class

```
// MyClass.h:

#import <UIKit/UIKit.h>

@interface MyClass : NSObject
- (NSString*) sayGoodnightGracie;
@end

// MyClass.m:

#import "MyClass.h"
#import "MyOtherClass.h"

@implementation MyClass {
    // instance variable declarations go here
}
- (NSString*) sayGoodnightGracie {
    return @"Good night, Gracie!";
}
@end
```

The result of this arrangement is that everything has the right visibility. No file ever imports an implementation file; that way, what's inside a class's implementation file is private to that class. If one class needs to be able to speak of another class, it imports that other class's header file. In Example 4-1:

- The MyClass header file imports *UIKit.h*, because otherwise MyClass could not be declared as inheriting from NSObject.

- The MyClass implementation file imports *MyClass.h*, because otherwise the class declaration would be incomplete. As a useful side effect, MyClass can thus also speak of NSString and other classes built into UIKit, without itself importing *UIKit.h*.

- The MyClass implementation file imports *MyOtherClass.h*, because otherwise MyClass could not speak of MyOtherClass (which we are pretending it needs to do).

A slight problem arises when a header file needs to mention a class that it has no need to import. Suppose, for example, that MyClass has a public method that takes or returns an instance of MyOtherClass. So *MyClass.h* needs to speak of `MyOtherClass*`. But *MyClass.h* doesn't otherwise need to import *MyOtherClass.h*, and we would prefer that it not do so. Yet if *MyClass.h* doesn't know about MyOtherClass, the compiler will complain when we use its name here. To silence the compiler, use the `@class` directive. The word `@class` is followed by a comma-separated list of class names, ending with a semicolon. So *MyClass.h* might start out like this:

```
#import <UIKit/UIKit.h>
@class MyOtherClass;
```

Then the interface section would follow, as before. The `@class` directive simply tells the compiler, "Don't worry, MyOtherClass really is the name of a class." That's all the compiler needs to know in order to permit the mention of the type `MyOtherClass*` in the header file.

A header file is also an appropriate place to define constants. In Chapter 1, for example, I talked about the problem of mistyping the name of a notification or dictionary key, which is a literal NSString, and how you could solve this problem by defining a name for such a string:

```
#define MYKEY @"mykey"
```

The question then arises of where to put that definition. If only one class needs to know about it, the definition can go near the start of its implementation file (it doesn't need to be inside the implementation section). But if multiple classes need to know about this name, then a header file is an appropriate location; every implementation file that imports this header file will acquire the definition, and you can use the name `MYKEY` in that implementation file.

(If many files need to know about this definition, it may be more convenient to put it in the project's *.pch* file, the single "precompiled header" that is implicitly imported by all *.h* files. I'll talk more about the *.pch* file in Chapter 6.)

Class Methods

Class methods are useful in general for two main purposes:

Factory methods

A factory method is a method that dispenses (vends) an instance of that class. For example, the UIFont class has a class method `fontWithName:size:`. You supply a name and a size, and the UIFont class hands you back a UIFont instance corresponding to a font with that name and size. A class method that vends a singleton instance, such as appears at the end of Chapter 1, is also a factory method.

Global utility methods

Classes are global (visible from all code, Chapter 13), so a class is a good place to put a utility method that anyone might need to call and that doesn't require the overhead of an instance. For example, the UIFont class has a class method `family-Names`. It returns an array of strings (that is, an NSArray of NSString instances) consisting of the names of the font families installed on this device. Because this method has to do with fonts, the UIFont class is as good a place as any to put it.

Most methods that you write will be instance methods, but now and then you might write a class method. When you do, your purpose will probably be similar to those examples.

The Secret Life of Classes

A class method may be called by sending a message directly to the name of a class. For example, the `familyNames` class method of UIFont that I mentioned a moment ago might be called like this:

```
NSArray* fams = [UIFont familyNames];
```

Clearly, this is possible because a class is an object (Chapter 2), and the name of the class here represents that object.

You don't have to do anything to create a class object. One class object for every class your program defines is created for you automatically as the program starts up. (This includes the classes your program imports, so there's a MyClass class object because you defined MyClass, and there's an NSString class object because you imported *UIKit.h* and the whole Cocoa framework.) It is to this class object that you're referring when you send a message to the name of the class.

Your ability to send a message directly to the bare name of a class is due to a kind of syntactic shorthand. You can use the bare class name only in two ways (and we already know about both of them):

To send a message to
> In the expression [UIFont familyNames], the bare name UIFont is sent the family-Names message.

To specify an instance type
> In the expression NSString*, the bare name NSString is followed by an asterisk to signify a pointer to an instance of this class.

Otherwise, to speak of a class object, you need to obtain that object formally. One way to do this is to send the class message to a class or instance. For example, [MyClass class] returns the actual class object. Some built-in Cocoa methods expect a class object parameter, whose type is described as Class. To supply this class object as an argument, you'd need to obtain a class object formally.

Take, for example, introspection on an object to inquire what its class is. The isKindOf-Class: instance method is declared like this:

```
- (BOOL)isKindOfClass:(Class)aClass
```

So that means you could call it like this:

```
if ([someObject isKindOfClass: [MyClass class]]) // ...
```

A class object is not an instance, but it is definitely a full-fledged object. Therefore, a class object can be used wherever an object can be used. For example, it can be assigned to a variable of type id:

```
id classObject = [MyClass class];
```

You could then call a class method by sending a message to that object, because it is the class object:

```
id classObject = [MyClass class];
[classObject someClassMethod];
```

All class objects are also members of the Class class, so you could say this:

```
Class classObject = [MyClass class];
[classObject someClassMethod];
```

Those examples will compile as long as someClassMethod is a known class method of *any* class.

The Global Namespace

When defining classes, choose your class names wisely to prevent name collisions. Objective-C has no namespaces; there's a single vast namespace containing all names. You don't want your own class name (or any top-level constant name) to match a name defined in Cocoa. Instead of namespaces, there's a convention: each Cocoa framework prefixes its names with a particular group of capital letters (NSString and NSArray, CGFloat and CGRect, and so on). Apple suggests that you use a prefix of your own as well; in fact, when you create a new project in Xcode, you're offered an opportunity to specify a prefix, which will appear before the automatically created class names. Don't use any of Apple's prefixes. Nothing limits your prefix to two letters, or requires that both letters be uppercase. In fact, because all of Apple's own prefixes *are* uppercase letters, "My" as a prefix is safe.

An object reference is a pointer (Chapter 3), and this is true of a reference to a class object just as much as a reference to an instance. Like id, the term Class is already typed as a pointer, so you don't use an asterisk with it.

CHAPTER 5

Objective-C Instances

Instances are the heart of the action in an Objective-C program. Obtaining and manipulating instances will be crucial to just about everything you do. Nearly every line of code that you write will be concerned with one or more of these activities:

- Referring to an instance that already exists
- Creating a new instance that didn't exist previously
- Assigning an instance to a variable
- Sending a message to an instance
- Passing an instance as an argument in a method call

How Instances Are Created

Your class objects are created for you automatically as your program starts up, but instances must be created individually as the program runs. Ultimately, every instance comes into existence in just one way: someone asks a class to instantiate itself (see Chapter 4). But there are three different ways in which this can occur: ready-made instances, instantiation from scratch, and nib-based instantiation.

Ready-Made Instances

One way to create an instance is indirectly, by calling code that does the instantiation for you. You can think of an instance obtained in this indirect manner as a "ready-made instance." (That's my made-up phrase, not an official technical term.) Consider this simple code:

```
NSString* s2 = [s uppercaseString];
```

The documentation for the NSString instance method uppercaseString says that it returns "a string with each character from the receiver changed to its corresponding uppercase value." In other words, you send the uppercaseString message to an NSString instance, and you get back a *different*, newly created NSString instance. After that line of code, s2 points to an NSString instance that didn't exist before.

The NSString instance produced by the uppercaseString method comes to you ready-made. Your code didn't say anything about instantiation; it just sent the uppercase-String message. But clearly *someone* said something about instantiation, because instantiation took place; this is a newly minted NSString instance. That "someone" is presumably some code inside the NSString class. But we don't have to worry about the details. We are guaranteed of receiving a complete brand spanking new ready-to-roll NSString instance, and that's all we care about.

Similarly, any class factory method instantiates the class and dispenses the resulting instance as a ready-made instance. So, for example, the NSString class method string-WithContentsOfFile:encoding:error: reads a file and produces an NSString instance representing its contents. All the work of instantiation has been done for you. You just accept the resulting string and away you go.

Instantiation from Scratch

The alternative to requesting a ready-made instance is to tell a class explicitly to instantiate itself. To do so, you send a class the alloc message. The alloc class method is implemented by the NSObject class, the root class from which all other classes inherit. It causes memory to be set aside for the instance so that an instance pointer can point to it. (Management of that memory is a separate issue, discussed in Chapter 12.)

You must never, never, *never* call alloc by itself. You must *immediately* call another method, an instance method that *initializes* the newly created instance, placing it into a known valid state so that it can be sent other messages. Such a method is called an *initializer*. Moreover, an initializer returns an instance — usually the same instance, initialized. Therefore you can, and always should, call alloc and the initializer in the same line of code. The minimal initializer is init. So the basic pattern, known informally as "alloc-init," looks like Example 5-1.

Example 5-1. The basic pattern for instantiation from scratch

```
SomeClass* aVariable = [[SomeClass alloc] init];
```

You cannot instantiate from scratch if you do not also know how to initialize, so we turn immediately to a discussion of initialization.

Initialization

Every class defines or inherits at least one initializer. This is an instance method; the instance has just been created, by calling `alloc` on the class, and it is to this newly minted instance that the initializer message must be sent. An initializer message must be sent to an instance immediately after that instance is created by means of the `alloc` message, and it must not be sent to an instance at any other time.

The basic initialization pattern, as shown in Example 5-1, is to nest the `alloc` call in the initializer call, assigning the result of the initialization (not the `alloc`!) to a variable. One reason for this nested structure is that if something goes wrong and the instance can't be created or initialized, the initializer will return nil; therefore it's important to capture the result of the initializer and treat that, not the result of `alloc`, as the pointer to the instance.

To help you identify initializers, all initializers are named in a conventional manner. The convention is that all initializers, and only initializers, begin with the word `init`. The ultimate bare-bones initializer is called simply `init`, and takes no parameters. Other initializers do take parameters, and usually begin with the phrase `initWith` followed by descriptions of their parameters. For example, the NSArray class documentation lists these methods:

```
- initWithArray:
- initWithArray:copyItems:
- initWithContentsOfFile:
- initWithContentsOfURL:
- initWithObjects:
- initWithObjects:count:
```

Let's try a real example. In Chapter 3, we created an NSArray from three strings constituting its elements, by means of a class factory method, `arrayWithObjects:`, taking a nil-terminated list of objects and returning a ready-made instance:

```
NSArray* pep =
    [NSArray arrayWithObjects:@"Manny", @"Moe", @"Jack", nil];
```

It turns out, however, that there is also an initializer for NSArray, `initWithObjects:`, that works exactly the same way as `arrayWithObjects:`. The difference is that the latter is a class method, a factory method that returns a ready-made instance, while the former is an initializer, an instance method, that may be used only in the same breath with `alloc`. Thus we can now do exactly the same thing that we did in Chapter 3, except that we are now creating the instance ourselves, from scratch:

```
NSArray* pep =
    [[NSArray alloc] initWithObjects:@"Manny", @"Moe", @"Jack", nil];
```

In modern Objective-C, as I mentioned in Chapter 3, you are unlikely to call `arrayWith-Objects:` or `initWithObjects:`, because there is now a convenient literal array syntax that generates an array based on a list of its contents:

```
NSArray* pep = @[@"Manny", @"Moe", @"Jack"];
```

So I'll give another example. Suppose that, one way or another, you now have an array pep containing the three strings @"Manny", @"Moe", and @"Jack", and that you want to instantiate a second array based on it and containing those same three strings. Note that it is *not* sufficient to assign pep to another NSArray variable:

```
NSArray* pep2 = pep; // no, that isn't another array
```

Object references are pointers, and pointer assignment merely points two references at the same thing (Chapter 3). So pep2 in that code isn't a second array; it's the same array, which isn't what we said we wanted. To make a second array instance based on the first, we can call the class method `arrayWithArray:`, like this:

```
NSArray* pep2 = [NSArray arrayWithArray: pep];
```

Now pep2 is a newly minted instance, separate from pep. It's a ready-made instance, returned from a class factory method. Once again, though, it turns out that there's a corresponding initializer, `initWithArray:`. To create the instance ourselves from scratch, therefore, we might instead use that initializer:

```
NSArray* pep2 = [[NSArray alloc] initWithArray: pep];
```

It is often the case that a built-in Cocoa class will offer both a factory method and an initializer that start from the same kind of data and produce the same kind of result. Ultimately, it makes no difference which you use; given the same arguments, both approaches result in instances that are indistinguishable from one another. (The two approaches do have differing implications for memory management, as I'll explain in Chapter 12, but under ARC those differences will probably not matter to you.)

In looking through the documentation for an initializer, don't forget to look upward through the class hierarchy. For example, the class documentation for UIWebView lists no initializers, but UIWebView inherits from UIView, and in UIView's class documentation you'll discover `initWithFrame:`. Moreover, the `init` method is defined as an instance method of the NSObject class, so every class inherits it and every newly minted instance can be sent the `init` message. Thus it is a given that if a class defines no initializers of its own, you can initialize an instance of it with `init`. For example, the UIResponder class documentation lists no initializers at all (and no factory methods). So to create a UIResponder instance from scratch, you'd call `alloc` and `init`.

When `init` is the initializer you want to call, you can collapse the successive calls to `alloc` and `init` into a call to the class method `new`. In other words, `[MyClass new]` is a synonym for `[[MyClass alloc] init]`. This is a convenient shorthand, but it applies *only* when the initializer is `init`, plain and simple; to use any other initializer, you'll have to call `alloc` and the initializer explicitly.

The designated initializer

If a class defines initializers, one of them may be described in the documentation as the *designated initializer*. (There's nothing about a method's name that tells you it's the designated initializer; you must peruse the documentation to find out.) For example, in the UIView class documentation, the `initWithFrame:` method is described as the designated initializer. A class that does not define a designated initializer inherits its superclass's designated initializer; the ultimate designated initializer, inherited by all classes without any other designated initializer anywhere in their superclass chain, is `init`. Thus, every class has exactly one designated initializer.

A class's designated initializer *must* be called in the course of instantiating that class. If a class has more than one initializer, whether inherited or defined within the class, its designated initializer is the initializer on which its other initializers depend: ultimately, they *must* call it.

Other initializers can relate to the designated initializer in various ways. The designated initializer might have the most parameters, allowing the most instance variables to be set explicitly (with the other initializers supplying default values for some instance variables). Or it might just be the most basic form of initialization. Here are some real-life examples:

- The NSDate class documentation says that `initWithTimeIntervalSince-ReferenceDate:` is the designated initializer, and that other initializers (such as `initWithTimeIntervalSinceNow:`) call it.

- The UIView class documentation says that `initWithFrame:` is the designated initializer. UIView contains no other initializers, but some of its subclasses do. UIWebView, a UIView subclass, has no initializer, so `initWithFrame:` is its designated initializer (by inheritance). UIImageView, a UIView subclass, has initializers such as `initWithImage:`, but none of them is a designated initializer; so `initWithFrame:` is its inherited designated initializer as well, and `initWithImage:` must call `initWithFrame:`.

A class that implements a designated initializer of its own must override the designated initializer inherited from the superclass, so that the latter calls the former. Thus:

Figure 5-1. Dragging a button into a view

- NSDate overrides the inherited `init` to call its own designated initializer, `initWith-TimeIntervalSinceReferenceDate:`, with a value that will generate a date specifying the current date and time.

- UIView overrides the inherited `init` to call its own designated initializer, `initWith-Frame:`, with a frame value of `CGRectZero`.

Nib-Based Instantiation

The third means of instantiation is through a nib file. A nib file is a file within the built app, generated from a *.storyboard* file or *.xib* file in which you have "drawn" parts of the user interface. Most Xcode projects will include at least one *.storyboard* file or *.xib* file, and thus most apps will contain at least one nib file inside the app bundle. A nib file, to be used, must be explicitly loaded, by some mechanism, as the app runs. A nib file consists, in a sense, of the names of classes along with instructions for instantiating and initializing them. When the app runs and a nib file is loaded, those instructions are carried out — those classes *are* instantiated and initialized. Thus the running app ends up generating instances based on what you originally drew in the *.storyboard* file or *.xib* file.

For example, suppose you'd like the user to be presented with a view containing a button whose title is "Howdy!" Xcode lets you arrange this graphically by editing a *.storyboard* file or *.xib* file. You drag a button from the Object library into the view, as in Figure 5-1. Then you place it at its desired position in the view, and set its title to "Howdy!", as in Figure 5-2. In effect, you create a drawing of what you want the view and its contents to look like.

When the app runs, the nib file loads, and that drawing is turned into reality. To do this, the drawing is treated as a set of instructions for instantiating objects. The button that you dragged into the view is treated as a representative of the UIButton class. The UIButton class is told to instantiate itself, and that instance is then initialized, giving it the same position you gave it in the drawing (the instance's `frame`), the same title you gave it in the drawing (the instance's `title`), and putting it into the view. In effect, the loading

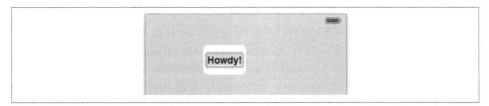

Figure 5-2. Configuring a button graphically

of your nib file is equivalent to code like this (assuming that `self.view` is a reference
to the view object):

```
UIButton* b =
    [UIButton buttonWithType:UIButtonTypeSystem];        // instantiate
[b setTitle:@"Howdy!" forState:UIControlStateNormal];    // set up title
[b setFrame: CGRectMake(100,100,52,30)];                 // set up frame
[self.view addSubview:b];                                // place button in view
```

In that code, the UIButton instance is created as a ready-made instance by calling a class
factory method, and is then assigned to a variable b. But in the case of nib-based instantiation, getting an instance from the nib to be assigned to a variable is quite a tricky
business, involving considerable preparation and a device called an *outlet*. The fact that
nib files are a source of instances, and that those instances are brought into existence as
the nib file is loaded, along with the problem of how to assign such instances to variables,
is a source of confusion to beginners. I'll discuss the matter in detail in Chapter 7.

Polymorphism

Given a subclass and its superclass, you are free to supply a subclass instance wherever
an instance of the superclass is expected. For example, UIButton is a subclass of UI-
Control, which is a subclass of UIView. So it would be perfectly legal and acceptable to
say this:

```
UIButton* b = [UIButton buttonWithType:UIButtonTypeSystem];
UIView* v = b;
```

The variable b is declared as a UIButton, but I'm assigning it to a variable declared as a
UIView. That's legal and acceptable because UIView is an ancestor (up the superclass
chain) of UIButton. Putting it another way, I'm behaving as if a UIButton were a UIView,
and the compiler accepts this because a UIButton *is* a UIView.

What's important when the app runs, however, is not the *declared* class of a variable,
but the *actual class of the object* to which that variable refers. After I assign the UIButton
instance to the variable v, the object to which the variable v points is a UIButton. So
even though v is not typed as a UIButton, it can do no harm to send it messages appropriate to a UIButton, because it *is* a UIButton. For example:

```
UIButton* b = [UIButton buttonWithType:UIButtonTypeSystem];
UIView* v = b;
[v setTitle:@"Howdy!" forState:UIControlStateNormal];
```

There is no UIView message `setTitle:forState:`. Nevertheless, that code is perfectly reasonable and safe; v may be typed as a mere UIView, but in reality, when the code runs, it will be pointing to a UIButton — and there *is* a UIButton message `setTitle:forState:`. The compiler, however, doesn't know anything about what v will be pointing to when the code runs, so (under ARC) it declares a compile error. I can allay the compiler's fears by typecasting the receiver:

```
UIButton* b = [UIButton buttonWithType:UIButtonTypeSystem];
UIView* v = b;
[(UIButton*)v setTitle:@"Howdy!" forState:UIControlStateNormal];
```

The typecast calms the compiler's fears, and the code now compiles. And when the code runs, it works just fine! It works not because I typecast v to a UIButton (typecasting doesn't magically convert anything to anything else; it's just a hint to the compiler), but because v really *is* a UIButton. I typecast the receiver, and the compiler always takes your word for it when you typecast; moreover, my typecast told the truth, so when the message `setTitle:forState:` arrives at the object pointed to by v, everything is fine. If v had been a UIView but *not* a UIButton, on the other hand, the program would have crashed at that instant.

Now let's turn the tables. We called a UIButton a UIView and sent it a UIButton message. Now we're going to call a UIButton a UIButton and send it a UIView message.

What an object really is depends not just upon its class but also upon that class's inheritance. A message is acceptable even if an object's own class doesn't implement a corresponding method, provided that the method is implemented somewhere up the superclass chain. For example:

```
UIButton* b = [UIButton buttonWithType:UIButtonTypeSystem];
[b setFrame: CGRectMake(100,100,52,30)];
```

That code works fine. But you won't find `setFrame:` in the documentation for the UIButton class. That's because you're looking in the wrong place. A UIButton is a UIControl, and a UIControl is a UIView. To find out about `setFrame:`, look in the UIView class's documentation. (Okay, it's more complicated than that; you won't find `setFrame:` there either. But you will find a term `frame` which is called a "property," and this amounts to the same thing, as I'll explain later in this chapter.) So the `setFrame:` message is sent to a UIButton, but it corresponds to a method defined on a UIView. Yet it works fine, because a UIButton *is* a UIView.

A common beginner mistake is to consult the documentation without following the superclass chain. If you want to know what you can say to a UIButton, don't just look in the UIButton class documentation: also look in the UIControl class documentation, the UIView class documentation, and so on.

We treated a UIButton object as a UIView, yet (by typecasting) we were still able to send it a UIButton message. We treated a UIButton as a UIButton, yet (by inheritance) we were still able to send it a UIView message.

An object responds to a message sent to it, not on the basis of anything said in code about what it is, but on the basis of what it really is when the program runs and the message is actually sent to that object. What matters when a message is sent to an object is not how the variable pointing to that object is declared or typecast, but what class the object really is. What an object really is depends upon its class, along with that class's inheritance from the superclass chain; these facts are innate to the object and are independent of how your code characterizes the variable pointing to the object. This independent maintenance of object type integrity is the basis of what is called *polymorphism*.

But it is not quite the whole of polymorphism. To understand the whole of polymorphism, we must go further into the dynamics of message sending.

The Keyword self

A common situation is that code in an instance method defined in a class must call another instance method defined within the same class. We have not yet discussed how to do this. A method is called by sending a message to an object; in this situation, what object would that be? The answer is supplied by a special keyword, self. Here's a simple example:

```
@implementation MyClass
- (NSString*) greeting {
    return @"Goodnight, Gracie!";
}
- (NSString*) sayGoodnightGracie {
    return [self greeting];
}
@end
```

When the sayGoodnightGracie message is sent to a MyClass instance, the say-GoodnightGracie instance method runs. It sends the greeting message to self. As a result, the greeting instance method is called; it returns the string @"Goodnight, Gracie!", and this same string is then returned from the sayGoodnightGracie method.

The example seems straightforward enough, and it is. In real life, your code for a class will often consist of a few public instance methods along with lots of other instance methods on which they rely. The instance methods within this class will be calling each other constantly. They do this by sending messages to self.

Behind this simple example, though, is a subtle and important mechanism having to do with the real meaning of the keyword self. The keyword self does not actually mean "in the same class." It's an instance, after all, not a class. What instance? It's this same instance. The same as what? The same instance to which the message was sent that resulted in the keyword self being encountered in the first place.

So let's consider in more detail what happens when we instantiate MyClass and send the sayGoodnightGracie message to that instance:

```
MyClass* thing = [MyClass new];
NSString* s = [thing sayGoodnightGracie];
```

We instantiate MyClass and assign the instance to a variable thing. We then send the sayGoodnightGracie message to thing, the instance we just created. The message arrives, and it turns out that this instance is a MyClass. Sure enough, MyClass implements a sayGoodnightGracie instance method, and this method is called. As it runs, the keyword self is encountered. It means "the instance to which the original message was sent in the first place." That, as it happens, is the instance pointed to by the variable thing. So now the greeting message is sent to that instance (Figure 5-3).

This mechanism may seem rather elaborate, considering that the outcome is just what you'd intuitively expect. But the mechanism *needs* to be elaborate in order to get the right outcome. This is particularly evident when superclasses are involved and a class overrides a method of its superclass.

To illustrate, suppose we have a class Dog with an instance method bark. And suppose Dog also has an instance method speak, which simply calls bark. Now suppose we subclass Dog with a class Basenji, which overrides bark (because Basenjis can't bark). What happens when we send the speak message to a Basenji instance, as in Example 5-2?

Example 5-2. Polymorphism in action

```
@implementation Dog
- (NSString*) bark {
    return @"Woof!";
}
- (NSString*) speak {
    return [self bark];
}
@end

@implementation Basenji : Dog
- (NSString*) bark {
```

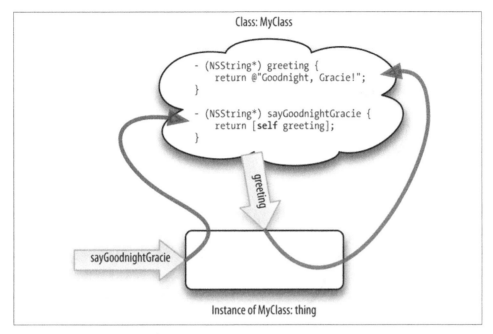

Figure 5-3. The meaning of self

```
    return @""; // empty string, Basenjis can't bark
}
@end

// So, in some other class:
Basenji* b = [Basenji new];
NSString* s = [b speak];
```

If the keyword self meant merely "the same class where this keyword appears," then when we send the speak message to a Basenji instance, we would arrive at the implementation of speak in the Dog class (because that's where speak is implemented), and the Dog class's bark method would be called. This would be terrible, because it would make nonsense of the notion of overriding; we'd return @"Woof!", which is wrong for a Basenji. But that is *not* what the keyword self means. It has to do with the instance, not the class.

So here's what happens. The speak message is sent to our Basenji instance, b. The Basenji class doesn't implement a speak method, so we look upward in the class hierarchy and discover that speak is implemented in the superclass, Dog. We call Dog's instance method speak, the speak method runs, and the keyword self is encountered. It means "the instance to which the original message was sent in the first place." That instance is still our Basenji instance b. So we send the bark message to the Basenji instance b. The

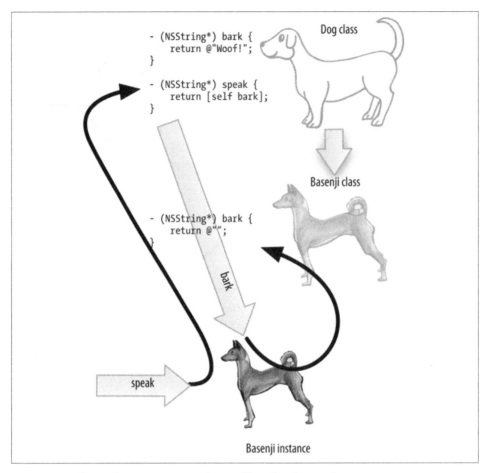

```
- (NSString*) bark {
    return @"Woof!";
}
```
Dog class

```
- (NSString*) speak {
    return [self bark];
}
```

Basenji class

```
- (NSString*) bark {
    return @"";
}
```

bark

speak

Basenji instance

Figure 5-4. Class inheritance, overriding, self, and polymorphism

Basenji class implements a bark instance method, so this method is found and called, and the empty string is returned (Figure 5-4).

Of course, if the Basenji class had *not* overridden bark, then when the bark message was sent to the Basenji instance, we would have looked upward in the class hierarchy *again* and found the bark method implemented in the Dog class and called that. Thus, thanks to the way the keyword self works, inheritance works correctly both when there is overriding and when there is not.

If you understand that example, you understand polymorphism. The mechanism I've just described is crucial to polymorphism and is the basis of object-oriented programming. (Observe that I now speak of object-oriented programming, not just object-based programming as in Chapter 2. That's because, in my view, the addition of polymorphism is what turns object-based programming into object-oriented programming.)

The Keyword super

Sometimes (quite often, in Cocoa programming) you want to override an inherited method but still access the overridden functionality. To do so, you'll use the keyword super. Like self, the keyword super is something you send a message to. But its meaning has nothing to do with "this instance" or any other instance. The keyword super is class-based, and it means: "Start the search for messages I receive in the superclass of this class" (where "this class" is the class where the keyword super appears).

You can do anything you like with super, but its primary purpose, as I've just said, is to access overridden functionality — typically from within the very functionality that does the overriding, so as to get both the overridden functionality and some additional functionality.

For example, suppose we define a class NoisyDog, a subclass of Dog. When told to bark, it barks twice:

```
@implementation NoisyDog : Dog
- (NSString*) bark {
    return [NSString stringWithFormat: @"%@ %@", [super bark], [super bark]];
}
@end
```

That code calls super's implementation of bark, twice; it assembles the two resulting strings into a single string with a space between (using the stringWithFormat: method), and returns that. Because Dog's bark method returns @"Woof!", NoisyDog's bark method returns @"Woof! Woof!". Notice that there is no circularity or recursion here: Noisy-Dog's bark method will never call itself.

A nice feature of this architecture is that by sending a message to the keyword super, rather than hard-coding @"Woof!" into NoisyDog's bark method, we ensure maintainability: if Dog's bark method is changed, the result of NoisyDog's bark method will change to match. For example, if we later go back and change Dog's bark method to return @"Arf!", NoisyDog's bark method will return @"Arf! Arf!" with no further change on our part.

In real Cocoa programming, it will very often be Cocoa's own methods that you're overriding. For example, the UIViewController class, which is built into Cocoa, implements a method viewDidAppear:, described in the documenation as follows:

```
- (void)viewDidAppear:(BOOL)animated
```

The documentation says that UIViewController is a class for which you are very likely to define a subclass. The documentation proceeds to suggest that in your subclass of

UIViewController you might want to override this method, but cautions that if you do, "you must call super at some point in your implementation." The phrase "call super" is a kind of shorthand, meaning "pass on to super the very same call and arguments that were sent to you."

So let's say you're overriding viewDidAppear: in your UIViewController subclass, called MyViewController. Your implementation might look like this:

```
- (void) viewDidAppear: (BOOL) animated {
    [super viewDidAppear: animated];
    // ... do more stuff here ...
}
```

The result is that when viewDidAppear: is called in a MyViewController instance, we do both the standard stuff that its superclass UIViewController does in response to view-DidAppear: and the custom stuff pertaining to our own class MyViewController. In this particular case, we don't even know exactly what the UIViewController stuff is, and we don't care. When the documentation tells you to call super when overriding, call super when overriding! Neglecting to call super when told by the documentation to do so can cause your app to behave incorrectly in unpredictable ways, and is a common beginner mistake.

Instance Variables and Accessors

In Chapter 3, I explained that one of the main reasons there are instances and not just classes is that instances can have instance variables. Instance variables, you remember, are declared when you define the class, and in Chapter 4 I said that these declarations go into curly braces at the start of the class's interface section or, in modern Objective-C, its implementation section. But for every instance variable defined in a class, each individual instance of that class keeps its instance variables individually; the value of any instance variable of any instance can be set and maintained and fetched and changed for as long as the instance itself persists.

 The term "instance variable" arises so often that it is often abbreviated to *ivar*. I'll use both terms indiscriminately from now on.

Let's write a class that uses an instance variable. Suppose we have a Dog class and we want every Dog instance to have a number, which should be an int. (For example, this number might correspond to the dog's license number.) In modern Objective-C, we would probably declare number in the implementation section for the Dog class, like this:

```
@implementation Dog {
    int number;
}
// method implementations go here
@end
```

(You might ask why, for this example, I don't use instead the concept of giving the dog a name. The reason is that a name would be an NSString instance, which is an object; instance variables that are pointers to objects raise some additional issues I don't want to discuss just now. But instance variables that are simple C data types raise no such issues. We'll return to this matter in Chapter 12.)

Within a class, that class's own instance variables are global to all instance methods. Any Dog instance method can just use the variable name number and access this instance variable, just like any other variable. But code that does this can be confusing when you're reading it; suddenly there's a variable called number and you don't understand what it is, because there's no nearby declaration for it. So I often use a different notation, like this: self->ivarName. The "arrow" operator, formed by a minus sign and a greater-than sign, is called the *structure pointer* operator, because of its original use in C (K&R 6.2).

Another conventional device is to start the name of an instance variable with an underscore: _ivarName. That way, even if you don't write self->_ivarName, the bare name _ivarName provides a clue as to where this variable might be declared.

The fact that ivars are global to all instance methods within a class, and that they persist for as long as the instance itself, is often a perfectly sufficient reason for having ivars. Think of ivars as a convenient and powerful way of sharing values across different instance methods of the same class. You will often, in one instance method, stick a value into an instance variable, exactly so that some other instance method can come alone later and retrieve it. An instance method here functions as a kind of drop box, and this is a very important function indeed (especially in the event-driven world of the Cocoa framework; see Chapter 11).

However, ivars can also be a means of communication with an instance from outside that instance. You may, as you construct the code for a class and think about its place in your program, want to allow instances of other classes to get or even set the value of an instance variable of an instance of this class. By default, however, instance variables are *protected*, meaning that other classes, except for subclasses of this one, can't see them. And if instance variables are declared in a class's implementation section, *no* other classes, not even subclasses of this one, can see them. So if, somewhere else, I instantiate a Dog, I won't be able to access that Dog instance's number instance variable. This is a deliberate feature of Objective-C; you can work around it if you like, but in general you should not. Instead, you will want to provide *accessor* methods.

There's a convention for the naming of such methods: they should be named setXxx: and xxx, where "xxx" are the same as one another (and may well be the same as the name of an instance variable). For example, we might name our accessor methods set-Number: and number.

Let's write, then, in Dog's implementation section, an accessor method setNumber: that allows setting a value for the number ivar (that is, this method is a *setter*):

```
- (void) setNumber: (int) n {
    self->number = n;
}
```

Of course, to make setNumber: public to any other class that imports Dog's interface file *Dog.h*, we must also declare it in Dog's interface section:

```
@interface Dog : NSObject
- (void) setNumber: (int) n;
@end
```

We can now, in any class that imports *Dog.h*, instantiate a Dog and assign that instance a number:

```
Dog* fido = [Dog new];
[fido setNumber: 42];
```

We can now set a Dog's number, but we can't get it (from outside that Dog instance). To correct this problem, we'll write a second accessor method, number, that allows for getting the value of the number ivar (this method is a *getter*):

```
- (int) number {
    return self->number;
}
```

Again, we declare the number method in Dog's interface section. We can now, in any class that imports *Dog.h*, both set and get a Dog instance's number:

```
Dog* fido = [Dog new];
[fido setNumber: 42];
int n = [fido number];
// sure enough, n is now 42!
```

Luckily, modern Objective-C provides a mechanism for generating accessor methods automatically (discussed in Chapter 12), so you won't have to go through the tedium of writing them by hand every time you want to make an ivar publicly accessible. (Though, to be honest, I don't see why you shouldn't have to go through that tedium; before Objective-C 2.0, we all had to, so why shouldn't you? We also had to clean the roads with our tongues on the way to school. And we liked it! You kids today, you don't know what real programming is.)

In my code, Dog now has both a number method and a number instance variable. This fact should not confuse you. It doesn't confuse the compiler, because the method name and the instance variable name are used in completely different ways in code. If the compiler can tell the difference, so can you. Still, elimination of any such confusion is another benefit of the convention that I mentioned a moment ago, where we begin our ivar names with an underscore: _number, not number. If we follow this convention and rename our ivar, we'll also have to rewrite (but not rename) the methods that access it:

```
@implementation Dog {
    int _number;
}
- (void) setNumber: (int) n {
    self->_number = n;
}
- (int) number {
    return self->_number;
}
@end
```

All instance variables are set to some form of zero when the instance comes into existence (as part of the call to the class method alloc). This is important, because it means that, unlike a local automatic variable, mere declaration of an instance variable without providing an initial value is not dangerous — which is good, because it's also impossible. We can't say:

```
@implementation Dog {
    int _number = 42; // no, sorry, that's not Objective-C!
}
```

However, at least we know that _number will start out life as 0, not as some dangerous indeterminate value. By the same token, a BOOL instance variable will start out life as NO, the BOOL form of 0, and an instance variable typed as an object will start out life as nil, the object form of 0. If you want an instance variable to have a nonzero value early in the lifetime of the instance, it is up to your code to give it that nonzero value. It can be important to remember to test an instance variable for 0 (or nil) to see whether this has happened yet.

Key–Value Coding

Objective-C provides a means for translating from a string to an accessor call, called *key–value coding*. Such translation is useful, for example, when the name of the desired accessor will not be known until runtime. The string is the *key*. The key–value coding equivalent of calling a getter is valueForKey:; the equivalent of calling a setter is set-Value:forKey:.

Thus, for example, suppose we wish to call the number method on the fido instance. We can do this by sending valueForKey: to fido, with a key @"number". However, even though the number method returns an int, the value returned by valueForKey: is an object — in this case, an NSNumber, the object equivalent of a number (see Chapter 10). If we want the actual int, NSNumber provides an instance method, `intValue`, that lets us extract it:

```
NSNumber* num = [fido valueForKey: @"number"];
int n = [num intValue];
```

Similarly, to use key–value coding to call the `setNumber:` method on the `fido` instance, we would say:

```
NSNumber* num = [NSNumber numberWithInt:42];
[fido setValue: num forKey: @"number"];
```

Before handing off the number 42 as the `value` argument in `setValue:forKey:`, we had to wrap it up as an object — in this case, an NSNumber object. Starting with LLVM compiler version 4.0 (Xcode 4.4), there's a syntactic shorthand for doing that; just as we can create an NSString by wrapping text in a compiler directive `@"..."`, we can create an NSNumber by wrapping a numeric expression in a compiler directive `@(...)` — or, if the numeric expression is just a literal number, by preceding that literal number with `@`. So we can rewrite the previous example like this:

```
NSNumber* num = @42;
[fido setValue: num forKey: @"number"];
```

In real life, you'd probably omit the intermediate variable `num` and write the whole thing as a single line of code:

```
[fido setValue: @42 forKey: @"number"];
```

In these examples there is no advantage to using key–value coding over just calling the accessors. But suppose we had received the value `@"number"` in a variable (as the result of a method call, perhaps). Suppose that variable is called `something`. Then we could say:

```
id result = [fido valueForKey: something];
```

Thus we could access a different accessor under different circumstances. This powerful flexibility is possible because Objective-C is such a dynamic language that a message to be sent to an object does not have to be formed until the program is already running.

When you call `valueForKey:` or `setValue:forKey:`, the correct accessor method is called if there is one. Thus, when we use `@"number"` as the key, a `number` method and a `setNumber:` method are called if they exist. This is one reason why your accessors should be properly named. On the other hand, if there isn't an accessor method, but there is an instance variable with the same name as the key, *the instance variable is accessed directly* (even if its name starts with an underscore)! Such direct access violates the privacy of instance variables, so there's a way to turn off this feature for a particular class if you don't like it. (I'll explain what it is, with more about key–value coding, in Chapter 12.)

Properties

A *property* is a syntactic feature of modern Objective-C designed to provide an alternative to the standard syntax for calling an accessor method. As syntactic sugar for formally calling an accessor, you can append the property name to an instance reference using dot-notation. You can use the resulting expression either on the left side of an equal sign (to call the corresponding setter) or elsewhere (to call the corresponding getter). The name of the property relies, by default, on the accessor naming conventions.

I'll use the Dog class as an example. If the Dog class has a public getter method called number and a public setter method called setNumber:, then the Dog class also has a number property that can be used on the left side of an equal sign or elsewhere. This means that, instead of saying things like this:

```
[fido setNumber: 42];
int n = [fido number];
```

You can talk like this:

```
fido.number = 42;
int n = fido.number;
```

Your use of property syntax is entirely optional. The existence of a property is equivalent to the existence of the corresponding getter and setter methods; using the property is equivalent to calling the accessor method. You're free to call an accessor method by either syntax. In the case of Dog, you can call the getter and setter methods (number and setNumber:), or you can use the property (number).

To use a property within the class that has that property, you must write self explicitly. So, for example:

```
self.number = 42;
```

Do not confuse a property with an instance variable. An expression like self->number = n, or even simply number = n, sets the instance variable directly (and is possible only within the class, because instance variables are protected by default). An expression like fido.number or self.number involves a property and is equivalent to calling a getter or setter method. That getter or setter method may access an instance variable, and that instance variable may even have the same name as the property, but that doesn't make them the same thing.

Properties will be taken up again in Chapter 12, where it will turn out that they are much more powerful and interesting beasts than I'm suggesting here. But I'm telling you about properties now because they are so widely used in Cocoa and because you'll encounter them so frequently in the documentation.

For example, earlier in this chapter I called UIView's `setFrame:` instance method on a UIButton instance:

```
[b setFrame: CGRectMake(100,100,52,30)];
```

I mentioned that `setFrame:` is not documented under UIButton; you have to look in the UIView documentation. But in fact, no such method is mentioned there either. What the UIView documentation does say is this:

frame

The frame rectangle, which describes the view's location and size in its superview's co-ordinate system.

```
@property(nonatomic) CGRect frame
```

The documentation is telling me about the UIView property name `frame`. That last line is a *property declaration*. From the point of view of the UIView class's client — in this case, that's me — the property declaration is simply a shorthand, telling me that such a property exists. (Never mind for now what `nonatomic` means.) But that's the same thing as telling me about the existence of UIView instance methods `frame` and `setFrame:`; I can use these methods either through the `frame` property and dot-notation or by calling them explicitly. That's how I knew there was a setter `setFrame:`. In my code, I called `setFrame:` explicitly; now you know that I could have used the `frame` property:

```
b.frame = CGRectMake(100,100,52,30);
```

Objective-C uses dot-notation for properties, and C uses dot-notation for structs; these can be chained. So, for example, UIView's `frame` is a property whose value is a struct (a CGRect); thus, you can say `myView.frame.size.height`, where `frame` is a property that returns a struct, `size` is an element of that struct, and `height` is an element of *that* struct. But there are limitations on this syntax; you cannot (for example) *set* a frame's height directly through a chain starting with the UIView, like this:

```
myView.frame.size.height = 36.0; // error, "Expression is not assignable"
```

Instead, if you want to change a component of a struct property, you must fetch the property value into a struct variable, change the struct variable's value, and set the entire property value from the struct variable:

```
CGRect f = myView.frame;
f.size.height = 0;
myView.frame = f;
```

How to Write an Initializer

Now that you know about `self` and `super` and instance variables, we can return to a topic that I blithely skipped over earlier. I described how to initialize a newly minted instance by calling an initializer, and emphasized that you must always do so, but I said

Dot-Notation Wars

Naturally, there is quasi-religious debate over properties and dot-notation syntax, with one side claiming that property syntax is convenient and compact, and makes Objective-C more like other languages that use dot-notation, and the other side retorting that it does no such thing, because it is so limited.

For example, property syntax opponents would argue, a UIScrollView has a `content-View` property, but when *setting* it you are most likely to want to animate the scroll view at the same time, which you do by calling `setContentView:animated:`. That's a kind of setter, but it takes two parameters; property syntax can't express that, so we're back to using an explicit method call, and property syntax has saved us nothing, and in fact is more likely to mislead us into forgetting to add the animation.

Another objection to property notation is that the compiler restricts its use; for example, you can use a formal method call to send the `number` message to a Dog instance typed as an `id`, but you can't append the `number` property with dot-notation to such an instance.

Yet another problem is that it is permitted to misuse property syntax to call a method that isn't, strictly speaking, a getter. For example, the `lastObject` instance method of NSArray is just a method; it isn't listed as a property. Nevertheless, programmers will often write `myArray.lastObject` just because it's simpler and faster to write than `[my-Array lastObject]` — and because it works. But, again, you can't do that with methods that don't return a value or that take any parameters; the method in question has to be getter-like, even if it isn't really a getter. Such misuse of property syntax may seem abominable, but it is also overwhelmingly tempting, as is proven by the fact that even Apple's own example code sometimes does it.

nothing about how to write an initializer in your own classes. You will wish to do this when you want your class to provide a convenient initializer that goes beyond the functionality of the inherited initializers. Often your purpose will be to accept some parameters and use them to set the initial values of some instance variables.

For example, in the case of a Dog with a number, let's say we don't want any Dog instances to come into existence without a number; every Dog *must* have one. So having a value for its `number` ivar is a *sine qua non* of a Dog being instantiated in the first place. An initializer publicizes this rule and helps to enforce it — especially if it is the class's designated initializer. So let's decide that this initializer will be Dog's designated initializer.

Moreover, let's say that a Dog's number should not be changed. Once the Dog has come into existence, along with a number, that number should remain attached to that Dog instance for as long as that Dog instance persists.

So delete the setNumber: method and its declaration, thus destroying any ability of other classes to set a Dog instance's number after it has been initialized. Instead, we're going to set a Dog's number as it is initialized, using a method we'll declare like this:

```
- (id) initWithNumber: (int) n;
```

Our return value is typed as id, not as a pointer to a Dog, even though in fact we will return a Dog object. This is a convention that we should obey. The name is conventional as well; as you know, the init beginning tells the world this is an initializer.

Now I'm just going to show you the actual code for the initializer (Example 5-3). Much of this code is conventional — a dance you are required to do. You should not question this dance: just do it. I'll describe the meaning of the code, but I'm not going to try to justify all the parts of the convention.

Example 5-3. Conventional schema for an initializer

```
- (id) initWithNumber: (int) n {
    self = [super init]; ❶ ❷
    if (self) {
        self->_number = n; ❸
    }
    return self; ❹
}
```

The parts of the convention are:

❶ We send some sort of initialization message, calling a designated initializer. If the method we are writing is our class's designated initializer, this message is sent to super and calls the superclass's designated initializer. Otherwise, it is sent to self and calls either this class's designated initializer or another initializer that calls this class's designated initializer. In this case, the method we are writing is our class's designated initializer, and the superclass's designated initializer is init.

❷ We capture the result of the initialization message we send, and assign that result to self. It comes as a surprise to many beginners (and not-so-beginners) that one can assign to self at all or that it would make sense to do so. But one can assign to self (because of how Objective-C messaging works behind the scenes), and it makes sense to do so because in certain cases the instance returned from the initialization message we send might not be same as the self we started with.

❸ If self is not nil, we initialize any instance variables we care to. This part of the code is typically the only part you'll customize; the rest will be according to the pattern. Observe that I don't use any setter methods (or properties); in initializing an instance variable not inherited from the superclass, you should assign directly to the instance variable.

(Earlier, I mentioned that instance variables start out life with a zero value, and that if you don't like that, giving them a different value is up to you. Clearly, writing a designated initializer is one way to do that! Conversely, if the default zero values are satisfactory initial values for some of your instance variables, you won't bother to set them in your designated initializer.)

❹ We return self.

But we are not finished. Recall from earlier in this chapter that a class that defines a designated initializer should also override the inherited designated initializer (in this case, init). And you can see why: if we don't, someone could say [[Dog alloc] init] (or [Dog new]) and create a dog without a number — the very thing our initializer is trying to prevent. Just for the sake of the example, I'll make the overridden init assign a negative number as a signal that there's a problem. Notice that we're still obeying the rules: this initializer is not the designated initializer, so it calls this class's designated initializer:

```
- (id) init {
    return [self initWithNumber: -9999];
}
```

Just to complete the story, here's some code showing how we now would instantiate a Dog:

```
Dog* fido = [[Dog alloc] initWithNumber:42];
int n = fido.number;
// n is now 42; our initialization worked!
```

 Even though an initializer returns an id, and even though id is the universal donor, the compiler warns if we assign the result to an inappropriately typed variable:

```
NSString* s = [[Dog alloc] initWithNumber:42]; // compiler warns
```

This magic is performed by the modern LLVM compiler, which infers, from the fact that the name of this method starts with init, that it is an initializer, and effectively substitutes for id the keyword instancetype, indicating that the value returned from this method should be of the same type as its receiver (here, a Dog).

Referring to Instances

This chapter has largely concentrated on the mechanics of instance creation. Often, however, your code will be concerned, not with creating a new instance, but with referring to an instance that already exists. An instance can be referred to either by using the name of an object reference to which it has previously been assigned (a variable, which may be an ivar) or by producing it as the result of a method call — and in no other way. If you haven't already got a named reference to a certain instance (by way of a variable or ivar), there may be a method call that returns the desired instance. For example, this is how you ask an array (an NSArray) for its last element:

```
id myThing = [myArray lastObject];
```

The NSArray myArray didn't *create* the object that it hands you. That object already existed; myArray was merely containing it, as it were — it was holding the object, pointing to it. Now it's sharing that object with you, that's all.

Similarly, many classes dispense one particular object repeatedly. For example, your app has exactly one instance of the UIApplication class (we call this the *singleton* UIApplication instance); to access it, you send the sharedApplication class method to the UIApplication class:

```
UIApplication* theApp = [UIApplication sharedApplication];
```

This singleton instance existed before you asked for it; indeed, it existed before any code of yours could possibly run. You don't care how it was brought into being; all you care is that you can get hold of it when you want it. I'll talk more about globally available singleton objects of this kind in Chapter 13.

In both those examples, the code is concerned with two things: finding a way to specify an already existing instance, and assigning that existing instance to a variable, thus creating (not a new instance, but) a new name under which to refer to that already existing instance. These are both aspects of the same thing — referring to an instance.

The business of referring to an instance is something with which you will be intimately concerned while programming iOS. The matter may sound trivial, but it is not. Indeed, the problem of referring to an already existing instance is so important that I will devote much of Chapter 13 to it. An instance does you no good if you can't refer to it. If you can't refer to it, you can't send a message to it. If you can't refer to it, you can't use it as an argument in a method call. If you can't refer to it, you can't find out anything about or do anything to or with it. You will quite often find yourself in a situation where you know an instance exists but you have to sweat in order to refer to it. You may even have to rewrite or rearchitect your program, changing what happens earlier in the program so that you'll be able to get a reference to a particular instance later in the program at the moment when you need it.

Moreover, once you *do* have a reference to a desired instance, you may very well be concerned to *keep* it. In the case of a singleton instance such as [UIApplication shared-Application], this is not really an issue. There is just one shared application instance, and the UIApplication class will be happy to hand it to you over and over again whenever you ask for it. Thus, you could just keep saying [UIApplication shared-Application] in various places in your program, and you probably will. Assigning the shared application instance to a variable of your own, such as theApp in the earlier example, is merely a convenience. It's just a short, easy name for this same instance.

Not so, though, with an instance like [myArray lastObject]. Here, we already had a reference to an array (myArray), and now we are concerned with obtaining a reference to one of its elements, namely, the last one. The instance that currently functions as the last element of myArray might not always be the last element of myArray. It might not always be an element of myArray at all. In fact, the array myArray might itself go out of existence. If the particular instance that we are presently able to refer to as [myArray lastObject] is going to be important to us in the future, we may need to take steps now to maintain some other reference to it, one that does not depend upon the status or state of some array. That is a likely reason for assigning the instance returned by [myArray lastObject] to a variable myThing. Now, regardless of what happens to the array, the name myThing will continue on as a reference to this instance.

In the preceding code, though, myThing is obviously just a local automatic variable; the variable will go out of scope when the current scope ends (for example, when the current method finishes executing), and the ability to refer to this instance will be lost. What can we do about that? Well, all this is happening within the class code running within some instance: let's say it's a Dog instance. If we need the myThing instance to live longer within this Dog instance, we will want to assign it to an instance variable. And doing so has an additional benefit: thereafter, other instance methods of this Dog instance will have a reference to it! What's more, if there's an accessor, other objects, if they have a reference to the Dog instance, will have a reference to the myThing instance as well! By this technique, we promote or extend the life of an instance, while broadening and ensuring our own future ability to get a reference to it. That, indeed, is such an important and valuable thing to be able to do that it will often be our reason for giving a class an instance variable in the first place.

PART II

IDE

By now, you're doubtless anxious to jump in and start writing an app. To do that, you need a solid grounding in the tools you'll be using. The heart and soul of those tools can be summed up in one word: Xcode. In this part of the book we explore Xcode, the *IDE* (integrated development environment) in which you'll be programming iOS. Xcode is a big program, and writing an app involves coordinating a lot of pieces; this part of the book will help you become comfortable with Xcode. Along the way, we'll generate a simple working app through some hands-on tutorials.

- Chapter 6 tours Xcode and explains the architecture of the *project*, the collection of files from which an app is generated.

- Chapter 7 is about nibs. A *nib* is a file containing a drawing of your interface. Understanding nibs — knowing how they work and how they relate to your code — is crucial to your use of Xcode and to proper development of just about any app.

- Chapter 8 pauses to discuss the Xcode documentation and other sources of information on the API.

- Chapter 9 explains editing your code, testing and debugging your code, and the various steps you'll take on the way to submitting your app to the App Store. You'll probably want to skim this chapter quickly at first, returning to it as a detailed reference later while developing and submitting an actual app.

CHAPTER 6

Anatomy of an Xcode Project

Xcode is the application used to develop an iOS app. An Xcode *project* is the source for an app; it's the entire collection of files and settings used to construct the app. To create, develop, and maintain an app, you must know how to manipulate and navigate an Xcode project. So you must know something about Xcode, and you must know something about the nature and structure of Xcode projects and how Xcode shows them to you. That's the subject of this chapter.

 The term "Xcode" is used in two ways. It's the name of the application in which you edit and build your app, and it's the name of an entire suite of utilities that accompanies it — in the latter sense, for example, Instruments and the Simulator are part of Xcode. This ambiguity should generally present little difficulty.

Xcode is a powerful, complex, and extremely large program. My approach in introducing Xcode is to suggest that you adopt a kind of deliberate tunnel vision: if you don't understand something, don't worry about it — don't even look at it, and don't touch it, because you might change something important. Our survey of Xcode will chart a safe, restricted, and essential path, focusing on aspects of Xcode that you most need to understand immediately, and resolutely ignoring everything else.

For full information, study Apple's own documentation (choose Help → Xcode User Guide); it may seem overwhelming at first, but what you need to know is probably in there somewhere. There are also entire books devoted to describing and explaining Xcode.

The structure of the Xcode installation changed starting with Xcode 4.3. The Developer folder in Xcode 4.2 and before was a top-level install folder containing Xcode and a lot of other files and folders. In Xcode 4.3 and later, the Developer folder is inside the Xcode application bundle itself, *Xcode.app/Contents/Developer*.

New Project

Even before you've written any code, an Xcode project is quite elaborate. To see this, let's make a new, essentially "empty" project; you'll find that it isn't empty at all.

1. Start up Xcode and choose File → New → Project.

2. The "Choose a template" dialog appears. The *template* is your project's initial set of files and settings. When you pick a template, you're really picking an existing folder full of files; basically, it will be one of the folders inside *Xcode.app/Contents/ Developer/Platforms/iPhoneOS.platform/Developer/Library/Xcode/Templates/ Project Templates/Application*. This template folder will essentially be copied, and a few values will be filled in, in order to create your project.

   So, in this case, on the left, under iOS (not OS X!), choose Application. On the right, select Single View Application. Click Next.

3. You are now asked to provide a name for your project (Product Name). Let's call our new project *Empty Window*.

   In a real project, you should give some thought to the project's name, as you're going to be living in close quarters with it. As Xcode copies the template folder, it's going to use the project's name to "fill in the blank" in several places, including some filenames and some settings, such as the name of the app. Thus, whatever you type at this moment is something you'll be seeing throughout your project. You are not locked into the name of your project forever, though, and there's a separate setting allowing you to change at any time the name of the app that it produces. I'll talk at the end of this chapter about name changes.

   It's fine to use spaces in a project name. Spaces are legal in the folder name, the project name, the app name, and the various names of files that Xcode will generate automatically; and in the few places where spaces are problematic (such as the bundle identifier, discussed in the next paragraph), the name you type as the Product Name will have its spaces converted to hyphens.

4. Note the Company Identifier field. The first time you create a project, this field will be blank, and you should fill it in. The goal here is to create a unique string identifying you or your company. The convention is to start the company identifier with com. and to follow it with a string (possibly with multiple dot-components) that no one else is likely to use. For example, I use com.neuburg.matt. Every app on a device

or submitted to the App Store needs a unique bundle identifier. Your app's bundle identifier, which is shown in gray below the company identifier, will consist of the company identifier plus a version of the project's name; if you give every project a unique name within your personal world, the bundle identifier will uniquely identify this project and the app that it produces (or you can change the bundle identifier manually later if necessary).

5. Make sure the Devices pop-up menu is set to iPhone. (Ignore the Class Prefix field for now; it should be empty, with its default value "XYZ" shown in gray. For its purpose, see "The Global Namespace" on page 84.) Click Next.

6. You've now told Xcode how to construct your project. Basically, it's going to copy the *Single View Application.xctemplate* folder from within the *Project Templates/ Application* folder I mentioned earlier. But you need to tell it where to copy this template folder to. That's why Xcode is now presenting a Save dialog. You are to specify the location of a folder that is about to be created — a folder that will be the *project folder* for this project.

   The project folder can go just about anywhere, and you can move it after creating it. I usually create new projects on the Desktop.

7. Xcode also offers to create a git repository for your project. In real life, this can be a great convenience (see Chapter 9), but for now, uncheck that checkbox. Click Create.

8. The *Empty Window* project folder is created on disk (on the Desktop, if that's the location you just specified), and the project window for the Empty Window project opens in Xcode.

The project we've just created is a working project; it really does build an iOS app called Empty Window. To see this, make sure that the scheme and destination in the project window's toolbar are listed as Empty Window → iPhone Retina (3.5-inch). (The scheme and destination are actually pop-up menus, so you can click on them to change their values if needed.) Choose Product → Run. After some delay, the iOS Simulator application eventually opens and displays your app running — an empty white screen.

To *build* a project is to compile its code and assemble the compiled code, together with various resources, into the actual app. Typically, if you want to know whether your code compiles and your project is consistently and correctly constructed, you'll build the project (Product → Build). New in Xcode 5, you can compile an individual file (choose Product → Perform Action → Compile [Filename]). To *run* a project is to launch the built app, in the Simulator or on a connected device; if you want to know whether your code works as expected, you'll run the project (Product → Run), which automatically builds first if necessary.

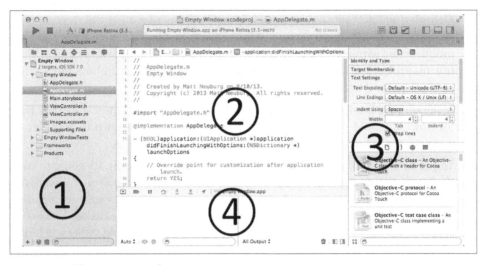

Figure 6-1. The project window

The Project Window

An Xcode project embodies a lot of information about what files constitute the project and how they are to be used when building the app, such as:

- The source files (your code) that are to be compiled

- Any *.storyboard* or *.xib* files, graphically expressing interface objects to be instantiated as your app runs

- Any resources, such as icons, images, or sound files, that are to be part of the app

- All settings (instructions to the compiler, to the linker, and so on) that are to be obeyed as the app is built

- Any frameworks that the code will need when it runs

A single Xcode project window presents all of this information, as well as letting you access, edit, and navigate your code, plus reporting the progress and results of such procedures as building or debugging an app and more. This window displays a lot of information and embodies a lot of functionality! A project window is powerful and elaborate; learning to navigate and understand it takes time. Let's pause to explore this window and see how it is constructed.

A project window has four main parts (Figure 6-1):

1. On the left is the Navigator pane. Show and hide it with View → Navigators → Show/Hide Navigator (Command-0) or with the first View button at the right end of the toolbar.

2. In the middle is the Editor pane (or simply "editor"). This is the main area of a project window. A project window nearly always displays an Editor pane, and can display multiple Editor panes simultaneously.

3. On the right is the Utilities pane. Show and hide it with View → Utilities → Show/Hide Utilities (Command-Option-0) or with the third View button at the right end of the toolbar.

4. At the bottom is the Debugger pane. Show and hide it with View → Show/Hide Debug Area (Command-Shift-Y) or with the second View button at the right end of the toolbar.

 All Xcode keyboard shortcuts can be customized; see the Key Bindings pane of the Preferences window. Keyboard shortcuts that I cite are the defaults.

The Navigator Pane

The Navigator pane is the column of information at the left of the project window. Among other things, it's your primary mechanism for controlling what you see in the main area of the project window (the editor). An important use pattern for Xcode is: you select something in the Navigator pane, and that thing is displayed in the editor.

It is possible to toggle the visibility of the Navigator pane (View → Navigators → Hide/Show Navigator, or Command-0); for example, once you've used the Navigator pane to reach the item you want to see or work on in the editor, you might hide the Navigator pane temporarily to maximize your screen real estate (especially on a smaller monitor). You can change the Navigator pane's width by dragging the vertical line at its right edge.

The Navigator pane itself can display eight different sets of information; thus, there are actually eight navigators. These are represented by the eight icons across its top; to switch among them, use these icons or their keyboard shortcuts (Command-1, Command-2, and so on). You will quickly become adept at switching to the navigator you want; their keyboard shortcuts will become second nature. If the Navigator pane is hidden, pressing a navigator's keyboard shortcut both shows the Navigator pane and switches to that navigator.

Depending on your settings in the Behaviors pane of Xcode's preferences, a navigator might show itself automatically when you perform a certain action. For example, by default, when you build your project, if warning messages or error messages are generated, the Issue navigator will appear. This automatic behavior will not prove troublesome, because it is generally precisely the behavior you want, and if it isn't, you can change it; plus you can easily switch to a different navigator at any time.

Let's begin experimenting immediately with the various navigators:

Project navigator (Command-1)

Click here for basic navigation through the files that constitute your project. For example, in the Empty Window folder (these folder-like things in the Project navigator are actually called *groups*), click *AppDelegate.m* to view its code in the editor (Figure 6-2).

At the top level of the Project navigator, with a blue Xcode icon, is the Empty Window project itself; click it to view the settings associated with your project and its targets. Don't change anything here without knowing what you're doing! I'll talk later in this chapter about what these settings are for.

The filter bar at the bottom of the Project navigator lets you limit what files are shown; when there are many files, this is great for quickly reaching a file with a known name. For example, try typing "delegate" in the filter bar search field. Don't forget to remove your filter when you're done experimenting.

 Once you've filtered a navigator, it stays filtered until you remove the filter — even if you close the project! A common mistake is to filter a navigator, forget that you've done so, fail to notice the filter (because you're looking at the navigator itself, not down at the bottom where the filter bar is), and wonder, "Hey, where did all my files go?"

Symbol navigator (Command-2)

A *symbol* is a name, typically the name of a class or method. Depending on which of the three icons in the filter bar at the bottom you highlight, you can view Cocoa's built-in symbols or the symbols defined in your project. The former can be a useful form of documentation; the latter can be helpful for navigating your code. For example, highlight the first two icons in the filter bar (the first two are blue, the third is dark), and see how quickly you can reach the definition of AppDelegate's `applicationDidBecomeActive:` method.

Try highlighting the filter bar icons in various ways to see how the contents of the Symbol navigator change. Type in the search field in the filter bar to limit what appears in the Symbol navigator; for example, try typing "active" in the search field, and see what happens.

Search navigator (Command-3)

This is a powerful search facility for finding text globally in your project, and even in the headers of Cocoa frameworks. You can also summon the Search navigator

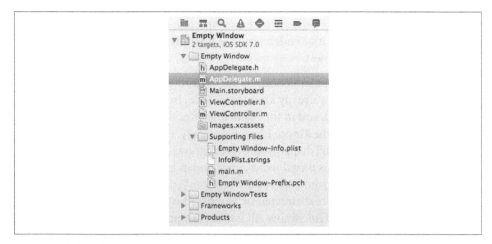

Figure 6-2. The Project navigator

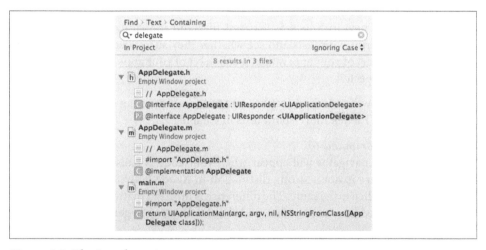

Figure 6-3. The Search navigator

with Find → Find in Project (Command-Shift-F). The words above the search field show what options are currently in force; they are pop-up menus, so click one to change the options. Try searching for "delegate" (Figure 6-3). Click a search result to jump to it in your code.

You can type in the other search field, the one in the filter bar at the bottom, to limit further which search results are displayed. (I'm going to stop calling your attention to the filter bar now, but every navigator has it in some form.)

Issue navigator (Command-4)

You'll need this navigator primarily when your code has issues. This doesn't refer to emotional instability; it's Xcode's term for warning and error messages emitted when you build your project.

To see the Issue navigator in action, you'll need to give your code an issue. For example, navigate (as you already know how to do, in at least three different ways) to the file *AppDelegate.m*, and in the blank line after the last comment at the top of the file's contents, above the `#import` line, type howdy. Build the project (Command-B). The Issue navigator will display some error messages, showing that the compiler is unable to cope with this illegal word appearing in an illegal place. Click an issue to see it within its file. In your code, issue "balloons" may appear to the right of lines containing issues; if you're distracted or hampered by these, toggle their visibility with Editor → Issues → Hide/Show All Issues (Command-Control-M).

Now that you've made Xcode miserable, select "howdy" and delete it; build again, and your issues will be gone. If only real life were this easy!

Test navigator (Command-5)

This navigator, new in Xcode 5, lists test files and individual test methods and permits you to run your tests and see whether they succeeded or failed. A test is code that isn't part of your app; rather, it calls a bit of your app's code to see whether it behaves as expected.

By default, a new Xcode 5 project has one test file containing one test method, to get you started. I'll talk more about tests in Chapter 9.

Debug navigator (Command-6)

By default, this navigator will appear when your code is paused while you're debugging it. There is not a strong distinction in Xcode between running and debugging; the milieu is the same. The difference is mostly a matter of whether breakpoints are obeyed (more about that, and about debugging in general, in Chapter 9).

To see the Debug navigator in action, you'll need to give your code a breakpoint. Navigate once more to the file *AppDelegate.m*, select in the line that says `return YES`, and choose Debug → Breakpoints → Add Breakpoint at Current Line to make a blue breakpoint arrow appear on that line. Run the project. By default, as the breakpoint is encountered, the Navigator pane switches to the Debug navigator, and the Debug pane appears at the bottom of the window. This overall layout (Figure 6-4) will rapidly become familiar as you debug your projects.

New in Xcode 5, the Debug navigator starts with two numeric and graphical displays of profiling information (CPU and Memory); click one to see extensive graphical information in the editor. This information allows you to track possible misbehavior of your app as you run it, without the added complexity of running the Instruments utility (discussed in Chapter 9). To toggle the visibility of the profiling

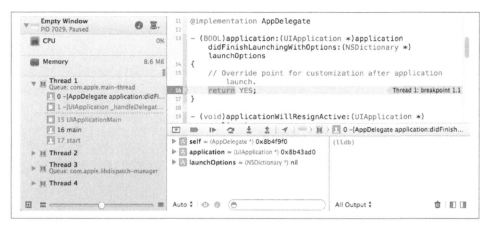

Figure 6-4. The Debug layout

information at the top of the Debug navigator, click the "gauge" icon (to the right of the process's name).

The Debug navigator also displays the call stack, with the names of the nested methods in which a pause occurs; as you would expect, you can click on a method name to navigate to it. You can shorten or lengthen the list with the slider at the bottom of the navigator. The second icon to the right of the process's name lets you toggle between display by thread and display by queue.

The Debug pane, which can be shown or hidden at will (View → Debug Area → Hide/Show Debug Area, or Command-Shift-Y), consists of two subpanes — the variables list and the console. Either of these can be hidden using the two buttons at the bottom right of the pane. The console can also be summoned by choosing View → Debug Area → Activate Console.

The variables list (on the left)
> It is populated with the variables in scope for the selected method in the call stack.

The console (on the right)
> Here the debugger displays text messages; that's how you learn of exceptions thrown by your running app, plus you can have your code deliberately send you log messages describing your app's progress and behavior. Such messages are important, so keep an eye on the console as your app runs. You can also use the console to enter commands to the debugger. This can often be a better way to explore values during a pause than the variables list.

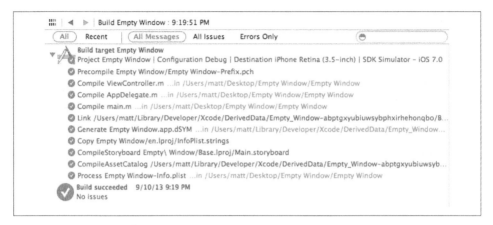

Figure 6-5. Viewing a log

Breakpoint navigator (Command-7)

This navigator lists all your breakpoints. At the moment you've only one, but when you're actively debugging a large project with many breakpoints, you'll be glad of this navigator. Also, this is where you create special breakpoints (such as symbolic breakpoints), and in general it's your center for managing existing breakpoints. We'll return to this topic in Chapter 9.

Log navigator (Command-8)

This navigator lists your recent major actions, such as building or running (debugging) your project. Click a listing to see (in the editor) the log file generated when you performed that action. The log file might contain information that isn't displayed in any other way, and also it lets you dredge up console messages from the recent past ("What was that exception I got while debugging a moment ago?").

For example, by clicking on the listing for a successful build, and by choosing to display All and All Messages using the filter switches at the top of the log, we can see the steps by which a build takes place (Figure 6-5). To reveal the full text of a step, click on that step and then click the Expand Transcript button that appears at the far right (and see also the menu items in the Editor menu).

When navigating by clicking in the Navigator pane, modifications to your click can determine where navigation takes place. By default, Option-click navigates in an assistant pane (discussed later in this chapter), double-click navigates by opening a new window, and Option-Shift-click summons the navigation window, a little heads-up pane where you can specify where to navigate (a new window, a new tab, or a new assistant pane). For the settings that govern these click modifications, see the Navigation pane of Xcode's preferences.

The Utilities Pane

The Utilities pane is the column at the right of the project window. It contains inspectors that provide information about the current selection or its settings; if those settings can be changed, this is where you change them. It also contains libraries that function as a source of objects you may need while editing your project. The Utilities pane's importance emerges mostly when you're editing a *.storyboard* or *.xib* file (Chapter 7). But it can be useful also while editing code, because Quick Help, a form of documentation (Chapter 8), is displayed here as well, plus the Utilities pane is the source of code snippets (Chapter 9). To toggle the visibility of the Utilities pane, choose View → Utilities → Hide/Show Utilities (Command-Option-0). You can change the Utilities pane's width by dragging the vertical line at its left edge.

The Utilities pane consists of numerous palettes, which are clumped into multiple sets, which are themselves divided into two major groups: the top half of the pane and the bottom half of the pane. You can change the relative heights of these two halves by dragging the horizontal line that separates them.

The top half

What appears in the top half of the Utilities pane depends on what's selected in the current editor. There are three main cases:

A code file is being edited

The top half of the Utilities pane shows either the File inspector or Quick Help. Toggle between them with the icons at the top of this half of the Utilities pane, or with their keyboard shortcuts (Command-Option-1, Command-Option-2). The File inspector is rarely needed, but Quick Help can be useful as documentation. The File inspector consists of multiple sections, each of which can be expanded or collapsed by clicking its header.

A .storyboard or .xib file is being edited

The top half of the Utilities pane shows, in addition to the File inspector and Quick Help, the Identity inspector (Command-Option-3), the Attributes inspector (Command-Option-4), the Size inspector (Command-Option-5), and the Connections inspector (Command-Option-6). These can consist of multiple sections, each of which can be expanded or collapsed by clicking its header.

An asset catalog is being edited

In addition to the File inspector and Quick Help, the Attributes inspector (Command-Option-4) lets you determine which variants of an image are listed.

The bottom half

The bottom half of the Utilities pane shows one of four libraries. Toggle between them with the icons at the top of this half of the Utilities pane, or with their keyboard shortcuts. They are the File Template library (Command-Option-Control-1), the Code Snippet library (Command-Option-Control-2), the Object library

(Command-Option-Control-3), and the Media library (Command-Option-Control-4). The Object library is the most important; you'll use it heavily when editing a *.storyboard* or *.xib* file.

To see a help pop-up describing the currently selected item in a library, press Spacebar.

The Editor

In the middle of the project window is the *editor*. This is where you get actual work done, reading and writing your code (Chapter 9), or designing your interface in a *.storyboard* or *.xib* file (Chapter 7). The editor is the core of the project window. You can hide the Navigator pane, the Utilities pane, and the Debug pane, but there is no such thing as a project window without an editor (though you can cover the editor completely with the Debug pane).

The editor provides its own form of navigation, the *jump bar* across the top. Not only does the jump bar show you hierarchically what file is currently being edited, but also it allows you to switch to a different file. In particular, each path component in the jump bar is also a pop-up menu. These pop-up menus can be summoned by clicking on a path component, or by using keyboard shortcuts (shown in the second section of the View → Standard Editor submenu). For example, Control-4 summons a hierarchical pop-up menu, which can be navigated entirely with the keyboard, allowing you to choose a different file in your project to edit. Moreover, each pop-up menu in the jump bar also has a filter field; to see it, summon a pop-up menu from the jump bar and start typing. Thus you can navigate your project even if the Project navigator isn't showing.

The symbol at the left end of the jump bar (Control-1) summons a hierarchical menu (the Related Files menu) allowing navigation to files related to the current one. What appears here depends not only on what file is currently being edited but on the current selection within that file. This is an extremely powerful and convenient menu, and you should take time to explore it. If this file is one of a pair of class files (*.m* or *.h*), you can switch to the other member of the pair (Counterparts). You can navigate to related class files and header files (Superclasses, Subclasses, and Siblings; siblings are classes with the same superclass). You can navigate to files included by this one, and to files that include this one; you can view methods called by the currently selected method, and that call the currently selected method.

The editor remembers the history of things it has displayed, and you can return to previously viewed content with the Back button in the jump bar, which is also a pop-up menu from which you can choose. Alternatively, choose Navigate → Go Back (Command-Control-Left).

It is extremely likely, as you develop a project, that you'll want to edit more than one file simultaneously, or obtain multiple views of a single file so that you can edit two areas of it simultaneously. This can be achieved in three ways: assistants, tabs, and secondary windows.

Assistants

> You can split the editor into multiple editors by summoning an *assistant* pane. To do so, click the second Editor button in the toolbar, or choose View → Assistant Editor → Show Assistant Editor (Command-Option-Return). Also, by default, adding the Option key to navigation opens an assistant pane; for example, Option-click in the Navigator pane, or Option-choose in the jump bar, to navigate by opening an assistant pane (or to navigate in an existing assistant pane if there is one). To remove the assistant pane, click the first Editor button in the toolbar, or choose View → Standard Editor → Show Standard Editor (Command-Return), or click the X button at the assistant pane's top right.

Tabs

> You can embody the entire project window interface as a tab. To do so, choose File → New → Tab (Command-T), revealing the tab bar (just below the toolbar) if it wasn't showing already. Use of a tabbed interface will likely be familiar from applications such as Safari. You can switch between tabs by clicking on a tab, or with Command-Shift-}. At first, your new tab will look largely identical to the original window from which it was spawned. But now you can make changes in a tab — change what panes are showing or what file is being edited, for example — without affecting any other tabs. Thus you can get multiple views of your project. You can assign a descriptive name to a tab: double-click on a tab name to make it editable.

Secondary windows

> A secondary project window is similar to a tab, but it appears as a separate window instead of a tab in the same window. To create one, choose File → New → Window (Command-Shift-T). Alternatively, you can promote a tab to be a window by dragging it right out of its current window.

You can determine how assistant panes are to be arranged. To do so, choose from the View → Assistant Editor submenu. I usually prefer All Editors Stacked Vertically, but it's purely a matter of taste. Once you've summoned an assistant pane, you can split it further into additional assistant panes. To do so, click the Plus button at the top right of an assistant pane. To move the contents of the current assistant pane into the main editor, choose Navigate → Open in Primary Editor. To dismiss an assistant pane, click the X button at its top right.

What makes an assistant pane an assistant, and not just a form of split-pane editing, is that it can bear a special relationship to the primary editor pane. The primary editor pane is the one whose contents, by default, are determined by what you click on in the Navigator pane; an assistant pane, meanwhile, can respond to what file is being edited in the primary editor pane by changing intelligently what file it (the assistant pane) is editing. This is called *tracking*.

Figure 6-6. Telling an assistant pane to track counterparts

To see tracking in action, open a single assistant pane and use the first component in its jump bar (Control-4). This is the Tracking menu. It's like the Related Files menu that I discussed a moment ago, but you can select a category to determine automatic tracking behavior. For example, choose Counterparts (Figure 6-6). Now use the Project navigator to select *AppDelegate.m*; the primary editor pane displays this file, and the assistant automatically displays *AppDelegate.h*. Next, use the Project navigator to select *App-Delegate.h*; the primary editor pane displays this file, and the assistant automatically displays *AppDelegate.m*. If a category has multiple files, the assistant navigates to the first one, and a pair of arrow buttons appears at the right end of the assistant's jump bar, with which you can navigate among the others (or use the second jump bar component, Control-5). There's a lot of convenience and power lurking here, which you'll explore as you need it. You can turn off tracking by setting the assistant's first jump bar component to Manual.

There isn't a strong difference between a tab and a secondary window; which you use, and for what, will be a matter of taste and convenience. I find that the advantage of a secondary window is that you can see it at the same time as the main window, and that it can be small. Thus, when I have a file I frequently want to refer to, I often spawn off a secondary window displaying that file, sized fairly small and without any panes other than the editor.

Tabs and windows come in handy in connection with custom behaviors. For example, as I mentioned before, it's important to be able to view the console while debugging; I like to see it at the full size of the project window, but I also want to be able to switch back to viewing my code. So I've created a custom behavior (click the Plus button at the bottom of the Behaviors pane of the Preferences window) that performs two actions: Show tab named Console in active window, and Show debugger with Console View.

Moreover, I've given that behavior a keyboard shortcut. Thus at any time I can press my keyboard shortcut, and we switch to the Console tab (creating it if it doesn't exist) displaying nothing but the console. This is just a tab, so I can switch between it and my code with Command-Shift-}.

 There are many ways to change what appears in an editor, and the navigators don't automatically stay in sync with those changes. To select in the Project navigator the file displayed in the current editor, choose Navigate → Reveal in Project Navigator. There are also Navigate menu items Reveal in Symbol Navigator and Reveal in Debug Navigator.

The Project File and Its Dependents

The first item in the Project navigator (Command-1) represents the project itself. (In the Empty Window project that we created earlier in this chapter, it is called Empty Window.) Hierarchically dependent upon it are items that contribute to the building of the project. Many of these items, including the project itself, correspond to items on disk in the project folder.

To survey this correspondence, let's examine the project folder in the Finder simultaneously with the Xcode project window. Select the project listing in the Project navigator and choose File → Show in Finder (Figure 6-7).

The Finder displays the contents of your project folder. The most important of these is *Empty Window.xcodeproj*. This is the *project file*, corresponding to the project listed in the Project navigator. All Xcode's knowledge about your project — what files it consists of and how to build the project — is stored in this file. To open a project from the Finder, double-click the project file. Alternatively, you can drag the project folder onto Xcode's icon (in the Finder, in the Dock, or in the application switcher) and Xcode will locate the project file and open it for you; thus, you might never need to open the project folder at all!

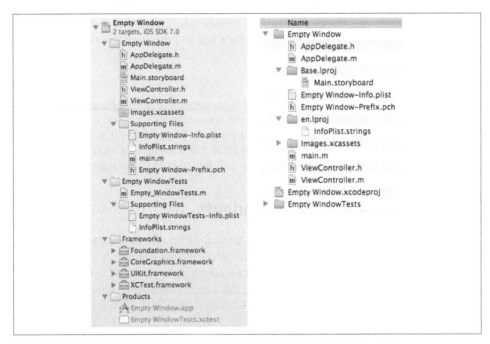

Figure 6-7. The Project navigator and the project folder

Never, never, *never* touch anything in a project folder by way of the Finder, except for double-clicking the project file to open the project. Don't put anything directly into a project folder. Don't remove anything from a project folder. Don't rename anything in a project folder. Don't touch anything in a project folder! Do all your interaction with the project through the project window in Xcode. (When you're an Xcode power user, you'll know when you can disobey this rule. Until then, just obey it blindly.)

The reason is that the project expects things in the project folder to be a certain way. If you make any alterations to the project folder directly in the Finder, behind the project's back, you can upset those expectations and break the project. When you work in the project window, it is Xcode itself that makes any necessary changes in the project folder, and all will be well.

Let's consider how the groups and files displayed hierarchically down from the project in the Project navigator correspond to reality on disk as portrayed in the Finder (Figure 6-7). (Recall that *group* is the technical term for the folder-like objects shown in the Project navigator.) Groups in the Project navigator don't necessarily correspond to folders on disk in the Finder, and folders on disk in the Finder don't necessarily correspond to groups in the Project navigator:

- The Empty Window group corresponds directly to the *Empty Window* folder on disk. Files within the Empty Window group, such as *AppDelegate.m*, correspond to real files on disk that are inside the *Empty Window* folder. If you were to create additional code files (which, in real life, you would almost certainly do in the course of developing your project), you would likely put them in the Empty Window group in the Project navigator, and they, too, would then be in the *Empty Window* folder on disk. (That, however, is not a requirement; your files can live anywhere and your project will still work fine.)

  Similarly, the Empty Window Tests group corresponds to the *Empty Window Tests* folder on disk, and the file *Empty_WindowTests.m* listed inside the Empty Window Tests group lives inside the *Empty Window Tests* folder.

  These two group–folder pairs correspond to the two *targets* of your project. I'll talk in the next section about what a target is. There is no law requiring that a target have a corresponding group in the Project navigator and a corresponding folder in the project folder, but the project template sets things up that way as an organizational convenience: it clarifies the project's structure in the Project navigator, and it prevents a lot of files from appearing at the top level of the project folder.

- The Supporting Files group inside the Empty Window group, on the other hand, corresponds to nothing on disk; it's just a way of clumping some items together in the Project navigator, so that they can be located easily and can be shown or hidden together. The things *inside* this group are real, however; you can see that the four files *Empty Window-Info.plist*, *InfoPlist.strings*, *main.m*, and *Empty Window-Prefix.pch* do exist on disk — they're just not inside anything called *Supporting Files*. (The Supporting Files group inside the Empty WindowTests group is similar.)

- Two files in the Empty Window group, *InfoPlist.strings* and *Main.storyboard*, appear in the Finder inside folders that don't visibly correspond to anything in the Project navigator: *Main.storyboard*, on disk, is inside a folder called *Base.lproj*, and *InfoPlist.strings*, on disk, is inside a folder called *en.lproj*. These folders have to do with *localization*, which I'll discuss in Chapter 9.

- The item *Images.xcassets* in the Project navigator corresponds to a specially structured folder *Images.xcassets* on disk. This is an *asset catalog* (new in Xcode 5); you add images to the asset catalog in Xcode, which maintains that folder on disk for you. This makes it easy for you to have multiple related images, such as app icons of different sizes, without having to see them all listed directly in the Project navigator. I'll talk more about the asset catalog later in this chapter, and in Chapter 9.

You may be tempted to find all this confusing. Don't! Remember what I said about not involving yourself with the project folder on disk in the Finder. Keep your attention on the Project navigator, make your modifications to the project there, and all will be well.

Feel free, as you develop your project and add files to it, to add further groups. The purpose of groups is to make the Project navigator work well for you. They don't affect how the app is built, and by default they don't correspond to any folder on disk; they are just an organizational convenience within the Project navigator. To make a new group, choose File → New → Group. To rename a group, select it in the Project navigator and press Return to make the name editable. For example, if some of your code files have to do with a login screen that your app sometimes presents, you might clump them together in a Login group. If your app is to contain some sound files, you might put them into a Sounds group. And so on.

The things in the Frameworks group and the Products group don't correspond to anything in the project folder, but they do correspond to real things that the project needs to know about in order to build and run:

Frameworks

This group, by convention, lists frameworks (Cocoa code) on which your code depends. Frameworks exist on disk, but they are not built into your app when it is constructed; they don't have to be, because they are present also on the target device (an iPhone, iPod touch, or iPad). Instead, the frameworks are *linked* to the app, meaning that the app knows about them and expects to find them on the device when it runs. Thus, all the framework code is omitted from the app itself, saving considerable space.

(Starting in Xcode 5, the new modules feature permits frameworks to be linked to your code without being listed here. I'll talk about modules at the end of this chapter.)

Products

This group, by convention, automatically holds a reference to the executable bundle generated by building a target.

The Target

A *target* is a collection of parts along with rules and settings for how to build a product from them. Whenever you build, what you're really building is a target.

Select the Empty Window project at the top of the Project navigator, and you'll see two things on the left side of the editor: the project itself, and a list of your targets. (This list can appear either as a column on the left side of the editor, as in Figure 6-8, or as a popup menu at the top left of the editor if that column is collapsed to save space.) Our Empty Window project comes with two targets: the app target, called Empty Window (just like the project itself), and the tests target, called Empty WindowTests. Under certain circumstances, you might add further targets to a project. For example, you might want to write an app that can be built as an iPhone app or as an iPad app — two different apps that share a lot of the same code. So you might want one project that builds both apps through separate targets.

If you select the project in the left column or pop-up menu of the editor, you *edit the project*. If you select a target in the left column or pop-up menu of the editor, you *edit the target*. I'll use those expressions a lot in later instructions.

Let's concentrate on the app target, Empty Window. This is the target that you use to build and run your app. Its settings are the settings that tell Xcode how your app is to be built; its product is the app itself. (The tests target, Empty WindowTests, creates a special executable whose purpose is to test your app's code. I'll talk more about testing in Chapter 9.)

Build Phases

Edit the Empty Window target and click Build Phases at the top of the editor (Figure 6-8). These are the stages by which your app is built. By default, there are three of them with content — Compile Sources, Link Binary With Libraries, and Copy Bundle Resources — and those are the only stages you'll usually need, though you can add others. The build phases are both a report to you on how the target will be built and a set of instructions to Xcode on how to build the target; if you change the build phases, you change the build process. Click each build phase to see a list of the files in your target to which that build phase will apply.

The meanings of the three build phases are pretty straightforward:

Compile Sources
    Certain files (your code) are compiled, and the resulting compiled code is copied into the app.

    This build phase typically applies to all of the target's *.m* files; those are the code files that constitute the target. Sure enough, it currently contains *ViewController.m*, *AppDelegate.m*, and *main.m*. If you add a new class to your project, you'll specify that it should be part of the app target, and the *.m* file will automatically be added to the Compile Sources build phase.

Link Binary With Libraries
    Certain libraries, usually frameworks, are linked to the compiled code (now referred to, following compilation, as the *binary*), so that it will expect them to be present on the device when the app runs.

    This build phase currently lists three frameworks. I'll talk later in this chapter about the mechanics of linking the binary with additional frameworks.

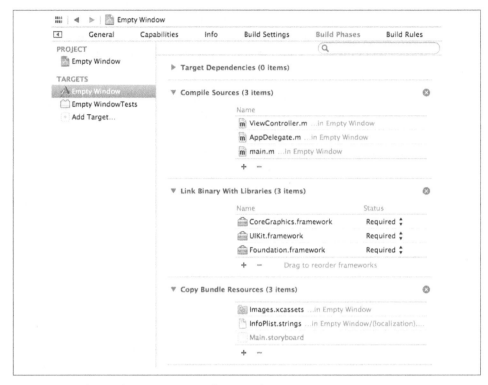

Figure 6-8. Editing the app target to show its phases

Copy Bundle Resources

Certain files are copied into the app, so that your code or the system can find them there when the app runs. For example, if your app had an icon image, it would need to be copied into the app so the device could find and display it.

This build phase currently applies to the asset catalog; any images you add to the asset catalog will be copied into your app as part of the catalog. It also currently lists *InfoPlist.strings* and your app's *.storyboard* file.

Copying doesn't necessarily mean making an identical copy. Certain types of file are automatically treated in special ways as they are copied into the app bundle. For example, copying the asset catalog means that icons and launch images in the catalog are written out to the top level of the app bundle; copying the *.storyboard* file means that it is transformed into a *.storyboardc* file, which is itself a bundle containing nib files.

You can alter these lists manually, and sometimes you may need to do so. For instance, if something in your project, such as a sound file, was not in Copy Bundle Resources and you wanted it copied into the app during the build process, you would drag it from

Setting	Resolved	Empty Win...	Empty Win...	iOS Default
▼ Architectures				
Additional SDKs				
Architectures	Standard ⬍		Standard ⬍	Standard ⬍
Base SDK	Latest iOS (iO... ⬍		Latest iOS (i... ⬍	iOS 7.0 ⬍
▼ Build Active Architecture Only	<Multiple val... ⬍		<Multiple va... ⬍	No ⬍
Debug	Yes ⬍		Yes ⬍	No ⬍
Release	No ⬍			No ⬍
Supported Platforms	iOS ⬍			iOS ⬍
Valid Architectures	arm64 armv7 a...			arm64 armv7 a...

Figure 6-9. Target build settings

the Project navigator into the Copy Bundle Resources list, or (easier) click the Plus button beneath the Copy Bundle Resources list to get a helpful dialog listing everything in your project. Conversely, if something in your project was in Copy Bundle Resources and you *didn't* want it copied into the app, you would delete it from the list; this would not delete it from your project, from the Project navigator, or from the Finder, but only from the list of things to be copied into your app.

A useful trick is to add a Run Script build phase, which runs a custom shell script late in the build process. To do so, choose Editor → Add Build Phase → Add Run Script Build Phase. Open the newly added Run Script build phase to edit the custom shell script. A minimal shell script might read:

```
echo "Running the Run Script build phase"
```

The "Show environment variables in build log" checkbox causes the build process's environment variables and their values to be listed in the build log during the Run Script build phase. This alone can be a good reason for adding a Run Script build phase; you can learn a lot about how the build process works by examining the environment variables.

Build Settings

Build phases are only one aspect of how a target knows how to build the app. The other aspect is build settings. To see them, edit the target and click Build Settings at the top of the editor (Figure 6-9). Here you'll find a long list of settings, most of which you'll never touch. But Xcode examines this list in order to know what to do at various stages of the build process. Build settings are the reason your project compiles and builds the way it does.

You can determine what build settings are displayed by clicking Basic or All. The settings are combined into categories, and you can close or open each category heading to save room. If you know something about a setting you want to see, such as its name, you can use the search field at the top right to filter what settings are shown.

You can determine how build settings are displayed by clicking Combined or Levels; in Figure 6-9, I've clicked Levels, in order to discuss what levels are. It turns out that not only does a *target* contain values for the build settings, but the *project* also contains values for the same build settings; furthermore, Xcode has certain built-in default build setting values. The Levels display shows all of these levels at once, so you can understand the derivation of the actual values used for every build setting.

To understand the chart, read from right to left. For example, the iOS default for the Build Active Architecture Only setting's Debug configuration (far right) is No. But then the project comes along (second column from the right) and sets it to Yes. The target (third column from the right) doesn't change that setting, so the result (fourth column from the right) is that the setting resolves to Yes.

You will rarely have occasion to manipulate build settings directly, as the defaults are usually acceptable. Nevertheless, you *can* change build setting values, and this is where you would do so. You can change a value at the project level or at the target level. You can select a build setting and show Quick Help in the Utilities pane to learn more about it. For further details on what the various build settings are, consult Apple's documentation, especially the *Xcode Build Setting Reference*.

Configurations

There are actually multiple lists of build setting values — though only one such list applies when a particular build is performed. Each such list is called a *configuration*. Multiple configurations are needed because you build in different ways at different times for different purposes, and thus you'll want certain build settings to take on different values under different circumstances.

By default, there are two configurations:

Debug
   This configuration is used throughout the development process, as you write and run your app.

Release
   This configuration is used for late-stage testing, when you want to check performance on a device.

Configurations exist at all because the project says so. To see where the project says so, edit the project and click Info at the top of the editor (Figure 6-10). Note that these configurations are just names. You can make additional configurations, and when you do, you're just adding to a list of names. The importance of configurations emerges only

Figure 6-10. Configurations

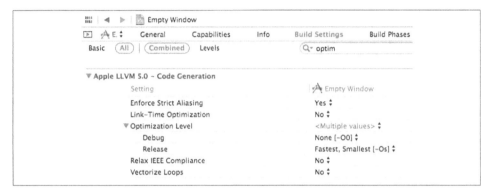

Figure 6-11. How configurations affect build settings

when those names are coupled with build setting values. Configurations can affect build setting values both at the project level and at the target level.

For example, return to the target build settings (Figure 6-9) and type "Optim" into the search field. Now you can look at the Optimization Level build setting (Figure 6-11). The Debug configuration value for Optimization Level is None: while you're developing your app, you build with the Debug configuration, so your code is just compiled line by line in a straightforward way. The Release configuration value for Optimization Level is Fastest, Smallest; when your app is ready to ship, you build it with the Release configuration, so the resulting binary is faster and smaller, which is great for your users installing and running the app on a device, but would be no good while you're developing the app because breakpoints and stepping in the debugger wouldn't work properly.

Schemes and Destinations

So far, I have not said how Xcode knows *which* configuration to use during a particular build. This is determined by a scheme.

A *scheme* unites a target (or multiple targets) with a build configuration, with respect to the purpose for which you're building. A new project comes by default with a single scheme, named after the project. Thus the Empty Window project's single scheme is currently called Empty Window. To see it, choose Product → Scheme → Edit Scheme. The scheme editor dialog opens.

On the left side of the scheme editor are listed various actions you might perform from the Product menu. Click an action to see its corresponding settings in this scheme.

The first action, the Build action, is different from the other actions, because it is common to all of them — the other actions all implicitly involve building. The Build action merely determines what target(s) will be built when each of the other actions is performed. For our project this means that the app target is always to be built, regardless of the action you perform, but the test target is to be built only if you elect to build in order to run the project's tests (by choosing Product → Test).

The second action, the Run action, determines the settings that will be used when you build and run (Figure 6-12). The Build Configuration pop-up menu is set to Debug. That explains where the current build configuration comes from: at the moment, whenever you build and run (Product → Run, or click the Run button in the toolbar), you're using the Debug build configuration and the build setting values that correspond to it, because you're using this scheme, and that's what this scheme says to do when you build and run.

You can edit the scheme, or create additional schemes. For example, suppose you wanted to build and run using the Release build configuration (in order to test the app as closely as possible to how an actual user would experience it). One way would be to edit this scheme, changing the build configuration for its Run action. Xcode makes it convenient to do this on the fly: hold the Option key as you choose Product → Run (or as you click the Run button in the toolbar). The scheme editor appears, containing a Run button. So now you can make alterations to the scheme and then proceed directly to build and run the app by clicking Run.

If you were to find yourself often wanting to switch between building and running with the Debug configuration and building and running with the Release configuration, you might create a distinct, additional scheme that uses the Release debug configuration for the Run action. This is easy to do: in the scheme editor, click Duplicate Scheme. The name of the new scheme is editable; let's call it Empty Window Release. Change the Build Configuration pop-up menu for the Run action in our new scheme to Release, and dismiss the scheme editor.

Now you have two schemes, Empty Window (whose build configuration for running is Debug) and Empty Window Release (whose build configuration for running is Release). To switch between them easily, you can use the Scheme pop-up menu in the project window toolbar (Figure 6-13) before you build and run.

Figure 6-12. The scheme editor

Figure 6-13. The Scheme pop-up menu

The Scheme pop-up menu lists each scheme, along with each destination on which you might run your built app. A *destination* is effectively a machine that can run your app. On any given occasion, you might want to run the app on a physical device or in the Simulator — and, if in the Simulator, you might want to specify that a particular type of device should be simulated. To make that choice, pick a destination in the Scheme pop-up menu.

Destinations and schemes have nothing to do with one another; your app is built the same way regardless of your chosen destination. The presence of destinations in the Scheme pop-up menu is intended as a convenience, allowing you to use this one pop-up menu to choose either a scheme or a destination, or both, in a single move. To switch easily among destinations without changing schemes, click the destination name in the Scheme pop-up menu. To switch among schemes, possibly also determining the destination (as shown in Figure 6-13), click the scheme name in the Scheme pop-up menu. You can also switch among schemes or among destinations by using the scheme editor or the Product menu.

If your app can run under more than one system version, you might also see a system version listed in the Scheme pop-up menu after a Simulator destination. For example, if your project's deployment target (see Chapter 9) is 6.1, the Scheme pop-up menu in the project window toolbar might say "iOS 7.0" or "iOS 6.1" after the destination name. In that case, when you summon the hierarchical pop-up menu for the scheme, as shown in Figure 6-13, it will have *three* levels. You can switch easily among system versions without changing schemes or destinations: click the version name in the Scheme pop-up menu. This changes nothing about how your app is built; it's a convenience, letting you determine the system version that the Simulator will use. (These system versions are technically SDKs; I'll discuss SDKs at the end of this chapter. On installing additional Simulator SDKs, see "Additional Simulator SDKs" on page 203.)

Further management of schemes is through the scheme management dialog (Product → Scheme → Manage Schemes, or use the Scheme pop-up menu). For example, if you created an Empty Window Release scheme and you no longer need it, you can delete it here.

Renaming Parts of a Project

The name assigned to your project at creation time is used in many places throughout the project, leading beginners to worry that they can never rename a project without breaking something. But fear not! To rename a project, select the project listing at the top of the Project navigator, press Return to make its name editable, type the new name, and press Return again. Xcode presents a dialog proposing to change some other names to match, including the target, the built app, the precompiled header file, and the *Info.plist* — and, by implication, the build settings specifying these. You can check or uncheck any name, and click Rename; your project will continue to work correctly.

You can freely change the target name independently of the project name. It is the target name, not the project name, that is used to derive the name of the product and thus the bundle name, bundle display name, and bundle identifier mentioned earlier in this chapter. Thus, when you settle on a real name for your app, it might be sufficient to change the target name.

Changing the project name (or target name) does not automatically change the scheme name to match. There is no particular need to do so, but you can change a scheme name freely; choose Product → Manage Schemes and click on the scheme name to make it editable.

Changing the project name (or target name) does not automatically change the main group name to match. There is no particular need to do so, but you can freely change the name of a group in the Project navigator, because these names are arbitrary; they have no effect on the build settings or the build process. However, the main group is special, because (as I've already said) it corresponds to a real folder on disk, the folder that sits beside your project file at the top level of the project folder. Beginners should not change the name of that folder on disk, as that folder name is hard-coded into several build settings.

You can change the name of the project folder in the Finder at any time, and you can move the project folder in the Finder at will, because all build setting references to file and folder items in the project folder are relative.

From Project to Running App

An app file is really a special kind of folder called a *package* (and a special kind of package called a *bundle*). The Finder normally disguises a package as a file and does not dive into it to reveal its contents to the user, but you can bypass this protection and investigate an app bundle with the Show Package Contents command. By doing so, you can study the internal structure of your built app bundle.

We'll use the Empty Window app that we built earlier as a sample minimal app to investigate. You'll have to locate it in the Finder; by default, it should be somewhere in your user *Library/Developer/Xcode/DerivedData* folder, as shown in Figure 6-14. (I presume you know how to reveal the user *Library* directory.) In theory, you should be able to select the app under Products in Xcode's Project navigator and choose File → Show in Finder, but there seems to be a long-standing bug preventing this.

In the Finder, Control-click the Empty Window app, and choose Show Package Contents from the contextual menu. Here you can see the results of the build process (Figure 6-15).

Think of the app bundle as a transformation of the project folder:

Empty Window
> Our app's compiled code. The build process has compiled *ViewController.m*, *App-Delegate.m*, and *main.m*, first performing precompilation so as to obey all #import directives (and also importing the results of precompiling *Empty Window-Prefix.pch*). The result is this single file, our app's binary. This is the heart of the app, its actual executable material. When the app is launched, the binary is linked to the various frameworks, and the code begins to run starting with the main function.

Main.storyboardc
> Our app's storyboard file. The project's *Main.storyboard* is where our app's interface comes from — in this case, an empty white view occupying the entire window. The

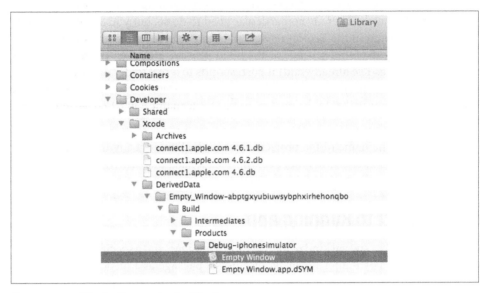

Figure 6-14. The built app, in the Finder

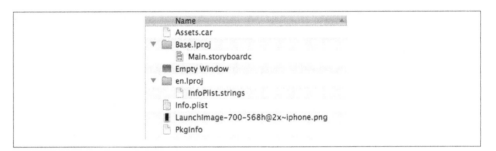

Figure 6-15. Contents of the app package

build process has compiled *Main.storyboard* (using the `ibtool` command-line tool) into a tighter format, resulting in a *.storyboardc* file, which is actually a bundle of nib files to be loaded as the app runs. One of these nib files, loaded as our app launches, will be the source of the white view displayed in the interface. *Main.storyboardc* occupies the same subfolder location (inside *Base.lproj*) as *Main.storyboard* does in the project folder; as I said earlier, this folder structure has to do with localization (to be discussed in Chapter 9).

InfoPlist.strings
This file has been copied directly from the project folder, maintaining the same subfolder location (inside *en.lproj*). This, too, has to do with localization.

Assets.car and LaunchImage-700-568h@2x~iphone.png

An asset catalog and a launch image. The original asset catalog *Images.xcassets* has been processed (using the `actool` command-line tool). This has resulted in a compiled asset catalog file (*.car*) containing any images that have been added to the catalog, along with a default black launch image (to be displayed momentarily during the animation when our app launches). If this were a real app, you'd probably see some additional app icon and launch image files written out from the asset catalog to the top level of the app bundle.

Info.plist

A configuration file in a strict text format (a *property list* file). It is derived from the project file *Empty Window-Info.plist*. It contains instructions to the system about how to treat and launch the app. For example, if our app had an icon, *Info.plist* would tell the system its name, so that the system could retrieve it from the app bundle and display it. It also tells the system things like the name of the binary, so that the system can find it and launch the app.

PkgInfo

A tiny text file reading `APPL????`, signifying the type and creator codes for this app. The *PkgInfo* file is something of a dinosaur; it isn't really necessary for the functioning of an iOS app and is generated automatically. You'll never need to touch it.

In real life, an app bundle will contain more files, but the difference will be mostly one of degree, not kind. For example, our project might have additional *.storyboard* or *.xib* files, icon image files, and image or sound files. All of these would make their way into the app bundle. In addition, an app bundle built to run on a device will contain some security-related files.

You are now in a position to appreciate, in a general sense, how the components of a project are treated and assembled into an app, and what responsibilities accrue to you, the programmer, in order to ensure that the app is built correctly. The rest of this chapter outlines what goes into the building of an app from a project, as well as how the constituents of that app are used at launch time to get the app up and running.

Build Settings

We have already talked about how build settings are determined. Xcode itself, the project, and the target all contribute to the resolved build setting values, some of which may differ depending on the build configuration. Before building, you, the programmer, will have specified a scheme; the scheme determines the build configuration, meaning the specific set of build setting values that will apply as this build proceeds.

Property List Settings

Your project contains a property list file that will be used to generate the built app's *Info.plist* file. The app target knows what file it is because it is specified in the Info.plist File build setting. For example, in our project, the value of the app target's Info.plist File build setting has been set to *Empty Window/Empty Window-Info.plist*. (Take a look at the build settings and see!)

 Because the name of the file in your project from which the built app's *Info.plist* file is generated will vary, depending on the name of the project, I'll refer to it generically as the project's *Info.plist*.

The property list file is a collection of key–value pairs. You can edit it, and you may well need to do so. There are three main ways to edit your project's *Info.plist*:

- Select the *Info.plist* file in the Project navigator and edit in the editor. By default, the key names (and some of the values) are displayed descriptively, in terms of their functionality; for example, it says "Bundle name" instead of the actual key, which is `CFBundleName`. But you can view the actual keys: click in the editor and then choose Editor → Show Raw Keys & Values, or use the contextual menu. In addition, you can see the *Info.plist* file in its true XML form: Control-click the *Info.plist* file in the Project navigator and choose Open As → Source Code from the contextual menu.

- Edit the target, and click Info at the top of the editor. The Custom iOS Target Properties section shows effectively the same information as editing the *Info.plist* in the editor.

- Edit the target, and click General at the top of the editor. Some of the settings here are effectively ways of editing the *Info.plist*. For example, when you click a Device Orientation checkbox here, you are changing the value of the "Supported interface orientations" key in the *Info.plist*. (Other settings here are effectively ways of editing build settings. For example, when you change the Deployment Target here, you are changing the value of the iOS Deployment Target build setting.)

Some values in the project's *Info.plist* require processing to transform them into their final values in the built app's *Info.plist*. This step is performed late in the build process. For example, the "Executable file" key's value in the project's *Info.plist* is `${EXECUTABLE_NAME}`; for this must be substituted the value of the `EXECUTABLE_NAME` build environment variable (which, as I mentioned earlier, you can discover by means of a Run Script build phase). Also, some additional key–value pairs are injected into the *Info.plist* during processing.

For a complete list of the possible keys and their meanings, see Apple's document *Information Property List Key Reference*. I'll talk more in Chapter 9 about *Info.plist* settings that you're particularly likely to edit.

Nib Files

A nib file is a description of a piece of user interface in a compiled format contained in a file with the extension *.nib*. Every app that you write is likely to contain at least one nib file. A nib file is generated during the build process by compilation (using the `ibtool` command-line tool) either from a *.xib* file, which results in a nib file, or from a *.storyboard* file, which results in a *.storyboardc* bundle containing multiple nib files. This compilation takes place by virtue of the *.storyboard* or *.xib* files being listed in the app target's Copy Bundle Resources build phase.

You edit the *.xib* or *.storyboard* file graphically in Xcode; in effect, you are describing graphically some objects that you want instantiated when the app runs and the nib file loads (Chapter 5). Thanks to this architecture, a nib file loads only when and if it is needed; this streamlines your app's launch time, when the only nib files loaded are those required to generate your app's initial interface, as well as your app's memory usage over time, because objects described in a nib are not instantiated until that nib is loaded, and can then be destroyed when they are no longer needed.

Our Empty Window project generated from the Single View Application template contains a single *.storyboard* file, called *Main.storyboard*. This one file is subject to special treatment as the app's main storyboard, not because of its name, but because it is pointed to in the *Info.plist* file by the key "Main storyboard file base name" (`UIMainStoryboard-File`), using its name ("Main") without the *.storyboard* extension — edit the *Info.plist* file and see! The result is that as the app launches, the first nib generated from this *.storyboard* file is loaded automatically to help create the app's initial interface.

If we had elected to use the Single View Application template to create a universal app — that is, an app that runs both on the iPad and on the iPhone — it would have had two *.storyboard* files, one to be used on the iPad (*Main_iPad.storyboard*) and the other to be used on the iPhone (*Main_iPhone.storyboard*). Thus the app can have different basic interfaces on the two different types of device. One of these storyboards is to be treated as the main storyboard file, depending on the device type at launch time, to create the app's initial interface. For this purpose, a second *Info.plist* key is used: the key "Main storyboard file base name" (`UIMainStoryboardFile`) points to "Main_iPhone", while the key "Main storyboard file base name (iPad)" (`UIMainStoryboardFile~ipad`) points to "Main_iPad".

I'll talk more about the app launch process and the main storyboard later in this chapter. See Chapter 7 for more about editing *.xib* and *.storyboard* files and how they create instances when your code runs.

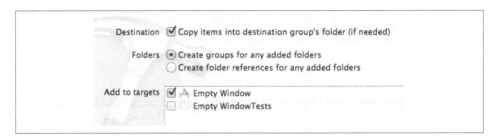

Figure 6-16. Options when adding a resource to a project

Additional Resources

Resources are ancillary files embedded in your app bundle, to be fetched as needed when the app runs, such as images you want to display or sounds you want to play. A real-life app is likely to involve many such additional resources. You'll add these resources to the project, making sure that they appear in the Copy Bundle Resources build phase. Making such resources available when your app runs will usually be up to your code (or to the code implied by the loading of a nib file): basically, the runtime simply reaches into your app bundle and pulls out the desired resource. In effect, your app bundle is being treated as a folder full of extra stuff.

To add a resource to your project, start in the Project navigator and choose File → Add Files to [Project], or drag the resource from the Finder into the Project navigator. A dialog appears (Figure 6-16) in which you make the following settings:

Copy items into destination group's folder (if needed)
> You should almost certainly check this checkbox. Doing so causes the resource to be copied into the project folder. If you leave this checkbox unchecked, your project will be relying on a file that's outside the project folder, where you might delete or change it unintentionally. Keeping everything your project needs inside the project folder is far safer.

Folders
> This choice matters only if what you're adding to the project is a folder; the difference is in how the project references the folder contents:

Create groups for any added folders
> The folder name becomes the name of an ordinary group within the Project navigator; the folder contents appear in this group, but they are listed individually in the Copy Bundle Resources build phase, so by default they will all be copied individually into the top level of the app bundle.

Create folder references for any added folders
> The folder is shown in blue in the Project navigator (a *folder reference*); moreover, it is listed as a folder in the Copy Bundle Resources build phase, meaning

that the build process will copy *the entire folder and its contents* into the app bundle. This means that the resources inside the folder won't be at the top level of the app bundle, but in a subfolder within it. Such an arrangement can be valuable if you have many resources and you want to separate them into categories (rather than clumping them all at the top level of the app bundle) or if the folder hierarchy among resources is meaningful to your app. The downside of this arrangement is that the code you write for accessing a resource will have to be specific about what subfolder of the app bundle contains that resource.

Add to Targets

Checking this checkbox for a target causes the resource to be added to that target's Copy Bundle Resources build phase. Thus you will almost certainly want to check it for the app target; why else would you be adding this resource to the project? Still, if this checkbox accidentally goes unchecked and you realize later that a resource listed in the Project navigator needs to be added to the Copy Bundle Resources build phase for a particular target, you can add it manually, as I described earlier.

Image resources for an iOS program tend to come in pairs, one for the single-resolution screen and one for the double-resolution screen. In order to work properly with the framework's image-loading methods, such pairs employ a special naming convention: for example, *listen_normal.png* and *listen_normal@2x.png*, where the @2x suffix in the second file's name means that it is the double-resolution variant of the first file. This can cause a confusing proliferation of image files in the Project navigator. That is one of the annoyances that asset catalogs, new in Xcode 5, are intended to alleviate.

Instead of adding *listen_normal.png* to my project in the way I've just described, I can decide to let an asset catalog help me manage it. I'll use the default catalog, *Images.xcassets*. I edit the default catalog, click the Plus button at the bottom of the first column, and choose New Image Set. The result is a placeholder called Image with a space for the single-resolution image and a space for the double-resolution image. I drag the two images *listen_normal.png* and *listen_normal@2x.png* into this space, where each is automatically assigned to its proper spot. Moreover, there's no dialog (as in Figure 6-16); the images have automatically been copied into the project folder (inside the asset catalog folder), and there is no need for me to specify the target membership of these image files, because they are part of an asset catalog which already has correct target membership. Finally, I can rename the placeholder to something more descriptive than Image and simpler than *listen_normal*; let's call it Listen (Figure 6-17).

The result is that my code can now load the correct image for the current screen resolution by referring to it as @"Listen", without regard to the original name (or extension) of the images. Moreover, these images do not need to appear separately in the built app bundle; for an iOS 7 app, they can remain inside the compiled asset catalog.

Another advantage of asset catalogs is that the naming conventions don't have to be followed. Suppose I have two images, *little.png* and *big.png*, where the latter is the

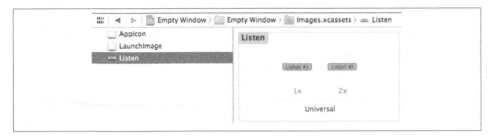

Figure 6-17. An image pair added to an asset catalog

double-resolution version of the former. We're not using the @2x naming convention, so the asset catalog can't tell that the two images are related in this way. But I can tell it, by dragging *little.png* onto my image set's "1x" space, and *big.png* onto its "2x" space.

The entries in an asset catalog can be inspected by selecting an image and using the Attributes inspector (Command-Option-4). This shows the name and size of the image. For example, in the case I just described, inspecting the "1x" variant of my image set tells me that this image is *little.png*, and gives its dimensions, showing that it is indeed half the size of its "2x" counterpart, *big.png*.

Code and the App Launch Process

The build process knows what code files to compile to form the app's binary because they are listed in the app target's Compile Sources build phase. (In the case of our Empty Window project, these are, as we've already seen, *ViewController.m*, *AppDelegate.m*, and *main.m*.) In addition, the project's *precompiled header* file is used during compilation; in fact, it is processed *before* any other code files. It isn't listed in the Compile Sources build phase; the target knows about it because it is pointed to by the Prefix Header build setting. (In the case of our Empty Window project, this file is called *Empty Window-Prefix.pch*.)

The precompiled header is a device for making compilation go faster. It's a header file; it is compiled once (or at least, very infrequently) and the results are cached (in the *DerivedData* folder) and are implicitly imported by all your code files. So the precompiled header should consist primarily of #import directives for headers that never change (such as the built-in Cocoa headers); it is also a reasonable place to put #defines that will never change and that are to be shared by all your code, as I mentioned in Chapter 4. The default precompiled header file imports *Foundation.h* (the Core Foundation framework header file) and *UIKit.h* (the Cocoa framework header file). I'll talk in the next section about what that means.

When the app launches, the system knows where to find the binary inside the app's bundle because the app bundle's *Info.plist* file has an "Executable file" key (CFBundle-

Executable) whose value tells the system the name of the binary; by default, the binary's name comes from the EXECUTABLE_NAME environment variable (here, "Empty Window").

The app is an Objective-C program, and Objective-C is C, so the entry point is the main function. This function is defined in the project's *main.m* file. Here are the main function's contents:

```
int main(int argc, char *argv[])
{
    @autoreleasepool {
        return UIApplicationMain(argc, argv, nil,
                                NSStringFromClass([AppDelegate class]));
    }
}
```

The main function does just two things:

- It sets up a memory management environment — the @autoreleasepool and the curly braces that follow it. I'll explain more about that in Chapter 12.
- It calls the UIApplicationMain function, which does the heavy lifting of helping your app pull itself up by its bootstraps and get running.

UIApplicationMain is responsible for solving some tricky problems. Where will your app get its initial instances? What instance methods will initially be called on those instances? Where will your app's initial interface come from? Here's what UIApplicationMain does:

1. UIApplicationMain creates your app's *first instance* — the shared application instance, which is to be subsequently accessible in code by calling [UIApplication sharedApplication]. The third argument in the call to UIApplicationMain specifies, as a string, what class the shared application instance should be an instance of. If nil, which will usually be the case, the default class is UIApplication. If, for some reason, you need to subclass UIApplication, you'll specify that subclass here by substituting something like this (depending on what the subclass is called) as the third argument in the call to UIApplicationMain:

   ```
   NSStringFromClass([MyUIApplicationSubclass class])
   ```

2. UIApplicationMain creates your app's *second instance* — the application instance's *delegate*. Delegation is an important and pervasive Cocoa pattern, described in detail in Chapter 11. It is crucial that every app you write have an app delegate instance. The fourth argument in the call to UIApplicationMain specifies, as a string, what class the app delegate instance should be. In our *main.m*, that specification is:

   ```
   NSStringFromClass([AppDelegate class])
   ```

This tells `UIApplicationMain` to create an instance of the AppDelegate class, and to associate that instance with the shared application instance as the latter's delegate. The code files defining this class, *AppDelegate.h* and *AppDelegate.m*, were created for you by the template; of course you can (and probably will) edit that code.

3. If the *Info.plist* file specifies a main storyboard file, `UIApplicationMain` loads it and looks inside it to find the view controller that is designated as this storyboard's *initial view controller*; it instantiates this view controller, thus creating your app's *third instance*. In the case of our Empty Window project, as constructed for us from the Single View Application template, that view controller will be an instance of the class called ViewController; the code files defining this class, *ViewController.h* and *ViewController.m*, were also created by the template.

4. If there was a main storyboard file, `UIApplicationMain` now creates your app's *window* by instantiating the UIWindow class — this is your app's *fourth instance*. It assigns this window instance as the app delegate's `window` property; it also assigns the initial view controller instance as the window instance's *root view controller* (`rootViewController` property).

   (I'm simplifying. In actual fact, `UIApplicationMain` first gives the app delegate instance a chance to create the window instance, by calling its `window` method. This is your code's opportunity to cause the window instance to come from a custom subclass of UIWindow.)

5. `UIApplicationMain` now turns to the app delegate instance and starts calling some of its code — in particular, it calls `application:didFinishLaunchingWith-Options:`. This is an opportunity for your own code to run! Thus, `application:did-FinishLaunchingWithOptions:` is a good place to put your code that initializes values and performs startup tasks, but you don't want anything time-consuming to happen here, because your app's interface still hasn't appeared.

   (I'm simplifying again. Starting in iOS 6, the sequence of calls to the app delegate's code actually begins with `application:willFinishLaunchingWithOptions:` if it exists.)

6. If there was a main storyboard, `UIApplicationMain` now causes your app's interface to appear. It does this by calling the UIWindow instance method `makeKeyAndVisible`.

7. The window is now about to appear. This, in turn, causes the window to turn to its root view controller and tell it to obtain its main view, which will occupy and appear in the window. If this view controller gets its view from a *.storyboard* or *.xib* file, the corresponding nib is now loaded; its objects are instantiated and initialized, and they become the objects of the initial interface.

The app is now launched and visible to the user. It has an initial set of instances — at a minimum, the shared application instance, the window, the initial view controller, and the initial view controller's view and whatever interface objects it contains. Some of your code (the app delegate's `application:didFinishLaunchingWithOptions:`) has run, and we are now off to the races: `UIApplicationMain` is still running (like Charlie on the M.T.A., `UIApplicationMain` never returns), and is just sitting there, watching for the user to do something, maintaining the *event loop*, which will respond to user actions as they occur.

In my description of the app launch process, I used several times the phrase "if there is a main storyboard." In most of the Xcode 5 app templates, such as the Single View Application template that we used to generate the Empty Window project, there *is* a main storyboard. It is also possible, though, not to have a main storyboard. In that case, things like creating a window instance, giving it a root view controller, assigning it to the app delegate's `window` property, and calling `makeKeyAndVisible` on the window to show the interface, must be done by your code.

To see what I mean, make a new iPhone project starting with the Empty Application template; let's call it Truly Empty. It has an App Delegate class, but no storyboard and no initial view controller. The app delegate's `application:didFinishLaunchingWith-Options:` in *AppDelegate.m* has code to create the window, assign it to the app delegate's `window` property, and show it:

```
self.window = [[UIWindow alloc] initWithFrame:[[UIScreen mainScreen] bounds]];
// Override point for customization after application launch.
self.window.backgroundColor = [UIColor whiteColor];
[self.window makeKeyAndVisible];
return YES;
```

If you build and run this app, it works and displays an empty white window; but there's a complaint in the console from the runtime engine, "Application windows are expected to have a root view controller at the end of application launch." We can prevent that complaint by creating a view controller and assigning it to the window's `rootView-Controller` property:

```
self.window = [[UIWindow alloc] initWithFrame:[[UIScreen mainScreen] bounds]];
// Override point for customization after application launch.
self.window.rootViewController = [UIViewController new]; // prevent complaint
self.window.backgroundColor = [UIColor whiteColor];
[self.window makeKeyAndVisible];
return YES;
```

That works: the complaint no longer appears when we build and run the app. However, we have left ourselves with no way customize our app's behavior meaningfully, as we have no UIViewController subclass. Moreover, we have no way to create the interface graphically; there is neither a *.storyboard* nor a *.xib* file. We can solve both problems by making a UIViewController subclass along with a *.xib* file:

1. Choose File → New → File. In the "Choose a template" dialog, under iOS, click Cocoa Touch on the left and select Objective-C Class. Click Next.

2. Name the class ViewController and specify that it is a subclass of UIViewController. Check the "With XIB for user interface" checkbox. Click Next.

3. The Save dialog appears. Make sure you are saving into the Truly Empty folder, that the Group pop-up menu is set to Truly Empty as well, and that the Truly Empty target is *checked* — we want these files to be part of the app target. Click Create.

   Xcode has created *three* files for us: *ViewController.h* and *ViewController.m*, defining ViewController as a subclass of UIViewController, and *ViewController.xib*, the source of the nib from which a ViewController instance will automatically obtain its view by default.

4. Now go back to the app delegate's `application:didFinishLaunchingWith-Options:`, in *AppDelegate.m*, and change the root view controller's class to View-Controller; you'll have to put `#import "ViewController.h"` at the top of this file as well:

   ```
   self.window = [[UIWindow alloc] initWithFrame:[[UIScreen mainScreen] bounds]];
   // Override point for customization after application launch.
   self.window.rootViewController = [ViewController new]; // our subclass
   self.window.backgroundColor = [UIColor whiteColor];
   [self.window makeKeyAndVisible];
   return YES;
   ```

We have thus created a perfectly usable minimal app project without a storyboard. Our code does some of the work that is done automatically by `UIApplicationMain` when there is a main storyboard: we instantiate UIWindow, we set the window instance as the app delegate's `window` property, we instantiate an initial view controller, we set that view controller instance as the window's `rootViewController` property, and we cause the window to appear. Moreover, the appearance of the window automatically causes the ViewController instance to fetch its view from the ViewController nib, which has been compiled from *ViewController.xib*; thus, we can use *ViewController.xib* to customize the app's initial interface.

Frameworks and SDKs

A *framework* is a library of compiled code used by your code. Most of the frameworks you are likely to use when programming iOS will be Apple's built-in frameworks. These frameworks are already part of the system on the device where your app will run; they live in */System/Library/Frameworks* on the device, though you can't tell that on an iPhone or iPad because there's no way (normally) to view the file hierarchy directly.

Your compiled code also needs to be connected to those frameworks when the project is being built, on your computer. To make this possible, the iOS device's *System/Library/*

Frameworks is duplicated on your computer, inside Xcode itself. This duplicated subset of the device's system is called an *SDK* (for "software development kit"). What SDK is used depends upon what destination you're building for.

Linking is the process of hooking up your compiled code with the frameworks that it needs, even though those frameworks are in one place at build time and in another place at runtime. Thus, for example:

When you build your code to run on a device:
> A copy of any needed frameworks is used. This copy lives in *System/Library/Frameworks/* inside the iPhone SDK, which is located at *Xcode.app/Contents/Developer/Platforms/iPhoneOS.platform/Developer/SDKs/iPhoneOS7.0.sdk.*

When your code runs on a device:
> The code, as it starts running, looks in the device's top-level */System* folder, located at */System/Library/Frameworks/*, for the frameworks that it needs.

Used in this way, the frameworks are part of an ingenious mechanism whereby Apple's code is effectively incorporated dynamically into your app when the app runs. The frameworks are the locus of all the stuff that every app might need to do; they are Cocoa. That's a lot of stuff, and a lot of compiled code. Your app gets to share in the goodness and power of the frameworks because it is linked to them. Your code works as if the framework code were incorporated into it. Yet your app is relatively tiny; it's the frameworks that are huge.

Linking takes care of connecting your compiled code to any needed frameworks, but it isn't sufficient to allow your code to compile in the first place. The frameworks are full of classes (such as NSString) and methods (such as `uppercaseString`) that your code will call. To satisfy the compiler, the frameworks do exactly what any C or Objective-C code would do: they publish their interface in header files (*.h*), which your code can import. Thus, for example, your code can speak of NSString and can call `uppercaseString` because it imports *NSString.h*. Actually, what your code imports is *UIKit.h*, which in turn imports *Foundation.h*, which in turn imports *NSString.h*. And you can see this happening at the top of any of your own code's header files:

```
#import <UIKit/UIKit.h>
```

(See Example 4-1 and the surrounding discussion for more about where framework headers are imported by class files and why.)

Thus, using a framework is a two-part process:

Import the framework's header
> Your code needs this information in order to *compile* successfully. Your code imports a framework's header by using the `#import` directive, specifying either that framework's header or a header that itself imports the desired header.

Link to the framework

The compiled executable binary needs to be connected to the frameworks it will use while running, effectively incorporating the compiled code constituting those frameworks. As your code is built, it is linked to any needed frameworks, in accordance with the list of frameworks in the target's Link Binary With Libraries build phase.

By default, the template has already linked three frameworks into your app target. It does this by listing them in the Link Binary With Libraries build phase (the frameworks then also appear in the Project Navigator, conventionally in the Frameworks group, and you can use these listings to navigate and examine their header files):

UIKit

Cocoa classes that are specialized for iOS, whose names begin with "UI," are part of the UIKit framework. The UIKit framework is imported (`<UIKit/UIKit.h>`) in the precompiled header file and in the class code header files that constitute the app templates, such as *AppDelegate.h*, as well as class code files that you create.

Foundation

Many basic Cocoa classes, such as NSString and NSArray and others whose names begin with "NS," are part of the Foundation framework. The Foundation framework is imported in the precompiled header file, but there is no need for this, because many headers imported by *UIKit.h* import the Foundation framework (`<Foundation/Foundation.h>`). In turn, *Foundation.h* includes the Core Foundation headers (`<CoreFoundation/CoreFoundation.h>`) and loads the Core Foundation framework as a subframework; thus, there is no need for you to import or link explicitly to the Core Foundation framework (which is full of functions and pointer types whose names begin with "CF," such as CFStringRef).

Core Graphics

The Core Graphics framework defines many structs and functions connected with drawing, whose names begin with "CG." It is imported by many UIKit headers, so you don't need to import it explicitly.

iOS has about 50 more frameworks, but the templates do not import them into your code or link them to your target. That's because extra frameworks mean extra work, both in order to compile your code and in order to launch your app. To use one of these additional frameworks, therefore, *you* must perform both the steps I listed a moment ago: you must import the framework's header wherever your code wants to use symbols published by that header, and you must link your code to the framework itself. This two-part process is rather inconvenient, and if you omit a step, things won't work properly.

For example, let's say you've just found out about the Address Book and you're raring to try it in your app. So, in your code, you create an ABNewPersonViewController:

```
ABNewPersonViewController* ab = [ABNewPersonViewController new];
```

The next time you try to build your app, the compiler complains that ABNewPerson-ViewController is an undeclared identifier. That's when you realize you need to import a framework header. The pair of letters at the start of ABNewPersonViewController's name might have provided a clue that it's provided by some additional framework; it doesn't start with "NS," "UI," or "CG". The ABNewPersonViewController class documentation informs us that it comes from the AddressBookUI framework. You might guess (correctly) that the way to import this framework's header is to put this line near the start of your implementation file:

```
#import <AddressBookUI/AddressBookUI.h>
```

This works to quiet the compiler, but your code *still* doesn't build. This time, you get a build error during the link phase of the build process complaining about _OBJC_CLASS_ $_ABNewPersonViewController and saying, "Symbol(s) not found." That mysterious-sounding error merely means that you've forgotten the second step: you have to link your target to *AddressBookUI.framework*.

To link your target to a framework, edit the target, click General at the top of the editor, and scroll down to the Linked Frameworks and Libraries section. (This is the same information that appears when you click Build Phases at the top of the editor and open the Link Binary With Libraries build phase.) Click the Plus button at the left just below the list of frameworks. A dialog appears listing the existing frameworks that are part of the active SDK. Select *AddressBookUI.framework* and click Add. The AddressBookUI framework is added to the target's Link Binary With Libraries build phase. (It also appears in the Project navigator.) Now you can build (and run) your app.

Starting in Xcode 5 and LLVM 5.0, you can elect to make the process of using additional frameworks much simpler, by using *modules*. Use of modules is a build setting, Enable Modules (C and Objective-C). By default, this setting is Yes for new projects constructed from the application templates.

Modules are cached information stored on your computer at *Library/Developer/Xcode/DerivedData/ModuleCache*. When you build an app that imports a framework header, if the information for that framework hasn't been cached as a module, it is cached as a module at that moment. Here are some benefits of using modules:

Smaller code files after precompilation
When precompilation is performed, whatever is imported is literally copied into your code. The UIKit headers, together with the headers that they import, constitute about 30,000 lines of code. This means that, in order to compile any *.m* file of yours, the compiler must deal with a file that is at least 30,000 lines longer than the code you wrote. When you're using modules, however, the imported header information lives in the modules, and the length of your code files is not significantly increased by precompilation. This might also mean that your code compiles faster.

Easier, shorter imports

Importing a framework's header can be tedious. The header name must be in brackets, and you have to provide both the framework's name (which is actually a folder name) and the name of the header file:

```
#import <AddressBookUI/AddressBookUI.h>
```

With modules, instead of the `#import` directive, you can use a new directive, `@import` (with an at-sign instead of a hash-sign), which requires only the bare name of the framework followed by a semicolon:

```
@import AddressBookUI;
```

Moreover, `#imports` are automatically converted to `@imports`, so you can express yourself either way, and your existing code using `#import` keeps working while taking advantage of modules.

Autolinking

Using a framework is a two-step process. Not only must you import the header, but also you must link to the framework. Modules permit you to omit the second step. This convenience is optional (it's a build setting, Link Frameworks Automatically), but it's turned on by default. The result is that once your code has imported a framework's header, your target *doesn't need to link to the framework*. Linking will be performed automatically during the build process.

Modules are ingenious and convenient, but they also have some aspects that might be considered disadvantages as opposed to the old regime of explicit importing and linking. For example, when a framework is explicitly linked into your project, you know it, because it is listed in the Link Binary With Libraries build phase and in the Project navigator. With modules, *you don't know what frameworks you're using*; there's no list of your autolinked frameworks.

Moreover, because autolinked frameworks are not listed in the Project navigator, their headers are not *navigable* in the Project navigator (whereas the headers of explicitly linked frameworks are), and their headers are not *searchable* in the Project navigator (whereas the headers of explicitly linked frameworks are, by using a search scope of "within workspace and frameworks").

Fortunately, if you miss those features, there's no harm in linking to a framework manually, to create a listing for it in the Project navigator, even if that framework is also being autolinked.

CHAPTER 7

Nib Management

The term *nib file*, or simply *nib*, has nothing to do with fountain pens or bits of chocolate; it originated as an acronym for "NeXTStep Interface Builder", which was used for the *.nib* file extension. Just about any iOS app you create will contain at least one nib file. This file will be generated from either a *.xib* file or a *.storyboard* file in your Xcode project (see Chapter 6). When you edit a *.xib* or *.storyboard* file in Xcode, you appear to be in a drawing program; it looks as if you're designing a piece of interface graphically, much as you might create and edit a drawing in Adobe Illustrator, OmniGraffle, Canvas, or any of a host of other similar drawing applications past and present. I'll refer to this aspect of Xcode's editing environment as the *nib editor*.

> Up through Xcode 3.2.x, nib editing was performed in a separate application, Interface Builder. Starting in Xcode 4, the functionality of Interface Builder was rolled into Xcode itself. Nevertheless, the nib editor environment within Xcode is still often referred to as Interface Builder.

When you work in the nib editor, you're not really creating a drawing. You're encoding instructions for *instantiating, initializing, and configuring objects*. As I said in Chapter 5 (see especially "Nib-Based Instantiation" on page 90), when you drag a button into a view in the nib editor, put that button into a certain position, give it a certain size, and double-click it and set its title to "Howdy!", you're putting instructions into the nib that will generate a UIButton instance and set its `frame` and `title` properties and make it a subview of the view you dragged it into, much as if you had performed the entire process of instantiation, initialization, and configuration of that button in code such as this:

```
UIButton* b =
    [UIButton buttonWithType:UIButtonTypeSystem];      // instantiate
[b setTitle:@"Howdy!" forState:UIControlStateNormal];  // set up title
[b setFrame: CGRectMake(100,100,52,30)];               // set up frame
[self.view addSubview:b];                              // put into view
```

The instructions that you create by working in the nib editor are embodied in a nib file in the built app. These instructions are effectively a collection of potential objects, also referred to as *nib objects*. Those potential objects encoded in the nib are not turned into real objects until and unless the nib is *loaded* in the course of the app's running. At that moment, the instructions embodied in the nib file are obeyed by the nib-loading mechanism, and the objects are reproduced into living instances, ready to become part of your running app. They are mostly interface objects, so the way in which they will usually manifest themselves is by being made subviews of a view that the user will see.

Thus there are three stages in the life of a nib with which you will be concerned while programming iOS:

- How to *edit* the nib as a *.xib* or *.storyboard* file in Xcode
- How the nib will come to be *loaded* as the app runs
- How, when the nib is loaded, the app will *use* the instances that it generates

These, and related matters, are the concerns of this chapter.

Are Nibs Necessary?

Since nibs are ultimately just sources of instances, you might wonder whether it is possible to do without them. Those same instances could be generated in code, so wouldn't it be possible to dispense with nibs altogether? The simple answer is: Yes, it would. It's quite possible to write a complex app that lacks a single *.storyboard* or *.xib* file (I've done it). The practical question, however, is one of balance. Most apps use nib files as a source of at least some interface objects; but there are some aspects of interface objects that can be customized only in code, and sometimes it's easier to generate those interface objects entirely in code at the outset. In real life your projects will probably involve a great deal of interplay between code and nib-generated objects.

A Tour of the Nib Editor Interface

Let's explore Xcode's nib editor interface. In Chapter 6, we created a simple iPhone project, Empty Window, directly from the Single View Application template; it contains a storyboard file, so we'll use that. In Xcode, open the Empty Window project, locate *Main.storyboard* in the Project navigator, and click to edit it.

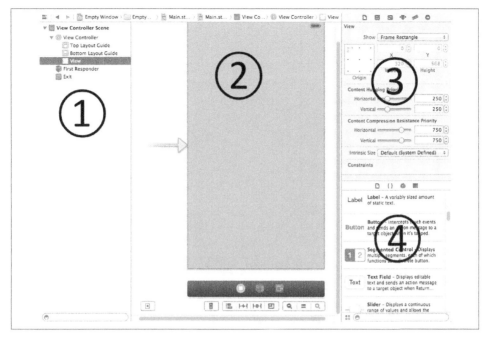

Figure 7-1. Editing a nib file

Figure 7-1 shows the project window after selecting *Main.storyboard* and making some additional adjustments. The Navigator pane is hidden; the Utilities pane is showing, containing the Size inspector and the Object library. The interface may be considered in four pieces:

1. At the left of the editor is the *document outline*, listing the storyboard's contents hierarchically by name. It can be hidden by dragging its right edge or by clicking the left-pointing-triangle button that sits near its bottom right corner.

2. The remainder of the editor is devoted to the *canvas*, where you physically design your app's interface. The canvas portrays views in your app's interface and things that can contain views. A *view* is an interface object, which draws itself into a rectangular area. The phrase "things that can contain views" is my way of including view controllers, which are represented in the canvas even though they are not drawn in your app's interface; a view controller isn't a view, but it *has* a view (and controls it).

3. The inspectors in the Utilities pane let you edit details of the currently selected object.

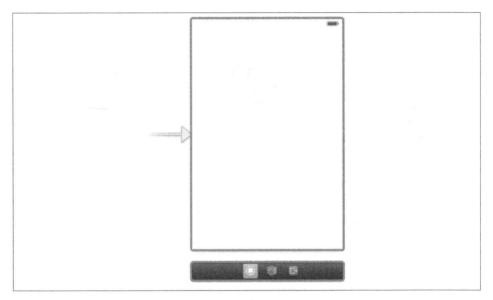

Figure 7-2. A view controller selected in a storyboard

4. The libraries in the Utilities pane, especially the Object library, are your source of interface objects to be added to the nib.

The Document Outline

The document outline portrays hierarchically the relationships between the objects in the nib. This structure differs slightly depending on whether you're editing a *.storyboard* file or a *.xib* file.

In a storyboard file, the primary constituents are *scenes*. A scene is, roughly speaking, a single view controller, along with some ancillary material; every scene has a single view controller at its top level.

A view controller isn't an interface object, but it manages an interface object, namely its view (or *main view*). A view controller in a nib doesn't have to have its main view in the same nib, but it usually does, and in that case, in the nib editor, the view usually appears inside the view controller in the canvas. Thus, in Figure 7-1, the large blue-highlighted rectangle in the canvas is a view controller's main view, and it is actually inside a view controller. The view controller itself is represented in the canvas by the rectangle containing the view, along with the black rounded rectangle below it, which is called the *scene dock*. This is easier to see if the view controller itself is selected, as in Figure 7-2: the view controller and its scene dock are highlighted together, with a heavy blue outline.

Each view controller in a storyboard file, together with its view and its scene dock, constitutes a scene. This scene is also portrayed as a hierarchical collection of names in the document outline. At the top level of the document outline are the scenes themselves. At the top level of each scene are names that designate the objects in the view controller's scene dock: the view controller itself, along with two *proxy objects*, the First Responder token and the Exit token. These objects — the ones displayed as icons in the scene dock, and shown at the top level of the scene in the document outline — are the scene's *top-level objects*.

Objects listed in the document outline are of two kinds:

Nib objects

> The view controller, along with its main view and any subviews that we care to place in that view, are real objects — potential objects that will be turned into actual instances when the nib is loaded by the running app. Such real objects to be instantiated from the nib are also called *nib objects*.

Proxy objects

> The proxy objects (here, the First Responder and Exit tokens) do *not* represent instances that will come from the nib when it is loaded. Rather, they represent other objects, and are present to facilitate communication between nib objects and other objects (I'll give examples later in this chapter). You can't create or delete a proxy object; the nib editor shows them automatically.

Aside from the top-level objects, most objects listed in a storyboard's document outline will depend hierarchically upon a scene's view controller. For example, in Figure 7-1, the view controller has a main view; that view is listed as hierarchically dependent on the view controller. That makes sense, because this view belongs to this view controller. Moreover, any further interface objects that we drag into the main view in the canvas will be listed in the document outline as hierarchically dependent on the view. That makes sense, too. A view can contain other views (its *subviews*) and can be contained by another view (its *superview*). One view can contain many subviews, which might themselves contain subviews. But each view can have only one immediate superview. Thus there is a hierarchical tree of subviews contained by their superviews with a single object at the top. The document outline portrays that tree (as an outline!).

In a *.xib* file, there are no scenes. What would be, in a *.storyboard* file, the top-level objects of a scene become, in a *.xib* file, the top-level objects of the nib itself. Nor is there any requirement that one of these top-level objects be a view controller; it can be, but more often the top-level interface object of a *.xib* file is a view. It might well be a view that is to serve as a view controller's main view, but that's not a requirement either. Figure 7-3 shows a *.xib* with a structure parallel to the single scene of Figure 7-1.

The document outline in Figure 7-3 lists three top-level objects. Two of them are proxy objects, termed Placeholders in the document outline: the File's Owner, and the First

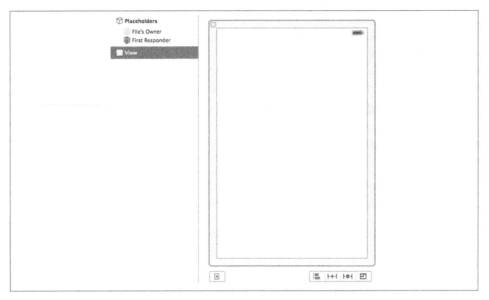

Figure 7-3. A .xib file containing a view

Figure 7-4. The dock in a .xib file

Responder. The third is a real object, a view; it will be instantiated when the nib is loaded as the app runs. The document outline in a *.xib* file can't be completely hidden; instead, it is collapsed into a set of icons representing the nib's top-level objects, similar to a scene dock in a storyboard file, and often referred to simply as the *dock* (Figure 7-4).

At present, the document outline may seem unnecessary, because there is very little hierarchy; all objects in Figure 7-1 and Figure 7-3 are readily accessibly in the canvas. But when a storyboard contains many scenes, and when a view contains many levels of hierarchically arranged objects (along with their autolayout constraints), you're going to be very glad of the document outline, which lets you survey the contents of the nib in a nice hierarchical structure, and where you can locate and select the object you're after. You can also rearrange the hierarchy here; for example, if you've made an object a subview of the wrong view, you can reposition it within this outline by dragging its name. You can also select objects using the jump bar at the top of the editor: the last jump bar path component (Control-6) is a hierarchical pop-up menu similar to the document outline.

If the names of nib objects in the document outline seem generic and uninformative, you can change them. The name is technically a *label*, and has no special meaning, so feel free to assign nib objects labels that are useful to you. Select a nib object's label in the document outline and press Return to make it editable, or select the object and edit the Label field in the Document section of the Identity inspector (Command-Option-3).

Canvas

The canvas provides a graphical representation of a top-level interface nib object along with its subviews, similar to what you're probably accustomed to in any drawing program. In a *.xib* file, you can remove the canvas representation of a top-level nib object (without deleting the object) by clicking the X at its top left (Figure 7-3), and you can restore the graphical representation to the canvas by clicking that nib object in the document outline. The canvas is scrollable and automatically accommodates however many graphical representations it contains; a storyboard canvas can also be zoomed (choose Editor → Canvas → Zoom, or use the zoom buttons at the lower right of the canvas; Figure 7-1).

Our simple Empty Window project's *Main.storyboard* contains just one scene, so it represents graphically in the canvas just one top-level nib object — the scene's view controller. Inside this view controller, and generally indistinguishable from it in the canvas, is its main view. It happens that this view controller will become our app's window's root view controller when the app runs; therefore its view will occupy the entire window, and will effectively be our app's initial interface (see Chapter 6). That gives us an excellent opportunity to experiment: any visible changes we make within this view should be visible when we run the app. To prove this, let's add a subview:

1. Start with the canvas looking more or less like Figure 7-1.

2. Look at the Object library (Command-Option-Control-3). If it's in icon view (a grid of icons without text), click the button at the left of the filter bar to put it into list view. Type "button" into the filter bar, so that only button objects are shown in the list. The Button object is listed first.

3. Drag the Button object from the Object library into the view controller's main view in the canvas (Figure 7-5), and let go of the mouse.

A button is now present in the view in the canvas. The move we've just performed — dragging from the Object library into the canvas — is extremely characteristic; you'll do it often as you design your interface.

Much as in a drawing program, the nib editor provides features to aid you in designing your interface. Here are some things to try:

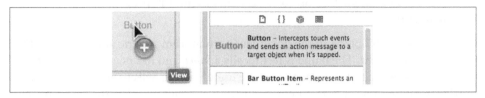

Figure 7-5. Dragging a button into a view

- Select the button: resizing handles appear. (If you accidentally select it twice and the resizing handles disappear, select the view and then the button again.)

- Using the resizing handles, resize the button to make it wider: dimension information appears.

- Drag the button near an edge of the view: a guideline appears, showing a standard margin space between the edge of the button and the edge of the view. Similarly, drag it near the center of the view: a guideline shows you when the button is centered.

- With the button selected, hold down the Option key and hover the mouse outside the button: arrows and numbers appear showing the distance between the button and the edges of the view. (If you accidentally clicked and dragged while you were holding Option, you'll now have two buttons. That's because Option-dragging an object duplicates it. Select the unwanted button and press Delete to remove it.)

- Control-Shift-click on the button: a menu appears, letting you select the button or whatever's behind it (in this case, the view, as well as the view controller because the view controller acts as a sort of top-level background to everything we're doing here).

- Double-click the button's title. The title becomes editable. Give it a new title, such as "Howdy!"

To prove that we really are designing our app's interface, we'll run the app:

1. Examine the Debug → Activate / Deactivate Breakpoints menu item. If it says Deactivate Breakpoints, choose it; we don't want to pause at any breakpoints you may have created while reading the previous chapter.

2. Make sure the destination in the Scheme pop-up menu is iPhone Retina (I don't care whether it's 3.5-inch or 4-inch).

3. Choose Product → Run (or click the Run button in the toolbar).

After a heart-stopping pause, the iOS Simulator opens, and presto, our empty window is empty no longer (Figure 7-6); it contains a button! You can tap this button with the

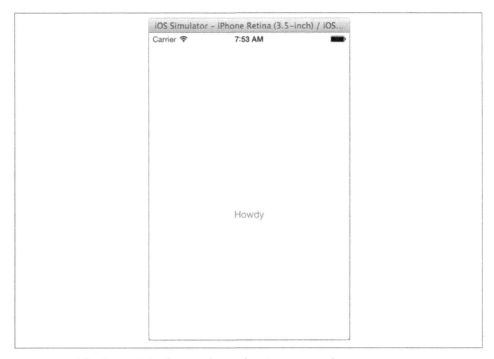

Figure 7-6. The Empty Window app's window is empty no longer

mouse, emulating what the user would do with a finger; the button highlights as you tap it.

Inspectors and Libraries

Four inspectors appear in conjunction with the nib editor, and apply to whatever object is selected in the document outline, dock, or canvas:

Identity inspector (Command-Option-3)
> The first section of this inspector, Custom Class, is the most important. Here you learn, and can change, the selected object's class. Some situations in which you'll need to change the class of an object in the nib appear later in this chapter.

Attributes inspector (Command-Option-4)
> Settings here correspond to properties and methods that you might use to configure the object in code. For example, selecting our view and choosing from the Background pop-up menu in the Attributes inspector corresponds to setting the view's `backgroundColor` property in code. Similarly, selecting our button and typing in the Title field is like calling the button's `setTitle:forState:` method.

The Attributes inspector has sections corresponding to the selected object's class inheritance. For example, the UIButton Attributes inspector has three sections: in addition to a Button section, there's a Control section (because a UIButton is also a UIControl) and a View section (because a UIButton is also a UIView).

Size inspector (Command-Option-5)
The X, Y, Width, and Height fields determine the object's position and size within its superview, corresponding to its `frame` property in code; you can equally do this in the canvas by dragging and resizing, but numeric precision can be desirable.

If Autolayout is turned off (uncheck Use Autolayout in the File inspector), the Size inspector displays an Autosizing box that corresponds to the `autoresizingMask` property, along with an animation that demonstrates visually the implications of your `autoresizingMask` settings; plus, an Arrange pop-up menu contains useful commands for positioning the selected object.

If Autolayout is turned on (the default for new *.xib* and *.storyboard* files), the rest of the Size inspector has to do with the selected object's Autolayout constraints, plus a four-button cartouche at the lower right of the canvas helps you manage alignment, positioning, and constraints.

Connections inspector (Command-Option-6)
I'll discuss and demonstrate use of the Connections inspector later in this chapter.

Two libraries are of particular importance when you're editing a nib:

Object library (Command-Option-Control-3)
This library is your source for objects that you want to add to the nib.

Media library (Command-Option-Control-4)
This library lists media in your project, such as images that you might want to drag into a UIImageView — or directly into your interface, in which case a UIImageView is created for you.

Nib Loading

A nib file is a collection of potential instances — its nib objects. Those instances become real only if, while your app is running, the nib is *loaded*. At that moment, the nib objects contained in the nib are transformed into instances that are available to your app.

This architecture is a source of great efficiency. A nib usually contains interface; interface is relatively heavyweight stuff. A nib isn't loaded until it is needed; indeed, it might never be loaded. Thus this heavyweight stuff won't come into existence until and unless it is needed. In this way, memory usage is kept to a minimum, which is important because memory is at a premium in a mobile device. Also, loading a nib takes time, so loading fewer nibs at launch time — enough to generate just the app's initial interface — makes launching faster.

 Nib loading is a one-way street: there's no such thing as "unloading" a nib. As a nib is loaded, its instances come into existence, and the nib's work, for that moment, is done. Henceforward it's up to the running app to decide what to do with the instances that just sprang to life. It must hang on to them for as long as it needs them, and will let them go out of existence when they are needed no longer.

Think of the nib file as a set of instructions for generating instances; those instructions are followed each time the nib is loaded. The same nib file can thus be loaded numerous times, generating a new set of instances each time. For example, a nib file might contain a piece of interface that you intend to use in several different places in your app. A nib file representing a single row of a table might be loaded a dozen times in order to generate a dozen visible rows of that table.

Recall from Chapter 5 that instances come about in three ways: as ready-made instances (through a method call that vends an instance), by instantiation from scratch (by calling `alloc`), and through the loading of a nib. We are now ready to discuss this third way of making instances.

Here are some of the chief circumstances under which a nib file is commonly loaded while an app is running:

A view controller is instantiated from a storyboard
A storyboard is a collection of scenes. Each scene starts with a view controller. When that view controller is needed, it is instantiated from the storyboard. This means that a nib containing the view controller is loaded.

Most commonly, a view controller will be instantiated from a storyboard automatically. For example, as your app launches, if it has a main storyboard, the runtime looks for that storyboard's *initial view controller* and instantiates it (see Chapter 6). Similarly, a storyboard typically contains several scenes connected by segues; when a segue is performed, the destination scene's view controller is instantiated.

It is also possible for your code to instantiate a view controller from a storyboard, manually. You can instantiate the storyboard's initial view controller by calling `instantiateInitialViewController`, or any view controller whose scene is named within the storyboard by an identifier string by calling `instantiateViewControllerWithIdentifier:`.

(Note that this is not the only way in which a view controller can come into existence. Far from it. A view controller is an instance like any other instance, so it can be created by telling a view controller class to instantiate itself. We saw this in Chapter 6, where we created a view controller in our Truly Empty app by saying [View-Controller new]. No nib was loaded at that moment; that was instantiation from scratch, not nib-based instantiation.)

A view controller loads its main view from a nib

A view controller has a main view. But a view controller is a lightweight object (it's just some code), whereas its main view is a relatively heavyweight object. Therefore, a view controller, when it is instantiated, lacks its main view. It generates its main view later, when that view is needed because it is to be placed into the interface. A view controller can obtain its main view in several ways; one way is to load its main view from a nib.

If a view controller belongs to a scene in a storyboard, and if, as will usually be the case, it contains its view in that storyboard's canvas (as in our Empty Window example project), then there are two nibs involved: the nib containing the view controller, and the nib containing its main view. The nib containing the view controller was loaded when the view controller was instantiated, as I just described; now, when that view controller instance needs its main view, the main view nib is loaded, and the whole interface connected with that view controller springs to life.

In the case of a view controller instantiated in some other way, there may be a *.xib*-generated nib file associated with it, containing its main view. The view controller will automatically load this nib and extract the main view when it's needed. This association between a view controller and its main view nib file is made through the nib file's name, and can happen in one of two ways:

Automatically, based on the name of the view controller's class

We saw this in our Truly Empty app in Chapter 6. The view controller's class was ViewController. The *.xib* file, and hence the nib file, was also called View-Controller (ignoring the file extension). That's enough to tell the nib-loading mechanism where to find the view controller's main view nib file when it's needed.

Explicitly, through the view controller's nibName property

When a view controller is instantiated, if it is initialized with initWithNib-Name:bundle:, the name of the nib file containing its main view may be stated explicitly as the nibName: argument; this sets the view controller instance's nib-Name property, which is used to locate the nib when the main view is needed. Alternatively, the view controller may set its own nibName property in a custom initializer.

Your code explicitly loads a nib file

Up to now, I've been describing situations where a nib file is loaded automatically. If a nib file comes from a *.xib* file, however, your code can also load it manually, by calling one of these methods:

`loadNibNamed:owner:options:`

An NSBundle instance method. Usually, you'll direct it to [NSBundle main-Bundle].

`instantiateWithOwner:options:`

A UINib instance method. The nib in question was specified when UINib was instantiated and initialized with `nibWithNibName:bundle:`.

 To specify a nib file while the app is running actually requires two pieces of information — its name and the bundle containing it. And indeed, a view controller has not only a `nibName` property but also a `nibBundle` property, and the methods for specifying a nib, such as `init-WithNibName:bundle:` and `nibWithNibName:bundle:`, have a `bundle:` parameter as well as a `name:` parameter. In real life, however, the bundle will be the app bundle (or [NSBundle mainBundle], which is the same thing); this is the default, so there will be no need to specify a bundle.

Outlets and the Nib Owner

When a nib loads and its instances come into existence, there's a problem: those instances are useless. An instance is of no use unless you can get a reference to it (I devoted a section of Chapter 5 to this matter). Without a reference to them, the instances generated by the loading of a nib can't be used for anything: they can't be put into the interface; they can't be modified or further configured; in fact, they can't even be held on to, and might very well pop right back out of existence again without having served any purpose at all.

One of the main ways of solving this problem is by using an *outlet*. An outlet is something in a nib file: it's a connection from one object in a nib file to another. The connection has a direction: that's why I use the words "from" and "to" to describe it. I'll call the two objects the *source* and the *destination* of the outlet. The outlet has two aspects:

The outlet's name

Inside the nib file, the outlet has a name. This name is effectively just a string.

An instance variable in the source's class

The class of the outlet's source object has an instance variable (or, what amounts to the same thing, a setter accessor) that matches the outlet's name (in accordance with the rules of key–value coding, discussed in Chapter 5).

When the nib loads, something unbelievably clever happens. The source object and the destination object are no longer just potential objects in a nib; they are now real, full-fledged instances. The outlet's name is now immediately used, by key–value coding, to match it with the instance variable (or setter) in the source object, and *the destination object is assigned to it*.

For example, let's say that we've made a nib where the class of Nib Object A is Dog, and let's say that a Dog has a `master` instance variable, which is typed as a Person. And let's say that the class of Nib Object B is Person. Then:

1. Let's say that in the nib editor, you draw an outlet connection from Nib Object A (a potential Dog instance) to Nib Object B (a potential Person instance) — an outlet called `master`. This connection is now part of the nib.

2. The app runs, and somehow this nib loads (in one of the ways I described in the previous section).

3. Nib Object A is instantiated, and Nib Object B is instantiated. We now have an actual Dog instance and an actual Person instance.

4. But the nib-loading mechanism is not finished. It sees that the nib also contains an outlet from Nib Object A to Nib Object B, called `master`. Accordingly, it calls `setValue:forKey:` on the Dog instance, where the key is `@"master"` and the `value` is the Person instance. Presto, the Dog instance now has a reference to the Person instance — namely, as the value of its `master` instance variable!

To sum up: an outlet in the nib is just a name involving two *potential* objects. But when the nib is loaded, the nib-loading mechanism makes those objects real, and it turns that outlet into an actual reference from one object to the other by way of an instance variable (Figure 7-7).

The nib-loading mechanism won't *create* an instance variable — that is, it doesn't cause the source object, once instantiated, to have an instance variable of the correct name if it didn't have one before. The class of the source object has to have defined an instance variable (or setter accessor) *already*. Thus, for an outlet to work, preparation must be performed in *two different places*: in the class of the source object, and in the nib. This is a bit tricky. As we'll see, Xcode helps you by making it hard for you to create an outlet if the source object class *doesn't* have the necessary instance variable. However, it is still possible for you to mess things up, as I'll explain later in this chapter.

Outlets are a clever way of allowing one object in a nib to get a reference to another object in a nib when those objects are no longer in the nib, but have been turned into

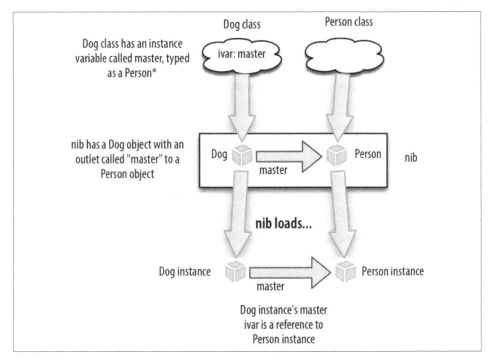

Figure 7-7. How an outlet provides a reference to a nib-instantiated object

real instances. But we still have not yet solved the problem we started with. A nib is going to load, and its objects are going to come into existence. The problem isn't how nib-instantiated objects can refer to one another (though it's great that they can do so); the problem is how an instance that *already* existed *before* the nib loaded can get a reference to an object that won't come into existence until *after* the nib has loaded. Otherwise, the objects generated from within the nib will be able to refer to one another, but nobody *else* will be able to refer to them, and they will still be useless.

We need a way for an outlet to cross the metaphysical barrier between the world of instances before the nib loads and the set of instances to be generated by the loading of the nib. That way is the *nib owner proxy object*. I mentioned earlier that your *.storyboard* or *.xib* file is populated automatically with some proxy objects, whose purpose I didn't divulge. Now I'm going to tell you what one of them is for, namely the nib owner proxy. First, you need to know where to find it:

- In a storyboard scene, the nib owner proxy is the top-level view controller. It is the first object listed for that scene in the document outline, and the first object shown in the scene dock.

- In a *.xib* file, the nib owner proxy is the first object shown in the document outline or dock; it is listed under Placeholders as the File's Owner.

The nib owner proxy is a proxy for an instance that *already* exists *outside* the nib at the time that the nib is loaded. When the nib is loaded, the nib-loading mechanism doesn't instantiate this object; it is *already* an instance. Instead, it substitutes the real, already existing instance for the proxy as it fulfills any connections that involve the proxy.

For example, suppose now that there is a Person nib object in our nib, but no Dog nib object. Instead, the nib owner proxy object's class is Dog — and a Dog, you remember, has a `master` instance variable. Then we can draw a `master` outlet in the nib editor from the nib owner proxy object (because its class is Dog) to the Person nib object. When the nib loads, the nib-loading mechanism will match the Dog nib owner proxy object with an already existing actual Dog instance, and will set the Person as that instance's `master`.

But how does the nib-loading mechanism know *which* already existing Dog instance is to be matched by the nib owner proxy object for this nib on this particular occasion when it loads? I thought you'd never ask. On every occasion when a nib is to be loaded, that nib is assigned an already existing object to be its *owner*. It is this already existing owner object that the nib owner proxy object represents within the nib (Figure 7-8).

How is the nib assigned an owner? In one of two ways:

- If your code loads the nib by calling `loadNibNamed:owner:options:` or `instantiateWithOwner:options:`, an owner object is specified as the `owner:` argument.
- If a view controller instance loads a nib automatically in order to obtain its main view, the view controller instance itself is specified as the nib's owner object.

Let's focus on the second case, because we already have two projects that demonstrate it. A view controller has a main view. This is expressed formally by the fact that a UIViewController has a `view` property — which means that, in effect, it has a `view` instance variable or corresponding accessors (or both). When a view controller loads a nib to get its main view, that view controller (as I just said) is the nib's owner.

So now we understand how a view controller, as it loads its main view nib, is able to *refer* to the main view instantiated from it and do something with it (like put it into the interface) — it does it through its `view` instance variable, which is matched by a `view` outlet in the nib. The situation is exactly parallel to Figure 7-8, showing the Dog instance that owns the nib with a Dog nib owner proxy that has a `master` outlet pointing to a Person — except that here we have a UIViewController instance that owns a nib with a UIViewController nib owner proxy that has a `view` outlet pointing to a UIView. (When I say "UIViewController" and "UIView" here, of course subclasses of these classes will do as well.)

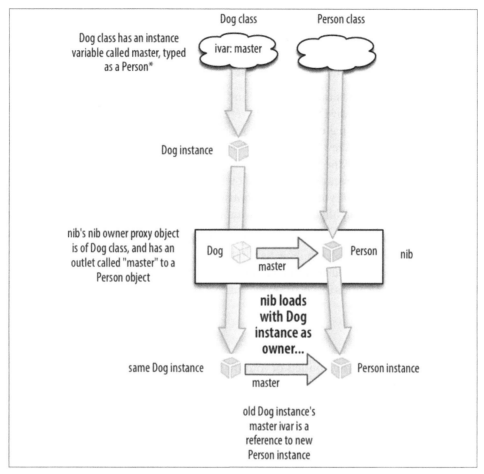

Dog class has an instance variable called master, typed as a Person*

Dog class

Person class

ivar: master

Dog instance

nib's nib owner proxy object is of Dog class, and has an outlet called "master" to a Person object

Dog

master

Person

nib

nib loads with Dog instance as owner...

same Dog instance

master

Person instance

old Dog instance's master ivar is a reference to new Person instance

Figure 7-8. An outlet from the nib owner proxy object

So if a nib is to contain a view controller's main view, two things had better be true inside that nib:

- The class of this nib's nib owner proxy object must be UIViewController, or some subclass thereof — preferably, the class of the view controller that will be loading this nib.

- This nib must have a view outlet from the nib owner proxy object to the main view nib object.

If both those things are true, all will be well. When the view controller needs its view, it will load the nib with itself as owner; the view described in the nib will come into existence as a full-fledged instance, and the view controller's view will be a reference to it. This will solve the problem that we set out to solve. All the other instances created from the nib depend upon that main view (as subviews of it, and so forth), so this one view instance variable of the view controller is now a reference to the main view along with the entire kit and caboodle of instances that depend upon it. The view controller is now ready and able to put its view into the interface.

If you look at the projects that we created in Chapter 6, you'll find that their nibs are indeed set up in just the way I've outlined here! First, look at our Empty Window project. Edit *Main.storyboard*. It has one scene, whose nib owner proxy object is the View Controller object. Select the View Controller in the document outline. Switch to the Identity inspector. It tells us that the nib owner proxy object's class is indeed ViewController. Now switch to the Connections inspector. It tells us that there is an Outlet connection to the View object (and if you hover the mouse over that outlet connection, the View object in the canvas is highlighted, to help you identify it).

Now look at our Truly Empty project. Edit *ViewController.xib*. The nib owner proxy object is the File's Owner placeholder. Select the File's Owner placeholder. Switch to the Identity inspector. It tells us that the nib owner proxy object's class is ViewController. Switch to the Connections inspector. It tells us that there is an Outlet connection to the View object.

Creating an Outlet

You will often want to create outlets of your own. To demonstrate how this is done, let's use the Empty Window project. Earlier in this chapter, we added a button to its initial view controller's main view. Now let's create an outlet from the view controller to the button. We propose to call this outlet button.

1. Start by considering the source and destination for this proposed outlet. In the Empty Window project, in *Main.storyboard*, select, and use the Identity inspector to identify the classes of, the objects involved. The class of the source object is ViewController. The class of the destination object is UIButton. This tells us that the ViewController class is going to need a button instance variable typed as a UIButton* (or some superclass of UIButton).

2. Now we'll make it so. Edit *ViewController.h*. Inside the @interface section, enter this line of code:

   ```
   @property IBOutlet UIButton* button;
   ```

   That's a property declaration. I haven't discussed property declarations yet (the details will appear in Chapter 12), so you'll just have to take my word that this will work — that it effectively equates to declaring an instance variable and accessor methods for it, in a single line. It isn't exactly the declaration I'd use in real life, but it will do for now. The key term here is IBOutlet; that's a hint to Xcode itself, a request saying that you'd like to be able to use this property as the name of an outlet

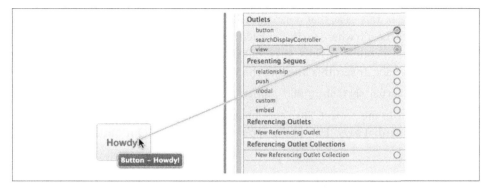

Figure 7-9. Connecting an outlet from the Connections inspector

when the source is a ViewController instance. The term `IBOutlet` is linguistically legal because, although Xcode can see the hint in your code, the compiler will treat it as equivalent to an empty string.

3. Edit *Main.storyboard* once again. Select View Controller and switch to the Connections inspector. An amazing thing has happened — there is now a `button` outlet listed here! That's because we used the magic word `IBOutlet` in our property declaration in the ViewController class. However, this outlet isn't yet hooked up to anything. In other words, the Connections inspector is telling us that the selected object (the View Controller) *can* be the source of a `button` outlet, but we have not in fact made it the source of a `button` outlet in this nib. To do so, drag from the circle, to the right of the word `button` in the Connections inspector, to the button — either the button in the canvas or its name in the document outline. A kind of stretchy line symbolizing the connection follows the mouse as you drag, and the button will be highlighted when the mouse is over it. At that moment, let go of the mouse (Figure 7-9).

The Connections inspector now reports that the `button` outlet is connected to our button. That's good, but we have not done anything to *prove* that this is the case. We have *made* an outlet, but we are not *using* the outlet for anything.

How can we use the outlet? Well, if our outlet is properly set up, then when our code runs, after our ViewController's main view is loaded from the nib, its `button` property will be a reference to the button that was instantiated from the nib and is now in the app's visible interface. So let's write some code that uses that `button` property to *change* something about that button. As the button is in the interface, we should be able to see the evidence of our change. We'll change the button's title:

1. Edit *ViewController.m*.

2. The `viewDidLoad` method runs *after* the view controller instance has obtained its main view. In this case, that means it will have loaded the nib containing its main view. That's the nib where we just created the `button` outlet, referring to our button. So by the time code here runs, `self.button` should point to the actual button that's in our interface. Insert this line into the `viewDidLoad` method:

   ```
   [self.button setTitle:@"Hi!" forState:UIControlStateNormal];
   ```

3. Build and run the project. Sure enough, even though the button says "Howdy!" in the storyboard, it says "Hi!" in the app's visible interface. Our outlet is working!

Misconfiguring an Outlet

Setting up an outlet to work correctly involves several things being true at the same time. I guarantee that at some point in the future you will fail to get this right, and your outlet won't work properly. Don't be offended, and don't be afraid; be prepared! This happens to everyone. The important thing is to recognize the symptoms so that you know what's gone wrong.

Wrong source class

Start with our working Empty Window example. Edit the storyboard. Use the Identity inspector to change the class of the scene's view controller to UIView-Controller. Run the project. We crash at launch time: "UIViewController ... class is not key value coding-compliant for the key button."

The wrong class is being instantiated as the outlet's source: instead of View-Controller, we're making a UIViewController instance. UIViewController, the built-in superclass of ViewController, has no `button` property (no `button` instance variable, no `setButton:` setter method). When we load the second nib to obtain the view controller's main view, it contains an outlet named `button`. The runtime can't match that up with anything in the outlet's source — the UIViewController instance — and we crash.

No instance variable in the source class

Fix the problem from the previous example by using the Identity inspector to change the class of the scene's view controller back to ViewController. Run the project to prove that all is well. Now comment out the `@property` declaration in *ViewController.h*; also comment out the `self.button` line in *ViewController.m*. Run the project. We crash at launch time: "ViewController ... class is not key value coding-compliant for the key button."

This is obviously the same problem in a different guise. We are instantiating the right class for the outlet's source, namely ViewController. But after having created an outlet named `button` in the nib, we have gone behind the nib editor's back and removed the corresponding instance variable from the outlet source's class. Again, when the nib loads, the runtime can't match the outlet's name with anything in the outlet's source — the ViewController instance — and we crash.

No outlet in the nib

Fix the problem from the previous example by uncommenting the line you commented out in *ViewController.h* and the line you commented out in *View-Controller.m*. Run the project to prove that all is well. Now edit the storyboard. Select the view controller and, in the Connections inspector, disconnect the `button` outlet by clicking the X at the left end of the second cartouche. Run the project. The app runs, but the button's title is still "Howdy!" — our attempt to change it to "Hi!" in ViewController's `viewDidLoad` method is *failing silently*.

This one is particularly insidious, and unbelievably common. We've set up the source object's class with the correct instance variable, and the nib editor is listing the outlet, but the outlet has no destination object. The result is that after the nib loads, the source object's `button` instance variable is nil. We then refer to `self.button` but it is nil. We send it the `setTitle:forState:` message, but this is a message to nil. Messages to nil don't cause any error, but they don't do anything either (see Chapter 3).

No view outlet

For this one, you'll have to use the Truly Empty example, because the storyboard editor guards against it. In the Truly Empty project, edit the *.xib* file. Select the File's Owner proxy object, switch to the Connections inspector, and disconnect the `view` outlet. Run the project. We crash at launch time: "loaded the 'ViewController' nib but the view outlet was not set."

The console message says it all. A nib that is to serve as the source of a view controller's main view *must* have a connected `view` outlet from the view controller (the nib owner proxy) to the view.

 A view controller has a `view` outlet because UIViewController's `view` property is marked as an outlet. Unfortunately, you can't see that marking. Nothing in the documentation for a built-in Cocoa class tells you *which* of its properties are also available as outlets! In general, the only way to learn what outlets a built-in class provides is to examine a representative of that class in the nib editor.

Deleting an Outlet

Deleting an outlet coherently — that is, without causing one of the problems described in the previous section — involves working in several places at once, just as creating an outlet does. I recommend proceeding in this order:

1. Disconnect the outlet in the nib.

2. Remove the outlet declaration from the code.

3. Attempt compilation and let the compiler catch any remaining issues for you.

Let's suppose, for example, that you decide to delete the button outlet from the Empty Window project. You would follow the same three-step procedure that I just outlined:

1. Disconnect the outlet in the nib. To do so, edit the storyboard, select the source object (the view controller), and disconnect the button outlet in the Connections inspector by clicking the X.

2. Remove the outlet declaration from the code. To do so, edit *ViewController.h* and delete or comment out the @property declaration line.

3. Remove other references to the property. The easiest way is to attempt to build the project; the compiler issues an error on the line referring to self.button in *ViewController.m*, because there is now no such property. Delete or comment out that line, and build again to prove that all is well.

More Ways to Create Outlets

Earlier, we created an outlet by manually declaring a property in a class's header file, and then dragging from the outlet's circle in the Connections inspector in the nib editor to connect the outlet. Xcode provides many other ways to create outlets — too many to list here. I'll survey some of the most interesting.

Start by deleting the outlet in our Empty Window project (if you haven't already done so). Instead of using the Connections inspector to specify the outlet in the nib, we'll use the HUD (heads-up display) attached to the destination object:

1. In *ViewController.h*, create (or uncomment) the property declaration:

   ```
   @property IBOutlet UIButton* button;
   ```

2. In the storyboard, Control-drag from the view controller itself to the button. The view controller is represented either by its label in the document outline (View Controller) or by the first icon in the scene dock. The button is represented either by its label in the document outline or by its graphical representation in the canvas.

3. When you release the mouse, a HUD appears, listing button as a possible outlet (Figure 7-10). Click button.

Again, delete the outlet. This time, we'll start in the HUD attached to the source object:

1. In *ViewController.h*, create (or uncomment) the property declaration.

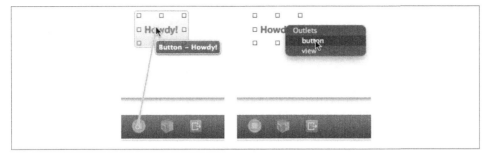

Figure 7-10. Connecting an outlet by Control-dragging from the source object

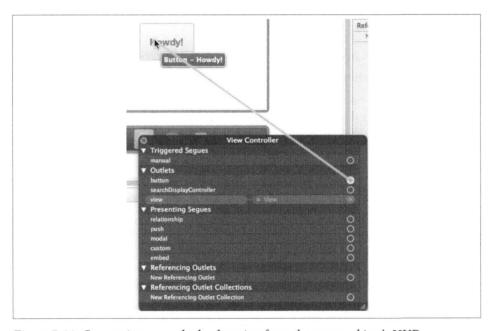

Figure 7-11. Connecting an outlet by dragging from the source object's HUD

2. Control-click the view controller. The view controller is represented either by its label in the document outline (View Controller) or by the first icon in the scene dock. A HUD appears, looking a lot like the Connections inspector.

3. Drag from the circle to the right of button to the button (Figure 7-11). Release the mouse.

Again, delete the outlet. This time, we'll start with the HUD attached to the destination object:

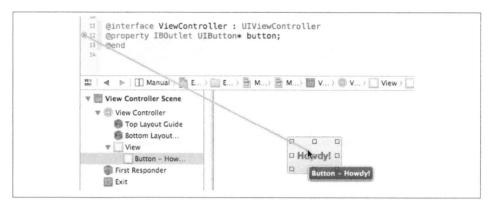

Figure 7-12. Connecting an outlet by dragging from code to nib editor

1. In *ViewController.h*, create (or uncomment) the property declaration.

2. Control-click the button. A HUD appears, looking a lot like the Connections inspector.

3. Locate the listing that says New Referencing Outlet. This means an outlet *from* something else *to* the thing we're inspecting, the button. Drag from the circle at its right to the view controller.

4. A second HUD appears, listing outlet names from the view controller. Click `button`.

Again, delete the outlet. Now we're going to create the outlet by dragging between the code and the nib editor. This will require that you work in two places at once: you're going to need an assistant pane. In the main editor pane, show *ViewController.h*. In the assistant pane, show the storyboard, in such a way that the button is visible.

1. In *ViewController.h*, create (or uncomment) the property declaration.

2. To the left of the property declaration, a circle appears in the gutter.

3. Drag from that circle across the pane boundary to the button in the nib editor (Figure 7-12), and release the mouse.

Again, delete the outlet. This time, we're going to create the code and connect the outlet, all in a single move! Use the two-pane arrangement from the preceding example.

1. Control-drag from the button in the nib editor across the pane boundary to the empty `@interface` section of *ViewController.h*.

2. A HUD offers to Insert Outlet, Action, or Outlet Collection (Figure 7-13). Release the mouse.

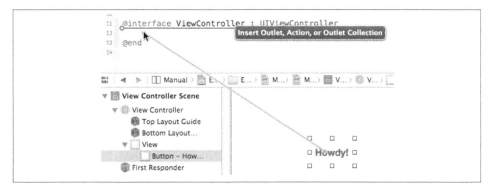

Figure 7-13. Creating an outlet by dragging from nib editor to code

Figure 7-14. Configuring a property declaration

3. A popover appears, where you can configure the declaration to be inserted into your code. Configure it as shown in Figure 7-14. Click Connect.

4. The property declaration is inserted into your code, and the outlet is connected in the nib, in a single move.

Making an outlet by connecting directly between code and the nib editor is extremely cool and convenient, but don't be fooled: there's no such direct connection. There are always, if an outlet is to work properly, *two distinct and separate things* — an instance variable in a class, and an outlet in the nib, *with the same name* and *coming from an instance of that class*. It is the identity of the names and classes that allows the two to be matched at runtime when the nib loads, so that the instance variable is properly set at that moment. Xcode tries to help you get everything set up correctly, but it is not in fact magically connecting the code to the nib.

When Xcode believes that an outlet is correctly set up, with an appropriate declaration in code and an appropriate connection in a nib, the circle to the left of the declaration in code is filled in. In addition to serving as a sign to you that the outlet should be working, you can click the filled circled to summon a pop-up menu telling you what's at the other end of the connection: click that menu item and you're switched to the nib editor, with the destination object selected.

Outlet Collections

An *outlet collection* is an NSArray instance variable (in code) matched (in a nib) by multiple connections to objects of the same type.

For example, suppose a class contains this property declaration:

```
@property IBOutletCollection(UIButton) NSArray* buttons;
```

Note the rather odd syntax: the term `IBOutletCollection` is accompanied by parentheses containing the name of a class, without an asterisk. The property itself is declared as an NSArray.

The outcome is that, in the nib editor, using an instance of this class as a source object, you can form *multiple* buttons outlets, each one connected to a different UIButton object in the nib. When the nib loads, those UIButton instances become the elements of the NSArray buttons; the order in which the outlets are formed is the order of the elements in the array.

The advantage of this arrangement is that your code can refer to multiple interface objects instantiated from the nib by number (the index into the array) rather than having to devise and manipulate a separate name for each one. This turns out to be particularly useful when forming outlets to such things as autolayout constraints and gesture recognizers.

Action Connections

In addition to outlet connections in a nib, there are also action connections. An action connection, like an outlet connection, is a way of giving one object in a nib a reference to another.

An *action* is a message emitted automatically by a Cocoa UIControl interface object (a *control*), and sent to another object, when the user does something to it, such as tapping the control. The various user behaviors that will cause a control to emit an action message are called *events*. To see a list of possible events, look at the UIControl class documentation, under "Control Events." For example, in the case of a UIButton, the user tapping the button corresponds to the `UIControlEventTouchUpInside` event.

For this architecture to work, the control object must know three things:

- What control event to respond to
- What message to send (method to call) when that control event occurs (the *action*)

- What object to send that message to (the *target*)

An action connection in a nib has the control object as its source; its destination is the target, to which the source will send the action message. Configuring the class of the destination object so that it has a method suitable as an action message is up to you.

As an example, let's arrange to use the view controller in our Empty Window project as a target for an action message emitted by the button's `UIControlEventTouchUpInside` event (meaning that the button was tapped). We'll need a method in the view controller that will be called by the button when the button is tapped. To make this method dramatic and obvious, we'll have the view controller put up an alert window. Insert this method into the implementation section in *ViewController.m*:

```
- (IBAction) buttonPressed: (id) sender {
    UIAlertView* av = [[UIAlertView alloc] initWithTitle:@"Howdy!"
                                            message:@"You tapped me."
                                            delegate:nil
                                    cancelButtonTitle:@"Cool"
                                    otherButtonTitles:nil];
    [av show];
}
```

The term `IBAction` is like `IBOutlet`: it's a hint to Xcode itself, and is linguistically legal because, although Xcode can see the hint in your code, the compiler will treat it as equivalent to `void`. It asks Xcode to make this method available in the nib editor as the selector of an action message, when an object of the class where this method is defined is the destination of an action connection. And indeed, if we look in the nib editor, we find that it *is* now available: select the View Controller object and switch to the Connections inspector, and you'll find that `buttonPressed:` is now listed under Received Actions.

As with an outlet connection, constructing an action connection is a two-step process. We have performed the first step: we've defined an action method. But we have not yet arranged for anything in the nib to call that method. To do so:

1. Starting in the View Controller object's Connections inspector, drag from the circle at the right of `buttonPressed:` to the button. Release the mouse.
2. A HUD listing control events appears. Click Touch Up Inside.

The action connection has now been formed. This means that when the app runs, any time the button gets a Touch Up Inside event — meaning that it was tapped — it will send the action message `buttonPressed:` to the target, which is the view controller instance. We know what that method should do: it should put up an alert. Try it! Build and run the app, and when the app appears running in the simulator, tap the button. It works!

As with outlet connections, action connections can be formed in many different ways. These are quite parallel to the ways in which outlet connections can be formed. For example, having created the action method in *ViewController.m*, you can connect the action:

- By Control-clicking the view controller. A HUD appears, similar to the Connections inspector. Proceed as in the previous case.

- By selecting the button and using the Connections inspector. Drag from the Touch Up Inside circle to the view controller. A HUD appears, listing the known action methods in the view controller; click buttonPressed:.

- By Control-clicking the button. A HUD appears, similar to the Connections inspector. Proceed as in the previous case.

It is also possible to connect between the code editor and the nib editor. Arrange to see *ViewController.m* in one pane and the storyboard in the other. The buttonPressed: method in *ViewController.m* has a circle to its left, in the gutter. You can drag from that circle across the pane boundary to the button in the nib.

As with an outlet connection, the most impressive way to make an action connection is to drag from the nib editor to your code, inserting the action method and forming the action connection in the nib in a single move. To try this, first delete the button-Pressed: method in your code so that there's no action connection in the nib. Now:

1. Control-drag from the button in the nib editor to an empty area in the @implementation section of *ViewController.m*. A HUD offering to Insert Action appears. Release the mouse.

2. A popover view appears, where you configure the action method you're about to create. Name it buttonPressed:, make sure the Event is set to Touch Up Inside (the default), and click Connect.

Xcode creates a stub method, and forms the corresponding action in the nib, in a single move:

```
- (IBAction)buttonPressed:(id)sender {
}
```

The method is just a stub (Xcode can't read your mind and guess what you want the method to do), so in real life, at this point, you'd insert some functionality between those curly braces.

As with an outlet connection, the filled circle next to the code in an action method tells you that Xcode believes that this connection is correctly configured, and you can click the filled circle to learn what object is (and navigate to) the source of the connection.

Connections Between Nibs

You cannot draw an outlet connection or an action connection between an object in one nib and an object in another nib, or (in a storyboard) between an object in one scene and an object in another scene. If you expect to be able to do this, you haven't understood what a nib is (or what a scene is, or what a connection is). The reason is simple: objects in a nib together will become instances together, at the moment when the nib loads, so it makes sense to connect them in the nib, because we know what instances we'll be talking about when the nib loads. If an outlet connection or an action connection were drawn from an object in one nib to an object in another nib, there would be no way to understand what actual future instances the connection is supposed to connect, because they are different nibs and will be loaded at different times (if ever). The problem of communicating between an instance generated from one nib and an instance generated from another nib is a special case of the more general problem of how to communicate between instances in a program, discussed in Chapter 13.

 A nib editor's Related Files menu includes actions and outlets connected to the currently selected object. This can be a rapid way to navigate, or simply to ascertain what's at the other end of a connection. An assistant pane, when there's a nib editor in the main pane, includes the same items in its Tracking menu; thus you can, for example, select an interface object in the nib editor to see instantly in the assistant pane the action method to which it is connected.

Additional Initialization of Nib-Based Instances

By the time a nib finishes loading, its instances are fully fledged; they have been initialized and configured with all the attributes dictated through the Attributes and Size inspectors, and their outlets have been used to set the values of the corresponding instance variables. Nevertheless, you might want to append your own code to the initialization process as an object is instantiated from a loading nib. This section describes some ways you can do that.

A common architecture is the one we've been using throughout this chapter, where a view controller, functioning as the owner when a nib containing its main view loads (and therefore represented in the nib by the nib owner proxy object), has an outlet to an interface object instantiated from the nib. In this architecture, the view controller can perform further configuration on that interface object, because it has a reference to it after the nib loads. The earliest place where it can do this is in its viewDidLoad method. That's why we used viewDidLoad, earlier in this chapter, as a place to put our code changing the button's title from "Howdy!" to "Hi!".

Another possibility is that you'd like the nib object to configure itself, over and above whatever configuration has been performed in the nib. Often, this will be because you've got a custom subclass of a built-in interface object class — in fact, you might want to create a custom class, just so you have a place to put this self-configuring code. The problem you're trying to solve might be that the nib editor doesn't let you perform the configuration you're after, or that you have many objects that need to be configured in some identical, elaborate way, so that it makes more sense for them to configure themselves by virtue of sharing a common class than to configure each one individually in the nib editor.

One approach is to implement `awakeFromNib` in your custom class. The `awakeFromNib` message is sent to all nib-instantiated objects just after they are instantiated by the loading of the nib: the object has been initialized and configured and its connections are operational.

For example, let's make a button whose background color is always red, regardless of how it's configured in the nib. (This is a nutty example, but it's dramatically effective.) In the Empty Window project, we'll create a button subclass, MyRedButton:

1. In the Project navigator, choose File → New → File. Specify an iOS Cocoa Touch Objective-C class. Click Next.

2. Call the new class MyRedButton. Make it a subclass of UIButton. Click Next.

3. Make sure you're saving into the project folder, with the Empty Window group, and make sure the Empty Window app target is checked. Click Create. Xcode creates *MyRedButton.h* and *MyRedButton.m*.

4. In *MyRedButton.m*, in the implementation section, implement `awakeFromNib`:
   ```
   - (void) awakeFromNib {
       [super awakeFromNib];
       self.backgroundColor = [UIColor redColor];
   }
   ```

We now have a UIButton subclass that turns itself red when it's instantiated from a nib. But we have no instance of this subclass in any nib. Let's fix that. Edit the storyboard, select the button, and use the Identity inspector to change this button's class to MyRedButton.

Now build and run the project. Sure enough, the button is red!

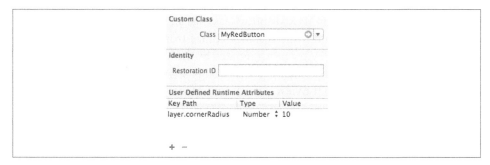

Figure 7-15. Rounding a button's corners with a runtime attribute

OS X Programmer Alert

If you're an experienced OS X programmer, you may be accustomed to rarely or never calling `super` from `awakeFromNib`; doing so used to raise an exception, in fact. In iOS, you must always call `super` in `awakeFromNib`. Another major difference is that in OS X, a nib owner's `awakeFromNib` is called when the nib loads, so it's possible for an object to be sent `awakeFromNib` multiple times; in iOS, `awakeFrom-Nib` is sent to an object only once, namely when that object is itself instantiated from a nib.

A further possibility is to take advantage of the User Defined Runtime Attributes in the nib object's Identity inspector. This allows to you to send a `setValue:forKey:` message to the object as it is instantiated from the nib. (Actually, it's a `setValue:forKeyPath:` message; key paths are discussed in Chapter 12.) This can allow you to configure, in the nib editor, aspects of a nib object for which the nib editor itself provides no built-in interface. Naturally, the object needs to be prepared to respond to the given key, or your app will crash when the nib loads.

For example, one of the disadvantages of the nib editor is that it provides no way to configure layer attributes. Let's say we'd like to use the nib editor to round the corners of our red button. In code, we would do that by setting the button's `layer.corner-Radius`. The nib editor gives no access to this property. Instead, we can select the button in the nib and use the User Defined Runtime Attributes. We set the Key Path to `layer.cornerRadius`, the Type to Number, and the Value to whatever value we want — let's say 10 (Figure 7-15). Now build and run; sure enough, the button's corners are now rounded.

To intervene with a nib object's initialization even earlier, if the object is a UIView (or a UIView subclass) or a UIViewController (or a UIViewController subclass), you can implement `initWithCoder:`. Note that `initWithCoder:` is *not* the initializer that is stubbed out for you by the template; instead, for a UIView subclass, you are given `init-WithFrame:`. For example, our MyRedButton class has an `initWithFrame:` stub. However, this will do you no good if the instance comes from a nib, because `initWith-Frame:` is *not called* when a UIView is instantiated by the loading of a nib — `initWith-Coder:` is called instead. (Implementing `initWithFrame:`, and then wondering why your code isn't working when the view is instantiated from a nib, is a common beginner mistake.)

A possible reason for implementing `initWithCoder:` would be the same reason why you'd implement any initializer — namely, to initialize additional instance variables declared by your subclass. The structure of `initWithCoder:` is much like the structure of any initializer (see Chapter 5): you'll call `super` at the start, and return `self` at the end:

```
- (id) initWithCoder:(NSCoder *)aDecoder {
    self = [super initWithCoder:aDecoder];
    if (self) {
        self->_myIvar = // whatever
    }
    return self;
}
```

CHAPTER 8

Documentation

> *Knowledge is of two kinds. We know a subject*
> *ourselves, or we know where we can find*
> *information upon it.*
>
> —Samuel Johnson, *Boswell's Life of Johnson*

No aspect of iOS programming is more important than a fluid and nimble relationship with the documentation. There is a huge number of built-in classes, with many methods and properties and other details. Apple's documentation, whatever its flaws, is the definitive official word on how you can expect Cocoa Touch to behave and on the contractual rules incumbent upon you in working with this massive framework whose inner workings you cannot see directly.

The Xcode documentation installed on your machine comes in large chunks called *documentation sets* (or *doc sets*, also called *libraries*). You do not merely install a documentation set; you subscribe to it, so that when Apple releases a documentation update, you can obtain the updated version.

When you first install Xcode, the bulk of the documentation is *not* installed on your machine; viewing the documentation in the documentation window (discussed in the next section) may require an Internet connection, so that you can see the online docs at Apple's site. This situation is untenable; you're going to want a copy of the documentation locally, on your own machine.

Therefore, you should start up Xcode immediately after installation to let it download and install your initial documentation sets. The process can be controlled and monitored, to some extent, in the Downloads pane of the Preferences window (under Documentation); you can also specify here whether you want updates installed automatically or whether you want to click Check and Install Now manually from time to time. This is also where you specify which doc sets you want; I believe that the iOS 7 doc set and the Xcode 5 doc set are all you need for iOS development, but I have also heard rumors that the documentation window (discussed in the next section) does not work properly unless you also install the OS X 10.8 or 10.9 doc set. You may have to provide your machine's admin password when a doc set is first installed.

In Xcode 5, doc sets are installed in your home *Library/Developer/Shared/Documentation/DocSets* directory.

 Unlike earlier versions of Xcode, Xcode 5 doesn't let you access older doc sets. A third-party application such as Dash can be helpful here (*http://kapeli.com/dash*).

The Documentation Window

Your primary access to the documentation is in Xcode, through the documentation window (Help → Documentation and API Reference, Command-Option-Shift-?). Within the documentation window, the primary way into the documentation is to do a search; for example, press Command-Option-Shift-? (or Command-L if you're already in the documentation window), type NSString, and press Return to select the top hit, which is the NSString Class Reference. Click the magnifying glass icon to limit the results to the iOS-related doc sets if desired.

There are two ways to see the results of a search in the documentation window:

Pop-up results window
> If you're actively typing in the search field, a dozen or so primary results are listed in a pop-up window. Click with the mouse, or navigate with arrow keys and press Return, to specify which result you want to view. You can also summon and hide this pop-up window whenever the search field has focus, by pressing Esc.

Full results page
> When the search field has focus and the pop-up results window is *not* showing, press Return to see a page listing *all* results of the search; these results are listed on four separate pages, by category: API Reference, SDK Guides, Tools Guides, and Sample Code.

You can also perform a documentation window search starting from within your code. You'll very often want to do this: you're looking right at a symbol actually being used in your code (a class name, a method name, a property name, and so on) and you want to know more about it. Hold Option and hover the mouse over a term in your code until a blue dotted underline appears; then (still holding Option) double-click the term. The documentation window opens, and you are taken directly to the explanation of that term within its class documentation page. (Similarly, during code completion — discussed in Chapter 9 — you can click the More link to make this same move, jumping directly to the documentation on the current symbol.)

Alternatively, you can select text in your code (or anywhere else) and choose Help →
Search Documentation for Selected Text (Command-Option-Control-/). This is the
equivalent of typing that text into the search field in the documentation window and
asking to see the full results page.

The documentation window behaves basically as a glorified web browser, because the
documentation consists essentially of web pages. Indeed, most of the same pages can
be accessed at Apple's developer site, *http://developer.apple.com*; and you can open in
your web browser the page you're currently viewing in the documentation window:
choose Editor → Share → Open in Browser, or click the Share button in the window
toolbar and choose Open in Safari. Multiple pages can appear simultaneously as tabs in
the documentation window: hold Command as you navigate, to navigate to a new tab
— for example, Command-click a link, or Command-click your choice in the pop-up
results window — or choose Open Link in New Tab from the contextual menu. You can
navigate between tabs (Window → Select Next Tab), and each tab remembers its navigation history (Navigate → Go Back, or use the Back button in the window toolbar,
which is also a pop-up menu).

A documentation page may be accompanied by an additional table of contents or additional details, or both. These are displayed in the Info pane at the right of the documentation window; to see it if it isn't showing, choose Editor → Show Info, or click the
rightmost button in the toolbar. The Table of Contents and Details are separate subpanes
within the Info pane; to switch between them, click one of the icons at the top of the
Info pane. For example, the NSString Class Reference page has a table of contents subpane linking to all the topics within the page, and a Details subpane linking to NSString's
class inheritance, its adopted protocols, and so forth. I'll talk more about a class's details
later in this chapter. Some documentation pages may use the table of contents subpane
to show the page's place within a larger group of pages; for example, the String Programming Guide consists of multiple pages, and when you're viewing one, the Table of
Contents subpane lists all the pages of the String Programming Guide along with each
page's main topics.

When you encounter a documentation page to which you're likely to want to return,
make it a bookmark: choose Editor → Share → Add Bookmark or click the Share button
in the toolbar and choose Add Bookmark, or (easiest of all) click the bookmark icon in
the left margin of the documentation page. Bookmarks are displayed in a pane at the
left of the documentation window; to see it if it isn't showing, choose Editor → Show
Bookmarks, or click the second-from-the-right button in the toolbar. Documentation
bookmark management is simple but effective: you can rearrange bookmarks or delete
a bookmark, and that's all.

To search for text *within* the current documentation page, use the Find menu commands. Find → Find (Command-F) summons a find bar, as in Safari.

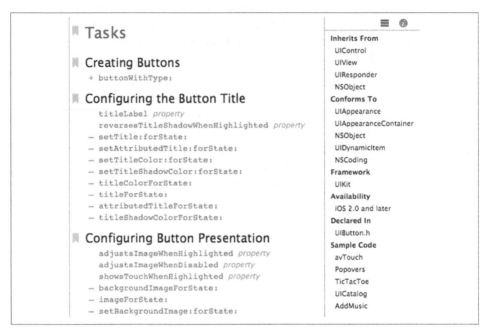

Figure 8-1. *The start of the UIButton class documentation page*

 Unlike earlier versions of Xcode, Xcode 5 provides no overall documentation table of contents, and it doesn't let you access a doc set's "home page" listing all of that doc set's documents. That page is present, however, and you can view it in your browser. I recommend that you locate the iOS 7 doc set inside your home *Library/Developer/Shared/Documentation/DocSets* folder, open it in the Finder with the Show Package Contents contextual menu command, drill down to *Contents/Resources/Documents/navigation/index.html*, drag that file into your browser, and bookmark it.

Class Documentation Pages

In the vast majority of cases, your target documentation page will be the documentation for a class. It's important to be comfortable and conversant with the typical features and information provided by a class documentation page, so let's pause to notice them (Figure 8-1).

A class documentation page makes particularly good use of the Details subpane of the documentation window's Info pane, and it's important to keep an eye on the Details information when you're studying the class (in the web browser presentation, this information appears at the top of the class documentation page itself):

Inherits From

Lists, and links to, the chain of superclasses. One of the biggest beginner mistakes is failing to consult the documentation up the superclass chain. A class inherits from its superclasses, so the functionality or information you're looking for may be in a superclass. You won't find out about `addTarget:action:forControlEvents:` from the UIButton class page; that information is in the UIControl class page. You won't find out that a UIButton has a `frame` property from the UIButton class page; that information is in the UIView class page.

Conforms To

Lists, and links to, the protocols adopted by this class. Protocols are discussed in Chapter 10.

Framework

Tells what framework this class is part of. Your code must link to this framework, and import this framework's header, in order to use this class (see Chapter 6).

Availability

States the earliest version of the operating system where this class is implemented. For example, UIDynamicAnimator (along with UIKit dynamics in general) wasn't invented until iOS 7. So if you want to use this feature in your app, you must make sure either that your app targets only iOS 7 or later, or that your code never uses this class when your app is running on an earlier system.

Declared In

The header(s) where this class is declared. Unfortunately this is not a link; I have not found any quick way to view a header starting from within the documentation. That's a pity, as it can often be worth looking at the header file, which may contain helpful comments or other details. You can open the header file from your project window, as explained later in this chapter.

Sample Code

If a class documentation page links to sample code, you might want to examine that code. (But see my remarks on sample code in the next section of this chapter.)

Related

If a class documentation page lists a related guide, you might want to click that link and read that guide. For example, the UIView class documentation page lists (and links to) the *View Programming Guide for iOS*. Guides are broad surveys of a topic; they provide important information (including, often, useful code examples), and they can serve to orient your thinking and make you aware of your options.

The body of the class documentation page is divided into sections, which are listed in the Table of Contents subpane of the Info pane:

Overview

Some class pages provide extremely important introductory information in the Overview section, including links to related guides and further information. (See the UIView class documentation page for an example.)

Tasks

This section lists in categorical order, and links to, the properties and methods that appear later on the page. Often, just looking over this list can give you the hint you're looking for.

Properties, Class Methods, Instance Methods

These sections provide the full documentation for this class's properties and methods. (A property *is* a method — usually two methods, a getter accessor and a setter accessor — but the documentation lists the property rather than the accessors.)

Constants

Many classes define constants that accompany particular methods. For example, to create a UIButton instance in code, you can call the `buttonWithType:` class method; the argument value will be a constant, listed under UIButtonType in the Constants section. (To help you get there, there's a link from the `buttonWithType:` method to the UIButtonType section in Constants.) There's a formal definition of the constant; you won't usually care about this (but do see Chapter 1 if you don't know how to read it). Then each value is explained, and the value name is suitable for copying and pasting into your code.

Finally, let's talk about how a class documentation page lists and explains individual properties and methods. In recent years, this part of the documentation has become quite splendid, with good hyperlinks. Note the following subsections, after the property or method name:

Description

A short summary of what the property or method does.

Formal declaration

Read this to learn things like the method's parameters and return type. (Chapter 12 explains how to read a property declaration.)

Parameters and Return Value

Precise information on the meaning and purpose of these.

Discussion

Often contains extremely important further details about how this method behaves. Always pay attention to this section!

Availability

An old class can acquire new methods as the operating system advances; if a newer method is crucial to your app, you might want to exclude your app from running on older operating systems that don't implement the method.

See Also

Lists and links to related methods. Very helpful for giving you a larger perspective on how this method fits into the overall behavior of this class.

Related Sample Code

It can sometimes be worth consulting the sample code to see how this method is used in real life.

Declared In

The relevant header file.

 Methods injected into a class by a category (Chapter 10) are often *not* listed on that class's documentation page and can be very difficult to discover. For example, awakeFromNib (discussed in Chapter 7) isn't mentioned in the documentation for UIButton or for any of its superclasses or protocols. This is a major weakness in Apple's organization and display of the documentation. A third-party documentation display application such as AppKiDo (*http://appkido.com*) can be helpful here.

Sample Code

Apple provides plenty of sample code projects. You can view the code directly in the documentation window; sometimes this will be sufficient, but you can see only one class implementation or header file at a time, so it's difficult to get an overview. The alternative is to open the sample code project in Xcode; click the Open Project button at the top of a sample code page in the documentation window. If you're looking at the sample code in your browser at *http://developer.apple.com*, there's a Download Sample Code button. With the sample code project open as a project window, you can read the code, navigate it, edit it, and of course run the project.

As a form of documentation, sample code is both good and bad. It can be a superb source of working code that you can often copy and paste and use with very little alteration in your own projects. It is usually heavily commented, because the Apple folks are aware, as they write the code, that it is intended for instructional purposes. Sample code also illustrates concepts that users have difficulty extracting from the documentation. (Users who have not grasped UITouch handling, for instance, often find that the lightbulb goes on when they discover the MoveMe example.) But the logic of a project is often spread over multiple files, and nothing is more difficult to understand than someone else's code (except, perhaps, your own code). Moreover, what learners most need is not the *fait accompli* of a fully written project but the reasoning process that constructed the project, which no amount of commentary can provide.

My own assessment is that Apple's sample code is uneven. Some of it is a bit careless or even faulty, while some of it is astoundingly well-written. It is generally thoughtful and instructive, though, and is definitely a major component of the documentation; it deserves more appreciation and usage than it seems to get. But it is most useful, I think, after you've reached a certain level of competence and comfort.

Other Resources

Here is a survey of other useful resources that supplement the documentation.

Quick Help

Quick Help is a condensed rendering of the documentation on some single topic, usually a symbol name (a class or method). It appears with regard to the current selection or insertion point automatically in the Quick Help inspector (Command-Option-2) if the inspector is showing. Thus, for example, if you're editing code and the insertion point or selection is within the term CGPointMake, documentation for CGPointMake appears in the Quick Help inspector if it is visible.

Quick Help is also available in the Quick Help inspector for interface objects selected in the nib editor, for build settings while editing a project or target, and so forth.

Quick Help documentation can also be displayed as a popover window, without the Quick Help inspector. Select a term and choose Help → Quick Help for Selected Item (Command-Control-Shift-?). Alternatively, hold down Option and hover the mouse over a term until the cursor becomes a question mark (and the term turns blue with a dashed underline); then Option-click the term.

The Quick Help documentation contains links. For example, click the Reference link to open the full documentation in the documentation window; click the header link to open the appropriate header file.

New in Xcode 5, you can inject documentation for your own methods into Quick Help. To do so, you'll need to write a comment in either doxygen format (see *http://www.stack.nl/~dimitri/doxygen/*) or HeaderDoc format (search on "HeaderDoc" at *http://developer.apple.com*). I recommend doxygen, as being a *de facto* standard. The comment will precede the declaration or definition of a method (or the declaration of a property). For example:

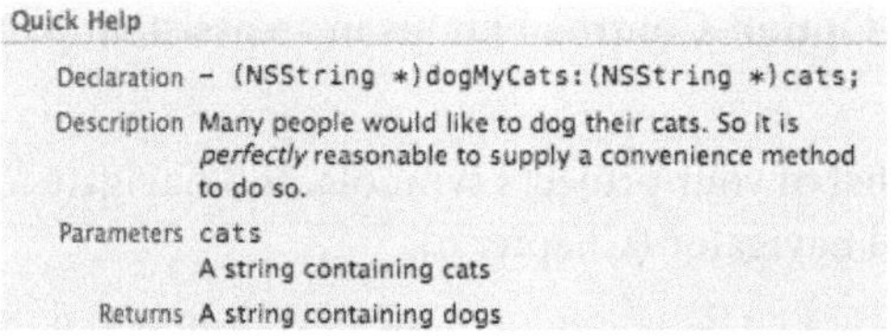

Quick Help	
Declaration	– (NSString *)dogMyCats:(NSString *)cats;
Description	Many people would like to dog their cats. So it is *perfectly* reasonable to supply a convenience method to do so.
Parameters	cats
	A string containing cats
Returns	A string containing dogs

Figure 8-2. Documentation for a custom method, injected into Quick Help

```
/*!
 Many people would like to dog their cats. So it is \e perfectly
 reasonable to supply a convenience method to do so.

 \param cats A string containing cats
 \return A string containing dogs
 */

- (NSString*) dogMyCats: (NSString*) cats {
    return @"Dogs";
}
```

The exclamation mark in the opening comment delimiter denotes that this is a doxygen comment, and the comment's location automatically associates it with the dogMy-Cats: method whose definition follows. The backslashed expressions \e, \param, and \return are doxygen commands. The outcome is that when dogMyCats: is selected anywhere in my code, its documentation is displayed in Quick Help (Figure 8-2). The doxygen method description (or a \brief description if you supply one) is also displayed as part of code completion (see Chapter 9).

Symbols

A *symbol* is a nonlocally defined term, such as the name of a class, method, or instance variable. If you can see the name of a symbol in your code in an editor in Xcode, you can jump quickly to the definition of the symbol. Select text and choose Navigate → Jump to Definition (Command-Control-J). Alternatively, hold down Command and hover the mouse over a prospective term, until the cursor becomes a pointing finger (and the term becomes blue with a solid underline); Command-click the term to jump to the definition for that symbol.

If the symbol is defined in a Cocoa framework, you jump to the declaration in the header file. If the symbol is defined in your code, you jump to the class or method definition; this can be very helpful not only for understanding your code but also for navigating it.

The precise meaning of the notion "jump" depends upon the modifier keys you use in addition to the Command key, and on your settings in the Navigation pane of Xcode's preferences. By default, Command-click jumps in the same editor, Command-Option-click jumps in an assistant pane, and Command-double-click jumps in a new window. Similarly, Command-Option-Control-J jumps in an assistant pane to the definition of the selected term.

Another way to see a list of your project's symbols, and navigate to a symbol definition, is through the Symbol navigator (Chapter 6).

An important and often neglected way to jump to a symbol definition whose name you know, even if you can't see the name in the code before you, is to choose File → Open Quickly (Command-Shift-O). In the search field, type key letters from the name, which will be interpreted intelligently; for example, to search for `applicationDidFinish-Launching:`, you might type "appdid". Possible matches are shown in a scrolling list below the search field; you can navigate this list with the mouse or by keyboard alone. Definitions in your own code are listed before declarations from Cocoa headers, so this, too, can be a rapid way of navigating your code.

Header Files

Sometimes a header file can be a useful form of documentation. It compactly summarizes a class's instance variables and methods and may contain comments with helpful information that might be provided nowhere else. A single header file can contain declarations for multiple class interfaces and protocols. So it can be an excellent quick reference.

There are various ways to see a header file from an Xcode editor:

- If the class is your own and you're in the implementation file, choose Navigate → Jump to Next Counterpart (Command-Control-Up).
- Show the jump bar's Related Files menu (Control-1). The menu lets you jump to any header files imported in the current file (as well as any files that import the current file) and to the header files of the current class file's superclasses and subclasses and so forth. Hold Option to jump in an assistant pane.
- Select text and choose File → Open Quickly (Command-Shift-O), as I explained in the previous section.
- Command-click a symbol, choose Navigate → Jump to Definition, or pass through Quick Help, as described in the previous sections.
- Use the Symbol navigator.

All of these approaches require that a project window be open; File → Open Quickly requires an active SDK for effective operation, and the others all operate on specific windows or words in an open project. An alternative that works under all circumstances, even when no project is open, is to switch to the Terminal and use the `open -h` command to open a header file in Xcode. The argument may represent part of a header file's name.

The command is interactive if there's an ambiguity; for example, `open -h NSString` proposes to open *NSString.h* or *NSStringDrawing.h* (or both, or neither). I wish this command were built into Xcode itself.

Internet Resources

Programming has become a lot easier since the Internet came along and Google started indexing it. It's amazing what you can find out with a Google search. Your problem is very likely one that someone else has faced, solved, and written about on the Internet. Often you'll find sample code that you can paste into your project and adapt.

Apple's documentation resources are available at *http://developer.apple.com*. These resources are updated before the changes are rolled into your doc sets for download. There are also some materials here that aren't part of the Xcode documentation on your computer. As a registered iOS developer, you have access to iTunes videos, including the videos for all WWDC 2013 sessions (as well as for some earlier years), and to Apple's developer forums (*https://devforums.apple.com*). Also, much of Apple's documentation comes in an alternative PDF format, convenient for storing and viewing on an iPad. Even better, Ole Zorn's Docsets app will let you download and browse entire doc sets on an iPad or iPhone; it isn't freeware, but it's open source (*https://github.com/omz/DocSets-for-iOS*), so it's free if you're willing to build it yourself.

Apple maintains some public mailing lists (*http://lists.apple.com/mailman/listinfo*). I have long subscribed to the Xcode-users group (for questions about use of the Xcode tools) and the Cocoa-dev group (for questions about programming Cocoa). The lists are searchable, but Apple's own search doesn't work very well; you're better off using Google with a `site:lists.apple.com` term, or *http://www.cocoabuilder.com*, which archives the lists. Apple has not added a mailing list devoted to iOS programming; that's what the developer forums are supposed to be for, but the interface for these is extraordinarily clunky, and this — plus the lack of openness (to Google and to the world in general) — has limited their usefulness.

Other online resources, such as forums, have sprung up spontaneously as iOS programming has become more popular, and lots of iOS and Cocoa programmers blog about their experiences. I am particularly fond of Stack Overflow (*http://www.stackoverflow.com*); it isn't devoted exclusively to iOS programming, of course, but lots of iOS programmers hang out there, questions are answered succinctly and correctly, and the interface lets you focus on the right answer quickly and easily.

CHAPTER 9

Life Cycle of a Project

This chapter surveys some of the main stages in the life cycle of an Xcode project, from inception to submission at the App Store. This survey will provide an opportunity to discuss some additional features of the Xcode development environment. You already know how to create a project, define a class, and link to a framework (Chapter 6), as well as how to create and edit a nib (Chapter 7) and how to use the documentation (Chapter 8).

Device Architecture and Conditional Code

As you create a project (File → New → Project), after you pick a project template, in the screen where you name your project, the Devices pop-up menu offers a choice of iPad, iPhone, or Universal. You can change this setting later (using the Devices pop-up menu in the General tab when you edit the app target), but your life will be simpler if you decide correctly here, at the outset, because it affects the details of the template on which your new project will be based.

The iPhone and iPad differ in their physical characteristics as well as their programming interfaces. The iPad has a larger screen size, along with some built-in interface features that don't exist on the iPhone, such as split views and popovers. A universal app runs on both iPhone and iPad natively, typically with a different interface on each type of device.

Your choice in the Devices pop-up menu also affects your project's Targeted Device Family build setting:

iPad
    The app will run only on an iPad.

iPhone
> The app will run on an iPhone or iPod touch; it can also run on an iPad, but not as a native iPad app (it runs in a reduced enlargeable window, which I call the *iPhone Emulator*; Apple sometimes refers to this as "compatibility mode").

iPhone/iPad
> The app will run natively on both kinds of device, and should be structured as a universal app.

 If you're updating an older app for iOS 7, and if you want it to run natively on a 64-bit device, change the Architectures build setting for your app target to "Standard architectures (including 64-bit)."

Two additional project-level build settings determine what systems your device will run on:

Base SDK
> The *latest* system your app can run on. As of this writing, in Xcode 5.0, you have just two choices, iOS 7.0 and Latest iOS (iOS 7.0). They sound the same, but the latter is better (and is the default for a new project). If you update Xcode to develop for a subsequent system, any existing projects that are already set to Latest iOS will use that newer system's most recent SDK as their Base SDK automatically, without your also having to update their Base SDK setting.

iOS Deployment Target
> The *earliest* system your app can run on: in Xcode 5.0, this can be any major iOS system all the way back to 4.3. To change the project's iOS Deployment Target setting easily, edit the project and switch to the Info tab, and choose from the iOS Deployment Target pop-up menu. (To change the target's iOS Deployment Target setting easily, edit the target and switch to the General tab, and choose from the Deployment Target pop-up menu; usually, however, you'll change this setting at project level and let the target adopt the project's setting automatically.)

Writing an app whose Deployment Target differs from its Base SDK is something of a challenge. There are two chief problems:

Unsupported features
> With each new system, Apple adds new features. Xcode will happily allow you to compile using any features of the Base SDK, even if they don't exist on the Deployment Target system; but your app will crash if execution encounters features not supported by the system on which it is actually running. Thus, if you were to set the project's Deployment Target to iOS 6, your project would compile and your app would run on iOS 6 even if it contained iOS 7–only features, but your app would crash on iOS 6 if any of those features were actually *encountered*.

Changed behavior

With each new system, Apple permits itself to change the way some features work. The result is that such features work differently on different systems. In some cases, the very same method may do two quite different things, depending on what system the app runs on. In other cases, an area of functionality may be handled differently on different systems, requiring you to implement or call a different set of methods.

Thus, backwards compatibility will probably require that you write *conditional code* — that is, code such that one set of code executes when running on one system, another when running on another. But it isn't merely a matter of code. A project can contain other resources, such as a nib file, that might not be compatible with earlier systems. (For example, a nib file that uses autolayout will crash when it is loaded on iOS 5.1 or earlier, because autolayout uses the NSLayoutConstraint class, which didn't exist back then.)

Even if you're *not* attempting backwards compatibility, you *still* might need to grapple with the problem of conditional code — if you want to write a universal app. Although you'll probably want to reduce duplication by sharing code between the iPhone and the iPad version of the app, nevertheless some code will likely have to be kept separate, because your app will need to behave differently on the different types of device. As I already mentioned, you can't summon a popover on an iPhone; and the complexities can run considerably deeper, because the overall interfaces might be quite different, and might behave very differently — tapping a table cell on the iPhone might summon an entire new screenful of stuff, whereas on the larger iPad, it might only alter what appears in one region of the screen.

Various programming devices help govern dynamically what code is encountered, based on what system or device type the app is running on; thus you can steer your code away from a crash or from undesirable behavior based on the runtime environment:

Explicit environment test

The UIDevice class lets you query the current device (`currentDevice`) to learn its system version (`systemVersion`) and type (`userInterfaceIdiom`).

For an actual example, make a Universal project from the Master–Detail Application template and look in *AppDelegate.m*. You'll see code in `application:did-FinishLaunchingWithOptions:` that configures the initial interface differently depending on the device type we're running on.

Info.plist key name suffix

Info.plist settings can be made to apply only to one device type or the other, by adding `~iphone` or `~ipad` to the name of the key. If the suffix is present, this setting overrides the general setting (without any suffix) on the appropriate device.

A Universal project based on the Master–Detail Application template is a case in point. You'll see that the *Info.plist* contains two sets of "Supported interface orientations" settings, a general set (`UISupportedInterfaceOrientations`) and an iPad-only set that overrides the general case when the app launches on an iPad (`UISupportedInterfaceOrientations~ipad`).

Similarly, a Universal project based on the Master-Detail Application template contains two storyboards, one supplying the interface for running on an iPhone, the other for an iPad. The choice between them is made through the *Info.plist* setting "Main storyboard file base name", which appears twice, once for the general case (`UIMainStoryboardFile`) and once for iPad only (`UIMainStoryboardFile~ipad`), the latter overriding the former when the app launches on an iPad.

Resource name suffix

Many calls that load resources by name from your app's bundle will use the same name-and-suffix rules as for *Info.plist* keys, automatically selecting an alternative resource whose name (before the extension) ends with ~iphone or ~ipad as appropriate to the device type, if there is such an alternative resource. For example, UIImage's `imageNamed:` method, if you specify the image name as `@"linen.png"`, will load an image called *linen~ipad.png* if it finds one and if we're running on an iPad.

(New in Xcode 5, however, if the image lives in an asset catalog, you won't have to worry about this naming convention: the image's use is determined by its place in the catalog. Select an image set in the catalog and choose Device Specific from the Devices pop-up menu in the Attributes inspector to create distinct slots for iPhone and iPad versions of an image. This is one reason among many for using asset catalogs!)

Weak-linked frameworks

If your app is linked to a framework and tries to run on a system that lacks that framework, it will crash at launch time. The solution is to link to that framework optionally, by changing the Required pop-up menu item in its listing in the target's Linked Frameworks and Libraries build phase to Optional; this is technically referred to as *weak-linking* the framework.

(This technique works even if you're using the new Xcode 5 modules feature — see Chapter 6 — but you'll have to link explicitly to any frameworks you want to weak-link, to make them appear in the Linked Frameworks and Libraries list; there's no way to specify weak autolinking.)

Method testing

You can test for the existence of a method using `respondsToSelector:` and related NSObject calls:

```
if ([UIButton respondsToSelector: @selector(appearance)]) {
    // ok to call appearance class method
} else {
    // don't call appearance class method
}
```

Class testing

You can test for the existence of a class using the `NSClassFromString` function, which yields nil if the class doesn't exist. Also, if the Base SDK is 5.0 or later, and if the class's framework is present or weak-linked, you can send the class any message (such as `class`) and test the result for nil; this works because classes are themselves weak-linked starting in iOS 5:

```
// assume Core Image framework is weak-linked
if ([CIFilter class]) { // ok to do things with CIFilter
```

Constant and function testing

You can test for the existence of a constant name, including the name of a C function, by taking the name's address and testing against zero. For example:

```
if (&UIApplicationWillEnterForegroundNotification) {
    // OK to refer to UIApplicationWillEnterForegroundNotification
```

Version Control

Sooner rather than later in the life of any real app, you should consider putting your project under version control. Version control is a way of taking periodic snapshots (technically called *commits*) of your project. Its purpose might be:

Security

Version control can help you store your commits in a repository offsite, so that your code isn't lost in case of a local computer glitch or some equivalent "hit by a bus" scenario.

Collaboration

Version control allows multiple developers ready and rational access to the same code.

Freedom from fear

A project is a complicated thing; often, changes must be made experimentally, sometimes in many files, possibly over a period of many days, before a new feature can be tested. Version control means that I can easily retrace my steps (to some previous commit) if things go badly; this gives me confidence to start down some tentative programmatic road whose outcome may not be apparent until much later. Also, if I'm confused about what programmatic road I seem to be taking, I can ask a version control system to list the changes I've made recently. If an ancillary bug is introduced, I can use version control to pinpoint when it happened and help discover the cause.

Xcode provides various version control facilities, which are geared chiefly to git (*http://git-scm.com*) and Subversion (*http://subversion.apache.org*, also called svn). This doesn't mean you can't use any other version control system with your projects! It means only that you can't use any other version control system in an integrated fashion from inside Xcode. That's no disaster; there are many other ways to use version control, and even with git and Subversion, it is perfectly possible to ignore Xcode's integrated version control and rely on the command line in Terminal, or use a specialized third-party GUI front end such as svnX for Subversion (*http://www.lachoseinteractive.net/en/products*) or SourceTree for git (*http://www.sourcetreeapp.com*).

If you *don't* want to use Xcode's integrated version control, you can turn it off more or less completely. If you uncheck Enable Source Control in the Source Control preference pane, the only thing you'll be able to do is choose Check Out from the Source Control menu, to fetch code from a remote server. If you check Enable Source Control, three additional checkboxes let you select which automatic behaviors you want. Personally, I like to check Enable Source Control along with "Refresh local status automatically", so that Xcode displays a file's status in the Project navigator; I leave the two additional checkboxes unchecked, because I'm a manual control kind of person. (The ability to uncheck "Add and remove files automatically" in Xcode 5 is particularly welcome; Xcode 4's habit of adding files to the git index the moment I added them to the project was an annoyance.)

When you create a new project, the Save dialog includes a checkbox that offers to place a git repository into your project folder from the outset. This can be purely local to your computer, or you can choose a remote server. If you have no reason to decide otherwise, I suggest that you check that checkbox!

When you open an existing project, if that project is already managed with Subversion or git, Xcode detects this and is ready instantly to display version control information in its interface. If a remote repository is involved, Xcode automatically enters information for it in the Accounts preference pane, which in Xcode 5 is the unified interface for repository management. To use a remote server without having a working copy checked out from it, enter its information manually in the Accounts preference pane.

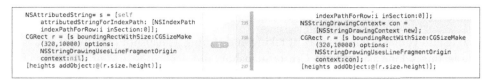

```
NSAttributedString* s = [self                                        indexPathForRow:i inSection:0]];
    attributedStringForIndexPath: [NSIndexPath       235  NSStringDrawingContext* con =
    indexPathForRow:i inSection:0]];                                  [NSStringDrawingContext new];
CGRect r = [s boundingRectWithSize:CGSizeMake       236  CGRect r = [s boundingRectWithSize:CGSizeMake
    (320,10000) options:                                              (320,10000) options:
    NSStringDrawingUsesLineFragmentOrigin                             NSStringDrawingUsesLineFragmentOrigin
    context:nil];                                                     context:con];
[heights addObject:@(r.size.height)];               237  [heights addObject:@(r.size.height)];
```

Figure 9-1. Version comparison

If you've checked "Refresh local status automatically", files in the Project navigator are marked with their status. For example, if you're using git, you can distinguish modified files (M), new untracked files (?), and new files added to the index (A).

Actual source control actions are available in two places: the Source Control menu (newly promoted to top level in Xcode 5), and the contextual menu in the Project navigator. To check out and open a project stored on a remote server, choose Source Control → Check Out. Other items in the Source Control menu are obvious, such as Commit, Push, Pull (or Update), Refresh Status, and Discard Changes. Note particularly the first item in the Source Control menu (new in Xcode 5), which lists all open working copies by name and branch; its hierarchical menu items let you perform branch management.

When you choose Source Control → Commit, you're shown a comparison view of all changes in all changed files. Each change can be excluded from this commit (or reverted entirely), so it's possible to group related file hunks into meaningful commits. A similar comparison view is available for any commit by choosing Source Control → History. (But Xcode still has nothing like the visual branch representation of git's own gitk tool.) Merge conflicts are also presented in a useful graphical comparison interface.

You can also see a comparison view for the file being currently edited, at any time, through the Version editor; choose View → Version Editor → Show Version Editor, or click the third Editor button in the project window toolbar. The Version editor actually has three modes: Comparison view, Blame view, and Log view (choose from View → Version Editor, or use the pop-up menu from the third Editor button in the toolbar when the Version editor is showing).

For example, in Figure 9-1, I can see that in the more recent version of this file (on the left) I've stopped using an explicit NSStringDrawingContext as the context: argument and have used nil instead. If I choose Editor → Copy Source Changes, the corresponding diff text is placed on the clipboard. If I switch to Blame view I can see my own commit message: "eliminated NSStringDrawingContext". The jump bar at the bottom of the Version editor permits me to view any commit's version of the current file in the editor.

Another way to learn how a line was changed, new in Xcode 5, is to select within that line (in the normal editor) and choose Editor → Show Blame For Line. A popover appears, describing the commit where this line changed to its current form; using buttons in that popover, you can see a version comparison for that commit, or switch to Blame view or Comparison view.

Xcode also contains its own way of taking and storing a snapshot of your project as a whole; this is done using File → Create Snapshot (and, according to your settings, some mass operations such as find-and-replace or refactoring may offer to take a snapshot first). Although these snapshots are not to be treated as full-fledged version control, they are in fact maintained as git repositories, and can certainly serve the purpose of giving confidence in advance of performing some change that might subsequently engender regret. Snapshots themselves are managed in the Projects tab of the Organizer window; here you can export a snapshot, thus resurrecting an earlier state of your project folder.

Editing Your Code

Many aspects of Xcode's editing environment can be modified to suit your tastes. Your first step should be to pick a Source Editor font face and size you like in Xcode's Fonts & Colors preference pane. Nothing is so important as being able to read and write code comfortably! I like a largish size (13, 14 or even 16) and a pleasant monospaced font such as Monaco, Menlo, or Consolas (or the freeware Inconsolata).

Xcode has some formatting, autotyping, and text selection features adapted for Objective-C. Exactly how these behave depends upon your settings in the Editing and Indentation tabs of Xcode's Text Editing preference pane. I'm not going to describe these settings in detail, but I urge you to take advantage of them. Under Editing, I like to check just about everything, including Line Numbers; visible line numbers are useful when debugging. Under Indentation, I like to have just about everything checked too; I find the way Xcode lays out Objective-C code to be excellent with these settings.

If you like Xcode's smart syntax-aware indenting, but you find that once in a while a line of code isn't indenting itself correctly, try choosing Editor → Structure → Re-Indent (Control-I), which autoindents the current line. (Autoindent problems can also be caused by incorrect syntax earlier in the file, so hunt for that too.)

Under Editing, notice "Automatically balance brackets in Objective-C method calls." If this option is checked, then when you type a closing square bracket after some text, Xcode intelligently inserts the opening square bracket before the text. I like this feature, as it allows me to type nested square brackets without planning ahead. For example, I type this:

```
UIAlertView* av = [UIAlertView alloc
```

I now type the right square bracket *twice*. The first right square bracket closes the open left square bracket (which highlights to indicate this). The second right square bracket also inserts a space before itself, *plus the missing left square bracket*, and the insertion point is positioned before the second right square bracket, ready for me to type init:

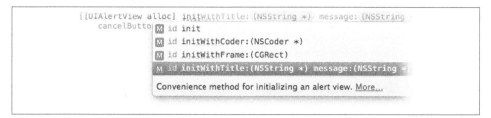

Figure 9-2. The autocompletion menu

```
UIAlertView* av = [[UIAlertView alloc] ]
//              insertion point is here: ^
```

With "Enable type-over completions" checked, Xcode goes even further. As I start to type that same line of code:

```
UIAlertView* av = [U
```

Xcode automatically appends the closing right square bracket, with the insertion point still positioned before it:

```
UIAlertView* av = [U]
```

That closing right square bracket, however, is tentative; it's in gray. Now I finish typing the first nested method call; the right square bracket is *still* gray:

```
UIAlertView* av = [UIAlertView alloc]
//      I have typed up to this c: ^
```

I can now confirm the closing right square bracket in any of several ways. I can actually type a right square bracket; or I can type Tab or Right arrow. The tentative right square bracket is replaced by a real right square bracket, and the insertion point is now positioned after it, ready for me to continue typing.

Autocompletion

As you write code, you'll take advantage of Xcode's autocompletion feature. Objective-C is a verbose language, and whatever reduces your time and effort typing will be a relief. However, I personally do *not* check "Suggest completions while typing" under Editing; instead, I check "Use Escape key to show completion suggestions", and when I want autocompletion to happen, I ask for it manually, by pressing Esc.

For example, suppose my code is as displayed in the previous example, with the insertion point before the second right square bracket. I now type `init` and then press Esc, and a little menu pops up, listing the four `init` methods appropriate to a UIAlertView (Figure 9-2). You can navigate this menu, dismiss it, or accept the selection, using only the keyboard. So, if it were not already selected by default, I would navigate to `initWith-Title:...` with the Down arrow key, and press Return to accept the selected choice.

Alternatively, I might press Control-Period instead of Esc. Pressing Control-Period repeatedly cycles through the alternatives. Again, press Return to accept the selected choice. Another possibility is to press Tab, which performs a partial completion without dismissing the autocompletion menu; in Figure 9-2, if I were to press Tab at this moment, initWith would be completed in my code — that's what the dashed underlines are telling me — and bare init, no longer an eligible completion, would be eliminated from the menu.

Observe also that there is a reduced form of Quick Help at the bottom of the autocompletion menu; click the More link to view (in the documentation window) the full documentation for the currently selected method (Chapter 8). If the selected method is defined in your code, and you've used doxygen to document that method in a comment as I described in Chapter 8, what appears here is the \brief description if there is one, and the full description otherwise; for this reason, it's good to define a \brief description, to keep the code completion window compact.

When I choose an alternative from the autocompletion menu, the template for the method call is entered in my code (I've broken it into multiple lines here):

```
[[UIAlertView alloc] initWithTitle:<#(NSString *)#>
                           message:<#(NSString *)#>
                          delegate:<#(id)#>
                 cancelButtonTitle:<#(NSString *)#>
                 otherButtonTitles:<#(NSString *), ...#>, nil]
```

The expressions in <#...#> are *placeholders*, showing the type of each parameter; you can select the next placeholder with Tab (if the insertion point precedes a placeholder) or by choosing Navigate → Jump to Next Placeholder (Control-/). Thus I can select a placeholder and type in its place the actual argument I wish to pass, select the next placeholder and type that argument, and so forth.

 Placeholders are delimited by <#...#> behind the scenes, but they appear in Xcode as "text tokens" to prevent them from being edited accidentally. To convert a placeholder to a normal string without the delimiters, select it and press Return, or double-click it.

Autocompletion also works for method declarations. You don't have to know or enter a method's return type beforehand. Just type the initial - or + (to indicate an instance method or a class method) followed by the first few letters of the method's name. For example, in my app delegate I might type:

```
- appli
```

If I then press Esc, I see a list of methods such as application:didChangeStatusBar-Frame:; these are methods that might be sent to my app delegate (by virtue of its being the app delegate, as discussed in Chapter 11). When I choose one, the declaration is filled in for me, including the return type and the parameter names:

```
- (void)application:(UIApplication *)application
    didChangeStatusBarFrame:(CGRect)oldStatusBarFrame
```

At this point I'm ready to type the left curly brace, followed by a Return character; this causes the matching right curly brace to appear, with the insertion point positioned between them, ready for me to start typing the body of this method.

Snippets

Code autocompletion is supplemented by code snippets. A code snippet is a bit of text with an abbreviation. Code snippets are kept in the Code Snippet library (Command-Option-Control-2), but a code snippet's abbreviation is globally available, so you can use it without showing the library. You type the abbreviation and the snippet's name is included among the possible completions.

For example, to enter an `if` block, I would type `if` and press Esc, to get autocompletion, and select "If Statement". When I press Return, the `if` block appears in my code, and the condition area (between the parentheses) and statements area (between the curly braces) are placeholders.

To learn a snippet's abbreviation, you must open its editing window — double-click the snippet in the Code Snippet library — and click Edit. If learning a snippet's abbreviation is too much trouble, simply drag it from the Code Snippet library into your text.

You can add your own snippets, which will be categorized as User snippets; the easiest way is to drag text into the Code Snippet library. Edit to suit your taste, providing a name, a description, and an abbreviation; use the `<#...#>` construct to form any desired placeholders.

Fix-it and Live Syntax Checking

Xcode's extremely cool Fix-it feature can actually make *and implement* positive suggestions on how to avert a problem. To summon it, click on an issue badge in the gutter. Such an issue badge will appear after compilation if there's a problem.

For instance, in Figure 9-3 I've omitted the `@` before an Objective-C NSString literal, and the compiler is complaining (because what I've typed is a C string literal, a very different thing). By clicking on the warning badge in the gutter, I've summoned a little dialog that not only describes the mistake but tells me how to fix it. Not only that: it has tentatively (in grey) implemented that solution; it has inserted the missing `@` into my code. Not only *that*: if I press Return, or double-click the "Fix-it" button in the dialog, Xcode *really* inserts the missing `@` into my code — and the warning vanishes, because the problem is solved. If I'm confident that Xcode will do the right thing, I can choose

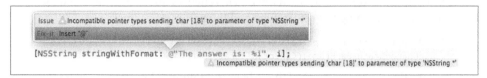

Figure 9-3. A warning with a Fix-it suggestion

Editor → Fix All in Scope (Command-Option-Control-F), and Xcode will implement *all* nearby Fix-it suggestions without my even having to show the dialog.

Live syntax checking is like a form of constant compilation. Even if you don't compile or even save, live syntax checking can detect the presence of a problem, and can suggest the solution with Fix-it. This feature can be toggled on or off using the "Show live issues" checkbox in the General preference pane. Personally, I keep it turned off, as I find it intrusive. My code is almost never valid while I'm typing, because the terms and parentheses are always half-finished; that's what it means to be typing. For example, merely typing a left parenthesis will instantly cause the syntax checker to complain of a parse error (until I type the corresponding right parenthesis).

Navigating Your Code

Developing an Xcode project involves editing code in many files at once. Fortunately, Xcode provides numerous ways to navigate your code, many of which have been mentioned in previous chapters.

Here are some of Xcode's chief forms of navigation:

The Project navigator
If you know something about the name of a file, you can find it quickly in the Project navigator (Command-1) by typing into the search field in the filter bar at the bottom of the navigator (Edit → Filter → Filter in Navigator, Command-Option-J). For example, type story to see just your *.storyboard* files. Moreover, after using the filter bar, you can press Tab and then the Up or Down arrow key to navigate the Project navigator; thus you can reach the desired file with the keyboard alone.

The Symbol navigator
If you highlight the first two icons in the filter bar (the first two are blue, the third is dark), the Symbol navigator lists your project's classes and their methods. Now you can navigate to a desired method. As with the Project navigator, the filter bar's search field can help get you where you want to go.

The jump bar
Every path component of the code editor's jump bar is a menu:

The bottom level

At the bottom level (farthest right) in the jump bar is a list of your file's method and function declarations and definitions, in the order in which they appear (hold Command while choosing the menu to see them in alphabetical order); choose one to navigate to it.

You can inject bold section titles into this bottom-level menu using the `#pragma mark` directive. For example, try modifying *ViewController.m* in our Empty Window project:

```
#pragma mark - View lifecycle

- (void)viewDidLoad
{
    [super viewDidLoad];
    // Do any additional setup after loading the view...
}
```

The result is that the "viewDidLoad" item in the bottom-level menu falls within a "View lifecycle" section.

To make a section divider line in the menu, type a `#pragma mark` directive whose value is a hyphen; in the preceding example, both a hyphen (to make a section divider line) and a title (to make a bold section title) are used. Similarly, comments outside of any method and starting with `TODO:`, `FIXME:`, `???:`, or `!!!:` will appear in the bottom-level menu.

Higher levels

Higher-level path components are hierarchical menus; thus you can use any of them to work your way down the file hierarchy.

History

Each editor pane remembers the names of files you've edited in it. The Back and Forward triangles are both buttons and pop-up menus (or choose Navigate → Go Back and Navigate → Go Forward, Command-Control-Left and Command-Control-Right).

Related items

The leftmost button in the jump bar summons the Related Items menu, a hierarchical menu of files related to the current file, such as counterparts, superclasses, and included files. This list even includes methods that call or are called by the currently selected method.

A path component menu in the jump bar can be filtered! Start typing while a jump bar menu is open, to filter what the menu displays. This filtering uses an "intelligent" search, not a strict text containment search; for example, typing "adf" will find `application:didFinish-LaunchingWithOptions:` (if it's present in the menu).

The Assistant pane
> The Assistant lets you be in two places at once. Hold Option while navigating to open something in an Assistant pane instead of the primary editor pane. The Tracking menu in an Assistant pane's jump bar sets its automatic relationship to the main pane; see the discussion of tracking in Chapter 6.

Tabs and windows
> You can also be in two places at once by opening a tab or a separate window (again, see Chapter 6).

Jump to definition
> Navigate → Jump to Definition (Command-Control-J) lets you jump to the declaration or definition of the symbol already selected in your code.

Open quickly
> File → Open Quickly (Command-Shift-O) searches in a dialog for a symbol in your code and the Cocoa headers.

Breakpoints
> The Breakpoint navigator lists all breakpoints in your code. Xcode lacks code bookmarks, but you can misuse a disabled breakpoint as a bookmark. Breakpoints are discussed later in this chapter.

Finding
> Finding is a form of navigation. In Xcode 5, the Find menu has been promoted from being an Edit submenu to a top-level menu. Xcode has both a global find (Find → Find in Project/Workspace, Command-Shift-F), which is the same as using the Search navigator, and an editor-level find (Find → Find, Command-F); don't confuse them.
>
> Find options are all-important. Additional options and capabilities appear in a pop-up menu when you click the magnifying glass icon in the search field. The global find options include a scope ("In project" in Figure 6-3), allowing you to specify in sophisticated ways which files will be searched: click the current scope to see a dialog where you can select a different scope or even create a custom scope. You can also find using regular expressions. There's a lot of power lurking here.
>
> To replace text, click on the word Find at the left end of the search bar to summon the pop-up menu, and choose Replace. You can replace all occurrences (Replace

All), or select particular find results in the Search navigator and replace only those (Replace); new in Xcode 5, you can also *delete* find results from the Search navigator, to protect them from being affected by Replace All. The Search navigator's Preview button summons a dialog that shows you the effect of each possible replacement, and lets you check or uncheck particular replacements in advance of performing the replacement. For editor-level find, hold Option before clicking Replace All, to find-and-replace within only the current selection.

A sophisticated form of editor-level find is Editor → Edit All In Scope, which finds simultaneously all occurrences of the currently selected term (usually a variable name) within the current set of curly braces; you can use this to change a variable's name throughout its scope, or just to survey how the name is used.

 To change a symbol's name throughout your code, as well as for automated, intelligent assistance in performing various code rearrangements that commonly arise in Objective-C programming, use Xcode's Refactoring feature (see "Make Projectwide Changes" in Apple's *Xcode User Guide*).

Running in the Simulator

When you build and run with the Simulator as the destination, you run in the iOS Simulator application. The Simulator window represents a device. Depending on your app target's Base SDK, Deployment Target, and Targeted Device Family build settings, you may have choices about the device and system to be represented by the Simulator as you choose your destination before running (see Chapter 6).

You can also switch device types from within the Simulator, by choosing Hardware → Device. This quits your app running in the Simulator; you can relaunch it by building and running in Xcode again, or by clicking your app's icon in the Simulator. In the latter case there is no longer any connection to Xcode (you aren't using the debugger, so you won't stop at breakpoints, and log messages won't be relayed to the Xcode console); still, you might do this just to check quickly on how your app looks or behaves on a different device.

The Simulator window can be displayed at half, three-quarter, or full size (choose from Window → Scale). This is a matter of display merely, comparable to zooming the window, so your app running in the Simulator does not quit when you change this setting. For example, you might run a Retina device in the Simulator at full size to see every double-resolution pixel, or at half size to save space.

You can interact with the Simulator in some of the same basic ways as you would a device. Using the mouse, you can tap on the device's screen; hold Option to make the mouse represent two fingers moving symmetrically around their common center, and

Option-Shift to represent two fingers moving in parallel. Some Simulator representations display a Home button, which you can click with the mouse, but the most reliable way to click the Home button is to choose Hardware → Home (Command-Shift-H). (Because of multitasking, clicking the Home button to switch from the app you're running in Xcode to the home screen does *not* stop your app running, in Xcode or on the Simulator. To quit your app in the Simulator, quit the Simulator, or switch to Xcode and choose Product → Stop.) Items in the Hardware menu also let you perform hardware gestures such as rotating the device, shaking it, and locking its screen; you can also test your app by simulating certain rare events, such as a low-memory situation.

The Debug menu in the Simulator is useful for detecting problems with animations and drawing. You can choose from this menu while your app is running in the Simulator, without causing the app to quit. Toggle Slow Animations makes animations unfold in slow motion so that you can see just what's happening. The next four menu items (their names begin with Color) are similar to features available when running on a device using Instruments, under the Core Animation instrument, revealing possible sources of inefficiency in screen drawing.

The Debug menu also lets you open the log in the Console application, and lets you set the simulated device's location (useful when testing a Core Location app).

Debugging

Debugging is the art of figuring out what's wrong with the behavior of your app as it runs. I divide this art into two main techniques: caveman debugging and pausing your running app.

Caveman Debugging

Caveman debugging consists of altering your code, usually temporarily, typically by adding code to dump informative messages into the console. You can view the console in the Debug pane; Chapter 6 describes a technique for displaying the console in a tab of its own.

The standard command for sending a message to the console is NSLog. It's a C function, and it takes an NSString which operates as a format string, followed by the format arguments.

A *format string* is a string (here, an NSString) containing symbols called *format specifiers*, for which values (the format arguments) will be substituted at runtime. All format specifiers begin with a percent sign (%), so the only way to enter a literal percent sign in a format string is as a double percent sign (%%). The character(s) following the percent sign specify the type of value that will be supplied at runtime. The most common format specifiers are %@ (an object reference), %d (an integer) and %f (a double). For example:

```
NSLog(@"the window: %@", self.window);
```

In that example, `self.window` is the first (and only) format argument, so its value will be substituted for the first (and only) format specifier, `%@`, when the format string is printed in the console. Thus the console output looks something like this (I've formatted it for clarity here):

```
the window: <UIWindow: 0x8a68a60;
            frame = (0 0; 320 480);
            hidden = YES;
            gestureRecognizers = <NSArray: 0x8a69fd0>;
            layer = <UIWindowLayer: 0x8a697b0>>
```

We learn the object's class, its address in memory (important for confirming whether two instances are in fact the same instance), and the values of some additional properties. That nice summary of information is due to UIWindow's implementation of the `description` method: an object's `description` method is called when that object is used with the `%@` format specifier. For this reason, you will probably want to implement `description` in your own classes, so that you can summarize an instance with a simple `NSLog` call.

For the complete repertory of format specifiers available in a format string, read Apple's document *String Format Specifiers* (in the *String Programming Guide*). The format specifiers are largely based on those of the C `printf` standard library function; see K&R B1.2, the `sprintf` man page, and the IEEE `printf` specification linked from the documentation.

The main ways to go wrong with `NSLog` (or any format string) are to supply a different number of format arguments from the number of format specifiers in the string, or to supply an argument value different from the type declared by the corresponding format specifier. I often see beginners claim that logging shows a certain value to be nonsense, when in fact it is their `NSLog` call that is nonsense; for example, a format specifier was `%d` but the value of the corresponding argument was a float. Another common mistake is treating an NSNumber as if it were the type of number it contains; an NSNumber isn't any kind of number — it's an object (`%@`). Problems with signed vs. unsigned integers can be tricky as well. Fortunately, the compiler will try to help you with warnings.

C structs are not objects, so to see a struct's value with `NSLog` you must somehow deconstruct the struct. Common Cocoa structs usually supply convenience functions for this purpose. For example:

```
NSLog(@"%@", NSStringFromCGRect(self.window.frame)); // {{0, 0}, {320, 480}}
```

Purists may scoff at caveman debugging, but I use it heavily: it's easy, informative, and lightweight. And sometimes it's the only way. Unlike the debugger, `NSLog` works with any build configuration (Debug or Release) and wherever your app runs (in the Simulator or on a device). It works when pausing is impossible (because of threading issues, for example). It even works on someone else's device, such as a tester to whom you've distributed your app. It's a little tricky for a tester to get a look at the console so as to be able to report back to you, but it can be done: for example, the tester can connect the device to a computer and view its log in Xcode's Organizer window or with Apple's iPhone Configuration Utility.

Remember to remove or comment out NSLog calls before shipping your app, as you probably don't want your finished app to dump lots of messages into the console. A useful trick (shamelessly stolen from Jens Alfke) is to call MyLog instead of NSLog, and define MyLog like this in your precompiled header (and when it's time to stop logging, change the 0 to 1):

```
#define MyLog if(0); else NSLog
```

A useful fact when logging is that the variable name _cmd holds the selector for the current method. Thus a single form of statement can signal where you are:

```
NSLog(@"Logging %@ in %@", NSStringFromSelector(_cmd), self);
```

(Similarly, in a C function, NSLog(@"%s", __FUNCTION__) logs the name of the function.)

Another sort of logging call with which you can pepper your code is *asserts*. Asserts are conditions that you claim (assert) are true at that moment — and you feel so strongly about this that you want your app to crash if you're wrong. Asserts are a very good way to confirm that the situation matches your expectations, not just now as you write your code, but in the future as the app develops.

The simplest form of assert is the C function (actually it's a macro) assert, to which you pass one argument, a condition — something that can be evaluated as false (0) or true (some other value). If it's false, your app will crash when this line is encountered, along with a nice explanation in the log. For example, suppose we assert NO, which is false and will certainly cause a crash. Then when this line is encountered we crash with this log message:

```
Assertion failed: (NO),
function -[AppDelegate application:didFinishLaunchingWithOptions:],
file /Users/mattleopard/Desktop/testing/testing/AppDelegate.m, line 20.
```

That's plenty for us to track down the assertion failure: we know the assertion condition, the method in which the assertion occurred, the file containing that method, and the line number.

For higher-level asserts, look at NSAssert (used in Objective-C methods) and NSCAssert (used in C functions). They allow you to form your own log message, which is to appear in the console in addition to the native assert logging; the log message can be a format string followed by values corresponding to the format specifiers, as with NSLog.

Some developers think that asserts should be allowed to remain in your code even when your app is finished. By default, however, higher-level `NSAssert` and `NSCAssert` are disabled in a Release build, thanks to the Enable Foundation Assertions build setting, which is set to No for the Release configuration in Apple's project templates. To keep asserts working in a Release build, change that value to Yes for your app target.

The Xcode Debugger

When you're building and running in Xcode, you can pause in the debugger and use Xcode's debugging facilities.

 The debugger in Xcode 5 is LLDB. For full technical details, see *http:// lldb.llvm.org*.

There isn't a strong difference between running and debugging in Xcode; the main distinction is whether breakpoints are effective or ignored. The effectiveness of breakpoints can be toggled at two levels:

Globally
> Breakpoints as a whole are either *active or inactive*. If breakpoints are inactive, we won't pause at any breakpoints.

Individually
> A given breakpoint is either *enabled or disabled*. Even if breakpoints are active, we won't pause at this one if it is disabled. Disabling a breakpoint allows you to leave in place a breakpoint that you might need later without pausing at it every time it's encountered.

A breakpoint, then, is ignored if it is disabled or if breakpoints as a whole are inactive.

The important thing, if you want to use the debugger, is that the app should be built with the Debug build configuration (the default for a scheme's Run action). The debugger is not very helpful against an app built with the Release build configuration, not least because compiler optimizations can destroy the correspondence between steps in the compiled code and lines in your code.

To create a breakpoint (Figure 9-4), select in the editor the line where you want to pause, and choose Debug → Breakpoints → Add Breakpoint at Current Line (Command-\). This keyboard shortcut toggles between adding and removing a breakpoint for the current line. The breakpoint is symbolized by an arrow in the gutter. Alternatively, a simple click in the gutter adds a breakpoint; to remove a breakpoint gesturally, drag it out of the gutter.

Figure 9-4. A breakpoint

Figure 9-5. A disabled breakpoint

To disable a breakpoint at the current line, click on the breakpoint in the gutter to toggle its enabled status. Alternatively, Control-click on the breakpoint and choose Disable Breakpoint in the contextual menu. A dark breakpoint is enabled; a light breakpoint is disabled (Figure 9-5).

Once you have some breakpoints in your code, you'll want to survey and manage them. That's what the Breakpoint navigator is for. Here you can navigate to a breakpoint, enable or disable a breakpoint by clicking on its arrow in the navigator, and delete a breakpoint.

You can also edit a breakpoint's behavior. Control-click on the breakpoint, in the gutter or in the Breakpoint navigator, and choose Edit Breakpoint; or Command-Option-click the breakpoint. This is a very powerful facility: you can have a breakpoint pause only under a certain condition or after it has been encountered a certain number of times, and you can have a breakpoint perform one or more actions when it is encountered, such as issuing a debugger command, logging, playing a sound, speaking text, or running a script.

A breakpoint can be configured to continue automatically after performing its action when it is encountered. This can be an excellent alternative to caveman debugging: instead of inserting an NSLog call, which must be compiled into your code and later removed when the app is released, you can set a breakpoint that logs and continues. By definition, such a breakpoint operates only when you're actively debugging the project; it won't dump any messages into the console when the app runs on a user's device.

In the Breakpoint navigator, you can create certain kinds of breakpoint that you can't create in the code editor. Click the Plus button at the bottom of the navigator and choose from its pop-up menu. The most important types are:

Exception breakpoint
> An exception breakpoint causes your app to pause at the time an exception is thrown or caught, without regard to whether the exception would crash your app later. I recommend that you create an exception breakpoint to pause on all exceptions when they are thrown, because this gives the best view of the call stack and variable values at the moment of the exception (rather than later when the crash actually

occurs); you can see where you are in your code, and you can examine variable values, which may help you understand the cause of the problem. If you do create such an exception breakpoint, I also suggest that you use the contextual menu to say Move Breakpoint To → User, which makes this breakpoint permanent and global to all your projects.

The only problem with an exception breakpoint is that sometimes Apple's code will throw an exception and catch it, deliberately. This isn't a crash, and nothing has gone wrong; but your app pauses in the debugger anyway, which can be confusing.

Symbolic breakpoint

A symbolic breakpoint causes your app to pause when a certain method or function is called, regardless of what object called it or to what object the message is sent. A method may be specified using the instance method or class method symbol (- or +) followed by square brackets containing the class name and the method name (see "A Useful Shorthand" on page 55). For example, to learn where in my app the `beginReceivingRemoteControlEvents` message was being sent to my shared application instance, I configured a symbolic breakpoint like this:

```
-[UIApplication beginReceivingRemoteControlEvents]
```

New in Xcode 5, you can specify a method name by typing its name alone, and it will be resolved into individual breakpoints for all the matching class-specific methods; you can then enable just the ones you want to pause at. This feature is useful also for confirming that you've entered the method name correctly. Thus, I can now create a symbolic breakpoint for `beginReceivingRemoteControlEvents`, and Xcode itself will resolve this to `-[UIApplication beginReceivingRemote-ControlEvents]` for me.

To toggle the active status of breakpoints as a whole, click the Breakpoints button in the bar at the top of the Debug pane, or choose Debug → Activate/Deactivate Breakpoints (Command-Y). The active status of breakpoints as a whole doesn't affect the enabled or disabled status of any breakpoints; if breakpoints are inactive, they are simply ignored en masse, and no pausing at breakpoints takes place. Breakpoint arrows are blue if breakpoints are active, gray if they are inactive.

When the app runs with breakpoints active and an enabled breakpoint is encountered (and assuming its conditions are met, and so on), the app pauses. In the active project window, the editor shows the file containing the point of execution, which will usually be the file containing the breakpoint. The point of execution is shown as a green arrow; this is the line that is *about* to be executed (Figure 9-6). Depending on the settings for Running → Pauses in the Behaviors preference pane, the Debug navigator and the Debug pane may also appear.

Here are some things you might like to do while paused at a breakpoint:

Figure 9-6. Paused at a breakpoint

See where you are

One common reason for setting a breakpoint is to make sure that the path of execution is passing through a certain line. You can see where you are in any of your methods by clicking on the method name in the call stack, shown in the Debug navigator.

Methods listed in the call stack with a User icon, with the text in black, are yours; click one to see where you are paused in that method. Other methods, with the text in gray, are methods for which you have no source code, so there would be little point clicking one unless you know something about assembly language. The slider in the filter bar hides chunks of the call chain, to save space, starting with the methods for which you have no source.

You can also view and navigate the call stack using the jump bar at the top of the Debug pane.

Study variable values

This is a very common reason for pausing. In the Debug pane, variable values for the current scope (corresponding to what's selected in the call stack) are visible in the variables list. You can see additional object features, such as collection elements, instance variables, and even some private information, by opening triangles. Local variable values are shown even if, at the point where are paused, those variables have not yet been initialized; such values are meaningless, so ignore them.

Switch the pop-up menu below the variables list to Auto to see only those variables that Xcode thinks will interest you (because their value has been recently changed, for instance); if you're after completeness, Local will probably be the best setting. You can use the search field to filter variables by name or value. If a formatted summary isn't sufficiently helpful, you can send `description` (or, if you've implemented it, `debugDescription`) to an object variable and view the output in the console: choose Print Description of [Variable] from the contextual menu, or select the variable and click the Info button below the variables list.

Xcode 5 introduces a powerful new way of viewing a variable's value graphically: select the variable and click the Quick Look button (an eye icon) below the variables list, or press Spacebar. For example, in the case of a CGRect, the graphical representation is a correctly proportioned rectangle.

Figure 9-7. A data tip

Also, data tips have been revised in Xcode 5 to make them more useful. To see a data tip, hover the mouse over the name of a variable in your code. The data tip is much like the display of this value in the variables list: there's a flippy triangle that you can open to see more information, plus an Info button that displays the value description here and in the console, and a Quick Look button for showing a value graphically (Figure 9-7).

You can also *change* variable values while paused in the debugger. Select a line in the variables list and press Return to make it editable, or double-click a value in a data tip; simple scalar values (such as floats and ints, including pointers) can be changed in this way. You can also use the expr command in the console to set a value. Use this feature with care (if at all).

Set a watchpoint

A watchpoint is like a breakpoint, but instead of depending on a certain line of code it depends on a variable's value: the debugger pauses whenever the variable's value changes. You can set a watchpoint only while paused in the debugger. Control-click on the variable in the variables list and choose Watch [Variable]. Watchpoints, once created, are listed and managed in the Breakpoint navigator. Because of the overhead required to maintain a watchpoint, you can only have a few of them at a time.

Manage expressions

An expression is code to be added to the variables list and evaluated every time we pause. Choose Add Expression from the contextual menu in the variables list. The expression is evaluated within the current context in your code, so be careful of side effects.

Talk to the debugger

You can communicate directly with the debugger through the console. Xcode's debugger interface is a front end to LLDB; by talking directly to LLDB, you can do everything that you can do through the Xcode debugger interface, and much more.

A common command is po (for "print object") followed by an object variable's name or a method call that returns an object; it calls the object's description method (or, if you've implemented it, debugDescription). Another valuable command is expr, which evaluates an Objective-C expression in the current context — meaning, among other things, that you can call a method, or change the value of a variable in scope! For a good list of other things you're likely to say, see *http://lldb.llvm.org/ lldb-gdb.html*. Any LLDB console command is also eligible to be used as a breakpoint's Debugger Command action.

Fiddle with breakpoints

You are free to create, destroy, edit, enable and disable, and otherwise manage breakpoints dynamically even while your app is running, which is useful because where you'd like to pause next might depend on what you learn while you're paused here.

Indeed, this is one of the main advantages of breakpoints over caveman debugging. To change your caveman debugging, you have to stop the app, edit it, rebuild it, and start running the app all over again. But to fiddle with breakpoints, you don't have to be stopped; you don't even have to be paused! An operation that went wrong, if it doesn't crash your app, can probably be repeated in real time; so you can just add a breakpoint and try again. For example, if tapping a button produces the wrong results, you can add a breakpoint and tap the button again; this time through the same code, you can work out what the trouble is.

Step or continue

To proceed with your paused app, you can either resume running until the next breakpoint is encountered (Debug → Continue) or take one step and pause again. Also, you can select in a line and choose Debug → Continue to Current Line (or Continue to Here from the contextual menu), which effectively sets a breakpoint at the chosen line, continues, and removes the breakpoint.

The stepping commands (in the Debug menu) are:

Step Over

Pause at the next line.

Step Into

Pause in your method that the current line calls, if there is one; otherwise, pause at the next line.

Step Out
> Pause when we return from the current method.

You can access these commands through convenient buttons in the bar at the top of the Debug pane. Even if the Debug pane is collapsed, the bar containing the buttons appears while running.

 If Step Over fails to reach the next line because it hits and pauses at a breakpoint inside a method called in the current line, Continue will then pause automatically at that next line — you don't have to say Step Out just to pause where you would have paused if it weren't for the unexpected breakpoint.

Start over, or abort
> To kill the running app, click Stop in the toolbar (Product → Stop, Command-Period). Clicking the Home button in the Simulator (Hardware → Home) or on the device does *not* stop the running app in the multitasking world of iOS 4 and later. To kill the running app and relaunch it without rebuilding it, Control-click Run in the toolbar (Product → Perform Action → Run Without Building, Command-Control-R).

You can make changes to your code while the app is running or paused, but those changes are not magically communicated to the running app; there are languages and programming milieus where that sort of thing is possible, but Xcode and Objective-C are not among them. You must stop the app and run in the normal way (which includes building) to see your changes in action.

Unit Testing

A *unit test* is code that isn't part of your app target, whose purpose is to exercise code that *is* part of your app target, making sure that it works as expected. For example, a unit test might call some method in your app target code, handing it various parameters and looking to see if the expected result is returned each time, not just under normal conditions but also when incorrect or extreme inputs are supplied. It can even be useful to write unit tests *before* writing the real code, as a way of developing a working algorithm. In addition, having initially ascertained that your code passes your tests, you continue to run those tests from time to time, to detect whether a bug has been introduced during the course of development.

Unit tests are *not* a means of exercising your app as a whole, guiding it through various scenarios by effectively tapping buttons with a ghost finger to make sure that the interface behaves as expected. You can perform tests of that sort — for example, you might make your app accessible, so that its user interface elements are visible to code, and then use the Automation instrument of Instruments to run Java-Script scripts that act like a ghost user — but that would not be unit testing. Unit tests are for probing your code's business logic, not for verifying its interface.

In the past, configuring your app for unit testing has been forbiddingly difficult, but in Xcode 5, unit tests are promoted to the level of first-class citizens: the application templates generate projects with a test target in addition to the app target, and tests can be managed and run easily from the Test navigator (Command-5) as well as from within a test class file.

A *test class* in Xcode 5 is a subclass of XCTestCase (which is itself a subclass of XCTest). A *test method* is an instance method of a test class, returning no value (`void`) and taking no parameters, whose name starts with `test`. The test target depends upon the app target, meaning that before a test class can be compiled and built, the app target must be compiled and built. Running a test also runs the app; the test target's product is a bundle, which is loaded into the app as it launches. Each test method will call one or more asserts; in Xcode 5, their names begin with `XCTAssert`. (To find out more about them, see `XCTestAssertions.h`.)

 The asserts whose names begin with `XCTAssert` are actually macros. Keep your syntax simple to avoid problems. For example, an array literal starting with @ doesn't work here.

In addition to test methods, a test class may contain utility methods that are called by the test methods. It may also contain any of four special methods inherited from XCTestCase:

`setUp` *class method*
Called once before *all* test methods in the class.

`setUp` *instance method*
Called before *each* test method.

`tearDown` *instance method*
Called after *each* test method.

`tearDown` *class method*
Called once after *all* test methods in the class.

The test target is a target, and what it produces is a bundle, with build phases like an app target. This means that resources, such as test data, can be included in the bundle. You might use setUp to load such resources; you can refer in code to the test bundle like this:

```
[NSBundle bundleForClass:[MyTestClass class]]
```

As an example, let's use our Empty Window project. Give the ViewController class a (nonsensical) instance method dogMyCats:, like this:

```
- (NSString*) dogMyCats: (NSString*) cats {
    return nil;
}
```

The method dogMyCats: is supposed to receive any string and return the string @"dogs". At the moment, though, it doesn't; it returns nil instead. That's a bug. Now we'll write a test method to ferret out this bug.

Empty Window comes with a single test class, Empty_WindowTests. Unlike a normal class, Empty_WindowTests is declared entirely in a single file, *Empty_WindowTests.m* — it has no corresponding header (*.h*) file, but contains both the @interface section and the @implementation section in the *.m* file. (This, as I said in Chapter 4, is perfectly legal.)

In *Empty_WindowTests.m*, delete the existing test method testExample. We're going to replace it with a test method that calls dogMyCats: and makes an assertion about the result. Since dogMyCats: is a ViewController instance method, we're going to need a ViewController instance. In order to speak of a ViewController instance and call a ViewController method, we'll need to import ViewController's header file:

```
#import "ViewController.h"
```

We're going to want to call dogMyCats:; to get that call past the compiler, we're going to need a knowledge of dogMyCats:. This means that dogMyCats: must be declared in the header file we just imported, *ViewController.h*.

Let's prepare an instance variable in the Empty_WindowTests class to store our View-Controller instance. Declare the property in the @interface section:

```
@interface Empty_WindowTests : XCTestCase
@property ViewController* viewController;
@end
```

Let's set the value of that property in our setUp method:

```
- (void)setUp {
    [super setUp];
    self.viewController = [ViewController new];
}
```

Now we can write our test method. Call it `testDogMyCats`. It has access to a View-Controller instance as `self.viewController`, because `setUp` will run before this test method does:

```
- (void)testDogMyCats {
    NSString* input = @"cats";
    XCTAssertEqualObjects([self.viewController dogMyCats:input], @"dogs",
        @"ViewController dogMyCats: fails to produce dogs from \"%@\"",
        input);
}
```

We are now ready to run our test. There are many ways to do this. Observe that the Test navigator lists our test target, our test class, and our test method. Hover the mouse over any name, and a button appears to its right. By clicking the appropriate button, you can thus run all tests in every class, all tests in the Empty_WindowTests class, or just the `testDogMyCats` test. But wait, there's more! Back in *Empty_WindowTests.m*, there's also a diamond-shaped indicator in the gutter to the left of the `@interface` line and the test method name; you can also click one of those to run, respectively, all tests in this class or an individual test. Or, to run all tests, you can choose Product → Test.

Make sure the scheme pop-up menu shows the destination as the Simulator, and run `testDogMyCats`. The app target is compiled and built; the test target is compiled and built. (We can't test if any of those steps fails, and you'll be back on familiar ground with a compile error or a build error.) The app launches in the Simulator, and the test runs.

The test fails! (Well, we knew that was going to happen, didn't we?) The app stops running in the Simulator. The error is described in a banner next to the assert that failed in our code, as well as in the Issue navigator; it is easiest to read, perhaps, in the Log navigator (there's a More button that exposes the entire error description). Moreover, red X marks appear everywhere — in the Test navigator next to `testDogMyCats`, in the Issue navigator, in the Log navigator, and in *Empty_WindowTests.m* next to the `@implementation` line and the first line of `testDogMyCats`. Most of these red X marks are buttons! You can click one to run the test again. (After running an individual test, you can also choose Product → Perform Action → Test [TestMethod] Again from wherever you happen to be.)

There's no point doing that, though, until we've fixed our code. In *ViewController.m*, modify `dogMyCats` to return `@"dogs"` instead of nil. Now run the test again. It passes!

When a test failure occurs, you might like to pause at the point where the assertion is about to fail. To do so, in the Breakpoint navigator, click the Plus button at the bottom and choose Add Test Failure Breakpoint. This is like an Exception breakpoint, pausing on the assert line in your test method just before it reports failure. You could then switch to the method being tested, for example, and examine its variables and so forth, to work out the reason for the impending failure.

There's a helpful feature allowing you to navigate between a method and a test that calls it: when the selection is within a method, the Related Files menu in the jump bar includes Test Callers. The same is true of the Tracking menu in an assistant pane situation.

The test code runs inside a bundle that is effectively injected into your running app. This means that it can see app globals such as [UIApplication sharedApplication]. Thus, for example, instead of making a new ViewController instance in order to initialize Empty_WindowTests's self.viewController, we could have accessed the application's already existing ViewController instance:

```
self.viewController =
    (ViewController*)[[[[UIApplication sharedApplication]
        delegate] window] rootViewController];
```

Organization of your test methods into test targets (suites) and test classes is largely a matter of convenience: it makes a difference to the layout of the Test navigator and which tests will be run together, plus each test class has its own instance variables, its own setUp method, and so on. To make a new test target or a new test class, click the Plus button at the bottom of the Test navigator.

> When you rename a project that contains a test target ("Renaming Parts of a Project" on page 138), the test target will break: several of its build settings still specify the app by its old name, so the test target cannot be built, and tests cannot be run. If you're uncomfortable editing the test target's build settings by hand, the easiest solution is to copy the test code to somewhere safe, delete the test target, make a new test target (which will have the right settings), and restore the test code.

Static Analyzer

From time to time, you should use the static analyzer to look for possible sources of error in your code; choose Product → Analyze (Command-Shift-B). This command causes your code to be compiled, and the static analyzer studies it in depth, reporting its findings in the Issue navigator and in your code. As with compiling, Xcode 5 can also analyze an individual file (choose Product → Perform Action → Analyze [Filename]).

The static analyzer is static (it's analyzing your code, not debugging in real time), but it is remarkably intelligent and thorough, and may well alert you to potential problems that could otherwise escape your notice. You might think that the compiler alone should be sufficient in this regard. It's true that *some* of the static analyzer's intelligence has indeed been migrated over into the compiler, which in Xcode 5 is providing more intelligent and helpful warnings than ever before. Moreover, one of the main reasons for using the static analyzer, namely, to assist with manual memory management of Objective-C instances, is largely gone if you're using ARC. Still, not all of your memory management will be taken care of by ARC; ARC doesn't handle CFTypeRef memory management, for example (Chapter 12), and the analyzer will alert you to your possible mistakes. And the static analyzer takes the time to study in depth the possible values and paths of execution in your code, and can detect potential sources of trouble in your program's *logic* that no mere compiler would worry about.

For example, not long ago I found the analyzer complaining about this code:

```
-(void) newGameWithImage:(id)imageSource song:(NSString*)song {
    CGImageSourceRef src;
    if ([imageSource isKindOfClass:[NSURL class]])
        src = CGImageSourceCreateWithURL(
                (__bridge CFURLRef)imageSource, nil);
    if ([imageSource isKindOfClass:[NSData class]])
        src = CGImageSourceCreateWithData(
                (__bridge CFDataRef)imageSource, nil);
    // ...
    if (nil != src)
        CFRelease(src);
}
```

First, the analyzer warned that `src` was a garbage value. This seemed unlikely to me; after all, the variable `src` was going to be initialized by one of the two `isKindOf-Class:` conditions. But then it occurred to me that the analyzer didn't know that for a fact — and neither did I. My *intention* was certainly that this method should be called with an `imageSource` value that was either an NSURL or an NSData; but what if some idiot (my future self) called it with some other type of value? Then, sure enough, `src` would never be initialized. So I initialized it to nil:

```
CGImageSourceRef src = nil;
```

I ran the analyzer again, but it still complained, saying that `src` was potentially leaking at the end of the method. But how could *that* be? The rules for CFTypeRef memory management require that if you make a CGImageSourceRef with a call to `CGImage-SourceCreateWithURL` or `CGImageSourceCreateWithData`, you must later call `CFRelease` on that object — and I was doing that.

When the static analyzer warns, if you click on the icon at the start of the warning, the analyzer draws a diagram displaying its logic step by step, complete with arrows showing the path of execution. I did that, and saw that the analyzer was imagining that *both* `isKindOfClass:` conditions might succeed (Figure 9-8). Sure enough, if that were to happen, the first value of `src` would leak: it would be replaced, without memory management, by the second value!

Based on the facts of class inheritance, both `isKindOfClass:` conditions *can't* succeed; `imageSource` must be an NSURL or an NSData (or neither). But the analyzer is concerned with *logic* and the flow of execution. If I believe that only one of these conditions will succeed, it's up to me to express that fact logically and structurally. I did so, by changing the second `if` to `else if`:

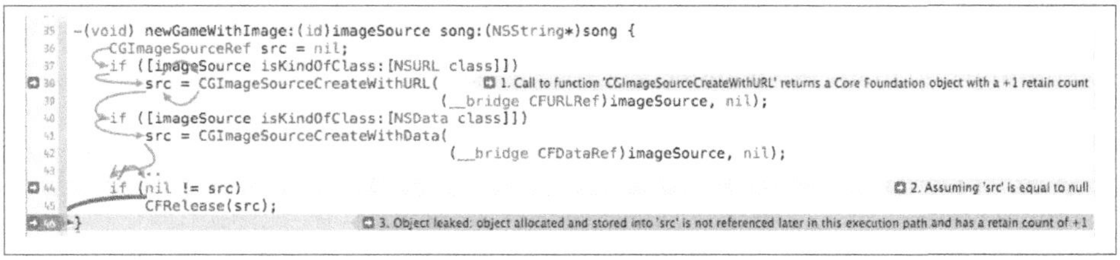

```
35  -(void) newGameWithImage:(id)imageSource song:(NSString*)song {
36     CGImageSourceRef src = nil;
37     if ([imageSource isKindOfClass:[NSURL class]])
38        src = CGImageSourceCreateWithURL(     ▣ 1. Call to function 'CGImageSourceCreateWithURL' returns a Core Foundation object with a +1 retain count
39                                    (__bridge CFURLRef)imageSource, nil);
40     if ([imageSource isKindOfClass:[NSData class]])
41        src = CGImageSourceCreateWithData(
42                                    (__bridge CFDataRef)imageSource, nil);
43     ...
44     if (nil != src)                                              ▣ 2. Assuming 'src' is equal to null
45        CFRelease(src);
46  }                            ▣ 3. Object leaked: object allocated and stored into 'src' is not referenced later in this execution path and has a retain count of +1
```

Figure 9-8. The static analyzer draws a diagram

```
if ([imageSource isKindOfClass:[NSURL class]])
    src = CGImageSourceCreateWithURL(
            (__bridge CFURLRef)imageSource, nil);
else if ([imageSource isKindOfClass:[NSData class]])
    src = CGImageSourceCreateWithData(
            (__bridge CFDataRef)imageSource, nil);
```

And that was that; running the analyzer once again, I found it was perfectly happy. The static analyzer had seen more deeply into the logical structure of my code than I did, and helped me to tighten that logical structure to make my code both clearer and safer.

If you'd like to run the static analyzer automatically as part of ordinary compilation when you do a build, you can: there's a build setting, Analyze During 'Build'. If you set that to Yes, you probably want Mode of Analysis for 'Build' to be Shallow; a full analysis (Deep) could be too time-consuming.

For more about the static analyzer, see *http://clang-analyzer.llvm.org*.

Clean

From time to time, during repeated testing and debugging, and before making a different sort of build (switching from Debug to Release, or running on a device instead of the Simulator), it is a good idea to *clean* your target. This means that existing builds will be removed and caches will be cleared, so that all code will be considered to be in need of compilation and the next build will build your app from scratch.

The first build of your app, after you clean, may take longer than usual. But it's worth it, because cleaning removes the cruft, quite literally. For example, suppose you have been including a certain resource in your app, and you decide it is no longer needed. You can remove it from the Copy Bundle Resources build phase (or from your project as a whole), but that doesn't remove it from your built app. This sort of leftover resource can cause all kinds of mysterious trouble. The wrong version of a nib may seem to appear in your interface; code that you've edited may seem to behave as it did before the edit. Cleaning removes the built app, and very often solves the problem.

I think of cleaning as having several levels or degrees:

Shallow clean

> Choose Product → Clean, which removes the built app and some of the intermediate information in the build folder.

Deeper clean

> Hold Option and choose Product → Clean Build Folder, which removes the entire build folder.

Complete clean

> Close the project. Open the Organizer window (Window → Organizer) and find your project listed at the left side of the Projects window; click it. On the right, click Delete. This removes the project's entire folder inside your user *Library/Developer/ Xcode/DerivedData* folder. The project's index will have to be rebuilt the next time the project is opened, which takes some time, but certain obscure issues can be solved only by forcing this to happen.

Total clean

> Quit Xcode. Open your user *Library/Developer/Xcode/DerivedData* folder and move all its contents to the trash. This is a complete clean for every project you've opened recently (plus the module information if you're using modules). The space savings can be significant.

In addition to cleaning your project, you should also remove your app from the Simulator. This is for the same reason as cleaning the project: when the app is built and copied to the Simulator, existing resources inside the built app may not be removed (in order to save time), and this may cause the app to behave oddly. To clean out the Simulator while running the Simulator, choose iOS Simulator → Reset Content and Settings. Alternatively, you can clean out apps from the Simulator by working in the Finder. Quit the Simulator if it's running. Then open your user *Library/Application Support/iPhone Simulator* folder and look for a folder named after the system version of the SDK (for example, there might be a folder called *7.0*); within this, find the *Applications* folder, and move the contents of that folder to the trash.

Running on a Device

Sooner or later, you're going to want to advance from running and testing and debugging in the Simulator to running and testing and debugging on a real device. The Simulator is nice, but it's only a simulation; there are many differences between the Simulator and a real device. The Simulator is really your computer, which is fast and has lots of memory, so problems with memory management and speed won't be exposed until you run on a device. User interaction with the Simulator is limited to what can be done with a mouse: you can click, you can drag, you can hold Option to simulate use of two fingers, but more elaborate gestures can be performed only on an actual device. And many iOS facilities, such as the accelerometer and access to the music library, are not present on the Simulator at all, so that testing an app that uses them is possible *only* on a device.

 Don't even think of developing an app without testing it on a device. You have no idea how your app *really* looks and behaves until you run it on a device. Submitting to the App Store an app that you have not run on a device is asking for trouble.

Before you can run your app on a device, even just to test, you must join the iOS Developer Program by paying the annual fee. (Yes, this is infuriating. Now get over it.) Only in this way can you obtain and provide to Xcode the credentials for running on a device. You'll go to the iOS Developer Program web page (*http://developer.apple.com/programs/ios*). This requires filling out a form and paying the annual fee. When you're starting out, the Individual program is sufficient. The Company program costs no more, but adds the ability to privilege additional developers in various roles. (You do *not* need the Company program in order to distribute your built app to other users for testing.)

Your iOS Developer Program membership involves two things:

An Apple ID

The user ID that identifies you at Apple's site (along with the corresponding password).

You'll use your Developer Program Apple ID for all kinds of things. In addition to letting you prepare an app to run on a device, this same Apple ID lets you enter Apple's development forums, download Xcode beta versions, view WWDC videos, and so forth.

A team name

You, under the same Apple ID, can belong to more than one *team*. On each team, you will have a *role* dictating your privileges.

For example, on the Matt Neuburg team, of which I am the sole member, my role is Agent, meaning that I can do everything: I can develop apps, run them on my device, submit apps to the App Store, and receive the money for any paid apps that sell any copies there. But I'm also a member of the TidBITS team, for which I write the TidBITS News app; for this team, I'm just an Admin, meaning that I can't submit to the App Store or see the app's details at iTunes Connect — someone else is the Agent for that team, and does those things.

Having established your Developer Program Apple ID, you should enter it into the Accounts preference pane in Xcode. (This is new in Xcode 5.) Click the Plus button at the bottom left and choose Add Apple ID. Provide the Apple ID and password. From now on, Xcode will identify you through the team name(s) associated with this Apple ID; you shouldn't need to tell Xcode this password again.

To run an app on a device, you will need to *sign* the app as you build it. An app that is not properly signed for a device will not run on that device (assuming you haven't jailbroken the device). Signing an app requires two things:

An identity

An identity represents Apple's permission for a given team to develop, on a particular computer, apps that can run on a device. It consists of two parts:

A private key

The private key is stored in the keychain on your computer. Thus, it identifies the computer as one where this team can *potentially* develop device-targeted apps.

A certificate

A certificate is a virtual permission slip from Apple. It contains the public key matching the private key (because you told Apple the public key when you asked for the certificate). With a copy of this certificate, any machine holding the private key can *actually* be used to develop device-targeted apps under the name of this team.

A provisioning profile

A provisioning profile is another virtual permission slip from Apple. It unites four things:

- An identity.
- An app, identified by its bundle id.
- A list of eligible devices.
- A list of entitlements. An *entitlement* is a special privilege that not every app needs, such as the ability to talk to iCloud. You won't concern yourself with entitlements unless you write an app that needs one.

Thus, a provisioning profile is sufficient for signing an app as you build it. It says that on this Mac it is permitted to build this app such that it will run on these devices.

There are two types of identity, and hence two types of certificate, and hence two kinds of provisioning profile: *development* and *distribution* (a distribution certificate is also called a *production* certificate). We are concerned here with the development identity, certificate, and profile; I'll talk about the distribution side later in this chapter.

Apple is the ultimate keeper of all information: your certificates, your provisioning profiles, what apps and what devices you've registered. Your communication with Apple, when you need to verify or obtain a copy of this information, will take place through one of two means:

The Member Center

A set of web pages. You need a Developer Program membership to log in. At the Member Center page (*https://developer.apple.com/membercenter*) or at the iOS Dev Center page (*https://developer.apple.com/devcenter/ios/*) click Certificates, Identifiers, & Profiles. You'll have access to all features and information to which you are entitled by your membership type and role. This is the area of Apple's site formerly known as the Portal; the interface was heavily revamped in April 2013.

Xcode

Except for obtaining a distribution provisioning profile, just about everything you would need to do at the Member Center can be done through Xcode instead. When all goes well, using Xcode is a lot simpler! If there's a problem, you can head for the Member Center to iron it out.

Obtaining a Certificate

Setting up an identity and obtaining a certificate is something you only have to do once (or, perhaps, once a year at most; you might have to do it again when your Developer Program membership is renewed). The certificate, you remember, depends upon a private–public key pair. The private key will live in your keychain; the public key will be handed over to Apple, to be built into the certificate. The way you give Apple your public key is through a *request* for the certificate. Thus, the procedure for obtaining a certificate is as follows:

1. Through the Keychain Access program on your computer, you generate the private–public key pair. Your keychain keeps the private key.

2. You embed the public key in a certificate request, and submit the request to Apple at the Member Center, identifying yourself through your Apple ID and (if necessary) your team, and specifying a development or distribution certificate.

3. Apple provides the certificate itself, which also contains the public key.

4. The certificate is downloaded, and is imported by the keychain, which uses the public key to match it up with the correct private key. Your keychain keeps the certificate.

5. Henceforward, Xcode can see the certificate in the keychain, and thus grants you an identity for development or distribution under the appropriate team name.

If that sounds complicated, that's because it is. However, in Xcode 5, all of those steps are performed for you automatically when you request a certificate! Here's what to do:

1. Open Xcode's Accounts preference pane.

2. If you haven't entered your developer Apple ID and password, do so now.

3. On the left, select your Apple ID. On the right, select your team. Click View Details.

4. If you had a certificate and it was revoked from the portal but is still valid, you may see a dialog offering to request and download the certificate. Click Request.

   Otherwise, click the Plus button and choose iOS Development (at the lower left under the Signing Identities column).

Everything then happens automatically: the private–public key pair is generated, and the certificate is requested, generated, downloaded, stored in your keychain, and listed under Signing Identities in the View Details dialog.

(Moreover, a wildcard team development provisioning profile may also be generated, as shown in Figure 9-10. Thus you may now have everything you need to run on a device!)

If that works, then skip the rest of this section. Just in case it doesn't, I'll now describe the more elaborate manual procedure for generating the private–public key pair and the certificate request. Instructions are also available at the Member Center as you initiate the process (go to the Certificates page and click the Plus button at the top right).

You launch Keychain Access and choose Keychain Access → Certificate Assistant → Request a Certificate from a Certificate Authority. Using your name and email address as identifiers, you generate and save to disk a 2048-bit RSA certificate request file. Your private key is stored in your keychain then and there; the certificate request containing your public key has been saved temporarily onto your computer. (For example, you might save it to the desktop.)

At the Member Center, you are presented with an interface allowing you to upload the saved certificate request file. You upload it, and the certificate is generated; click its listing at the Member Center to expose the Download button, and click Download. Locate and double-click the file you just downloaded; Keychain Access automatically imports the certificate and stores it in your keychain. You do not need to keep the certificate request file or the downloaded certificate file; your keychain now contains all the needed credentials. If this has worked, you can see the certificate in your keychain, read its details, and observe that it is valid and linked to your private key (Figure 9-9). Moreover, you should be able to confirm that Xcode now knows about this certificate: in the Accounts preference pane, click your Apple ID on the left and your team name on the right, and click View Details; a dialog opens where you should see an iOS Development signing identity listed at the top, with a Valid status.

Figure 9-9. A valid development certificate, as shown in Keychain Access

 If this is your very, very first time obtaining any certificate from the Member Center, you will need *another* certificate: the WWDR Intermediate Certificate. This is the certificate that certifies that certificates issued by WWDR (the Apple Worldwide Developer Relations Certification Authority) are to be trusted. (You can't make this stuff up.) Xcode should automatically install this in your keychain; if not, you can obtain a copy of it manually by clicking a link at the bottom of the page at the Member Center where you begin the process of adding a certificate.

Obtaining a Development Provisioning Profile

A provisioning profile, as I've already mentioned, unites an identity, a device, and an app bundle id. If things go well, in the simplest case, you'll be able to obtain a development provisioning profile in a single step from within Xcode. If an app doesn't require special entitlements or capabilities, a single development profile associated with your team is sufficient for all your apps, so you might only have to do this step once.

You already have a development identity, from the previous section. You may also have a universal development provisioning profile, from the previous section! If not, do this:

1. Connect a device to your computer.

2. Open the Organizer window in Xcode (Window → Organizer).

3. Switch to the Devices tab.

4. Select the connected device.

Provisioning Profiles	Expiration	Entitlements
iOS Team Provisioning Profile: *	9/19/14	

Done

Figure 9-10. A universal development profile

5. Click Add to Member Center or Use for Development at the bottom of the window.

The device is registered with Apple by its unique identifier number, and a universal development provisioning profile targeted for this device is created and downloaded.

To confirm that the device has been added to the Member Center, go there in your browser and click Devices.

To confirm that you have the universal development provisioning profile, click View Details in the Accounts preference pane (for the appropriate team). Certificates and profiles are listed here. The universal development profile, in addition to the title "iOS Team Provisioning Profile", will have a nonspecific app bundle id associated with it, indicated by an asterisk (Figure 9-10).

The universal development profile allows you to run *any* app on the targeted device for testing purposes, provided that the app doesn't require special entitlements (such as using iCloud).

Additional devices can be introduced through Xcode. Connect the device to your computer. When you click Add to Member Center or Use for Development, the device is automatically registered at the Member Center and added to any team development profiles, and those profiles are automatically regenerated and downloaded into Xcode.

Sometimes, Xcode will generate individual development provisioning profiles for *every* app ID listed at the Member Center for a team. These will then be listed in the Accounts preference pane in the View Details dialog for that team, with the title "iOS Team Provisioning Profile" and a specific app bundle id. For running on a device, these extra team provisioning profiles are probably superfluous.

It is also possible to obtain a development profile manually at the Member Center:

1. At the Member Center, make sure your target device is listed under Devices. If it isn't, click the Plus button and enter a name for this device along with its UDID.

You can copy the device's UDID from its listing in the Devices tab of the Organizer window.

2. For a specific app, make sure your app is registered at the Member Center under Identifiers → App IDs. If it isn't, add it. Click Plus. Enter a name for this app. Don't worry about the nonsense letters and numbers that the Member Center adds as a prefix to your bundle identifier; use the Team ID. Enter the bundle identifier under Explicit App ID exactly as shown in Xcode, in the Bundle Identifier field under General when you edit the app target. (Unfortunately, if the bundle identifier is automatically generated, you can't copy it from the Bundle Identifier field.)

3. Under Provisioning Profiles, click Plus. Ask for an iOS App Development profile. On the next screen, choose the App ID. On the next screen, check your development certificate. On the next screen, select the device(s) you want to run on. On the next screen, give this profile a name, and click Generate. Click the Download button. Find the downloaded profile, and double-click it to open it in Xcode. You can then throw the downloaded profile away; Xcode has made a copy.

Running the App

Once you have a development profile applicable to an app and a device (or, in the case of the universal team profile, all apps and all registered devices), connect the device, choose it as the destination in the Scheme pop-up menu, and build and run the app. You may be asked for permission to access your keychain; grant it. If necessary, Xcode will install the associated provisioning profile onto the device.

The app is built, loaded onto your device, and runs there. As long as you launch the app from Xcode, everything is just as when running in the Simulator: you can run, or you can debug, and the running app is in communication with Xcode, so that you can stop at breakpoints, read messages in the console, and so on. The outward difference is that to interact physically with the app, you use the device (tethered physically to your computer), not the Simulator.

Running the app from Xcode on the device can also be used simply as a way of copying the current version of the app to the device. You can then stop the app (in Xcode), disconnect the device from your computer, and launch the app on the device and play with it. This is a good way of testing. You are not debugging, so you can't get any feedback in Xcode, but NSLog messages are written to the console internally and can be retrieved later.

Profile and Device Management

In Xcode 5, the central location for surveying identities and provisioning profiles is the Accounts preference pane. Select an Apple ID and a team and choose View Details.

An important feature of the Accounts preference pane is the ability to export account information. You'll need this if you want to be able to develop on a different computer. Select an Apple ID and use the Gear menu at the bottom of the pane to choose Export Accounts. You'll be asked for a file name and a place to save, along with a password; this password is associated solely with this file, and is needed only to open the file later on another computer. On the other computer, to which you have copied the exported file, run Xcode and double-click the exported file; Xcode asks for its password. When you provide it, like magic the entire suite of teams and identities and certificates and provisioning profiles springs to life in that other copy of Xcode, including the entries in your keychain.

Alternatively, you might need to export just an identity, without any provisioning profiles. You can do that with the gear menu in the Accounts preference pane's View Details dialog.

If the provisioning profiles listed in the Accounts preference pane's View Details dialog get out of sync with the Member Center, click the Refresh button at the bottom left. If that doesn't help, quit Xcode and, in the Finder, open your user *Library/MobileDevice/ Provisioning Profiles* folder, and delete everything that's in there. Relaunch Xcode. In Accounts, your provisioning profiles are gone! *Now* click the refresh button. Xcode will download fresh copies of all your provisioning profiles, and you'll be back in sync with the Member Center.

When a device is attached to the computer, it is listed with a green dot under Devices in the Organizer window. Click its name to access information on the device. You can see the device's unique identifier. You can see provisioning profiles that have been installed on the device. You can view the device's console log in real time, just as if you were running the Console application to view your computer's logs. You can see log reports for crashes that took place on the device. And you can take screenshots that image your device's screen; you'll need to do this for your app when you submit it to the App Store.

Gauges and Instruments

Xcode provides tools for probing the internal behavior of your app graphically and numerically, and you should keep an eye on those tools. The gauges in the Debug navigator, new in Xcode 5, allow you to monitor CPU and memory usage any time you run your app. And Instruments, a sophisticated and powerful utility application, collects profiling data that can help track down memory management problems and provide the numeric information you need to improve your app's performance and responsiveness. You'll probably want to spend some time with Instruments as your app approaches completion (optimizing prematurely is a waste of time and effort).

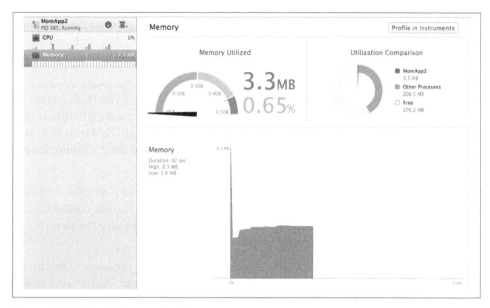

Figure 9-11. The Debug navigation gauges

The gauges in the Debug navigator are operating whenever you build and run your app. Keep an eye on them to track your app's CPU and memory usage. Click on a gauge to see further detail displayed in the editor. The gauges do not provide highly detailed information, but they are extremely lightweight and always active, so they provide an easy way to get a general sense of your running app's behavior at any time. In particular, if there's a problem, such as a prolonged period of unexpectedly high CPU usage or a relentless unchecked increase in memory usage, you can spot it in the gauges and then use Instruments to help track it down.

In Figure 9-11, I've been exercising my app for a few moments, repeatedly performing the typical actions I expect the user to perform most often. The Memory gauge in the Debug navigator looks fairly flat, which is a good sign, but just to be on the safe side I've clicked on it to view the larger memory usage charts in the editor. Certain actions, when performed for the first time, have caused memory to spike or increase, but as these actions are repeated my app's memory usage seems to have settled down and leveled off, so I don't suspect any memory issues.

You can use Instruments on the Simulator or the device. The device is where you'll do your ultimate testing, for maximum verisimilitude, and certain instruments (such as Core Animation) are available only for the device.

To get started with Instruments, set the desired destination in the Scheme pop-up menu in the project window toolbar, and choose Product → Profile. Your app builds using the Profile action for your scheme; by default, this uses the Release build configuration, which is probably what you want. If you're running on a device, you may see some validation warnings, but you can safely ignore them. Instruments launches; if your scheme's Instrument pop-up menu for the Profile action is set to Ask on Launch (the default), Instruments presents a dialog where you choose a trace template.

Alternatively, click Profile In Instruments in a Debug navigator gauge editor; this launches Instruments, selecting the appropriate trace template for you. A dialog offers two options: Restart stops your app and relaunches it with Instruments, whereas Transfer keeps your app running and hooks Instruments into it. Typically, Restart is what you want: you've noticed a possible problem in the gauges, and you want to reproduce it under the more detailed monitoring of Instruments.

With Instruments running, you should interact with your app like a user; Instruments will record its statistics. Once Instruments is running, it can be further customized to profile the kind of data that particularly interests you, and you can save the structure of the Instruments window as a custom template.

Use of Instruments is an advanced topic, which is largely beyond the scope of this book. Indeed, an entire book could (and really should) be written about Instruments alone. For proper information, you should read Apple's documents, especially the *Instruments User Reference* and *Instruments User Guide*. Also, many WWDC videos from current and prior years are about Instruments; look particularly for sessions with "Instruments" or "Performance" in their names. Here, I'll just demonstrate, without much explanation, the sort of thing Instruments can do.

I'll start by charting the memory usage of my TidBITS News app as it starts up and the user proceeds to work with it. Memory is a scarce resource on a mobile device, so it's important to be certain that we're not hogging too much of it. I'll set the destination to the Simulator and choose Product → Profile; Instruments launches, and I'll choose the Allocations trace template and click Profile. My app starts running in the Simulator, and I work with it for a while and then pause Instruments, which meanwhile has charted my memory usage (Figure 9-12). Examining the chart, I find there are a couple of spikes early on, first as the app launches and then as the app downloads and parses an RSS feed; but it's only 5.40 MB at its maximum, and the app settles down to use slightly over 2 MB pretty steadily thereafter. These are very gentle memory usage figures, and memory returns to the same level when the app's interface is returned to its base state, so I'm happy.

Another field of Instruments expertise is the ability to detect memory leaks. Memory leaks, discussed further in Chapter 12, remain possible even under ARC. In this trivial example, I have two classes, MyClass1 and MyClass2; MyClass1 has an `ivar` property which is a MyClass2 instance, and MyClass2 has an `ivar` property which is a MyClass1 instance. The app runs this code:

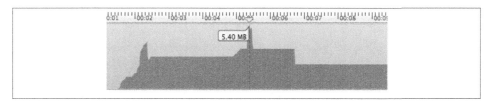

Figure 9-12. Instruments graphs memory usage over time

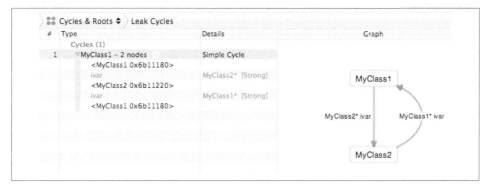

Figure 9-13. Instruments describes a leak

```
MyClass1* m1 = [MyClass1 new];
MyClass2* m2 = [MyClass2 new];
m1.ivar = m2;
m2.ivar = m1;
```

There are steps I could have taken to prevent this from being a memory leak, as I'll explain in Chapter 12; but I haven't taken those steps, so it *is* a memory leak. I'll set the destination to the Simulator and choose Product → Profile; Instruments launches, and I'll choose the Leaks trace template and click Profile. My app starts running in the Simulator, and after about 10 seconds (the default interval at which Instruments runs its leak analysis), a leak is detected. After some appropriate button-pushing, I'm actually shown a diagram of the mistake that's causing this leak (Figure 9-13)!

 When using Instruments to explore memory management, it may help to change the scheme so that the Profile action uses the Debug configuration; it defaults to using the Release configuration, which optimizes your code in ways that can obscure memory management details.

In this final example, I'm concerned with what's taking my Albumen app so long to switch from master view to detail view. I'll set the destination to a device, because that's

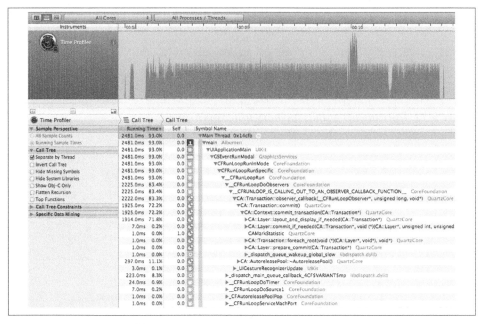

Figure 9-14. A time profile in Instruments

where speed matters and needs to be measured, and choose Product → Profile; Instruments launches, and I'll choose the Time Profiler trace template and click Profile. The master view appears; I'll tap a cell in the table view, and after a significant delay, the detail view appears. Now I'll pause Instruments and look at what it's telling me.

As we can see from Figure 9-14, this transition is taking nearly three seconds. Opening the triangles in the lower portion of the window, it turns out that much of this is spent in something described as `CA::Layer::layout_and_display_if_needed`. That's not my code; it's deep inside Cocoa. But by clicking the little arrow that appears to the right of that line when I hover the mouse over it, I can see the call stack and discover how my code is involved in this call (Figure 9-15).

One line of my code is involved in this call: `tableView:heightForRowAtIndexPath:`. This is where we work out the heights of the table view cells to be shown in the detail view. By double-clicking the listing of that line, I can see my own code, time-profiled (Figure 9-16).

This is really useful information. It's also fairly depressing. The bulk of the time is being spent in Cocoa's `systemLayoutSizeFittingSize:`. That call is how I calculate the height of the table view cell using autolayout. This approach is working perfectly, but clearly it is relatively expensive, and I need to decide whether to keep using it.

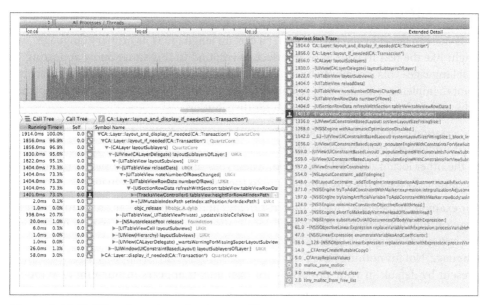

Figure 9-15. Drilling down into the time profile

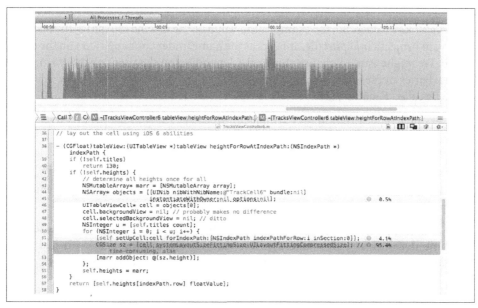

Figure 9-16. My code, time-profiled

Localization

A device can be set by the user to prefer a certain language as its primary language. You might like the text in your app's interface to respond to this situation by appearing in that language. This is achieved by *localizing* the app for that language. You will probably want to implement localization relatively late in the lifetime of the app, after the app has achieved its final form, in preparation for distribution.

Localization operates through localization folders in your project folder and in the built app bundle. Let's say that a resource in one of these localization folders has a counterpart in the other localization folders. Then, when your app goes to load such a resource, it automatically loads the one appropriate to the user's preferred language.

For example, if there's a copy of *InfoPlist.strings* in the English localization folder and a copy of *InfoPlist.strings* in the French localization folder, the latter will be used when the app needs a copy of *InfoPlist.strings* on a device on which French is the preferred language. Not for nothing have I used *InfoPlist.strings* as my example. This is a file that's present by default in your project — for example, it appears in our Empty Window example project — but its purpose wasn't discussed in Chapter 6, so presumably you've been on tenterhooks since then, wondering what it was for. Well, it's a *.strings* file; the purpose of a *.strings* file is to be localized.

The purpose of this particular *.strings* file, *InfoPlist.strings*, is to store localized versions of *Info.plist* key values. So, for example, the value of the `CFBundleDisplayName` key, as set in your project's *Info.plist* file, appears as the name under your app's icon on the user's device. We might want to change this name depending on the user's primary language setting. For example, on a French language device, we might like our Empty Window app to be called Fenêtre Vide.

As an example of localization, let's arrange for that very thing to happen. First we must set up our app for localization to French; then we must localize *InfoPlist.strings*.

1. Edit the project. Under Info, the Localizations table lists our app's localizations.

2. Click the Plus button under the Localizations table. From the pop-up menu that appears, choose French.

3. A dialog appears, listing files that are currently localized for English (because they came that way as part of the app template). We're dealing here with just *Info-Plist.strings*, so leave it checked but uncheck any other files that appear here. Click Finish.

We have now set up *InfoPlist.strings* to be localized for both English and French. This fact is reflected in two ways:

Figure 9-17. How a localized strings file is represented in Xcode

- In the Project navigator, the listing for *InfoPlist.strings* has acquired a flippy triangle. Open the triangle to reveal that our project now contains *two* copies of *Info-Plist.strings*, one for English and one for French (Figure 9-17). Thus we can now edit either one individually.

- In the Empty Window project folder on disk, there is now both an *en.lproj* folder and a *fr.lproj* folder. The former contains the copy of *InfoPlist.strings* destined for English language users; the latter contains the copy of *InfoPlist.strings* destined for French language users. Moreover, when we build, this folder structure is copied into the built app.

Now let's edit our *InfoPlist.strings* files. A *.strings* file is simply a collection of key–value pairs in the following format:

```
/* Optional comments are C-style comments */
"key" = "value";
```

In the case of *InfoPlist.strings*, the key is simply the key name from *Info.plist* — the raw key name, not the English-like name. So the English *InfoPlist.strings* should look like this:

```
"CFBundleDisplayName" = "Empty Window";
```

The French *InfoPlist.strings* should look like this:

```
"CFBundleDisplayName" = "Fenêtre Vide";
```

Now let's try it!

1. Build and run Empty Window on the iPhone Simulator.

2. In Xcode, stop the running project. In the Simulator, the home screen is revealed.

3. Examine the name of our app, as displayed in the Simulator home screen. It is Empty Window (perhaps truncated).

4. In the Simulator, launch the Settings app and change the language to French (General → International → Language → Français). Our app's name is now displayed as Fenêtre Vide.

Is this fun or what? When you're done marveling at your own cosmopolitanism, change the Simulator's language back to English.

Now let's talk about nib files. Before Xcode 4.5 and iOS 6, it was necessary to localize a copy of the entire nib. So, for example, if you wanted a French version of a nib file, you were constantly maintaining two separate nib files. If you created a button in one nib file, you had to create the same button in the other — except that in one, the title was in English, while in the other, the title was in French. And so on, for every interface object and every localization language. It doesn't sound like much fun, does it?

Nowadays, happily, there's a better way — *base internationalization*. If a project uses base internationalization, then a correspondence can be created between a nib file in a *Base.lproj* folder and a *.strings* file in a localization folder. Thus the developer has just one copy of the nib file to maintain. If the app runs on a device that's localized for a language for which a *.strings* file exists, the strings in the *.strings* file are substituted for the strings in the nib file.

By default, our Empty Window project does use base internationalization, and its *Main.storyboard* file is in a *Base.lproj* folder. So we're ready to localize the storyboard file for French:

1. Edit *Main.storyboard* and look at the File inspector. Under Localization, Base should be checked already. In addition, check French.

2. In the Project navigator, examine the listing for *Main.storyboard*. It now has a flippy triangle. Flip it open. Sure enough, there is now a base-localized *Main.storyboard* and a French-localized *Main.strings*.

3. Edit the French *Main.strings*. It has been created automatically, with keys corresponding to every interface item in *Main.storyboard* that has a title. You have to deduce, from comments and the key names, how this correspondence works. In our case, there's just one interface item in *Main.storyboard*, and anyway it's pretty easy to guess what interface item the key represents. It looks something like this:

   ```
   /* Class = "IBUIButton"; normalTitle = "Howdy!"; ObjectID = "Df5-YJ-JME"; */
   "Df5-YJ-JME.normalTitle" = "Howdy!";
   ```

4. In the second line, containing the key–value pair, change the value to "Bonjour!". *Don't change the key!* It has been generated automatically, and correctly, so as to specify the correspondence between this value and the title of the button.

Now we're going to run the project in the Simulator and test it under English and French localizations. Before doing that, if there's a self.button line in *ViewController.m*, comment it out! That line changes the title of the button from its title in the nib — but it's the title in the nib that we're localizing.

Run the project. You should see that when the device is localized for English, the button's title is "Howdy!", but when the device is localized for French, the button's title is "Bonjour!"

If we now modify the nib — let's say we add another button to the view in *Main.story-board* — there's no automatic change to the corresponding *.strings* file(s), which must be regenerated manually. Therefore, in real life it's a good idea not to start localizing your nib files until your interface is pretty much finished. Here's what to do:

1. Select *Main.storyboard* and choose File → Show in Finder.

2. Run Terminal. Type `ibtool --export-strings-file output.strings` followed by a space, and drag *Main.storyboard* from the Finder into the Terminal window. Press Return.

The result is that a new strings file called *output.strings* based on *Main.storyboard* is generated in your home directory (or whatever the current directory is). Merging this information with the existing localized *.strings* files based on *Main.storyboard* is up to you.

For completeness, let's talk about how to make your project use base initialization if it doesn't already. We can use as an example our Truly Empty project, which came from the Empty Application template and had no nib file to start with. We gave it a *View-Controller.xib* file. Let's say we'd like to localize it. Here's how:

1. Edit *ViewController.xib* and localize it for English by clicking the Localize button in the File inspector. A dialog appears asking if we want to start an *.lproj* file for English. We do, so click Localize.

2. Edit the project, and below the Localization table, check Use Base Internationalization.

3. A dialog appears, listing nib files that are currently localized only for English. At present, it lists just *ViewController.xib*, and it is checked. That's good! Click Finish.

After that, the project is ready for you to add localizations to it, as in our earlier examples.

Finally, what about strings that appear in your app's interface but whose value is generated in code? In the Empty Window app, an example would be the alert summoned by tapping the button. The approach is the same — a *.strings* file — but your code must be modified to use it explicitly. There are various ways to do this, but the simplest is to use the `NSLocalizedString` macro (which calls an NSBundle instance method, `localizedStringForKey:table:`). So, for example, we might modify our `button-Pressed:` method to look like this:

```
UIAlertView* av = [[UIAlertView alloc]
            initWithTitle:NSLocalizedString(@"AlertGreeting", nil)
            message:NSLocalizedString(@"YouTappedMe", nil)
            delegate:nil
            cancelButtonTitle:NSLocalizedString(@"Cool", nil)
            otherButtonTitles:nil];
```

The string provided as the first argument to `NSLocalizedString` is intended as the key in a *.strings* file. (The second argument, which I've given as nil, would be in real life a message to your localizer explaining what the string is supposed to say.) Our code is now broken, however, as there is no corresponding *.strings* file! By default, the *.strings* file expected here is called *Localizable.strings*. But no such file exists. There's no error, but these keys have no value either — so the key itself will be used when the alert appears, which is not what we want. You'll need to create the required *.strings* file. Here's how to do it:

1. Choose File → New → File.

2. The "choose a template" dialog appears. On the left, under iOS, select Resource. On the right, select Strings File. Click Next.

3. Name the file *Localizable.strings*. Pick an appropriate Group, and make sure this file is part of our Empty Window app target. Click Create.

4. Now we must localize the new file. In the Project navigator, select *Localizable.strings*. In the File inspector, under Localization, click the Localize button. In the resulting dialog, move the existing file into the English localization or the Base localization; they are the same in this project.

5. In the File inspector, you can now add localizations as desired. For example, check French.

You must now also provide our *Localizable.strings* files with content, in accordance with the localizable string keys specified in your code. You can do this by hand, or, just as we used the `ibtool` command-line tool to generate a *.strings* file from a nib, you can use the `genstrings` tool to generate a *.strings* file from a code file. For example, on my machine I would now say, in the Terminal:

```
$ genstrings /Users/matt/Desktop/Empty\ Window/Empty\ Window/ViewController.m
```

The result is a file *Localizable.strings* in the current directory, reading as follows:

```
/* No comment provided by engineer. */
"AlertGreeting" = "AlertGreeting";

/* No comment provided by engineer. */
"Cool" = "Cool";

/* No comment provided by engineer. */
"YouTappedMe" = "YouTappedMe";
```

Now you copy and paste that content into the English and French versions of our project's *Localizable.strings* files, and go through those pairs, changing the value in each case so that it reads correctly for the given localization. For example, in the English *Localizable.strings* file:

```
"AlertGreeting" = "Howdy!";
```

And in the French *Localizable.strings* file:

```
"AlertGreeting" = "Bonjour!";
```

And so forth.

Archiving and Distribution

By *distribution* is meant providing to others who are not developers on your team your built app for running on their devices. There are two kinds of distribution:

Ad Hoc distribution
> You are providing a copy of your app to a limited set of known users so that they can try it on their specific devices and report bugs, make suggestions, and so forth.

App Store distribution
> You are providing the app to the App Store so that anyone can download it (possibly for a fee) and run it.

> There is a registration limit of 100 devices per year per developer (not per app), which limits your number of Ad Hoc testers. Devices used for development are counted against this limit.

To create a copy of your app for distribution, you need first to build an *archive* of your app. It is this archive that will subsequently be exported for Ad Hoc or App Store distribution. An archive is basically a preserved build. It has three main purposes:

Distribution
> An archive will serve as the basis for an Ad Hoc distribution or an App Store distribution.

Reproduction
> Every time you build, conditions can vary, so the resulting app might behave slightly differently. But an archive preserves a specific built binary; every distribution from a particular archive is guaranteed to contain an identical binary, and thus will behave the same way. This fact is important for testing: if a bug report comes in based on an app distributed from a particular archive, you can Ad Hoc distribute that archive to yourself and run it, knowing that you are testing exactly the same app.

Symbolication
> The archive includes a *.dSYM* file which allows Xcode to accept a crash log and report the crash's location in your code. This allows you to deal with crash reports from users.

Here's how to build an archive of your app:

1. Set the destination in the Scheme pop-up menu in the project window toolbar to iOS Device. (Until you do this, the Product → Archive menu item will be disabled. You do *not* have to have a device connected; you are not building to run on a particular device, but saving an archive that will run on *some* device.)

2. If you like, edit the scheme to confirm that the Release build configuration will be used for the Archive action. (This is the default, but it does no harm to double-check.)

3. Choose Product → Archive. The app is compiled and built. The archive itself is stored in a date folder within your user *Library/Developer/Xcode/Archives* folder. Also, it is listed in the Organizer window under Archives, which may open spontaneously to show the archive you've just created. You can add a comment here; you can also change the archive's name (this won't affect the name of the app).

 In the past, I advised modifying your build project's settings, possibly by adding a configuration, so that an archive would be signed at build time with a distribution profile. That now appears to be unnecessary! By default, an archive will be signed with a development profile; you'll substitute a distribution profile when you export the archive later.

To perform any kind of distribution based on your archive, you will also need a distribution identity (a private key and a distribution certificate in your computer's keychain) and a distribution profile especially for this app. If you're doing an Ad Hoc distribution and an App Store distribution, you'll need a separate distribution profile for each.

You can obtain a distribution identity from within Xcode in exactly the same way as I described obtaining a development identity: in the Accounts preference pane, in the View Details dialog for your team, click the Plus button and choose iOS Distribution. If that doesn't work, obtain the certificate manually, just as I described for a development certificate.

You can't create a distribution profile from Xcode; you have to do it at the Member Center, in your browser. Here's how:

1. If this is to be an Ad Hoc distribution profile, collect the unique identifiers of all the devices where this build is to run, and add each of the device identifiers at the Member Center under Devices. (For an App Store distribution profile, omit this step.)

2. Make sure that the app is registered at the Member Center, as I described earlier in this chapter.

3. At the Member Center, under Provisioning Profiles, click the Plus button to ask for a new profile. In the Add iOS Provisioning Profile form, specify an Ad Hoc profile or an App Store profile. On the next screen, choose your app from the pop-up menu. On the next screen, choose your distribution certificate. On the next screen, for an Ad Hoc profile only, specify the devices you want this app to run on. On the next screen, give the profile a name.

   Be careful about the profile's name, as you will need to be able to recognize it later from within Xcode! My own practice is to assign a name containing both the name of the app and the term "AdHoc" or "AppStore".

4. Click Generate to generate the profile. To obtain the profile, either click Download and then find the downloaded profile and double-click it to get Xcode to see it, or else open the View Details dialog in Xcode's Accounts preference pane and click the Refresh button at the bottom left.

Ad Hoc Distribution

Apple's docs say that an Ad Hoc distribution build should include an icon that will appear in iTunes, but my experience is that this step, though it does work, is unnecessary. If you want to include this icon, it should be a PNG or JPEG file, 512×512 pixels in size, and its name should be *iTunesArtwork*, with *no file extension*. Make sure the icon is included in the build, being present in the Copy Bundle Resources build phase.

Here are the steps for creating an Ad Hoc distribution file:

1. Build an archive of your app, as described in the previous section.

2. In the Organizer window, under Archives, select the archive and click the Distribute button at the upper right of the window. A dialog appears. Here, you are to specify a procedure; choose Save for Enterprise or Ad-Hoc Deployment. Click Next.

3. You are now asked to code-sign the app. You should see a list of distribution profiles. Choose the Ad Hoc distribution profile for this app — you see now the value of creating a meaningful name for the distribution profile!

4. After a while, a Save dialog appears. Give the file a useful name; this won't affect the name of the app. Save the file to disk. It will have the suffix *.ipa* ("iPhone app").

5. Locate in the Finder the file you just saved. Provide this file to your users with instructions.

A user should copy the *.ipa* file to a safe location, such as the Desktop, and then launch iTunes and drag the *.ipa* file from the Finder onto the iTunes icon in the Dock. Then the user should connect the device to the computer, make certain the app is present in the list of apps for this device *and that it will be installed on the next sync*, and finally sync the device to cause the app to be copied to it. (If this isn't the first version of your app that you've distributed to your Ad Hoc testers, the user might need to delete the current version from the device beforehand; otherwise, the new version might not be copied to the device when syncing.)

If you listed your own device as one of the devices for which this Ad Hoc distribution profile was to be enabled, you can obey these instructions yourself to make sure the Ad Hoc distribution is working as expected. First, remove from your device any previous copies of this app (such as development copies) and any profiles that might be associated with this app (in the Settings app, under General → Profiles). Then copy the app onto your device by syncing with iTunes as just described. The app should run on your device, and you should see the Ad Hoc distribution profile on your device (in the Settings app). Because you are not privileged over your other Ad Hoc testers, what works for you should work for them.

Final App Preparations

As the big day approaches when you're thinking of submitting your app to the App Store, don't let the prospect of huge fame and massive profits hasten you past the all-important final stages of app preparation. Apple has a lot of requirements for your app, such as icons and launch images, and failure to meet them can cause your app to be rejected. Take your time. Make a checklist and go through it carefully. See the "App-Related Resources" chapter of Apple's *iOS App Programming Guide* for full details.

At various stages, you can obtain validation of your app to confirm that you haven't omitted certain requirements. For example, by default, a new project's Release build configuration has the Validate Build Product build setting set to Yes. Thus, when I do a build of the Empty Window app we've developed in previous chapters, if that build uses the Release build configuration, Xcode warns that the app has no icon. When you submit your app to the App Store, it will be subjected to even more rigorous validation.

Fortunately, Xcode 5 (unlike earlier versions) provides some decent information on the icon and launch image sizes you'll need. If you're not using an asset catalog, the sizes are listed when you edit the app target, in the General tab (Figure 9-18). Add PNG images of the correct sizes to the project and click the folder button at the right end of a line to select that image in a dialog.

If you're not using an asset catalog for icons or launch images and you'd like to switch to using one, click the Use Asset Catalog button (Figure 9-18). The Use Asset Catalog button then changes to a pop-up menu listing the asset catalog's name and the name of the image set within the catalog to be used for icons or launch images.

If you are using an asset catalog, the image sizes needed are listed in the asset catalog itself. Select an image slot and look in the Attributes inspector, under Expected Size. (Confusingly, "2x" means that the image should be double the listed dimensions for an

Figure 9-18. Icons and launch images, no asset catalog

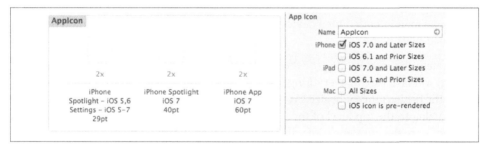

Figure 9-19. Icon slots in the asset catalog

icon, but not for a launch image.) You determine which slots should be displayed with checkboxes in the Attributes inspector when you select an icon set or launch image set (Figure 9-19). To add an image, drag it from the Finder into the appropriate slot.

I recommend using an asset catalog! It makes configuring your icons and launch images ridiculously simple, taking care of naming issues and correctly setting up your *Info.plist* at build time. I'll give examples in the next sections.

Icons in the App

An icon file must be a PNG file, without alpha transparency. It should be a full square; the rounding of the corners will be added for you. For iOS 7, Apple seems to prefer

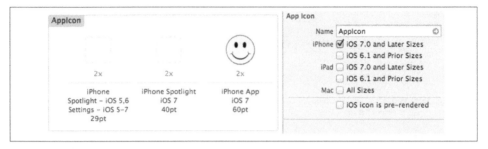

Figure 9-20. An icon in the asset catalog

simple, cartoony images with a few bright colors and possibly a gentle gradient background. Icon files must live at the top level of the app bundle.

On a device, the system uses the "Icon files" key (CFBundleIcons) in your app's *Info.plist* file to locate your icons, and it decides which icon to use under what circumstances by examining their sizes. Therefore, these sizes must be exactly correct. The structure and details for the "Icon files" entry in the *Info.plist* can be elaborate and confusing, especially if your app is to run on multiple device types, and even more so if it is to run on multiple systems. Moreover, there are naming rules: the double-resolution variant of an icon (that is, an icon intended for a device with a double-resolution screen) should have @2x appended to its name.

Fortunately, the asset catalog (or the app target General tab if you're not using an asset catalog) will take care of everything for you. When you provide an icon file, Xcode will balk if the file isn't the right size. At build time, Xcode will write the icons out from the asset catalog to the top level of the app bundle, it will give them correct names, and it will configure the built app's *Info.plist* to point to them correctly.

For example, let's take the simplest case: an iPhone-only, iOS 7-only app. This requires a single 120×120 double-resolution icon — there is no need for a single-resolution variant, because iOS 7 doesn't run on any single-resolution iPhone-type devices. Suppose I've dragged such an image from the Finder into the appropriate slot in my asset catalog, as shown in Figure 9-20.

Then, at build time, Xcode will write this image out to the top level of the app bundle, giving it the name *AppIcon60x60@2x.png* (the prefix "AppIcon" comes from the name of this image set in the catalog), and will insert the appropriate material into the *Info.plist* file, pointing to that image file so that the system on the device can find it:

```
<key>CFBundleIcons~iphone</key>
<dict>
    <key>CFBundlePrimaryIcon</key>
    <dict>
        <key>CFBundleIconFiles</key>
        <array>
```

```
            <string>AppIcon60x60</string>
        </array>
    </dict>
</dict>
```

It seems pointless to summarize the required icon sizes for various systems and devices, because the Xcode 5 interface summarizes them so well. The key requirements are these:

For an iPhone app to run under iOS 7
> One 120×120 double-resolution icon. iOS 7 doesn't run on any single-resolution iPhone-type devices.

For an iPhone app to run under iOS 6 or earlier
> A 57×57 icon and its 114×114 double-resolution variant.

For an iPad app to run under iOS 7
> A 76×76 icon and its 152×152 double-resolution variant.

For an iPad app to run under iOS 6 or earlier
> A 72×72 icon and its 144×144 double-resolution variant.

An app that is to run on multiple device types or on multiple systems (or both) will need all appropriate icons listed above. You can see why the asset catalog is a lifesaver!

Optionally, you may elect to include smaller versions of your icon to appear when the user does a search on the device (as well as in the Settings app if you include a settings bundle). The iOS 7 smaller icon sizes are 29×29 (58×58 double-resolution) for the Settings bundle, and 40×40 (80×80 double-resolution) for search results. However, I never include these icons.

Other Icons

When you submit an app to the App Store, you will be asked to supply a 1024×1024 PNG, JPEG, or TIFF icon to be displayed at the App Store. Have this icon ready before submission. Apple's guidelines say that it should not merely be a scaled-up version of your app's icon; but it must not differ perceptibly from your app's icon, either, or your app will be rejected (I know this from bitter experience).

The App Store icon does *not* need to be built into your app; indeed, it should not be, as it will merely swell the built app's size unnecessarily. On the other hand, you will probably want to keep it in your project (and in your project folder) so that you can find and maintain it easily. So I recommend that you import it into your project and copy it into your project folder, but do *not* add it to any target.

If you created an *iTunesArtwork* icon for Ad Hoc distribution, you may wish to delete it from the Copy Bundle Resources build phase now.

Launch Images

There is a delay between the moment when the user taps your app's icon to launch it and the moment when your app is up and running and displaying its initial window. To cover this delay and give the user a visible indication that something is happening, you must provide a launch image, a PNG file, to be displayed during that interval.

The launch image might be just a blank depiction of the main elements or regions of the interface that will be present when the app has finished launching. In this way, when the app *does* finish launching, the transition from the launch image to the real app will be a matter of those elements or regions being filled in. The best way to create such a launch image is to start with a screenshot of your app's actual initial interface. Typically, I insert some temporary code into my app such that it will launch into a blank version of its normal interface; I then take a screenshot of that, and remove the temporary code. Taking screenshots is covered in the next section.

In iOS 7, a launch image needs to be the full size of the screen. For an iPhone app, the height of the image should be the height of the screen, even if the app launches into landscape orientation (in that case, the launch image should be *turned sideways* to match the initial orientation). For an iPad app, you will usually supply a launch image for portrait orientation and another for landscape orientation (in both single and double resolution sizes).

In iOS 6 and before, an iPad launch image needs to have the status bar region trimmed off the top, unless the app launches into fullscreen mode with no status bar showing. The status bar region is the width of the image and 20 pixels high, meaning 40 pixels for a double-resolution image. (I use the shareware GraphicConverter, *http://www.lemkesoft.com*, to perform this trimming operation easily and precisely.)

Starting with the advent of the iPhone 5 (and fifth-generation iPod touch), whose screen has a taller height dimension than earlier devices, the launch image has a second purpose: it tells the system whether your app is to run "natively" on these devices. The rule is that if your app contains a launch image specifically targeted to this elongated screen size, your app will occupy the entire screen; if not, it will be displayed letterboxed, at the size of the iPhone 4 screen, with black bars at the top and bottom. This taller screen is what the asset catalog refers to as "R4".

(That's why, by default, as I mentioned in Chapter 6, the asset catalog generates a black launch image called *LaunchImage-700-568h@2x~iphone.png* at build time: if it didn't, your app would be letterboxed on the taller screen.)

The base name of a launch image file can be either *Default* or else some other name specified in the *Info.plist*, and there are various additional name qualifiers that must be applied: -568h for a taller iPhone image, @2x for a double resolution image, and ~iphone or ~ipad for a device type. Moreover, in iOS 7, there's a new UILaunchImages *Info.plist* key with a complex structure (see Apple's *Information Property List Key Reference* for the gory details). As with app icons, the simplest solution is to use the asset catalog and let it take care of the file naming and the *Info.plist* setup at build time.

Here are the pixel screen sizes for the current device types:

iPhone 4S and before
  640×960 (double-resolution; iOS 7 doesn't run on a single-resolution iPhone)

iPhone 5 and later
  640×1136 (double-resolution; there is no single-resolution iPhone 5)

iPad
  1024×768 and 2048×1536

Screenshots

When you submit the app to the App Store, you will be asked for one or more screenshots of your app in action to be displayed at the App Store. You should take these screenshots beforehand and be prepared to provide them during the app submission process.

The required screenshot sizes are listed in Apple's *iTunes Connect Developer Guide*, under "Adding New Apps"; look for the table, "Upload file sizes and format descriptions". The dimensions of a screenshot depend on its orientation and the screen size. You must provide at least one screenshot corresponding to the screen size of every device on which your app can run, except that all screenshots must be double-resolution — not because the target device will necessarily be double-resolution, but because there's a chance that this screenshot will be viewed on a double-resolution device.

In iOS 6 and before, unless an app hid the status bar so as to run fullscreen, it was required to trim the status bar region off a screenshot before submitting it (as with iPad launch images, discussed in the previous section). In iOS 7 this isn't necessary, since all apps are fullscreen apps.

You can obtain screenshots either from the Simulator or from a device connected to the computer:

Simulator
  Run the app in the Simulator, using the destination (and, if necessary, the Simulator's Hardware menu) to get the desired device type and resolution. Choose File → Save Screen Shot.

Device
  In Xcode, in the Organizer window, locate your connected device under Devices and click Screenshots. Click New Screenshot, at the lower right of the window. The screenshot is then available in the Organizer window, and you can click Export to get it to the desktop and make it available for upload to the App Store.

You can alternatively take a screenshot on the device by clicking the screen lock button and the Home button simultaneously. Now the screenshot is in the Camera Roll in the Photos app, and you can communicate it to your computer in any convenient way (such as by emailing it to yourself).

If a screenshot is listed in the Organizer window, you can turn it directly into a launch image (see the previous section): select it and click Save as Launch Image. A dialog will ask what name to assign to it and what open project to add it to.

Property List Settings

A number of settings in the *Info.plist* are crucial to the proper behavior of your app. You should peruse Apple's *Information Property List Key Reference* for full information. Most of the required keys are created as part of the template, and are given reasonable default values, but you should check them anyway. The following are particularly worthy of attention:

Bundle display name (`CFBundleDisplayName`)
>The name that appears under your app's icon on the device screen; this name needs to be short in order to avoid truncation.

Supported interface orientations (`UISupportedInterfaceOrientations`)
>This key designates the totality of orientations in which the app is ever permitted to appear. You can perform this setting with checkboxes in the General tab of the target editor. But you may also need to edit the *Info.plist* manually to rearrange the order of possible orientations, because on an iPhone the *first* orientation listed is the one into which the app will actually launch.

Required device capabilities (`UIRequiredDeviceCapabilities`)
>You should set this key if the app requires capabilities that are not present on all devices. Be sure to look over the list of possible values. Don't use this key unless it makes no sense for your app to run *at all* on a device lacking the specified capabilities.

Bundle version (`CFBundleVersion`)
>Your app needs a version number. The best place to set it is the General tab of the target editor. Things are a little confusing here because there is both a Version field and a Build field; the former corresponds in the *Info.plist* to "Bundle versions string, short" (`CFBundleShortVersionString`), while the latter corresponds to "Bundle version" (`CFBundleVersion`). As far as I can determine, Apple will pay attention to the former if it is set, and otherwise will fall back on the latter. In general I play it safe and set both to the same value when submitting to the App Store. The value needs to be a version string, such as "1.0". This version number will appear at the App Store. Failure to increment the version string when submitting an update will cause the update to be rejected.

Status bar style (`UIStatusBarStyle`*)*

Over the years, Apple has changed its policy on the status bar more often than Liberace changes costume. We've had the "grey or black" policy, the "automatic color" policy, the "basic black on iPad" policy, and so forth. The new policy for iOS 7 is simple in itself, but it also reflects the ruined wreck of those earlier accretions.

Basically, on iOS 7, all apps are fullscreen apps, on both iPhone and iPad, and the status bar, if visible, is a transparent overlay. There are just two status bar styles: `UIStatusBarStyleDefault`, meaning the status bar text is black, and `UIStatusBar-StyleLightContent`, meaning the status bar text is white. And the way you set the status bar style has changed in iOS 7; instead of setting it at application level, you set it at view controller level: your app's view controllers, if they don't want `UIStatus-BarStyleDefault`, are expected to set the status bar style by implementing the `preferredStatusBarStyle` method.

Thus, the modern approach is *not* to set the status bar style in your *Info.plist*, but to let your view controllers do it at runtime.

Nonetheless, you *still* might want to set the status bar style in the *Info.plist*, typically for backwards compatibility, because your app also runs on iOS 6 or earlier, or because you have old code that you can't adapt for iOS 7. In this case, continue to use the *Info.plist* status bar style setting as you did in the past; by default, this setting will be ignored on iOS 7.

It is also possible to ask that this setting *not* be ignored on iOS 7. To do so, set the *Info.plist* "View controller–based status bar appearance" key (`UIViewController-BasedStatusBarAppearance`) to NO. This means that your app will not use view controller calls such as `preferredStatusBarStyle` to determine the status bar style; instead, it will set the shared UIApplication's `statusBarStyle` property, as in iOS 6 and before. Now your `UIStatusBarStyle` setting in the *Info.plist* will *not* be ignored on iOS 7; the old Black Translucent ("Transparent black style", `UIStatusBar-StyleBlackTranslucent`) and Black Opaque ("Opaque black style", `UIStatusBar-StyleBlackOpaque`) settings will both be treated as equivalent to the new `UIStatus-BarStyleLightContent`. You can make these settings conveniently with the Status Bar Style pop-up menu in the General pane of the target editor.

Status bar is initially hidden (`UIStatusBarHidden`*)*

This is parallel to the status bar style. In iOS 7, you are expected to show and hide the status bar at the level of your individual view controllers, by implementing the `prefersStatusBarHidden` method. So this *Info.plist* setting will be ignored on iOS 7, unless you've also set the *Info.plist* "View controller–based status bar appearance" key (`UIViewControllerBasedStatusBarAppearance`) to NO. The `UIStatusBar-Hidden` key can be conveniently set, if you still need it, with the "Hide during application launch" checkbox in the General pane of the target editor.

Property list settings can adopt different values depending on what device type you're running on. To specify that a property list setting applies only on a particular type of device, you add to its key the suffix ~iphone, ~ipod, or ~ipad. This feature is typically useful in a universal app, as I described earlier in this chapter.

Submission to the App Store

Before submitting your app to the App Store, it's a good idea to build it as an archive, as described earlier in this chapter, and test it one last time as an Ad Hoc build. The archived build that appears in the Organizer window can be used to generate either an Ad Hoc build or an App Store build. You can't test an App Store build, so you use this archived build to generate an Ad Hoc build and test with that. When you generate the App Store build, you use this same archived build; it is the exact same binary, so you are guaranteed that its behavior will be exactly the same as the build you tested.

When you're satisfied that your app works well, and you've installed or collected all the necessary resources, you're ready to submit your app to the App Store for distribution. To do so, you'll need to make preparations at the iTunes Connect web site. You can find a link to it on the iOS developer pages when you've logged in at Apple's site. You can go directly to *http://itunesconnect.apple.com*, but you'll still need to log in with your iOS Developer username and password.

 The first time you visit iTunes Connect, you should go to the Contracts section and complete submission of your contract. You can't offer any apps for sale until you do, and even free apps require completion of a contractual form.

I'm not going to recite all the steps you have to go through to tell iTunes Connect about your app, as these are described thoroughly in Apple's *iTunes Connect Developer Guide*, which is the final word on such matters. But I'll just mention the main pieces of information you will have to supply:

Your app's name
> This is the name that will appear at the App Store; it need not be identical to the short name that will appear under the app's icon on the device, dictated by the "Bundle display name" setting in your *Info.plist* file. This name can be up to 255 characters long, though Apple recommends that you limit it to fewer than 70 and ideally to fewer than 35 characters. You can get a rude shock when you submit your app's information to iTunes Connect and discover that the name you wanted is already taken. There is no reliable way to learn this in advance, and such a discovery can necessitate a certain amount of last-minute scrambling on your part.

Description

You must supply a description of fewer than 4,000 characters; Apple recommends fewer than 580 characters, and the first paragraph is the most important, because this may be all that users see at first when they visit the App Store. It must be pure text, without HTML and without character styling.

Keywords

This is a comma-separated list shorter than 100 characters. These keywords will be used, in addition to your app's name, to help users discover your app through the Search feature of the App Store.

Support

This the URL of a web site where users can find more information about your app; it's good to have the site ready in advance.

Copyright

Do not include a copyright symbol in this string; it will be added for you at the App Store.

SKU number

This is unimportant, so don't get nervous about it. It's just a unique identifier, unique within the world of your own apps. It's convenient if it has something to do with your app's name. It needn't be a number; it can actually be any string.

Price

You don't get to make up a price. You have to choose from a list of pricing "tiers."

Availability Date

There's an option to make the app available as soon as it is approved, and this will typically be your choice. Alternatively, Apple will send you an email when the app is approved, and you can then return to iTunes Connect and make the app available manually.

 You cannot validate or upload your app until you've formally told iTunes Connect that you have finished your preparations. You do this by clicking Ready to Upload Binary at the top right corner of the iTunes Connect web page. Omitting this step and then wondering why you can't validate or submit is a common mistake.

When you've finished supplying the information for your app, you can do a final validation check: return to the Organizer window, select the archived build, and click Validate. (This feature has not worked well for me in the past, however.)

Finally, when you're ready to upload the app for which you've already submitted the information at iTunes Connect, and when the iTunes Connect status for your app is

"Waiting for Upload," you can perform the upload using Xcode. Select the archived build in the Organizer and click Distribute. In the dialog, choose "Submit to the iOS App Store." The upload will be performed, and the app will be validated at the far end.

Alternatively, you can use Application Loader. Export the archive as an *.ipa* file, as for an Ad Hoc distribution, but use the App Store distribution profile. Launch Application Loader by choosing Xcode → Open Developer Tool → Application Loader, and hand it the *.ipa* file.

You will subsequently receive emails from Apple informing you of your app's status as it passes through various stages: "Waiting For Review," "In Review," and finally, if all has gone well, "Ready For Sale" (even if it's a free app). Your app will then appear at the App Store.

PART III

Cocoa

When you program for iOS, you take advantage of a suite of frameworks provided by Apple. These frameworks, taken together, constitute *Cocoa*; the brand of Cocoa that provides the API for programming iOS is *Cocoa Touch*. Cocoa thus plays an important and fundamental role in iOS programming; your code will ultimately be almost entirely about communicating with Cocoa. The Cocoa Touch frameworks provide the underlying functionality that any iOS app needs to have. Your app can put up a window, show the interface containing a button, respond to that button being tapped by the user, and so forth, because Cocoa knows how to do those things. But with the great advantages of working with a framework come great responsibilities. You have to think the way the framework thinks, put your code where the framework expects it, and fulfill many obligations imposed on you by the framework.

- Chapter 10 picks up where Chapter 5 left off, describing some Objective-C linguistic features used by Cocoa, such as categories and protocols; it also surveys some important fundamental classes.

- Chapter 11 describes Cocoa's event-driven model, along with its major design patterns. An *event* is a message sent by Cocoa to your code. Cocoa is event-based; if Cocoa doesn't send your code an event, your code doesn't run. Getting your code to run at the appropriate moment is all about knowing what events you can expect Cocoa to send you and when.

- Chapter 12 describes your responsibilities for making your instances nicely encapsulated and good memory-management citizens in the world of Cocoa objects.

- Chapter 13 surveys some answers to the question of how your objects are going to see and communicate with one another within the Cocoa-based world.

CHAPTER 10

Cocoa Classes

Using the Cocoa Touch frameworks requires an understanding of how those frameworks organize their classes. Cocoa class organization depends upon certain Objective-C language features that are introduced in this chapter. The chapter also surveys some commonly used Cocoa utility classes, along with a discussion of the Cocoa root class.

Subclassing

Cocoa effectively hands you a large repertory of objects that already know how to behave in certain desirable ways. A UIButton, for example, knows how to draw itself and how to respond when the user taps it; a UITextField knows how to display editable text, how to summon the keyboard, and how to accept keyboard input.

Often, the default behavior or appearance of an object supplied by Cocoa won't be quite what you're after, and you'll want to customize it. This does *not* necessarily mean that you need to subclass! Cocoa classes are heavily endowed with methods that you can call, and properties that you can set, precisely in order to customize an instance, and these will be your first resort. Always study the documentation for a Cocoa class to see whether instances can already be made to do what you want. For example, the class documentation for UIButton shows that you can set a button's title, title color, internal image, background image, and many other features and behaviors, without subclassing.

Nevertheless, sometimes setting properties and calling methods won't suffice to customize an instance the way you want to. In such cases, Cocoa may provide methods that are called internally as an instance does its thing, and whose behavior you can customize by subclassing and overriding (Chapter 4). You don't have the code to any of Cocoa's built-in classes, but you can still subclass them, creating a new class that acts just like a built-in class except for the modifications you provide.

Oddly enough (and you might be particularly surprised by this if you've used another object-oriented application framework), subclassing is probably one of the less important ways in which your code will relate to Cocoa. Knowing when to subclass can be somewhat tricky, but the general rule is that you probably shouldn't subclass unless you're invited to. Some Cocoa Touch classes are subclassed very commonly; for example, a plain vanilla UIViewController, not subclassed, is very rare. But most built-in Cocoa Touch classes will never need subclassing (and some, in their documentation, downright forbid it).

Take, for instance, the case of UIView. Cocoa Touch is full of built-in UIView subclasses that behave and draw themselves as needed (UIButton, UITextField, and so on), and you will rarely need to subclass any of them. On the other hand, you might create your *own* UIView subclass, whose job would be to draw itself in some completely new way. You don't actually draw a UIView; rather, when a UIView needs drawing, its draw-Rect: method is called so that the view can draw itself. So the way to draw a UIView in some completely custom manner is to subclass UIView and implement drawRect: in the subclass. As the documentation says, "Implement this method if your view draws custom content." The word "implement" can only mean "implement in a subclass" — that is, subclass and override. The documentation is saying that you *need* to subclass UIView in order to draw content that is completely your own.

For example, suppose we want our window to contain a horizontal line. There is no horizontal line interface widget built into Cocoa, so we'll just have to roll our own — a UIView that draws itself as a horizontal line. Let's try it:

1. In our Empty Window example project, choose File → New → File and specify a Cocoa Touch Objective-C class, and in particular a subclass of UIView. Call the class MyHorizLine. Xcode creates *MyHorizLine.m* and *MyHorizLine.h*. Make sure, when creating them, that you make them part of the app target.

2. In *MyHorizLine.m*, replace the contents of the implementation section with this (without further explanation):

    ```
    - (id)initWithCoder:(NSCoder *)decoder {
        self = [super initWithCoder:decoder];
        if (self) {
            self.backgroundColor = [UIColor clearColor];
        }
        return self;
    }

    - (void)drawRect:(CGRect)rect {
        CGContextRef c = UIGraphicsGetCurrentContext();
        CGContextMoveToPoint(c, 0, 0);
        CGContextAddLineToPoint(c, self.bounds.size.width, 0);
        CGContextStrokePath(c);
    }
    ```

3. Edit the storyboard. Find UIView in the Object library (it is called simply "View"), and drag it into the View object in the canvas. You may resize it to be less tall.

4. With the UIView that you just dragged into the canvas still selected, use the Identity inspector to change its class to MyHorizLine.

Build and run the app in the Simulator. You'll see a horizontal line corresponding to the location of the top of the MyHorizLine instance in the nib. Our view has drawn itself as a horizontal line, because we subclassed it to do so.

In that example, we started with a bare UIView that had no drawing functionality of its own. That's why there was no need to call super; the default implementation of UIView's drawRect: does nothing. But you might also be able to subclass a built-in UIView subclass to modify the way it already draws itself. For example, the UILabel documentation shows that two methods are present for exactly this purpose. Both drawTextInRect: and textRectForBounds:limitedToNumberOfLines: explicitly tell us: "You should not call this method directly. This method should only be overridden by subclasses." The implication is that these are methods that will be called for us, automatically, by Cocoa, as a label draws itself; thus, we can subclass UILabel and implement these methods in our subclass to modify how a particular type of label draws itself.

Here's an example from one of my own apps, in which I subclass UILabel to make a label that draws its own rectangular border and has its content inset somewhat from that border, by overriding drawTextInRect:. As the documentation tells us: "In your overridden method, you can configure the current [graphics] context further and then invoke super to do the actual drawing [of the text]." Let's try it:

1. In the Empty Window project, make a new class file, a UILabel subclass; call the class MyBoundedLabel.

2. In *MyBoundedLabel.m*, insert this code into the implementation section:

   ```
   - (void)drawTextInRect:(CGRect)rect {
       CGContextRef context = UIGraphicsGetCurrentContext();
       CGContextStrokeRect(context, CGRectInset(self.bounds, 1.0, 1.0));
       [super drawTextInRect:CGRectInset(rect, 5.0, 5.0)];
   }
   ```

3. Edit the storyboard, add a UILabel to the interface, and change its class in the Identity inspector to MyBoundedLabel.

Build and run the app, and you'll see how the rectangle is drawn and the label's text is inset within it. (It may help to add an identical UILabel to the interface, whose class is UILabel, so as to observe the difference in how they draw themselves.)

Another reason why subclassing is rare in Cocoa is that so many built-in classes use the delegate mechanism (Chapter 11) as a way of letting you customize their behavior. You wouldn't subclass UIApplication (the class of the singleton shared application instance) just in order to respond when the application has finished launching, because the delegate mechanism provides a way to do that (application:didFinishLaunchingWith-

`Options:`). That's why the templates give us an AppDelegate class, which is *not* a UIApplication subclass. On the other hand, if you needed to perform certain tricky customizations of your app's fundamental event messaging behavior, you might subclass UIApplication in order to override `sendEvent:`. The documentation does tell you this, and it also tells you, rightly, that doing so would be very rare.

 If you do subclass UIApplication, you'll want to change the third argument in the call to `UIApplicationMain` in *main.m* from nil to the NSString name of your subclass. Otherwise your UIApplication subclass won't be instantiated as the shared application instance. See Chapter 6.

Categories

A *category* is an Objective-C language feature that allows you to reach right into an existing class and inject additional methods. You can do this even if you don't have the code for the class, as with Cocoa's classes. Your instance methods can refer to `self`, and this will mean the instance to which the message was originally sent, as usual. A category, unlike a subclass, cannot define additional instance variables; it can override methods, but you should probably not take advantage of this ability.

Defining a category is almost exactly like defining a class (Chapter 4). You'll need an interface section and an implementation section, and you'll typically distribute them into the standard *.h* and *.m* class file pair. But:

- There's no need, in the interface section, to declare a superclass; this class already exists, and its superclass has already been declared. Indeed, the interface section must have access to the declaration for the original class, typically by importing the header for the original class (or the header of the framework that defines it).

- At the start of both the interface section and the implementation section, where you give the class's name, you add a category name in parentheses.

If you're using a *.h* and *.m* file pair, the *.m* file will, as usual, import the *.h* file. Also, if any other *.m* file in your project needs to call any of your category's injected methods, those methods must be made public with a declaration in the category's *.h* file, and that *.m* file must import the category's *.h* file.

The easiest way to set up a *.h* and *.m* category file pair is to ask Xcode to do it for you. Choose File → New → File, and in the "Choose a template" dialog, among the iOS Cocoa Touch file types, pick "Objective-C category". You'll be asked to give a name for the category and the class on which you're defining this category.

On the other hand, if only one of your classes needs to call this category's injected methods, it is perfectly reasonable to put both the category's interface section and the category's implementation section into that class's *.m* file. In that case, the category's interface section can be empty; the *.m* file can see and use the methods defined in the category's implementation section.

For example, in one of my apps I found myself performing a bunch of string transformations in order to derive the path to various resource files inside the app bundle based on the resource's name and purpose. I ended up with half a dozen utility methods. Given that these methods all operated on an NSString, it was appropriate to implement them as a category of NSString, thus allowing *any* NSString, anywhere in my code, to respond to them.

The code was structured like this (I'll show just one of the methods):

```
// StringCategories.h:
#import <Foundation/Foundation.h>

@interface NSString (MyStringCategories)
- (NSString*) basePictureName;
@end

// StringCategories.m:
#import "StringCategories.h"

@implementation NSString (MyStringCategories)
- (NSString*) basePictureName {
    return [self stringByAppendingString:@"IO"];
}
@end
```

If basePictureName had been implemented as a utility method within some other class, it would need to take a parameter — we'd have to pass an NSString to it — and, if it were an instance method, we'd need to go to the extra trouble of obtaining a reference to an instance of that class. A category is neater and more compact. We've extended NSString itself to have basePictureName as an instance method, so, in any *.m* file that imports *StringCategories.h*, we can send the basePictureName message directly to any NSString we want to transform:

```
NSString* aName = [someString basePictureName];
```

A category is particularly appropriate in the case of a class like NSString, because the documentation warns us that subclassing NSString is a bad idea. That's because NSString is part of a complex of classes called a *class cluster*, which means that an NSString object's real class might actually be some other class. A category is a much better way to modify a class within a class cluster than subclassing.

A method defined through a category can equally be a class method. Thus you can inject utility methods into any appropriate class and call those methods without the overhead of instantiating anything at all. Classes are globally available, so your method becomes, in effect, a global method (see Chapter 13).

For example, in one of my apps I found myself frequently using a certain color (UIColor). Rather than repeating the instructions for generating that color every time I wanted to use it, I put those instructions in *one* place — a category's implementation section, in a *.m* file:

```
@implementation UIColor (MyColors)
+ (UIColor*) myGolden {
    return [self colorWithRed:1.000 green:0.894 blue:0.541 alpha:.900];
}
@end
```

I declared `myGolden` in the category's interface section in the corresponding *.h* file, and imported that *.h* file in my project's *.pch* file (the precompiled header). Since the pre-compiled header is automatically imported throughout my project, I could now call `[UIColor myGolden]` anywhere.

Splitting a Class

A category can be used to split a class over multiple *.h*/*.m* file pairs. If a class threatens to become long and unwieldy, yet it clearly needs to be a single class, you can define the basic part of it (including instance variables) in one file pair, and then add another file pair defining a category on your own class to contain further methods.

Cocoa itself does this. A good example is NSString. NSString is defined as part of the Foundation framework, and its basic methods are declared in *NSString.h*. Here we find that NSString itself, with no category, has just two methods, `length` and `characterAt-Index:`, because these are regarded as the minimum that a string needs to do in order to be a string. Additional methods — those that create a string, deal with a string's encoding, split a string, search in a string, and so on — are clumped into categories. The interface for some of these categories appears in this same file, *NSString.h*. But a string may serve as a file pathname, so we also find a category on NSString in *NSPath-Utilities.h*, where methods are declared for splitting a pathname string into its constituents and the like. Then, in *NSURL.h*, there's another NSString category, declaring methods for dealing with percent-escaping in a URL string. Finally, off in a completely different framework (UIKit), *NSStringDrawing.h* adds two further NSString categories, with methods about drawing a string in a graphics context.

This organization won't matter to you as a programmer, because an NSString is an NSString, no matter how it acquires its methods, but it can matter when you consult the documentation. The NSString methods declared in *NSString.h*, *NSPathUtilities.h*, and *NSURL.h* are documented in the NSString class documentation page, but the NSString methods declared in *NSStringDrawing.h* are not, presumably because they originate in a different framework. Instead, they appear in a separate document,

NSString UIKit Additions Reference. As a result, the string drawing methods can be difficult to discover, especially as the NSString class documentation doesn't link to the other document. I regard this as a major flaw in the structure of the Cocoa documentation. A third-party utility such as AppKiDo can be helpful here.

Class Extensions

A *class extension* is a nameless category that exists solely as an interface section, like this:

```
@interface MyClass ()
// stuff goes here
@end
```

Typically, the only classes that will be permitted to "see" a class extension will be the class that's being extended or a subclass of that class. If only the former is the case, the class extension will usually appear directly in the class's implementation (*.m*) file, like this:

```
// MyClass.m:

@interface MyClass ()
// stuff goes here
@end

@implementation MyClass {
    // ivars
}
// methods
@end
```

That's such a common arrangement that Xcode's project template files actually give you a class extension in certain classes. For example, our Empty Window project comes with a class extension at the start of *ViewController.m* — take a look and see!

What on earth sort of "stuff" could possibly go into a class extension to make it so useful that it appears in a template file? First, I'll tell you what a class extension *used* to be used for: it was the standard solution to the problem of method definition order.

Before the Objective-C language improvements introduced by LLVM compiler version 3.1 (Xcode 4.3), one method in an implementation section couldn't call another method in that same implementation section unless either the definition or a method declaration for that other method preceded it. It's finicky work trying to arrange all the method definitions in the right order, so the obvious solution is a method declaration. A method declaration can go only into an interface section. But to put a method declaration into the interface section in this class's header file is annoying — it means we must switch to another file — and, even worse, it makes that method public; any class that imports that header file can now see and call this method. That's fine if this method is supposed to be public; but what if we wanted to keep it private? The solution: a class extension at the start of this class's implementation file. Put the method declarations into that class extension; all the methods in the implementation section can now see those method declarations and can call one another, but no other class can see them.

Nowadays, though, that trick is unnecessary: methods (and functions) in a class implementation can see and call one another regardless of order.

In modern Objective-C, the usefulness of class extensions has to do mostly with property declarations (which I don't discuss until Chapter 12). Property declarations, like method declarations, must appear in an interface section; and, although some properties are intended to be public, it is also often the case that we would prefer certain properties to remain private to the class — they are global to all methods of the class, and are useful for preserving values and permitting those values to be accessed by multiple methods, but no other class can see them. The solution is to declare the private properties in a class extension.

(For example, in Chapter 7 we declared an IBOutlet property in a class's *.h* file. But in real life we are much more likely to declare such a property in a class extension of the *.m* file; a class's outlets are usually no other class's business.)

I'll describe yet another use of class extensions in the next section.

Protocols

Every reasonably sophisticated object-oriented language must face the fact that the hierarchy of subclasses and superclasses is insufficient to express the desired relationships between classes. For example, a Bee object and a Bird object might need to have certain features in common by virtue of the fact that both a bee and a bird can fly. But Bee might inherit from Insect, and not every insect can fly, so how can Bee acquire the aspects of a Flier in a way that isn't completely independent of how Bird acquires them?

Some object-oriented languages solve this problem through *mixin* classes. For example, in Ruby you could define a Flier module, complete with method definitions, and incorporate it into both Bee and Bird. Objective-C uses a simpler, lighter-weight approach — the *protocol*. Cocoa makes heavy use of protocols.

A protocol is just a named list of method declarations, with no implementation. A class may formally declare that it *conforms* to (or *adopts*) a protocol; such conformance is inherited by subclasses. This declaration satisfies the compiler when you try to send a corresponding message: if a protocol declares an instance method myCoolMethod, and if MyClass declares conformance to that protocol, then you can send the myCool-Method message to a MyClass instance and the compiler won't complain.

Actually implementing the methods declared in a protocol is up to the class that conforms to it. A protocol method may be required or optional. If a protocol method is required, then if a class conforms to that protocol, the compiler will warn if that class fails to implement that method. Implementing optional methods, on the other hand, is optional. (Of course, that's just the compiler's point of view; at runtime, if a message is sent to an object with no implementation for the corresponding method, a crash can result; see Chapter 3.)

Here's an example of how Cocoa uses a protocol. Some objects can be copied; some can't. This has nothing to do with an object's class heritage. Yet we would like a uniform method to which any object that *can* be copied will respond. So Cocoa defines a protocol named NSCopying, which declares just one method, copyWithZone: (required). A class that explicitly conforms to NSCopying is promising that it implements copyWithZone:.

Here's how the NSCopying protocol is defined (in *NSObject.h*, where your code can see it):

```
@protocol NSCopying
- (id)copyWithZone:(NSZone *)zone;
@end
```

That's all there is to defining a protocol. The definition uses the @protocol compiler directive; it states the name of the protocol; it consists entirely of method declarations; and it is terminated by the @end compiler directive.

A protocol definition will typically appear in a header file, so that classes that need to know about it, in order to adopt it or call its methods, can import it. A protocol section of a header file is not inside any other section (such as an interface section).

Any optional methods must be preceded by the @optional directive. A protocol definition may state that the protocol incorporates other protocols; these constitute a comma-separated list in angle brackets after the protocol's name, like this example from Apple's own code (*UIAlertView.h*):

```
@protocol UIAlertViewDelegate <NSObject>
@optional
- (void)alertView:(UIAlertView *)alertView
    clickedButtonAtIndex:(NSInteger)buttonIndex;
// ... more optional method declarations ...
@end
```

The NSCopying protocol definition in *NSObject.h* is just a definition; it is not a statement that NSObject conforms to NSCopying. Indeed, NSObject does *not* conform to NSCopying! To see this, try sending the copyWithZone: method to your own subclass of NSObject:

```
MyClass* mc = [MyClass new];
MyClass* mc2 = [mc copyWithZone: nil];
```

Under ARC, that code won't compile, because no implementation of copyWithZone: has been inherited.

To conform formally to a protocol, a class's interface section appends the name of the protocol, in angle brackets, after the name of the superclass (or, if this is a category declaration, after the parentheses). This will necessitate importing the header file that declares the protocol (or some header file that imports that header file). To state that a class conforms to multiple protocols, put multiple protocol names in the angle brackets, separated by comma.

Let's see what happens if you conform formally to the NSCopying protocol. Modify the first line of the interface section of your class as follows:

```
@interface MyClass : NSObject <NSCopying>
```

Now your code compiles, but the compiler warns that MyClass fails to implement copy-WithZone:, which it is contracted to do because copyWithZone: is a required method of the NSCopying protocol.

The name of a protocol may also be used when specifying an object type. Most often, the object will be typed as an id, but with the accompanying proviso that it conforms to a protocol, whose name appears in angle brackets.

To illustrate, let's look at another typical example of how Cocoa uses protocols, namely in connection with a table view (UITableView). A UITableView has a dataSource property, declared like this:

```
@property (nonatomic, assign) id<UITableViewDataSource> dataSource
```

This property represents an instance variable whose type is id <UITableViewData-Source>. This means "I don't care what class my data source belongs to, but whatever it is, it should conform to the UITableViewDataSource protocol." Such conformance constitutes a promise that the data source will implement at least the required instance methods tableView:numberOfRowsInSection: and tableView:cellForRowAtIndex-Path:, which the table view will call when it needs to know what data to display.

If you attempt to set a table view's dataSource property to an object that does *not* conform to UITableViewDataSource, you'll get a warning from the compiler. So, for example:

```
MyClass* mc = [MyClass new];
UITableView* tv = [UITableView new];
tv.dataSource = mc; // compiler warns
```

Under ARC, this warning is couched in rather confusing terms, along these lines: "Assigning to 'id<UITableViewDataSource>' from incompatible type 'MyClass *__strong'."

To quiet the compiler, MyClass's declaration should state that it conforms to UITable-ViewDataSource. Once it does so, MyClass *is* an id <UITableViewDataSource>, and the third line no longer generates a warning. Of course, you must also supply implementations of tableView:numberOfRowsInSection: and tableView:cellForRowAt-

`IndexPath:` in MyClass to avoid the other warning, namely that you're not implementing a required method of a protocol you've claimed to conform to.

In a very large percentage of cases, the object that you want to assign where conformity to a protocol is expected is `self`. In this situation, you can declare this class's conformity to the protocol in the implementation (.*m*) file as part of a class extension, like this:

```
// MyClass.m:
@interface MyClass () <UITableViewDataSource>
@end

@implementation MyClass
- (void) someMethod {
    UITableView* tv = [UITableView new];
    tv.dataSource = self;
}
@end
```

I prefer this arrangement, because it means that the declaration of conformity to the protocol is right there in the same file that uses the protocol.

A prevalent use of protocols in Cocoa is in connection with delegate objects (and indeed, it is primarily in order to implement delegation that you are most likely to define your own protocols). We'll talk in detail about delegates in Chapter 11, but you can readily see that many classes have a `delegate` property and that the class of this property is often `id <SomeProtocol>`. For example, in our Empty Window project, the App-Delegate class provided by the project template is declared like this:

```
@interface AppDelegate : UIResponder <UIApplicationDelegate>
```

The reason is that AppDelegate's purpose on earth is to serve as the shared application's delegate. The shared application object is a UIApplication, and UIApplication's `delegate` property is typed as an `id <UIApplicationDelegate>`. So AppDelegate announces its role by explicitly conforming to UIApplicationDelegate.

A slight chicken-and-egg problem arises in a header file containing a protocol definition and a class's interface section, each of which mentions the other. The class's interface section, it seems, cannot come first, because it mentions the protocol before the protocol has been defined; but the protocol definition can't come first either, because it mentions the class before the class has been defined. The usual solution is to put the class's interface section first, preceded by a *forward declaration* of the protocol, a single line introducing just the name of the protocol, whose definition will be forthcoming elsewhere — meaning, as it turns out, three lines from now:

```
@protocol MyProtocol;
@interface MyClass : NSObject
@property (nonatomic, weak) id<MyProtocol> delegate;
@end
@protocol MyProtocol
- (void) doSomething: (MyClass*) m;
@end
```

As a programmer, Cocoa's use of protocols will matter to you in two ways:

Conformity

If an object value that you wish to assign or pass as an argument is typed as id <Some-Protocol>, you must make sure that that object's class does indeed conform to SomeProtocol (and implements any methods required by that protocol).

Using the documentation

A protocol has its own documentation page. When the UIApplication class documentation tells you that the delegate property is typed as an id <UIApplication-Delegate>, it's implicitly telling you that if you want to know what messages a UIApplication's delegate might receive, you need to look in the UIApplication-Delegate protocol documentation.

Similarly, when a class's documentation mentions that the class conforms to a protocol, don't forget to examine that protocol's documentation, because the latter might contain important information about how the class behaves. To learn what messages can be sent to an object, as I already mentioned in Chapter 8, you need to look upward through the superclass inheritance chain; you also need to look at any protocols that this object's class (or superclass) conforms to.

Informal Protocols

You may occasionally see, online or in the documentation, a reference to an *informal protocol*. An informal protocol isn't really a protocol at all; it's just a way of providing the compiler with a method signature so that it will allow a message to be sent without complaining.

There are two complementary ways to implement an informal protocol. One is to define a category on NSObject; this makes any object eligible to receive the messages listed in the category. The other is to define a protocol to which no class formally conforms; instead, send any message listed in the protocol only to objects typed as id, thus suppressing any possible objections from the compiler.

These techniques were widespread before protocols could declare methods as optional; now they are largely unnecessary. (They are still used, but decreasingly so; in iOS 7 very few informal protocols remain.) They are also mildly dangerous, because you might accidentally define a method with the same name as an existing method but a different signature, with unpredictable results.

Optional Methods

A protocol can explicitly designate some or all of its methods as optional. The question thus arises: How, in practice, is such an optional method feasible? We know that if a message is sent to an object and the object can't handle that message, an exception is raised and your app will likely crash. But a method declaration is a contract suggesting that the object *can* handle that message. If we subvert that contract by declaring a method that might or might not be implemented, aren't we inviting crashes?

The answer is that Objective-C is not only dynamic but also introspective. You can ask an object whether it can really deal with a message without actually sending it that message. The key method here is NSObject's `respondsToSelector:`, which takes a selector parameter and returns a BOOL. With it, you can send a message to an object only if it would be safe to do so:

```
MyClass* mc = [MyClass new];
if ([mc respondsToSelector:@selector(woohoo)]) {
    [mc woohoo];
}
```

You wouldn't want to do this before sending just any old message, because it isn't necessary except for optional methods, and it slows things down a little. But Cocoa does in fact call `respondsToSelector:` on your objects as a matter of course. To see that this is true, implement `respondsToSelector:` on AppDelegate in our Empty Window project and instrument it with logging:

```
- (BOOL) respondsToSelector: (SEL) sel {
    NSLog(@"%@", NSStringFromSelector(sel));
    return [super respondsToSelector:(sel)];
}
```

The output on my machine, as the Empty Window app launches, includes the following (I'm omitting private methods and multiple calls to the same method):

```
application:handleOpenURL:
application:openURL:sourceApplication:annotation:
applicationDidReceiveMemoryWarning:
applicationWillTerminate:
applicationSignificantTimeChange:
application:willChangeStatusBarOrientation:duration:
application:didChangeStatusBarOrientation:
application:willChangeStatusBarFrame:
application:didChangeStatusBarFrame:
application:deviceAccelerated:
application:deviceChangedOrientation:
applicationDidBecomeActive:
applicationWillResignActive:
applicationDidEnterBackground:
applicationWillEnterForeground:
applicationWillSuspend:
```

```
application:didResumeWithOptions:
application:shouldSaveApplicationState:
application:supportedInterfaceOrientationsForWindow:
application:performFetchWithCompletionHandler:
application:didReceiveRemoteNotification:fetchCompletionHandler:
application:willFinishLaunchingWithOptions:
application:didFinishLaunchingWithOptions:
```

That's Cocoa, checking to see which of the optional UIApplicationDelegate protocol methods (including a couple of undocumented methods) are actually implemented by our AppDelegate instance — which, because it is the UIApplication object's delegate and formally conforms to the UIApplicationDelegate protocol, has explicitly agreed that it *might* be willing to respond to any of those messages. The entire delegate pattern (Chapter 11) depends upon this technique. Observe the policy followed here by Cocoa: it checks all the optional protocol methods once, when it first meets the object in question, and presumably stores the results; thus, the app is slowed a tiny bit by this one-time initial bombardment of respondsToSelector: calls, but now Cocoa knows all the answers and won't have to perform any of these same checks on the same object later.

Some Foundation Classes

The Foundation classes of Cocoa provide basic data types and utilities that will form the basis of much that you do in Cocoa. Obviously I can't list all of them, let alone describe them fully, but I can survey a few that I use frequently and that you'll probably want to be aware of before writing even the simplest Cocoa program. For more information, start with Apple's list of the Foundation classes in the *Foundation Framework Reference*.

Useful Structs and Constants

NSRange is a struct of importance in dealing with some of the classes I'm about to discuss. Its components are integers (NSUInteger), location and length. For example, a range whose location is 1 starts at the second element of something (because element counting is always zero-based), and if its length is 2 it designates this element and the next. Cocoa also supplies various convenience methods for dealing with a range; you'll use NSMakeRange frequently. (Note that the name, NSMakeRange, is backward compared to names like CGPointMake and CGRectMake.)

NSNotFound is a constant integer indicating that some requested element was not found. For example, if you ask for the index of a certain object in an NSArray and the object isn't present in the array, the result is NSNotFound. (The result could not be 0 to indicate the absence of the object, because 0 would indicate the first element of the array. Nor could it be nil, because nil is 0, and in any case is not appropriate when an integer is expected. Nor could it be -1, because an array index value is always positive.) The true numeric value of NSNotFound is of no concern to you; always compare against NSNot-Found itself, to learn whether a result is a meaningful index.

If a search returns a range and the thing sought is not present, the location component of the resulting NSRange will be NSNotFound.

NSString and Friends

NSString, which has already been used rather liberally in examples in this book, is the Cocoa object version of a string. You can create an NSString through a number of class methods and initializers, or by using the NSString literal notation @"...", which is really a compiler directive. Particularly important is stringWithFormat:, which lets you convert numbers to strings and combine strings; see Chapter 9, where I discussed format strings in connection with NSLog. Here are some strings in action:

```
int x = 5;
NSString* s = @"widgets";
NSString* s2 = [NSString stringWithFormat:@"You have %d %@.", x, s];
```

NSString has a modern, Unicode-based idea of what a string can consist of. A string's "elements" are its characters, whose count is its length. These are not bytes, because the numeric representation of a Unicode character could be multiple bytes, depending on the encoding. Nor are they glyphs, because a composed character sequence that prints as a single "letter" can consist of multiple characters. Thus the length of an NSRange indicating a single "character" might be greater than 1. See the "Characters and Grapheme Clusters" chapter of Apple's *String Programming Guide*.

An NSString can be searched using various rangeOf... methods, which return an NSRange. In addition, NSScanner lets you walk through a string looking for pieces that fit certain criteria; for example, with NSScanner (and NSCharacterSet) you can skip past everything in a string that precedes a number and then extract the number. The rangeOfString: family of search methods lets you look for a substring; using the option NSRegularExpressionSearch, you can search using a regular expression, and regular expressions are also supported as a separate class, NSRegularExpression (which uses NSTextCheckingResult to describe match results).

In this example from one of my apps, the user has tapped a button whose title is something like "5 by 4" or "4 by 3". I want to know both numbers; one tells me how many rows the layout is to have, the other how many columns. I use an NSScanner to locate the two numbers in the title:

```
NSString* s = // title of button, e.g. @"4 by 3"
NSScanner* sc = [NSScanner scannerWithString:s];
int rows, cols;
[sc scanInt:&rows];
[sc scanUpToCharactersFromSet:[NSCharacterSet decimalDigitCharacterSet]
                   intoString:nil];
[sc scanInt:&cols];
```

After that, `rows` and `cols` hold the desired numbers. Here's how I might do the same thing using a regular expression:

```
NSString* s = // title of button, e.g. @"4 by 3"
int rowcol[2]; int* prowcol = rowcol;
NSError* err = nil;
NSRegularExpression* r =
    [NSRegularExpression regularExpressionWithPattern:@"\\d"
                                              options:0
                                                error:&err];
// error-checking omitted
for (NSTextCheckingResult* match in
    [r matchesInString:s options:0 range:NSMakeRange(0, [s length])])
        *prowcol++ = [[s substringWithRange: [match range]] intValue];
```

After that, `rowcol[0]` and `rowcol[1]` hold the desired numbers. The syntax seems oddly tortured, though, because we must convert each match from an NSTextCheckingResult to a range, then to a substring of our original string, and finally to an integer.

More sophisticated automated textual analysis is supported by some additional classes, such as NSDataDetector, an NSRegularExpression subclass that efficiently finds certain types of string expression such as a URL or a phone number, and NSLinguisticTagger, which actually attempts to analyze text into its grammatical parts of speech.

An NSString object's string is immutable. You can use a string to generate another string in various ways, such as by appending another string or by extracting a substring, but you can't alter the string *itself*. For that, you need NSString's subclass, NSMutableString.

NSString has convenience utilities for working with a file path string, and is often used in conjunction with NSURL, which is another Foundation class worth looking into. NSString and some other classes discussed in this section provide methods for writing out to a file's contents or reading in a file's contents; when you call those methods, the file can be specified either as an NSString file path or as an NSURL.

An NSString carries no font and size information. Interface objects that display strings (such as UILabel) have a `font` property that is a UIFont; but this determines the *single* font and size in which the string will display. Before iOS 6, display of styled text — where different runs of text have different style attributes (size, font, color, and so forth) — was quite challenging. The NSAttributedString class, embodying a string along with style runs, required the use of Core Text, and you had to lay out the styled text by drawing it yourself; you couldn't display styled text in any standard interface object. Starting in iOS 6, however, NSAttributedString became a full-fledged Objective-C class. It has methods and supporting classes that allow you to style text and paragraphs easily in sophisticated ways — and the built-in interface objects that display text can display styled text.

String drawing in a graphics context can be performed with methods provided through the NSStringDrawing category on NSString (see the *String UIKit Additions Reference*) and on NSAttributedString (see the *NSAttributedString UIKit Additions Reference*).

NSDate and Friends

An NSDate is a date and time, represented internally as a number of seconds (NSTime-Interval) since some reference date. Calling [NSDate new] or [NSDate date] gives you a date object for the current date and time; other date operations may involve NSDate-Components and NSCalendar and can be a bit tricky because calendars are complicated (see the *Date and Time Programming Guide*). Here's an example of constructing a date based on its calendrical values:

```
NSCalendar* greg =
    [[NSCalendar alloc] initWithCalendarIdentifier:NSGregorianCalendar];
NSDateComponents* comp = [NSDateComponents new];
comp.year = 2013;
comp.month = 8;
comp.day = 10;
comp.hour = 15;
NSDate* d = [greg dateFromComponents:comp];
```

Similarly, the way to do correct date arithmetic is to use NSDateComponents. Here's how to add one day to a given date:

```
NSDate* d = // whatever
NSDateComponents* comp = [NSDateComponents new];
comp.day = 1;
NSCalendar* greg =
    [[NSCalendar alloc] initWithCalendarIdentifier:NSGregorianCalendar];
NSDate* d2 = [greg dateByAddingComponents:comp toDate:d options:0];
```

You will also likely be concerned with dates represented as strings. Creation and parsing of date strings involves NSDateFormatter, which uses a format string similar to NSString's stringWithFormat. A complication is added by the fact that the exact string representation of a date component or format can depend upon the user's locale, consisting of language, region format, and calendar settings. (Actually, locale considerations can also play a role in NSString format strings.)

In this example from one of my apps, I prepare the content of a UILabel reporting the date and time when our data was last updated. The app is not localized — the word "at" appearing in the string is always going to be in English — so I want complete control of the presentation of the date and time components as well. To get it, I have to insist upon a particular locale:

```
NSDateFormatter *df = [NSDateFormatter new];
if ([[NSLocale availableLocaleIdentifiers] indexOfObject:@"en_US"]
        != NSNotFound) {
    NSLocale* loc = [[NSLocale alloc] initWithLocaleIdentifier:@"en_US"];
    [df setLocale:loc]; // English month name and time zone name if possible
}
[df setDateFormat:@"'Updated' d MMMM yyyy 'at' h:mm a z"];
NSString* updatedString = [df stringFromDate: [NSDate date]]; // just now
```

At the other end of the spectrum, to surrender completely to the user's locale, generate an NSDateFormatter's format with `dateFormatFromTemplate:options:locale:` and the current locale. The "template" is a string listing the date components to be used, but their order, punctuation, and language are left up to the locale:

```
NSDateFormatter *df = [NSDateFormatter new];
NSString* format =
    [NSDateFormatter dateFormatFromTemplate:@"dMMMMyyyyhmmaz"
        options:0 locale:[NSLocale currentLocale]];
[df setDateFormat:format];
NSString* updatedString = [df stringFromDate: [NSDate date]]; // just now
```

On a device set to a French locale (Settings → General → International → Region Format), the result might be "20 juillet 2013 5:14 PM UTC–7". Observe that a locale is not a system language: that result is in French because of the device's locale setting, not its language setting. To learn more about locales in general, consult in your browser the documentation for ICU (International Components for Unicode), from which the iOS support for creating and parsing date strings is derived. To study what locales exist, use the locale explorer at *http://demo.icu-project.org/icu-bin/locexp*.

An extremely common beginner error is forgetting that a date has a time zone. For example, when logging an NSDate with `NSLog`, the time (and day) may appear to be wrong, because the value is being represented as GMT (London). To prevent this, call `descriptionWithLocale:`, supplying the desired locale (usually the current locale), or use a date formatter.

NSNumber

An NSNumber is an object that wraps a numeric value (including BOOL). Thus, you can use it to store and pass a number where an object is expected. An NSNumber is formed from an actual number with a method that specifies the numeric type; for example, you can call `numberWithInt:` to form a number from an int:

```
[[NSUserDefaults standardUserDefaults] registerDefaults:
    [NSDictionary dictionaryWithObjectsAndKeys:
        [NSNumber numberWithInt: 4],
        @"cardMatrixRows",
        [NSNumber numberWithInt: 3],
        @"cardMatrixColumns",
        nil]];
```

As I mentioned in Chapter 5, LLVM compiler version 4.0 (Xcode 4.4) brought with it a new syntax for forming a new NSNumber instance:

- Precede a literal number (or BOOL) with @. To specify further the numeric type, follow the literal number with U (unsigned integer), L (long integer), LL (long long integer), or F (float). For example, @3.1415 is equivalent to [NSNumber numberWith-Double:3.1415]; @YES is equivalent to [NSNumber numberWithBool:YES].

- If an expression yields a number, wrap it in parentheses and precede the left parenthesis with @. For example, if height and width are floats, @(height/width) is equivalent to [NSNumber numberWithFloat: height/width].

Thus, the preceding example can be rewritten like this:

```
[[NSUserDefaults standardUserDefaults] registerDefaults:
    [NSDictionary dictionaryWithObjectsAndKeys:
        @4,
        @"cardMatrixRows",
        @3,
        @"cardMatrixColumns",
        nil]];
```

(There is also an NSDictionary literal syntax, so it will turn out, a few pages from now, that we can rewrite that code even more compactly.)

An NSNumber is not itself a number, however, so you can't use it in calculations or where an actual number is expected. Instead, you must explicitly extract the number from its NSNumber wrapper using the inverse of the method that wrapped the number to begin with. Knowing what that method was is up to you. So, for example, if an NSNumber wraps an int, you can call intValue to extract the int:

```
NSUserDefaults* ud = [NSUserDefaults standardUserDefaults];
int therows = [[ud objectForKey:@"cardMatrixRows"] intValue];
int thecols = [[ud objectForKey:@"cardMatrixColumns"] intValue];
```

Actually, this is such a common transformation when communicating with NSUser-Defaults that convenience methods are provided. So I could have written the same thing this way:

```
NSUserDefaults* ud = [NSUserDefaults standardUserDefaults];
int therows = [ud integerForKey:@"cardMatrixRows"];
int thecols = [ud integerForKey:@"cardMatrixColumns"];
```

An NSNumber subclass, NSDecimalNumber, on the other hand, *can* be used in calculations, thanks to a bunch of arithmetic methods (or their C equivalent functions, which are faster). This is useful particularly for rounding, because there's a handy way to specify the desired rounding behavior.

NSValue

NSValue is NSNumber's superclass. Use it for wrapping nonnumeric C values such as structs where an object is expected — for storage in an NSArray, for example, or for use as a value with key–value coding.

Convenience methods provided through the NSValueUIGeometryExtensions category on NSValue (see the *NSValue UIKit Additions Reference*) allow easy wrapping and unwrapping of CGPoint, CGSize, CGRect, CGAffineTransform, UIEdgeInsets, and UIOffset; additional categories allow easy wrapping and unwrapping of NSRange, CATransform3D, CMTime, CMTimeMapping, CMTimeRange, MKCoordinate, and MKCoordinateSpan. You are unlikely to need to store any other kind of C value in an NSValue, but you can if you need to.

NSData

NSData is a general sequence of bytes; basically, it's just a buffer, a chunk of memory. It is immutable; the mutable version is its subclass NSMutableData.

In practice, NSData tends to arise in two main ways:

- When downloading data from the Internet. For example, NSURLConnection and NSURLSession supply whatever they retrieve from the Internet as NSData. Transforming it from there into (let's say) a string, specifying the correct encoding, would then be up to you.
- When storing an object as a file or in user preferences. For example, you can't store a UIColor value directly into user preferences. So if the user has made a color choice and you need to save it, you transform the UIColor into an NSData (using NSKeyedArchiver) and save that:

```
[[NSUserDefaults standardUserDefaults] registerDefaults:
    [NSDictionary dictionaryWithObjectsAndKeys:
        [NSKeyedArchiver archivedDataWithRootObject:[UIColor blueColor]],
        @"myColor",
        nil]];
```

Equality and Comparison

The foregoing types will quickly come to seem to you like basic data types, but of course they are actually object types — which means that they are pointers (Chapter 3). Therefore you cannot compare them using the C operators for testing equality as you would with actual numbers. That's because, in the case of object types, the C operators compare the pointers, not the object content of the instances. For example:

```
NSString* s1 = [NSString stringWithFormat:@"%@, %@", @"Hello", @"world"];
NSString* s2 = [NSString stringWithFormat:@"%@, %@", @"Hello", @"world"];
if (s1 == s2) // false
    // ...
```

The two strings are equivalent (@"Hello, world") but are not the same object. (The example is deliberately elaborate because Cocoa's efficient management of string literals sees to it that two strings initialized directly as @"Hello, world" *are* the same object, which wouldn't illustrate the point I'm making.)

It is up to individual classes to implement a test for equality. The general test, isEqual:, is inherited from NSObject and overridden, but some classes also define more specific and efficient tests. Thus, the correct way to perform the above test is like this:

```
if ([s1 isEqualToString: s2])
```

Similarly, it is up to individual classes to supply ordered comparison methods. The standard method is called compare:, and returns one of three constants: NSOrdered-Ascending (the receiver is less than the argument), NSOrderedSame (the receiver is equal to the argument), or NSOrderedDescending (the receiver is greater than the argument); see Example 3-2.

NSIndexSet

NSIndexSet expresses a collection of unique whole numbers; its purpose is to express element numbers of an ordered collection, such as an NSArray. Thus, for instance, to retrieve multiple objects simultaneously from an array, you specify the desired indexes as an NSIndexSet. It is also used with other things that are array-like; for example, you pass an NSIndexSet to a UITableView to indicate what sections to insert or delete.

To take a specific example, let's say you want to speak of elements 1, 2, 3, 4, 8, 9, and 10 of an NSArray. NSIndexSet expresses this notion in some compact implementation that can be readily queried. The actual implementation is opaque, but you can imagine that in this case the set might consist of two NSRange structs, {1,4} and {8,3}, and NSIndexSet's methods actually invite you to think of an NSIndexSet as composed of ranges.

An NSIndexSet is immutable; its mutable subclass is NSMutableIndexSet. You can form a simple NSIndexSet consisting of just one contiguous range directly, by passing an NSRange to indexSetWithIndexesInRange:; but to form a more complex index set you'll need to use NSMutableIndexSet so that you can append additional ranges.

To walk through (enumerate) the index values or ranges specified by an NSIndexSet, call `enumerateIndexesUsingBlock:` or `enumerateRangesUsingBlock:` or their variants.

NSArray and NSMutableArray

An NSArray is an ordered collection of objects. Its length is its `count`, and a particular object can be obtained by index number using `objectAtIndex:`. The index of the first object is zero, so the index of the last object is `count` minus one.

Starting with LLVM compiler version 4.0 (Xcode 4.5), it is no longer necessary to call `objectAtIndex:`; instead, you can use a notation reminiscent of C and other languages that have arrays, namely, append square brackets containing the index number to the array reference (*subscripting*).

So, for example, if pep consists of `@"Manny"`, `@"Moe"`, and `@"Jack"`, then `pep[2]` yields `@"Jack"`; it is equivalent to `[pep objectAtIndex:2]`. Okay, I lied; actually, `pep[2]` is equivalent to `[pep objectAtIndexedSubscript:2]`. That's because the subscripting notation causes *any* reference to which the subscript is appended to be sent `objectAtIndexedSubscript:`. This in turn means that *any* class can implement `objectAtIndexedSubscript:` and become eligible for subscripting notation — including your classes. Note that this method must be publicly declared for the compiler to permit the subscripting notation.

You can form an NSArray in various ways, but typically you'll start by supplying a list of the objects it is to contain. As I mentioned in Chapter 3, a literal syntax (starting with LLVM compiler version 4.0, Xcode 4.4 or later) lets you wrap this list in `@[ ... ]` as a way of generating the NSArray:

```
NSArray* pep = @[@"Manny", @"Moe", @"Jack"];
```

An NSArray is immutable. This doesn't mean you can't mutate any of the objects it contains; it means that once the NSArray is formed you can't remove an object from it, insert an object into it, or replace an object at a given index. To do those things, you can derive a new array consisting of the original array plus or minus some objects, or use NSArray's subclass, NSMutableArray.

NSMutableArray's `addObject:` and `replaceObjectAtIndex:withObject:` are supplemented by the same subscripting notation that applies to NSArray. In this case, though, the subscripted reference is an lvalue — you're assigning to it:

```
pep[3] = @"Zelda";
```

That causes the NSMutableArray to be sent `setObject:atIndexedSubscript:`. NSMutableArray implements this in such a way that, if pep has three elements, `pep[3] = @"Zelda"` is equivalent to `addObject:` (you're appending to the end of the array), but if pep has more than three elements, it's equivalent to replaceObjectAtIndex:with-Object:. (If pep has fewer than three elements, an exception is thrown.)

You can walk through (enumerate) every object in an array with the for...in construct described in Chapter 1. (You'll get an exception if you try to mutate an NSMutableArray while enumerating it.)

You can seek an object within an array with indexOfObject: or indexOfObject-IdenticalTo:; the former's idea of equality is to call isEqual:, whereas the latter uses pointer equality.

Those familiar with other languages may miss such utility array functions as map, which builds a new array of the results of calling a method on each object in the array. (make-ObjectsPerformSelector: requires a selector that returns no value, and enumerate-ObjectsUsingBlock: requires a block function that returns no value.) The usual work-around is to make an empty mutable array and then enumerate the original array, calling a method and appending each result to the mutable array (Example 10-1). It is also sometimes possible to use key–value coding as a map substitute (see Chapter 12).

Example 10-1. Building an array by enumerating another array

```
NSMutableArray* marr = [NSMutableArray new];
for (id obj in myArray) {
    id result = [obj doSomething];
    [marr addObject: result];
}
```

There are many ways to search or filter an array using a block:

```
NSArray* pep = @[@"Manny", @"Moe", @"Jack"];
NSArray* ems =
    [pep objectsAtIndexes: [pep indexesOfObjectsPassingTest:
    ^BOOL(id obj, NSUInteger idx, BOOL *stop) {
        return ([(NSString*)obj rangeOfString:@"m"
            options:NSCaseInsensitiveSearch].location == 0);
    }]];
```

You can derive a sorted version of an array, supplying the sorting rules in various ways, or if it's a mutable array, you can sort it directly; see Example 3-1 and Example 3-2.

Forming a new array from some or all of the elements of an existing array is *not* an expensive operation. The objects constituting the elements of the first array are not copied; the new array consists merely of a new set of pointers to the already existing objects. The same is true for the other collection types I'm about to discuss.

NSSet and Friends

An NSSet is an unordered collection of distinct objects. "Distinct" means that no two objects in a set can return YES when they are compared using isEqual:. Learning whether an object is present in a set is much more efficient than seeking it in an array, and you can ask whether one set is a subset of, or intersects, another set. You can walk through (enumerate) a set with the for...in construct, though the order is of course undefined. You can filter a set, as you can an array. Indeed, much of what you can do with a set is parallel to what you can do with an array, except that of course you can't do anything with a set that involves the notion of ordering.

To escape even that restriction, you can use an ordered set. An ordered set (NSOrdered-Set) is *very* like an array, and the methods for working with it are very similar to the methods for working with an array — NSOrderedSet even implements objectAt-IndexedSubscript:, so you can fetch an element by subscripting. But an ordered set's elements must be distinct. An ordered set provides many of the advantages of sets: for example, as with an NSSet, learning whether an object is present in an ordered set is much more efficient than for an array, and you can readily take the union, intersection, or difference with another set. Since the distinctness restriction will often prove no restriction at all (because the elements were going to be distinct anyway), it is worthwhile to use NSOrderedSet instead of NSArray wherever possible.

 Handing an array over to an ordered set *uniques* the array, meaning that order is maintained but only the first occurrence of an equal object is moved to the set.

An NSSet is immutable. You can derive one NSSet from another by adding or removing elements, or you can use its subclass, NSMutableSet. Similarly, NSOrderedSet has its mutable counterpart, NSMutableOrderedSet (which implements setObject:at-IndexedSubscript:). There is no penalty for adding to, or inserting into, a mutable set an object that the set already contains; nothing is added (and so the distinctness rule is enforced), but there's no error.

NSCountedSet, a subclass of NSMutableSet, is a mutable unordered collection of objects that are *not* necessarily distinct (this concept is usually referred to as a *bag*). It is implemented as a set plus a count of how many times each element has been added.

NSDictionary and NSMutableDictionary

An NSDictionary is an unordered collection of key–value pairs (what some languages would refer to as a *hash*). The key is usually an NSString, though it doesn't have to be. The value can be any object. An NSDictionary is immutable; its mutable subclass is NSMutableDictionary.

The keys of a dictionary are distinct (using `isEqual:` for comparison). If you add a key–value pair to an NSMutableDictionary, then if that key is not already present, the pair is simply added, but if the key is already present, then the corresponding value is replaced.

The fundamental use of an NSDictionary is to request an entry's value by key (using `objectForKey:`); if no such key exists, the result is nil, so this is also the way to find out whether a key is present. A dictionary is thus an easy, flexible data storage device, an object-based analogue to a struct. Cocoa often uses a dictionary to provide you with an extra packet of named values, as in the `userInfo` of an NSNotification, the `options:` parameter of `application:didFinishLaunchingWithOptions:`, and so on.

The same Objective-C modernizations that brought us array literals and subscripting have brought us dictionary literals and subscripting. In addition to forming a dictionary from an array of objects and an array of keys (`dictionaryWithObjects:forKeys:`) or as a nil-terminated list of alternating objects and keys (`dictionaryWithObjectsAndKeys:`), a dictionary may be formed literally as a comma-separated list of key–value pairs, each key followed by a colon and the value, and wrapped in `@{...}`. Thus, recall our earlier NSUserDefaults example:

```
[[NSUserDefaults standardUserDefaults] registerDefaults:
    [NSDictionary dictionaryWithObjectsAndKeys:
        @4,
        @"cardMatrixRows",
        @3,
        @"cardMatrixColumns",
        nil]];
```

That can be rewritten like this:

```
[[NSUserDefaults standardUserDefaults] registerDefaults:
    @{@"cardMatrixRows":@4, @"cardMatrixColumns":@3}];
```

To fetch a value from a dictionary by its key, instead of calling `objectForKey:`, you can subscript the key in square brackets to the dictionary reference: `dict[key]`. Similarly, to add a key–value pair to an NSMutableDictionary, instead of calling `setObject:forKey:`, you can assign to the subscripted dictionary reference. Parallel to NSArray, this is accomplished behind the scenes by calling `objectForKeyedSubscript:` and `setObject:forKeyedSubscript:`, and your own classes can declare these methods and be eligible for keyed subscripting notation.

Data structures such as an array of dictionaries, a dictionary of dictionaries, and so forth, are extremely common, and will often lie at the heart of an app's functionality. Here's an example from one of my own apps. The app bundle contains a text file laid out like this:

```
chapterNumber [tab] pictureName [return]
chapterNumber [tab] pictureName [return]
```

As the app launches, I load this text file and parse it into a dictionary, each entry of which has the following structure:

```
key: (chapterNumber, as an NSNumber)
value: [Mutable Array]
    (pictureName)
    (pictureName)
    ...
```

Thus we end up with all pictures for a chapter collected under the number of that chapter. This data structure is designed with its purpose in mind: it makes it trivially easy and extremely fast for me later to access all the pictures for a given chapter.

Here's the actual code by which I parse the text file into that data structure. For each line of the text file, if the dictionary entry for that chapter number doesn't exist, we create it, with an empty mutable array as its value. Whether that dictionary entry existed or not, it does now, and its value is a mutable array, so we append the picture name to that mutable array. Observe how this single typical example brings together many of the Foundation classes discussed in this section:

```
NSString* f = [[NSBundle mainBundle] pathForResource:@"index" ofType:@"txt"];
NSError* err = nil;
NSString* s = [NSString stringWithContentsOfFile:f
                            encoding:NSUTF8StringEncoding
                               error:&err];
// error-checking omitted
NSMutableDictionary* d = [NSMutableDictionary new];
for (NSString* line in [s componentsSeparatedByString:@"\n"]) {
    NSArray* items = [line componentsSeparatedByString:@"\t"];
    NSInteger chnum = [items[0] integerValue];
    NSNumber* key = @(chnum);
    NSMutableArray* marr = d[key];
    if (!marr) { // no such key, create key-value pair
        marr = [NSMutableArray new];
        d[key] = marr;
    }
    // marr is now a mutable array, empty or otherwise
    NSString* picname = items[1];
    [marr addObject: picname];
}
```

You can get from an NSDictionary a list of keys, a sorted list of keys, or a list of values. You can walk through (enumerate) a dictionary by its keys with the for...in construct, though the order is of course undefined. A dictionary also supplies an object-Enumerator, which you can use with the for...in construct to walk through just the values. You can also walk through the key–value pairs together using a block, and you can even filter an NSDictionary by a test against its values.

NSNull

NSNull does nothing but supply a pointer to a singleton object, [NSNull null]. Use this singleton object to stand for nil in situations where an actual object is required and nil is not permitted. For example, you can't use nil as the value of an element of a collection (such as NSArray, NSSet, or NSDictionary), so you'd use [NSNull null] instead.

Despite what I said earlier about equality, you can test an object against [NSNull null] using the C equality operator, because this is a singleton instance and therefore pointer comparison works.

Immutable and Mutable

Beginners sometimes have difficulty with the Foundation's immutable/mutable class pairs, so here are some hints.

The documentation may not make it completely obvious that the mutable classes obey and, if appropriate, override the methods of the immutable classes. Thus, for example, [NSArray array] generates an immutable array, but [NSMutableArray array] generates a mutable array. (You will look in vain for the expected [NSMutableArray mutableArray].) The same is true of all the initializers and convenience class methods for instantiation: they may have "array" in their name, but when sent to NSMutableArray, they yield a mutable array.

That fact also answers the question of how to make an immutable array mutable, and *vice versa*. If arrayWithArray:, sent to the NSArray class, yields a new immutable array containing the same objects in the same order as the original array, then the same method, arrayWithArray:, sent to the NSMutableArray class, yields a *mutable* array containing the same objects in the same order as the original. Thus this single method can transform an array between immutable and mutable in either direction. You can also use copy (produces an immutable copy) and mutableCopy (produces a mutable copy).

All of the above applies equally, of course, to the other immutable/mutable class pairs. You will often want to work internally and temporarily with a mutable instance but then store (and possibly vend to other classes) an immutable instance, thus protecting the value from being changed accidentally or behind your own back. What matters is not a variable's declared class but what class the instance really is (polymorphism; see Chapter 5), so it's good that you can easily switch between an immutable and a mutable version of the same data.

To test whether an instance is mutable or immutable, do *not* ask for its `class`. These immutable/mutable class pairs are all implemented as *class clusters*, which means that Cocoa uses a secret class, different from the documented class you work with. This secret class is subject to change without notice, because it's none of your business and you should never have looked at it in the first place. Thus, code of this form is subject to breakage:

```
if ([NSStringFromClass([n class]) isEqualToString: @"NSCFArray"]) // wrong!
```

Instead, to learn whether a collection is mutable, ask it whether it responds to a mutability method:

```
if ([n respondsToSelector:@selector(addObject:)]) // right
```

(Unfortunately, that technique works *only* for collections; it doesn't work, say, for distinguishing an NSString from an NSMutableString.)

 Here's a reminder: just because a collection class is immutable doesn't mean that the objects it collects are immutable. They are still objects and do not lose any of their normal behavior merely because they are pointed to by way of an immutable collection.

Property Lists

A *property list* is a string (XML) representation of data. The Foundation classes NSString, NSData, NSArray, and NSDictionary are the only classes that can be converted into a property list. Moreover, an NSArray or NSDictionary can be converted into a property list only if the only classes it collects are these classes, along with NSDate and NSNumber. (This is why, as I mentioned earlier, you must convert a UIColor into an NSData in order to store it in user defaults; the user defaults is a property list.)

The primary use of a property list is to store data as a file. NSArray and NSDictionary provide convenience methods `writeToFile:atomically:` and `writeToURL:atomically:` that generate property list files given a pathname or file URL, respectively; they also provide inverse convenience methods that initialize an NSArray object or an NSDictionary object based on the property list contents of a given file. For this very reason, you are likely to start with one of these classes when you want to create a property list. (NSString and NSData, with their methods `writeToFile:...` and `writeToURL:...`, just write the data out as a file directly, not as a property list.)

When you generate an NSArray or NSDictionary object from a property list file in this way, the collections, string objects, and data objects in the collection are all immutable. If you want them to be mutable, or if you want to convert an instance of one of the other property list classes to a property list, you'll use the NSPropertyListSerialization class (see the *Property List Programming Guide*).

The Secret Life of NSObject

Because every class inherits from NSObject, it's worth taking some time to investigate and understand NSObject. NSObject is constructed in a rather elaborate way:

- It defines some native class methods and instance methods having mostly to do with the basics of instantiation and of method sending and resolution. (See the *NSObject Class Reference*.)

- It adopts the NSObject protocol. This protocol declares instance methods having mostly to do with memory management, the relationship between an instance and its class, and introspection. Because all the NSObject protocol methods are required, the NSObject class implements them all. (See the *NSObject Protocol Reference*.) This architecture is what permits NSProxy to be a root class; it, too, adopts the NSObject protocol.

- It implements convenience methods related to the NSCopying, NSMutable-Copying, and NSCoding protocols, without formally adopting those protocols. NSObject intentionally doesn't adopt these protocols because this would cause all other classes to adopt them, which would be wrong. But thanks to this architecture, if a class does adopt one of these protocols, you can call the corresponding convenience method. For example, NSObject implements the copy instance method, so you can call copy on any instance, but you'll crash unless the instance's class adopts the NSCopying protocol and implements copyWithZone:.

- A large number of methods are injected into NSObject by more than two dozen categories on NSObject, scattered among various header files. For example, awake-FromNib (see Chapter 7) comes from the UINibLoadingAdditions category on NSObject, declared in *UINibLoading.h*. And performSelector:with-Object:afterDelay:, discussed in Chapter 11, comes from the NSDelayed-Performing category on NSObject, declared in *NSRunLoop.h*.

- A class object, as explained in Chapter 4, is an object. Therefore all classes, which are objects of type Class, inherit from NSObject. Therefore, *any method defined as an instance method by NSObject can be called on a class object as a class method!* For example, respondsToSelector: is defined as an instance method by NSObject, but it can (therefore) be treated also as a class method and sent to a class object.

The problem for the programmer is that Apple's documentation is rather rigid about classification. When you're trying to work out what you can say to an object, you don't care where that object's methods come from; you just care what you can say. But the documentation differentiates methods by where they come from. Even though NSObject is the root class, the most important class, from which all other classes inherit, *no single page of the documentation provides a conspectus of all its methods*. Instead, you have to look at both the *NSObject Class Reference* and the *NSObject Protocol Reference* simultaneously, plus the pages documenting the NSCopying, NSMutableCopying, and NSCoding protocols (in order to understand how they interact with methods defined by NSObject), plus you have to supply mentally a class method version of every NSObject instance method!

Then there are the methods injected into NSObject by categories. Some that are general in nature are documented on the NSObject class documentation page itself; for example, `cancelPreviousPerformRequestsWithTarget:` comes from a category declared in *NSRunLoop.h*, but it is documented under NSObject, quite rightly, since this is a class method, and therefore effectively a global method, that you might want to send at any time. Others are delegate methods used in restricted situations (so that these are really informal protocols), and do not need centralized documentation; for example, `animationDidStart:` is documented under the CAAnimation class, quite rightly, because you need to know about it only and exactly when you're working with CAAnimation. However, every object responds to `awakeFromNib`, and it's likely to be crucial to every app you write; yet you must learn about it outside of the NSObject documentation, sitting all by itself in the *NSObject UIKit Additions Reference* page, where you're extremely unlikely to discover it! The same goes, it might be argued, for all the key–value coding methods (Chapter 12) and key–value observing methods (Chapter 13).

Once you've collected, by hook or by crook, all the NSObject methods, you can see that they fall into a certain natural classification, much as outlined in Apple's documentation (see also "The Root Class" in the "Cocoa Objects" section of the *Cocoa Fundamentals Guide*):

Creation, destruction, and memory management

> Methods for creating an instance, such as `alloc` and `copy`, along with methods that you might override in order to learn when something is happening in the lifetime of an object, such as `initialize` (see Chapter 11) and `dealloc` (see Chapter 12), plus methods that manage memory (see Chapter 12).

Class relationships

> Methods for learning an object's class and inheritance, such as `class`, `superclass`, `isKindOfClass:`, and `isMemberOfClass:`.

> To check the class of an instance (or class), use methods such as `isKindOfClass:` and `isMemberOfClass:`. Direct comparison of two class objects, as in `[someObject`

class] == [otherObject class], is rarely advisable, especially because a Cocoa instance's class might be a private, undocumented subclass of the class you expect. I mentioned this already in connection with class clusters, and it can happen in other cases.

Object introspection and comparison
Methods for asking what would happen if an object were sent a certain message, such as respondsToSelector:; for representing an object as a string (description, used in debugging; see Chapter 9); and for comparing objects (isEqual:).

Message response
Methods for meddling with what does happen when an object is sent a certain message, such as doesNotRecognizeSelector:. If you're curious, see the *Objective-C Runtime Programming Guide*.

Message sending
Methods for sending a message dynamically. For example, performSelector: takes a selector as parameter, and sending it to an object tells that object to perform that selector. This might seem identical to just sending that message to that object, but what if you don't know what message to send until runtime? Moreover, variants on performSelector: allow you to send a message on a specified thread, or send a message after a certain amount of time has passed (performSelector:with-Object:afterDelay: and similar).

CHAPTER 11

Cocoa Events

None of your code runs until Cocoa calls it. The art of iOS programming consists largely of knowing when and why Cocoa will call your code. If you know this, you can put your code in the correct place, with the correct method name, so that your code runs at the correct moment, and your app behaves the way you intend.

In Chapter 7, for example, we wrote a method to be called when the user taps a certain button in our interface, and we also arranged things so that that method *would* be called when the user taps that button:

```
- (void) buttonPressed: (id) sender {
    // ... react to the button being pressed
}
```

This architecture typifies the underpinnings of a Cocoa program. Your code itself is like a panel of buttons, waiting for Cocoa to press one. If something happens that Cocoa feels your code needs to know about and respond to, it presses the right button — if the right button is there. You organize your code with Cocoa's behavior in mind. Cocoa makes certain promises about how and when it will dispatch messages to your code. These are Cocoa's *events*. You know what these events are, and you arrange for your code to be ready when Cocoa delivers them.

Thus, to program for iOS, you must, in a sense, surrender control. Your code never gets to run just whenever it feels like it. It can run *only* in response to some kind of event. Something happens, such as the user making a gesture on the screen, or some specific stage arriving in the lifetime of your app, and Cocoa dispatches an event to your code — if your code is prepared to receive it. So you don't write just any old code you want to and put it in any old place. You use the framework, by letting the framework use you. You submit to Cocoa's rules and promises and expectations, so that your code will be called at the right time and in the right way.

The specific events that you can receive are listed in the documentation. The overall architecture of how and when events are dispatched and the ways in which your code arranges to receive them is the subject of this chapter.

Reasons for Events

Broadly speaking, the reasons you might receive an event may be divided informally into four categories. These categories are not official; I made them up. Often it isn't completely clear which of these categories an event fits into; an event may well appear to fit two categories. But they are still generally useful for visualizing how and why Cocoa interacts with your code:

User events
> The user does something interactive, and an event is triggered directly. Obvious examples are events that you get when the user taps or swipes the screen, or types a key on the keyboard.

Lifetime events
> These are events notifying you of the arrival of a stage in the life of the app, such as the fact that the app is starting up or is about to go into the background, or of a component of the app, such as the fact that a UIViewController's view has just loaded or is about to be removed from the screen.

Functional events
> Cocoa is about to do something, and turns to you in case you want to supply additional functionality. I would put into this category things like UIView's `draw-Rect:` (your chance to have a view draw itself) and UILabel's `drawTextInRect:` (your chance to modify the look of a label), with which we experimented in Chapter 10.

Query events
> Cocoa turns to you to ask a question; its behavior will depend upon your answer. For example, the way data appears in a table (a UITableView) is that whenever Cocoa needs a cell for a row of the table, it turns to you and asks for the cell.

Subclassing

A built-in Cocoa class may define methods that Cocoa itself will call and that you are invited (or required) to override in a subclass, so that your custom behavior, and not (merely) the default behavior, will take place.

An example I gave in Chapter 10 was UIView's `drawRect:`. This is what I call a functional event. By overriding `drawRect:` in a UIView subclass, you dictate the full procedure by which a view draws itself. You don't know exactly when this method will be called, and you don't care; when it is, you draw, and this guarantees that the view will always appear the way you want it to. (You never call `drawRect:` yourself; if some underlying condition has changed and you want the view to be redrawn, you call `setNeedsDisplay` and let Cocoa call `drawRect:` in response.)

Built-in UIView subclasses may have other functional event methods you'll want to customize through subclassing. Typically this will be in order to change the way the view is drawn, without taking command of the entire drawing procedure yourself. In Chapter 10 I gave an example involving UILabel and its `drawTextInRect:`. A similar example is UISlider, which lets you customize the position and size of the slider's "thumb" by overriding `thumbRectForBounds:trackRect:value:`.

UIViewController is a good example of a class meant for subclassing. Of the methods listed in the UIViewController class documentation, just about all are methods you might have reason to override. If you create a UIViewController subclass in Xcode, you'll see that the template already includes a couple of method overrides to get you started. For example, `viewDidLoad` is called to let you know that your view controller's view has loaded, so that you can perform initializations; it's an obvious example of a lifetime event.

A UIViewController method like `supportedInterfaceOrientations` is what I call a query event. Your job is to return a bitmask telling Cocoa what orientations your view can appear in at this moment — whenever that may be. You trust Cocoa to call this method at the appropriate moments, so that if the user rotates the device, your app's interface will or won't be rotated to compensate, depending on what value you return.

When looking for events that you can receive through subclassing, be sure to look upward though the inheritance hierarchy. For example, if you're wondering how to be notified when your custom UILabel subclass is embedded into another view, you won't find the answer in the UILabel class documentation; a UILabel receives the appropriate event by virtue of being a UIView. In the UIView class documentation, you'll learn that you can override `didMoveToSuperview` to be informed when this happens.

Even further up the inheritance hierarchy, you'll find things like NSObject's `initialize` class method. Before any class is sent its first class message (including instantiation), it is sent the `initialize` message. Thus, `initialize` can be overridden in order to run code extremely early in a class's lifetime. Your project's application delegate class, such as AppDelegate in our Empty Window project, is instantiated very early in the app's lifetime, so its `initialize` can be a good place to perform very early app initializations, such as setting default values for any user preferences.

When implementing `initialize`, we must test, as a matter of course, whether `self` really is the class in question; otherwise there is a chance that `initialize` will be called again (and our code will run again) if a subclass of this class is used. This is one of the few situations in which we will compare two classes directly against one another;

`initialize` is a class method, so `self` means "the class to which the `initialize` message was sent":

```
// MyClass.m:
+ (void)initialize {
    if (self == [MyClass class]) {
        // do stuff
    }
}
```

Notifications

Cocoa provides your app with a single instance of NSNotificationCenter, informally called the *notification center*, and available as [NSNotificationCenter default-Center]. This instance is the basis of a mechanism for sending messages called *notifications*. A notification includes an instance of NSNotification (a *notification object*). The idea is that any object can be registered with the notification center to receive certain notifications. Another object can hand the notification center a notification object to send out (this is called *posting* the notification). The notification center will then send that notification object, in a notification, to all objects that are registered to receive it.

The notification mechanism is often described as a dispatching or broadcasting mechanism, and with good reason. It lets an object send a message without knowing or caring what object or how many objects receive it. This relieves your app's architecture from the formal responsibility of somehow hooking up instances just so a message can pass from one to the other (which can sometimes be quite tricky or onerous, as discussed in Chapter 13). When objects are conceptually "distant" from one another, notifications can be a fairly lightweight way of permitting one to message the other.

An NSNotification object has three pieces of information associated with it, which can be retrieved by instance methods:

name
: An NSString which identifies the notification's meaning.

object
: An instance associated with the notification; typically, the instance that posted it.

userInfo
: Not every notification has a userInfo; it is an NSDictionary, and can contain additional information associated with the notification. What information this NSDictionary will contain, and under what keys, depends on the particular notification; you have to consult the documentation. For example, the documentation tells us that UIApplication's UIApplicationDidChangeStatusBarFrame-Notification includes a userInfo dictionary with a key UIApplicationStatus-BarFrameUserInfoKey whose value is the status bar's frame. When you post a

notification yourself, you can put anything you like into the userInfo for the notification's recipient(s) to retrieve.

Cocoa itself posts notifications through the notification center, and your code can register to receive them. You'll find a separate Notifications section in the documentation for a class that provides them.

Receiving a Notification

To register to receive a notification, you send one of two messages to the notification center. One is addObserver:selector:name:object:. The parameters are as follows:

observer:
> The instance to which the notification is to be sent. This will typically be self; it isn't usual for one instance to register a different instance as the receiver of a notification.

selector:
> The message to be sent to the observer instance when the notification occurs. The designated method should return void and should take one parameter, which will be the NSNotification object (so the parameter should be typed as NSNotification* or id). Don't forget to implement this method! If the notification center sends a notification by sending the message specified as the selector: here, and there is no method implemented to receive this message, your app will crash (see Chapter 3).

name:
> The NSString name of the notification you'd like to receive. If this parameter is nil, you're asking to receive *all* notifications associated with the object designated in the object: parameter. A built-in Cocoa notification's name is usually a constant. As I explained in Chapter 1, this is helpful, because if you flub the name of a constant, the compiler will complain, whereas if you enter the name of the notification directly as an NSString literal and you get it wrong, the compiler won't complain but you will mysteriously fail to get any notifications (because no notification has the name you actually entered) — a very difficult sort of mistake to track down.

object:
> The object of the notification you're interested in, which will usually be the object that posted it. If this is nil, you're asking to receive *all* notifications with the name designated in the name: parameter. (If both the name: and object: parameters are nil, you're asking to receive all notifications!)

For example, in one of my apps I want to change the interface whenever the device's music player starts playing a different song. The API for the device's built-in music player belongs to the MPMusicPlayerController class; this class provides a notification to tell me when the built-in music player changes what song is being played, listed under

Notifications in the MPMusicPlayerController class documentation as `MPMusicPlayer-ControllerNowPlayingItemDidChangeNotification`.

It turns out, looking at the documentation, that this notification won't be posted at all unless I first call MPMusicPlayerController's `beginGeneratingPlayback-Notifications` instance method. This architecture is not uncommon; Cocoa saves itself some time and effort by not sending out certain notifications unless they are switched on, as it were. So my first job is to get an instance of MPMusicPlayerController and call this method:

```
MPMusicPlayerController* mp = [MPMusicPlayerController iPodMusicPlayer];
[mp beginGeneratingPlaybackNotifications];
```

Now I register myself to receive the desired playback notification:

```
[[NSNotificationCenter defaultCenter] addObserver:self
    selector:@selector(nowPlayingItemChanged:)
        name:MPMusicPlayerControllerNowPlayingItemDidChangeNotification
    object:nil];
```

So now, whenever an `MPMusicPlayerControllerNowPlayingItemDidChange-Notification` is posted, my `nowPlayingItemChanged:` method will be called:

```
- (void) nowPlayingItemChanged: (NSNotification*) n {
    MPMusicPlayerController* mp = [MPMusicPlayerController iPodMusicPlayer];
    self->_nowPlayingItem = mp.nowPlayingItem;
    // ... and so on ...
}
```

The other way to register to receive a notification is by calling `addObserverFor-Name:object:queue:usingBlock:`. It returns a value, whose purpose I'll explain in a moment. The `queue:` will usually be nil; a non-nil `queue:` is for background threading. The `name:` and `object:` parameters are just like those of `add-Observer:selector:name:object:`. Instead of an observer and a selector, you provide a block consisting of the actual code to be executed when the notification arrives. This block should take one parameter — the NSNotification itself.

This way of registering for a notification has some tremendous advantages. For `add-Observer:selector:name:object:` to work properly, you must get the selector right and make sure you implement the corresponding method. With a block, on the other hand, there is no selector and no separate method; everything happens right there in the block:

```
MPMusicPlayerController* mp = [MPMusicPlayerController iPodMusicPlayer];
[mp beginGeneratingPlaybackNotifications];
id ob = [[NSNotificationCenter defaultCenter]
addObserverForName:MPMusicPlayerControllerNowPlayingItemDidChangeNotification
object:nil queue:nil usingBlock:^(NSNotification *n) {
```

```
        self->_nowPlayingItem = mp.nowPlayingItem;
        // ... and so on ...
    }
}];
```

Consider how maintainable and understandable that code is. Heavy use of `add-`
`Observer:selector:name:object:` means that your code ends up peppered with
methods that exist solely in order to be called by the notification center. But there is
nothing about these methods that tells you what they are for — you will probably want
to use explicit comments in order to remind yourself — and the methods are separate
from the registration call, all of which makes your code very method-heavy and confusing. With a block, on the other hand, the whole purpose of the registration is crystal-
clear, because the block accompanies it. And notice how, in the block, I don't have to
redefine `mp` as I did in the separate method `nowPlayingItemChanged:`; it is still in scope
from where it was defined a couple of lines earlier. Blocks are so convenient!

Unregistering

It is up to you, for every object that you register as a recipient of notifications, to unregister that object before it goes out of existence. If you fail to do this, and if the object
does go out of existence, and if a notification for which that object is registered is posted,
the notification center will attempt to send the appropriate message to that object, which
is now missing in action. The result will be a crash at best, and chaos at worst.

To unregister an object as a recipient of notifications, send the notification center the
`removeObserver:` message. (Alternatively, you can unregister an object for just a specific
set of notifications with `removeObserver:name:object:`.) The object passed as the
`observer:` argument is the object that is no longer to receive notifications. What object
that is depends on how you registered in the first place:

You called `addObserver:...`
   You supplied an observer originally; that is the observer you must now unregister.

You called `addObserverForName:...`
   The call to `addObserverForName:...` returned an observer token object, which you
   captured as an `id` variable (its real class and nature are no concern of yours); that
   is the observer you must now unregister.

The trick is finding the right moment to unregister. The fallback solution is the registered
instance's `dealloc` method, this being the last lifetime event an instance is sent before
it goes out of existence. If you're using ARC and `addObserverForName:...`, there are
some additional memory management implications that I'll talk about in Chapter 12.

If you're calling `addObserverForName:...` multiple times from the same class, you're
going to end up receiving from the notification center multiple observer tokens, which
you need to preserve so that you can unregister all of them later. If your plan is to

unregister everything at once, one way to handle this situation is through an instance variable that is a mutable collection. So, for example, I might have an NSMutableSet instance variable called _observers. Early on, I initialize it to an empty set:

```
self->_observers = [NSMutableSet set];
```

Each time I register for a notification using a block, I capture the result and add it to the set:

```
id ob = [[NSNotificationCenter defaultCenter]
    addObserverForName:@"whatever" object:nil queue:nil
    usingBlock:^(NSNotification *note) {
        // ... whatever ...
    }];
[self->_observers addObject:ob];
```

When it's time to unregister, I enumerate the set:

```
for (id ob in self->_observers)
    [[NSNotificationCenter defaultCenter] removeObserver:ob];
```

The tedium of arranging all that is a price worth paying in order to take advantage of blocks when using notifications.

 NSNotificationCenter provides no kind of introspection: you cannot ask an NSNotificationCenter what objects are registered with it as notification recipients. This seems to me to be a major gap in Cocoa's functionality. I once had a devil of a time understanding why one of my instances was not receiving a notification for which it was registered. Caveman debugging didn't help. Eventually I realized that some code I'd forgotten about was unregistering my observer prematurely. The moral: keep your registration/unregistration logic extremely simple.

Posting a Notification

Although you'll mostly be interested in receiving notifications from Cocoa, you can also take advantage of the notification mechanism as a way of communicating between your own objects. As I mentioned before, one reason for doing this might be that two objects are conceptually distant or independent from one another.

To use notifications in this way, your objects must play both roles in the communication chain. One of your objects (or more than one) will register to receive a notification, identified by name or object or both, as I've already described. Another of your objects will post a notification, identified in the same way. The notification center will then pass the message along from the poster to the registered recipient.

To post a notification, send to the notification center the message `postNotification-`
`Name:object:userInfo:`.

For example, one of my apps is a simple card game. The game needs to know when a
card is tapped. But a card knows nothing about the game; when it is tapped, it simply
emits a virtual shriek by posting a notification:

```
- (void) singleTap: (id) g {
    [[NSNotificationCenter defaultCenter]
        postNotificationName:@"cardTapped" object:self];
}
```

The game object has registered for the `@"cardTapped"` notification, so it hears about
this and retrieves the notification's `object`; now it knows what card was tapped and can
proceed correctly.

 I am skipping over some other aspects of notifications that you probably won't need to know about. Read Apple's *Notification Program-*
ming Topics for Cocoa if you want the gory details.

NSTimer

A timer (NSTimer) is not, strictly speaking, a notification; but it behaves very similarly. It is an object that gives off a signal (*fires*) after the lapse of a certain time interval.
The signal is a message to one of your instances. Thus you can arrange to be notified
when a certain time has elapsed. The timing is not perfectly accurate, but it's pretty good.

Timer management is not exactly tricky, but it is a little unusual. A timer that is actively
watching the clock is said to be *scheduled*. A timer may fire once, or it may be a *repeat-*
ing timer. To make a timer go out of existence, it must be *invalidated*. A timer that is set
to fire once is invalidated automatically after it fires; a repeating timer repeats until *you*
invalidate it by sending it the `invalidate` message. An invalidated timer should be
regarded as off-limits: you cannot revive it or use it for anything further, and you should
probably not send any messages to it.

The straightforward way to create a timer is with the NSTimer class method `scheduled-`
`TimerWithTimeInterval:target:selector:userInfo:repeats:`. This creates the
timer and schedules it, so that it begins watching the clock immediately. The target and
selector determine what message will be sent to what object when the timer fires; the
method in question should take one parameter, which will be a reference to the timer.
The `userInfo` is just like the `userInfo` of a notification.

For example, one of my apps is a game with a score; I want to penalize the user, by
diminishing the score, for every ten seconds after each move that elapses without the
user making a further move. So each time the user makes a move, I create a repeating

timer whose time interval is ten seconds (and I also invalidate any existing timer); in the method that the timer calls, I diminish the score.

Starting in iOS 7, an NSTimer has a `tolerance` property, which is a time interval signifying a how long after the timer *would* fire you're willing to grant before it really *does* fire. The documentation suggests that you can improve device battery life and app responsiveness by supplying a value of at least 10 percent of the `timeInterval`.

Timers have some memory management implications that I'll discuss in Chapter 12, along with a block-based alternative to a timer.

Delegation

Delegation is an object-oriented design pattern, a relationship between two objects, in which the first object's behavior is customized or assisted by the second. The second object is the first object's *delegate*. No subclassing is involved, and indeed the first object is agnostic about the second object's class.

As implemented by Cocoa, here's how delegation works. A built-in Cocoa class has an instance variable, usually called `delegate` (it will certainly have `delegate` in its name). For some instance of that Cocoa class, you set the value of this instance variable to an instance of one of *your* classes. At certain moments in its activity, the Cocoa class promises to turn to its delegate for instructions by sending it a certain message: if the Cocoa instance finds that its delegate is not nil, and that its delegate is prepared to receive that message (see Chapter 10 on `respondsToSelector:`), the Cocoa instance sends the message to the delegate.

Recall the discussion of protocols from Chapter 10. Delegation is one of Cocoa's main uses of protocols. In the old days, delegate methods were listed in the Cocoa class's documentation, and their method signatures were made known to the compiler through an informal protocol (a category on NSObject). Now, though, a class's delegate methods are usually listed in a genuine protocol with its own documentation. There are over 70 Cocoa delegate protocols, showing how heavily Cocoa relies on delegation. Most delegate methods are optional, but in a few cases you'll discover some that are required.

Cocoa Delegation

To customize a Cocoa instance's behavior through delegation, you start with one of your classes, which, if necessary, declares conformance to the relevant delegate protocol. When the app runs, you set the Cocoa instance's `delegate` property (or whatever its name is) to an instance of your class. You might do this in code; alternatively, you might do it in a nib, by connecting an instance's `delegate` outlet (or whatever it's called) to an appropriate instance that is to serve as delegate. Your delegate class will probably do other things besides serving as this instance's delegate. Indeed, one of the nice things about delegation is that it leaves you free to slot delegate code into your class architecture however you like.

Here's a simple example, involving UIAlertView. If a UIAlertView's Cancel button is tapped, the alert view is dismissed. But if you want to *do* something in response to the alert view being dismissed, you need to give it a delegate so that you can receive an event (`alertView:didDismissWithButtonIndex:`) telling you that the alert view *was* dismissed. It's so common to give a UIAlertView a delegate that its designated initializer allows you to supply one; typically, the delegate will be the instance (`self`) that summoned the alert view in the first place:

```
- (void) gameWon {
    UIAlertView* av =
        [[UIAlertView alloc] initWithTitle:@"Congratulations!"
                                    message:@"You won the game. Another game?"
                                    delegate:self
                         cancelButtonTitle:@"No, thanks."
                         otherButtonTitles:@"Sure!", nil];
    [av show];
}

- (void) alertView:(UIAlertView*) av
        didDismissWithButtonIndex: (NSInteger) ix {
    if (ix == 1) { // user said "Sure!"
        [self newGame];
    }
}
```

An app's shared application instance ([`UIApplication sharedApplication`]) has a delegate, which serves such an important role in the life of the app that the Xcode app templates automatically supply one. I described in Chapter 6 how an app gets started by calling `UIApplicationMain`:

```
int main(int argc, char *argv[])
{
    @autoreleasepool {
        return UIApplicationMain(argc, argv, nil,
                        NSStringFromClass([AppDelegate class]));
    }
}
```

The template has provided the project with files defining an AppDelegate class; that line tells `UIApplicationMain` to instantiate AppDelegate and make that instance the delegate of the shared application instance (which it has also created). As I pointed out in Chapter 10, AppDelegate formally adopts the UIApplicationDelegate protocol, signifying that it is ready to serve in this role. And, as I also said in Chapter 10, `respondsTo-Selector:` is then sent to the app delegate to see what UIApplicationDelegate protocol methods it implements. If it implements `application:didFinishLaunchingWith-`

`Options:`, it will be sent `application:didFinishLaunchingWithOptions:`, which is thus one of the earliest opportunities for *your* code to run.

 The UIApplication delegate methods are also provided as notifications. This lets an instance other than the app delegate hear conveniently about application lifetime events, by registering for them. A few other classes provide duplicate events similarly; for example, UITableView's delegate method `tableView:didSelectRowAtIndexPath:` is matched by a notification `UITableViewSelectionDidChange-Notification`.

By convention, many Cocoa delegate method names contain the modal verbs `should`, `will`, or `did`. A `will` message is sent to the delegate just before something happens; a `did` message is sent to the delegate just after something happens. A `should` method is special: it returns a BOOL, and you are expected to respond with YES to permit something or NO to prevent it. The documentation tells you what the default response is; you don't have to implement a `should` method if the default response is always acceptable.

In many cases, a property will control some overall behavior, while a delegate message lets you modify that behavior based on circumstances at runtime. For example, whether the user can tap the status bar to make a scroll view scroll quickly to the top is governed by the scroll view's `scrollsToTop` property; but even if this property's value is YES, you can prevent this behavior for a particular tap by returning NO from the delegate's `scroll-ViewShouldScrollToTop:`.

When you're searching the documentation for how you can be notified of a certain event, be sure to consult the corresponding delegate protocol, if there is one. You'd like to know when the user taps in a UITextField to start editing it? You won't find anything relevant in the UITextField class documentation; what you're after is `textFieldDid-BeginEditing:` in the UITextFieldDelegate protocol. You want to respond when the user rearranges items on your tab bar? Look in UITabBarControllerDelegate. And so on.

Implementing Delegation

The Cocoa pattern of a delegate whose responsibilities are described by a protocol is one that you will want to imitate in your own code. Setting up this pattern takes some practice, and can be a little time-consuming, but it is often the most appropriate approach, because of the way it assigns knowledge and responsibility to the various objects involved. A very typical situation is a case of two-way communication: for example,

Object A creates and configures Object B; later, before Object B goes out of existence, Object A also needs to hear back from Object B.

The pattern here is that Class B defines a protocol SomeProtocol in its header, along with a delegate property typed as id <SomeProtocol>. That way, Class A imports Class B's header, which is right and proper because Object A is going to create Object B and configure it, but Class B needn't know anything about Class A, which is right and proper because it's just a servant, and should be able to serve *any* other object. Because Class A imports Class B's header, it knows about SomeProtocol and can adopt it and implement its required methods. When Object A creates Object B, it also sets itself as Object B's delegate. Now Object B knows all that it needs to know: it can send SomeProtocol messages to its delegate, regardless of that delegate's actual class.

To see why this pattern is a good one, consider an actual case. In one of my apps I present a view where the user can move three sliders to choose a color. Appropriately, its code is in a class called ColorPickerController. When the user taps Done or Cancel, the view should be dismissed; but first, the code that presented this view needs to hear about what color the user chose. So I need to send a message from the ColorPickerController instance back to the instance that presented it. Here is the declaration for that message:

```
- (void) colorPicker:(ColorPickerController*)picker
    didSetColorNamed:(NSString*)theName
             toColor:(UIColor*)theColor;
```

The question is: where should this declaration go?

Now, it happens that in my app I know the class of the instance that will in fact present the ColorPickerController's view: it is a SettingsController. So I could simply declare this method in the interface section of SettingsController's header file, and have Color-PickerController import SettingsController's header file. But this feels wrong:

- It should not be up to SettingsController to declare a method that it is implementing only in deference to ColorPickerController.
- If SettingsController declares this message in its header file, ColorPickerController will have to import that header file in order to send the message; but this means that ColorPickerController now knows all about SettingsController, whereas the *only* thing it needs to know about SettingsController is that it implements this one method.
- It is merely a contingent fact that the instance being sent this message *is* a Settings-Controller; it should be open to *any* class to present and dismiss a ColorPicker-Controller's view, and thus to be eligible to receive this message.

Therefore we want ColorPickerController *itself* to declare the method that *it itself is going to call*; and we want it to send the message blindly to some receiver, without regard to the class of that receiver. Thus there needs to be a linkage, as it were, between the declaration of this method in ColorPickerController and the implementation of this method in the receiver. That linkage is precisely what a protocol creates! The solution, then, is for ColorPickerController to define a protocol in its header file, with this method as part of that protocol, and for the class that presents a ColorPickerController's view to conform to that protocol. ColorPickerController also has an appropriately typed `delegate` property; this provides the channel of communication, and tells the compiler that sending this message is legal.

Here's ColorPickerController's header file (note the use of the forward declaration I mentioned in Chapter 10):

```
@protocol ColorPickerDelegate;
@interface ColorPickerController : UIViewController
@property (nonatomic, weak) id <ColorPickerDelegate> delegate;
@end
@protocol ColorPickerDelegate
// color == nil on cancel
- (void) colorPicker:(ColorPickerController *)picker
     didSetColorNamed:(NSString *)theName
             toColor:(UIColor*)theColor;
@end
```

When my SettingsController instance creates and configures a ColorPickerController instance, it also sets itself as that ColorPickerController's `delegate`. Now, when the user picks a color, the ColorPickerController knows to whom it should send `color-Picker:didSetColorNamed:toColor:`, namely, its delegate; and the compiler allows this, because the delegate has adopted the ColorPickerDelegate protocol:

```
- (void) dismissColorPicker: (id) sender { // user has tapped our Done button
    [self.delegate colorPicker:self
            didSetColorNamed:self.colorName
                   toColor:self.color];
}
```

If you create a project from Xcode's own Utility Application template, you will see that it, too, exemplifies exactly this same architecture. We start with a MainViewController. It eventually creates a FlipsideViewController. When the FlipsideViewController is ready to go out of existence, it is going to want to send the `flipsideViewController-DidFinish:` message back to whoever created it. So FlipsideViewController defines a FlipsideViewControllerDelegate protocol requiring the `flipsideViewControllerDid-Finish:` method, along with a `delegate` property typed as id `<FlipsideView-ControllerDelegate>`. When a MainViewController instance creates a FlipsideView-Controller instance, it specifies that it itself, the MainViewController instance, is the FlipsideViewController's `delegate`; and it can do this, because MainViewController does in fact adopt the FlipsideViewControllerDelegate protocol! Problem solved, mission accomplished. If you're in doubt about how to set up the delegation-and-protocol pattern, make a project based on the Utility Application template and study it.

Data Sources

A *data source* is like a delegate, except that its methods supply the data for another object to display. The chief Cocoa classes with data sources are UITableView, UICollection-View, UIPickerView, and UIPageViewController. In each case, the data source must formally conform to a protocol with required methods.

It comes as a surprise to some beginners that a data source is necessary at all. Why isn't a table's data just part of the table? Or why isn't there at least some fixed data structure that contains the data? The reason is that such an architecture would violate generality. Use of a data source separates the object that displays the data from the object that manages the data, and leaves the latter free to store and obtain that data however it likes (see on model–view–controller in Chapter 13). The only requirement is that the data source must be able to supply information quickly, because it will be asked for it in real time when the data needs displaying.

Another surprise is that the data source is different from the delegate. But this again is only for generality; it's an option, not a requirement. There is no reason why the data source and the delegate should not be the same object, and most of the time they probably will be. Indeed, in most cases, data source methods and delegate methods will work closely together; you won't even be conscious of the distinction.

In this simple example, we implement a UIPickerView that allows the user to select by name a day of the week (the Gregorian week, using English day names). The first two methods are UIPickerView data source methods; the third method is a UIPickerView delegate method. It takes all three methods to supply the picker view's content:

```
- (NSInteger) numberOfComponentsInPickerView: (UIPickerView*) pickerView {
    return 1;
}

- (NSInteger) pickerView: (UIPickerView*) pickerView
       numberOfRowsInComponent: (NSInteger) component {
    return 7;
}

- (NSString*) pickerView:(UIPickerView*)pickerView
             titleForRow:(NSInteger)row
           forComponent:(NSInteger)component {
    NSArray* arr = @[@"Sunday",
                     @"Monday",
                     @"Tuesday",
                     @"Wednesday",
                     @"Thursday",
                     @"Friday",
                     @"Saturday"];
    return arr[row];
}
```

Actions

An *action* is a message emitted by an instance of a UIControl subclass (a *control*) reporting a significant user event taking place in that control (see Chapter 7). The UIControl subclasses are all simple interface objects that the user can interact with directly, like a button (UIButton), a switch (UISwitch), a segmented control (UISegmented-Control), a slider (UISlider), or a text field (UITextField).

The significant user events (*control events*) are listed under UIControlEvents in the Constants section of the UIControl class documentation. Different controls implement different control events: for example, a segmented control's Value Changed event signifies that the user has tapped to select a different segment, but a button's Touch Up Inside event signifies that the user has tapped the button. Of itself, a control event has no external effect; the control responds visually (for example, a tapped button looks tapped), but it doesn't share the information that the event has taken place. If you want to know when a control event takes place, so that you can respond to it in your code, you must arrange for that control event to trigger an action message.

Here's how it works. A control maintains an internal dispatch table: for each control event, there can be any number of target–action pairs, in each of which the *action* is a message selector (the name of a method) and the *target* is the object to which that message is to be sent. When a control event occurs, the control consults its dispatch table, finds all the target–action pairs associated with that control event, and sends each action message to the corresponding target (Figure 11-1).

There are two ways to manipulate a control's action dispatch table: you can configure an action connection in a nib (as explained in Chapter 7), or you can use code. To use code, you send the control the message addTarget:action:forControlEvents:, where the target: is an object, the action: is a selector, and the controlEvents: are designated by a bitmask (see Chapter 1 if you've forgotten how to construct a bitmask). Unlike a notification center, a control also has methods for introspecting the dispatch table.

Recall the example from Chapter 7. We have a buttonPressed: method, whose purpose is to be called when the user taps a certain button in the interface:

```
- (void) buttonPressed: (id) sender {
    UIAlertView* av = [[UIAlertView alloc] initWithTitle:@"Howdy!"
                                                 message:@"You tapped me."
                                                delegate:nil
                                       cancelButtonTitle:@"Cool"
                                       otherButtonTitles:nil];
    [av show];
}
```

In Chapter 7, we arranged for that to happen by setting up an action connection in the nib: we connected the button's Touch Up Inside event to the ViewController buttonPressed: method. In reality, this meant that we were forming a target–action pair —

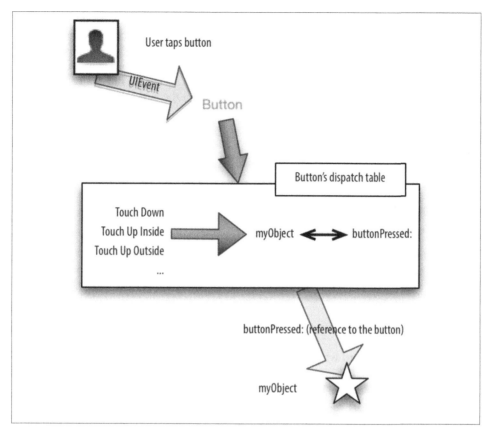

User taps button

UIEvent

Button

Button's dispatch table

Touch Down
Touch Up Inside
Touch Up Outside
...

myObject ⟷ buttonPressed:

buttonPressed: (reference to the button)

myObject

Figure 11-1. The target–action architecture

the target was the ViewController instance that would own the nib when it was loaded, and the action was the buttonPressed: selector — and adding it to the button's dispatch table for the Touch Up Inside control event.

Instead of making that arrangement in the nib, we could have done the same thing in code. Suppose we had never drawn that action connection. And suppose that, instead, we had an outlet connection from the view controller to the button, called button. (In Chapter 7, we did in fact create such an outlet connection.) Then the view controller, after the nib loads, can configure the button's dispatch table like this:

```
[self.button addTarget:self action:@selector(buttonPressed:)
                forControlEvents:UIControlEventTouchUpInside];
```

A control event can have multiple target–action pairs. You might configure it this way intentionally, but it is also possible to do so accidentally. Unintentionally giving a control event a target–action pair without removing its *existing* target-action pair is an easy mistake to make, and can cause some very mysterious behavior. For example, if we had formed an action connection in the nib *and* configured the dispatch table in code, a tap on the button would cause buttonPressed: to be called *twice*.

The signature for the action selector can be in any of three forms:

- The fullest form takes two parameters:
  — The control, usually typed as id.
  — The UIEvent that generated the control event.
- A shorter form, the one most commonly used, omits the second parameter. button-Pressed: is an example; it takes one parameter, sender. When buttonPressed: is called through an action message emanating from the button, sender will be a reference to the button.
- There is a still shorter form that omits both parameters.

What is the UIEvent, and what is it for? Well, a *touch event* is generated whenever the user does something with a finger (sets it down on the screen, moves it, raises it from the screen). UIEvents are the lowest-level objects charged with communication of touch events to your app. A UIEvent is basically a timestamp (a double) along with a collection (NSSet) of touch events (UITouch). The action mechanism deliberately shields you from the complexities of touch events, but by electing to receive the UIEvent, you can still deal with those complexities if you want to.

Curiously, none of the action selector parameters provide any way to learn *which* control event triggered the current action selector call! Thus, for example, to distinguish a Touch Up Inside control event from a Touch Up Outside control event, their corresponding target–action pairs must specify two different action handlers; if you dispatch them to the same action handler, that handler cannot discover which control event occurred.

OS X Programmer Alert

If you're an experienced OS X Cocoa developer, you'll note that there are some major differences between the OS X implementation of actions and the iOS implementation. In OS X, a control has just one action; in iOS, a control may respond to multiple control events. In OS X, an action has just one target; in iOS, a single event can trigger multiple action messages to multiple targets. In OS X, an action message selector comes in just one form; in iOS, there are three possible forms.

The Responder Chain

A *responder* is an object that knows how to receive UIEvents directly (see the previous section). It knows this because it is an instance of UIResponder or a UIResponder subclass. If you examine the Cocoa class hierarchy, you'll find that just about any class that has anything to do with display on the screen is a responder. A UIView is a responder. A UIWindow is a responder. A UIViewController is a responder. Even a UIApplication is a responder. In iOS 5 and later, the app delegate is a responder.

If you look in the documentation for the UIResponder class, you'll find that it implements four low-level methods for receiving touch-related UIEvents: touches-Began:withEvent:, touchesMoved:withEvent:, touchesEnded:withEvent: and touchesCancelled:withEvent:. These are called to notify a responder of a touch event. No matter how your code ultimately hears about a user-related touch event — indeed, even if your code *never* hears about a touch event (because Cocoa reacted in some automatic way to the touch, without your code's intervention) — the touch was initially communicated to a responder through one of these methods.

The mechanism for this communication starts by deciding which responder the user touched. The UIView methods hitTest:withEvent: and pointInside:withEvent: are called until the correct view (the *hit-test view*) is located. Then UIApplication's send-Event: method is called, which calls UIWindow's sendEvent:, which calls the correct method of the hit-test view (a responder).

The responders in your app participate in a *responder chain*, which essentially links them up through the view hierarchy. A UIView can sit inside another UIView, its *superview*, and so on until we reach the app's UIWindow (a UIView that has no superview). The responder chain, from bottom to top, looks like this:

1. The UIView that we start with (here, the hit-test view).
2. The UIViewController that controls that UIView, if there is one.
3. The UIView's superview, and then *its* UIViewController if there is one. Repeat this step, moving up the superview hierarchy one superview at a time, until we reach...

4. The UIWindow.

5. The UIApplication.

6. The UIApplication's delegate.

Deferring Responsibility

The responder chain can be used to let a responder defer responsibility for handling a touch event. If a responder receives a touch event and can't handle it, the event can be passed up the responder chain to look for a responder that *can* handle it. This can happen in two main ways:

- The responder doesn't implement the relevant method.
- The responder implements the relevant method to call `super`.

For example, a plain vanilla UIView has no native implementation of the touch event methods. Thus, by default, even if a UIView is the hit-test view, the touch event effectively falls through the UIView and travels up the responder chain, looking for someone to respond to it. In certain situations, it might make logical sense for you to defer responsibility for this touch to the main background view, or even to the UIView-Controller that controls it.

One of my apps is a game that's a simple jigsaw puzzle: a rectangular photo is divided into smaller pieces, and the pieces are shuffled. The background view is a UIView subclass called Board; the puzzle pieces are generic UIView objects, and are subviews of the Board. Knowledge of how a piece should respond when tapped resides in the Board, which knows the overall layout of the pieces; thus, I don't need a puzzle piece to contain any tap detection logic. Therefore I take advantage of the responder chain to defer responsibility: the puzzle pieces don't implement any touch methods, and a tap on a puzzle piece falls through to the Board, which *does* perform touch detection and handles the tap, and tells the tapped piece what to do. The user, of course, knows nothing about that: outwardly, you touch a piece and the piece responds.

Nil-Targeted Actions

A *nil-targeted action* is a target–action pair in which the target is nil. There is no designated target object, so the following rule is used: starting with the hit-test view (the view with which the user is interacting), Cocoa looks up the responder chain for an object that can respond to the action message.

Suppose, for example, that we were to configure a button in code, like this:

```
[self.button addTarget:nil action:@selector(buttonPressed:)
            forControlEvents:UIControlEventTouchUpInside];
```

That's a nil-targeted action. So what happens when the user taps the button? First, Cocoa looks in the UIButton itself to see whether it responds to buttonPressed:. If not, it looks in the UIView that is its superview. And so on, up the responder chain. If a responder is found that handles buttonPressed:, the action message is sent to that object; otherwise, the message goes unhandled (with no penalty).

Thus, in the app we posited earlier, where self is the view controller that owns the view that contains the button, and where the class of this view controller does in fact implement buttonPressed:, tapping the button will cause buttonPressed: to be called!

To create a nil-targeted action in a nib, you form a connection to the First Responder proxy object (in the dock). This is what the First Responder proxy object is for! The First Responder isn't a real object with a known class, so before you can connect an action to it, you have to define the action message within the First Responder proxy object, like this:

1. Select the First Responder proxy in the nib, and switch to the Attributes inspector.

2. You'll see a table (probably empty) of user-defined nil-targeted First Responder actions. Click the Plus button and give the new action a signature; it must take a single parameter (so that its name will end with a colon).

3. Now you can Control-drag from a control, such as a UIButton, to the First Responder proxy to specify a nil-targeted action with the signature you specified.

 Cocoa uses the term *first responder* in a confusing way. An arbitrary responder object can be assigned formal first responder status (by sending it becomeFirstResponder, provided that this responder returns YES from canBecomeFirstResponder). But this does not make the object first responder for purposes of handling nil-targeted actions! Cocoa's hunt for a responder that can handle a nil-targeted action still starts with the control that the user is interacting with (the hit-test view) and goes up the responder chain from there.

Swamped by Events

Your code runs only because Cocoa sends an event and you had previously set up a method ready to receive it. Cocoa has the potential to send lots of events, telling you what the user has done, informing you of each stage in the lifetime of your app and its objects, asking for your input on how to proceed. To receive the events that you need to hear about, your code is peppered with methods that are *entry points* — methods that you have written with just the right name and in just the right class so that they can be called by Cocoa through events. In fact, it is easy to imagine that in many cases your code for a class will consist almost entirely of entry points.

That fact is one of your primary challenges as an iOS programmer. You know what you want to do, but you have to divide it up and allocate it according to when Cocoa is going to call into your code. Before you've written a single line of your own code, the skeleton structure of a class is likely to have been largely mapped out for you by the need to be prepared to receive the events that Cocoa is going to want to send you.

Suppose, for example, that your iPhone app presents an interface consisting of a table view. (This is in fact an extremely probable scenario.) You're likely to have a corresponding UITableViewController subclass; UITableViewController is a built-in UIViewController subclass, and an instance of your UITableViewController subclass will own and control the table view, plus you'll probably use this same class as the table view's data source and delegate. In this single class, then, you're likely to want to implement *at a minimum* the following methods:

`initWithCoder:` *or* `initWithNibName:bundle:`
    UIViewController lifetime method, where you perform custom instance initializations.

`viewDidLoad`
    UIViewController lifetime method, where you perform view-related initializations.

`viewDidAppear:`
    UIViewController lifetime method, where you set up states that need to apply only while your view is onscreen. For example, if you're going to register for a notification or set up a timer, this is a likely place to do it.

`viewDidDisappear:`
    UIViewController lifetime method, where you reverse what you did in `viewDidAppear:`. For example, this would be a likely place to unregister for a notification or invalidate a repeating timer that you set up in `viewDidAppear:`.

`supportedInterfaceOrientations`
    UIViewController query method, where you specify what device orientations are allowed for this view controller's main view.

`numberOfSectionsInTableView:`
`tableView:numberOfRowsInSection:`
`tableView:cellForRowAtIndexPath:`
    UITableView data source query methods, where you specify the contents of the table.

`tableView:didSelectRowAtIndexPath:`
    UITableView delegate user action method, where you respond when the user taps a row of the table.

```
dealloc
```
NSObject lifetime method, where you perform end-of-life cleanup.

Suppose, further, that you did in fact use `viewDidAppear:` to register for a notification and to set up a timer. Then that notification has a selector (unless you used a block), and the timer has a selector; you must therefore also implement the methods described by those selectors.

We already have, then, about a dozen methods whose presence is effectively a matter of boilerplate. These are not *your* methods; *you* are never going to call them. They are *Cocoa's* methods, which you have placed here so that each can be called at the appropriate moment in the life story of your app.

The logic of a program laid out in this fashion is by no means easy to understand! I'm not criticizing Cocoa here — indeed, it's hard to imagine how else an application framework could work — but, purely as an objective matter of fact, the result is that a Cocoa program, even your own program, even *while you're developing it*, is hard to read, because it consists of numerous disconnected entry points, each with its own meaning, each called at its own set moment which is not in any way obvious from looking at the program. To understand what our hypothetical class does, you have to know *already* such things as when `viewDidAppear:` is called and how it is typically used; otherwise, you don't even know where to look to find the program's logic and behavior, let alone how to interpret what you see when you do look there. And this difficulty is greatly compounded when you try to read someone else's code (this is one reason why, as I mentioned in Chapter 8, sample code is not all that helpful to a beginner).

Looking at the code of an iOS program — even your own code — your eyes can easily glaze over at the sight of all these methods called automatically by Cocoa under various circumstances. To be sure, experience will teach you about such things as the overridden UIViewController methods and the table view delegate and data source methods. On the other hand, no amount of experience will tell you that a certain method is called as a button's action or through a notification. Comments really help, and I strongly advise you, as you develop any iOS app, to comment every method, quite heavily if need be, saying what that method does and under what circumstances you expect it to be called — especially if it is an entry point, where it is Cocoa itself that will do the calling.

Perhaps the most common kind of mistake in writing a Cocoa app is not that there's a bug in your code itself, but that you've put the code in the wrong place. Your code isn't running, or it's running at the wrong time, or the pieces are running in the wrong order. I see questions about this sort of thing all the time on the various online user forums (these are all actual examples that appeared over the course of just two days):

- "There's a delay between the time when my view appears and when my button takes on its correct title." That's because you put the code that sets the button's title in `viewDidAppear:`. That's *too late*; your code needs to run earlier, perhaps in `view-WillAppear:`.

- "My subviews are positioned in code and they're turning out all wrong." That's because you put the code that positions your subviews in `viewDidLoad`. That's *too early*; your code needs to run later, when your view's dimensions have been determined.

- "My view is rotating even though my view controller's `supportedInterfaceOrientations` says not to." That's because you implemented `supportedInterfaceOrientations` in the *wrong class*; it needs to be implemented in the UINavigationController that contains your view controller.

- "I set up an action connection for Value Changed on a text field, but my code isn't being called when the user edits." That's because you connected the *wrong action*; a text field emits Editing Changed, not Value Changed.

Adding to your challenges is that fact that you can't really know precisely when an entry point will be called. The documentation may give you a general sense, but in most cases there are no guarantees about when events will arrive and in what order. What you think is going to happen, and even what the documentation leads you to believe is going to happen, might not be quite what really does happen. Your own code can trigger unintended events. The documentation might not make it clear just when a notification will be sent. There could even be a bug in Cocoa such that events are called in a way that seems to contradict the documentation. And you have no access to the Cocoa source code, so you can't work out the underlying details. Therefore I also recommend that as you develop your app, you instrument your code heavily with caveman debugging (`NSLog`; see Chapter 9). As you test your code, keep an eye on the console output and check whether the messages make sense. You may be surprised at what you discover.

For example, in one app that I was developing, I suddenly found that in a UIViewController subclass, `viewDidLoad` was being called twice as the app started up, which should be impossible. Fortunately, my code was heavily instrumented with `NSLog` calls, or I would never have discovered this problem. Adding even more `NSLog` calls, I found that `viewDidLoad` was being called while I was still in the middle of executing `awakeFromNib`, which should *really* be impossible. The reason turned out to be my own mistake: I was referring to my view controller's `view` property during `awakeFromNib`, which was causing `viewDidLoad` to be called. The problem went away when I corrected my mistake.

Delayed Performance

Some of your code tells Cocoa what to do. But Cocoa is a black box, so what Cocoa actually will do, and precisely when it will do it, is out of your control. Your code was executed in response to some event; but your code in turn may trigger a new event or chain of events. Sometimes this causes bad things to happen: there might be a crash, or Cocoa might appear not to have done what you said to do. One of the chief causes of these difficulties is the chain of triggered events itself. Sometimes you just need to step outside that chain for a moment and wait for everything to settle down before proceeding.

The technique for doing this is called *delayed performance*. You tell Cocoa to do something not right this moment, but in a little while, when things have settled down. Perhaps you need only a very short delay, possibly even as short as zero seconds, just to let Cocoa finish doing something, such as laying out interface. Technically, you're allowing the current run loop to finish, completing and unwinding the entire current method call stack, before proceeding further with your own code.

You're likely to be using delayed performance a lot more than you might expect. With experience, you'll develop a kind of sixth sense for when delayed performance might be the solution to your difficulties. There are three chief implementations of delayed performance that I use in my own code:

performSelector:withObject:afterDelay:
> I mentioned this NSObject method at the end of Chapter 10. It limits you as to the signature of the selector — it must take one parameter or none — so you might have to restructure your own code slightly.

dispatch_after
> I mentioned this in Chapter 3. It takes a block, not a selector, which can result in more direct and readable code.

dispatch_async
> Often, the delay you're after doesn't need to be more than zero. What you're trying to do is postpone the next step until the consequences of the previous step have worked themselves out. So it suffices to wait until nothing is happening. You can do this with a call to dispatch_async onto the same queue where everything is happening now, namely the main queue.

In all three cases, what you propose to do will be done later on; you're deliberately breaking out of your own code's line-by-line sequence of execution. So a delayed performance call will be the last call in its method (or block), and cannot return any value.

In this example from one of my own apps, the user has tapped a row of a table, and my code responds by creating and showing a new view controller:

```
- (void) tableView:(UITableView *)tableView
        didSelectRowAtIndexPath:(NSIndexPath *)indexPath {
    TracksViewController *t =
        [[TracksViewController alloc]
         initWithMediaItemCollection:(self.albums)[indexPath.row]];
    [self.navigationController pushViewController:t animated:YES];
}
```

Unfortunately, the innocent-looking call to my TracksViewController method init-WithMediaItemCollection: can take a moment to complete, so the app comes to a stop with the table row highlighted — very briefly, but just long enough to startle the user. To cover this delay with a sense of activity, I've rigged my UITableViewCell subclass to show a spinning activity indicator when it's selected:

```
- (void)setSelected:(BOOL)selected animated:(BOOL)animated {
    if (selected) {
        [self.activityIndicator startAnimating]; // appear and spin
    } else {
        [self.activityIndicator stopAnimating]; // disappear
    }
    [super setSelected:selected animated:animated];
}
```

However, the spinning activity indicator never appears and never spins. The reason is that the events are stumbling over one another here. UITableViewCell's set-Selected:animated: isn't called until the UITableView delegate method table-View:didSelectRowAtIndexPath: has finished. But the delay we're trying to paper over is *during* tableView:didSelectRowAtIndexPath:; the whole problem is that it *doesn't* finish fast enough. Delayed performance to the rescue! I'll rewrite tableView:did-SelectRowAtIndexPath: so that it finishes immediately — thus triggering set-Selected:animated: immediately and causing the activity indicator to appear and spin — and I'll use delayed performance to call initWithMediaItemCollection: later on, when the interface has ironed itself out:

```
- (void) tableView:(UITableView *)tableView
        didSelectRowAtIndexPath:(NSIndexPath *)indexPath {
    // tiny delay to allow spinner to start spinning
    double delayInSeconds = 0.1;
    dispatch_time_t popTime =
        dispatch_time(DISPATCH_TIME_NOW, delayInSeconds * NSEC_PER_SEC);
    dispatch_after(popTime, dispatch_get_main_queue(), ^(void){
        TracksViewController *t =
            [[TracksViewController alloc]
             initWithMediaItemCollection:(self.albums)[indexPath.row]];
        [self.navigationController pushViewController:t animated:YES];
    });
}
```

CHAPTER 12

Accessors and Memory Management

This chapter returns to three aspects of Objective-C introduced briefly in Chapter 5 — accessors, key–value coding, and properties — discussing them more deeply and rigorously, and describing in particular the special role that they play in one of the most important and crucial aspects of Cocoa: memory management of Objective-C instances.

Accessors

An *accessor* is a method for getting or setting the value of an instance variable. An accessor that gets the instance variable's value is called a *getter*; an accessor that sets the instance variable's value is called a *setter*.

Accessors are important in part because instance variables, by default, are protected (Chapter 5), whereas publicly declared methods are public; without public accessor methods, a protected instance variable can't be accessed by any object whose class (or superclass) isn't the one that declares the instance variable.

You might be tempted to conclude from this that you needn't bother making an accessor for an instance variable that isn't intended for public access, and to some extent this is a reasonable conclusion. However, in modern Objective-C, making accessors is as easy as declaring an instance variable: you declare a property, and the instance variable along with the accessors come into existence automatically — you don't have to write any accessor code. Plus, if you *do* write accessor code, you can consistently perform additional tasks when the instance variable's value is touched.

There are naming conventions for accessors, and you should obey them. The conventions are simple:

The setter

A setter's name should start with set, followed by a capitalized version of the instance variable's name (without an initial underscore if the instance variable has one). The setter should take one parameter — the new value to be assigned to the instance variable. Thus, if the instance variable is named `myVar` (or `_myVar`), the setter should be named `setMyVar:`.

The getter

A getter should have the same name as the instance variable (without an initial underscore if the instance variable has one). This will not cause you or the compiler any confusion, because variable names and method names are used in completely different contexts. Thus, if the instance variable is named `myVar` (or `_myVar`), the getter should be named `myVar`.

If the instance variable's value is a BOOL, you may optionally start the getter's name with `is` (for example, an ivar `showing` or `_showing` can have a getter `isShowing`), though in fact I never do this.

The accessor naming conventions allow Objective-C features to call those accessors given only a single name. Key–value coding starts with a string and calls the accessors; you can use a property name as a way of calling an accessor. The naming conventions make such things possible.

Moreover, the naming conventions effectively give the accessors a life of their own, independent of any instance variable. Once you have accessors, no law requires that they use the name of a *real* instance variable! Quite the contrary: you might deliberately have methods `myVar` and `setMyVar:` when in fact there is no `myVar` (or `_myVar`) instance variable. (Perhaps the accessors are masking the real name of the instance variable, or perhaps there is no instance variable at all, and these accessors are really doing something quite different behind the scenes.) Nevertheless, thanks to the naming conventions, all the accessor-dependent features of Objective-C continue to work. Accessors effectively present a façade, as if there *were* a certain instance variable, while shielding the caller from any knowledge of the underlying details.

Key–Value Coding

Cocoa derives the name of an accessor from a string name at runtime through a mechanism called *key–value coding*, or simply *KVC*. The *key* is a string (an NSString) that names the value to be accessed. The basis for key–value coding is the NSKeyValue-Coding protocol, an informal protocol (it is actually a category) to which NSObject (and therefore every object) conforms. Key–value coding is a big subject; see Apple's *Key-Value Coding Programming Guide* for full information.

The fundamental key–value coding methods are `valueForKey:` and `setValue:for-Key:`. When one of these methods is called on an object, the object is introspected. In simplified terms, first the appropriate accessor is sought; if it doesn't exist, the instance variable is accessed directly.

A class is *key–value coding compliant* (or *KVC compliant*) on a given key if it implements the methods, or possesses the instance variable, required for access via that key. An attempt to access a key for which a class is *not* key–value coding compliant will cause an exception at runtime: "This class is not key value coding-compliant for the key key-Name." (The last word in that error message, despite the lack of quotes, is the key string that caused the trouble.)

So, for example, suppose the call is this:

```
[myObject setValue:@"Hello" forKey:@"greeting"];
```

First, a method `setGreeting:` is sought in `myObject`; if it exists, it is called, passing `@"Hello"` as its argument. If that fails, but if `myObject` has an instance variable called `greeting` (or `_greeting`), the value `@"Hello"` is assigned directly to that ivar. If *that* fails, an exception is thrown and the app will crash.

 The key–value coding mechanism can bypass completely the privacy of an instance variable! Cocoa knows that you might not want to allow that, so a class method `accessInstanceVariablesDirectly` is supplied, which you can override to return NO (the default is YES).

Both `valueForKey:` and `setValue:forKey:` require an object as the value. Your accessor's signature (or, if there is no accessor, the instance variable itself) might not use an object as the value, so the key–value coding mechanism converts for you. Numeric types (including BOOL) are expressed as an NSNumber; other types (such as CGRect and CGPoint) are expressed as an NSValue.

Another useful pair of methods is `dictionaryWithValuesForKeys:` and `setValuesFor-KeysWithDictionary:`, which allow you to get and set multiple key–value pairs by way of an NSDictionary with a single command.

Key–value coding allows you, in effect, to decide at runtime, based on an NSString, what accessor to call. By using an NSString instead of an actual accessor method call, you're throwing away compile-time checking as to the message you're sending. Moreover, KVC is agnostic about the actual class of the object you're talking to; you can send `valueFor-Key:` to *any* object and successfully get a result, provided the class of that object is KVC compliant for that key, so you're throwing away compile-time checking as to the object you're sending the message to. These are both strong advantages of key–value coding, and I often find myself using it because of them.

Here's an example of key–value coding used in my own code. In a flashcard app, I have a class Term, representing a Latin term, that defines many instance variables. Each card displays one term, with its instance variables shown in different text fields. If the user taps any of three text fields, I want the interface to change from the term that's currently showing to the next term whose value is different for the instance variable that this text field represents. Thus this code is the same for all three text fields; the only difference is what instance variable to consider as we hunt for the next term to be displayed. By far the simplest way to express this parallelism is through key–value coding:

```
NSInteger tag = g.view.tag; // the tag tells us which text field was tapped
NSString* key = nil;
switch (tag) {
    case 1: key = @"lesson"; break;
    case 2: key = @"lessonSection"; break;
    case 3: key = @"lessonSectionPartFirstWord"; break;
}
// get current value of corresponding instance variable
NSString* curValue = [[self currentCardController].term valueForKey: key];
// ...
```

A number of built-in Cocoa classes permit you to use key–value coding in a special way. For example:

- If you send valueForKey: to an NSArray, it sends valueForKey: to each of its elements and returns a new array consisting of the results, an elegant shorthand (and a kind of poor man's map). NSSet behaves similarly.

- NSDictionary implements valueForKey: as an alternative to objectForKey: (useful particularly if you have an NSArray of dictionaries). Similarly, NSMutable-Dictionary treats setValue:forKey: as a synonym for setObject:forKey:, except that value: can be nil, in which case removeObject:forKey: is called.

- NSSortDescriptor sorts an NSArray by sending valueForKey: to each of its elements. This makes it easy to sort an array of dictionaries on the value of a particular dictionary key, or an array of objects on the value of a particular instance variable.

- CALayer and CAAnimation permit you to use key–value coding to define and retrieve the values for arbitrary keys, as if they were a kind of dictionary; this is useful for attaching identifying and configuration information to one of these instances.

- NSManagedObject, used in conjunction with Core Data, is guaranteed to be key-value coding compliant for attributes you've configured in the entity model. Therefore, it's common to access those attributes with valueForKey: and setValue:for-Key:.

KVC and Outlets

Key–value coding lies at the heart of how outlet connections work (Chapter 7). The name of the outlet in the nib is a string. Key–value coding turns the string into a hunt for appropriate accessors.

Suppose you have a class MyClass with an instance variable `myVar`, and you've drawn a `myVar` outlet from that class's representative in the nib to a MyOtherClass nib object. When the nib loads, the outlet name `myVar` is translated to the accessor method name `setMyVar:`, and your MyClass instance's `setMyVar:` method, if it exists, is called with the MyOtherClass instance as its parameter, thus setting the value of your MyClass instance's `myVar` instance variable to the MyOtherClass instance (Figure 7-7).

If something goes wrong with the match between the outlet name in the nib and the name of the instance variable or accessor in the class, then at runtime, when the nib loads, Cocoa will attempt to use key–value coding to set a value in your object based on the name of the outlet, will fail, and will generate an exception, complaining that the class is not key–value coding compliant for the key (the outlet name) — that is, your app will crash at nib-loading time. A likely way for this to happen is that you form the outlet correctly but then later change the name of (or delete) the instance variable or accessor in the class (see "Misconfiguring an Outlet" on page 174).

Conversely, you should not use accessor names for methods that aren't accessors. For instance, returning to our example with MyClass and `myVar`, you probably would not want MyClass to have a method called `setMyVar:` if it is not the accessor for `myVar`. If it did have such a method, it would be called when the nib loads and key–value coding tries to resolve the `myVar` outlet in the nib. The MyOtherClass instance would be passed to this method, so there's no error, but the MyOtherClass instance would *not* be assigned to the `myVar` instance variable, because `setMyVar:` isn't its accessor. As a result, references in your code to `myVar` would be references to nil. The `setMyVar:` method has acted as a false façade, preventing the `myVar` instance variable from being set at nib-loading time. Making this kind of mistake is surprisingly common.

Key Paths

A *key path* allows you to chain keys in a single expression. If an object is key–value coding compliant for a certain key, and if the value of that key is itself an object that is key–value coding compliant for another key, you can chain those keys by calling `valueForKeyPath:` and `setValue:forKeyPath:`. A key path string looks like a succession of key names joined using dot-notation. For example, `valueForKeyPath:@"key1.key2"` effectively calls `valueForKey:` on the message receiver, with `@"key1"` as the key, and then takes the object returned from that call and calls `valueForKey:` on that object, with `@"key2"` as the key.

To illustrate this shorthand, imagine that our object `myObject` has an instance variable `theData` which is an array of dictionaries such that each dictionary has a `name` key and a `description` key. I'll show you the actual value of `theData` as displayed by `NSLog`:

```
(
    {
        description = "The one with glasses.";
        name = Manny;
    },
    {
        description = "Looks a little like Governor Dewey.";
        name = Moe;
    },
    {
        description = "The one without a mustache.";
        name = Jack;
    }
)
```

Then [myObject valueForKeyPath: @"theData.name"] returns an array consisting of the strings @"Manny", @"Moe", and @"Jack". If you don't see why, review what I said a few paragraphs ago about how NSArray and NSDictionary implement valueForKey:.

(Recall also the discussion of user-defined runtime attributes, in Chapter 7. The key you're entering when you define a runtime attribute in an object's Identity inspector in a nib is actually a key path.)

Array Accessors

Key–value coding allows an object to implement a key as if its value were an array (or a set), even if it isn't. This is similar to what I said earlier about how accessors function as a façade, putting an instance variable name in front of hidden complexities. To illustrate, I'll add these methods to the class of our object myObject:

```
- (NSUInteger) countOfPepBoys {
    return [self.theData count];
}

- (id) objectInPepBoysAtIndex: (NSUInteger) ix {
    return (self.theData)[ix];
}
```

By implementing countOf... and objectIn...AtIndex:, I'm telling the key–value coding system to act as if the given key (@"pepBoys" in this case) existed and were an array. An attempt to fetch the value of the key @"pepBoys" by way of key–value coding will succeed, and will return an object that can be treated as an array, though in fact it is a proxy object (an NSKeyValueArray). Thus we can now say [myObject valueForKey: @"pepBoys"] to obtain this array proxy, and we can say [myObject valueForKeyPath: @"pepBoys.name"] to get the same array of strings as before.

(This particular example may seem a little silly because the underlying implementation is already an array instance variable, but you can imagine an implementation whereby the result of `objectInPepBoysAtIndex:` is obtained through some completely different sort of operation.)

The proxy object returned through this sort of façade behaves like an NSArray, not like an NSMutableArray. If you want the caller to be able to manipulate the proxy object provided by a KVC façade as if it were a mutable array, you must implement two more methods, and the caller must obtain a different proxy object by calling `mutableArray-ValueForKey:`. So, for example (we are now presuming that `theData` is a mutable array):

```
- (void) insertObject: (id) val inPepBoysAtIndex: (NSUInteger) ix {
    [self.theData insertObject:val atIndex:ix];
}

- (void) removeObjectFromPepBoysAtIndex: (NSUInteger) ix {
    [self.theData removeObjectAtIndex: ix];
}
```

Now it is possible to call `[myObject mutableArrayValueForKey: @"pepBoys"]` to obtain something that acts like a mutable array. (The true usefulness of `mutableArray-ValueForKey:` will be clearer when we talk about key–value observing in Chapter 13.)

A complication for the programmer is that none of these methods can be looked up directly in the documentation, because they involve key names that are specific to your object. You can't find out from the documentation what `removeObjectFromPepBoysAt-Index:` is for; you have to know, in some other way, that it is part of the implementation of key–value coding compliance for a key `@"pepBoys"` that can be obtained as a mutable array. Be sure to comment your code so that you'll be able to understand it later.

Another complication, of course, is that getting a method name wrong can cause your object *not* to be key–value coding compliant. Figuring out why things aren't working as expected in a case like that can be tricky.

Memory Management

It comes as a surprise to many beginning coders that Cocoa objects require manual memory management, and that a memory management mistake can lead to runaway excessive memory usage, crashes, or mysterious misbehavior of your app. Fortunately, under ARC, your personal explicit memory management responsibilities are greatly reduced, which is a tremendous relief, as you are far less likely to make a mistake, and more of your time is liberated to concentrate on what your app actually does instead of dealing with memory management concerns. But even with ARC it is still possible to make a memory management mistake (I speak from personal experience), so you still need to understand Cocoa memory management, so that you know what ARC is doing for you, and so that you know how to interface with ARC in situations where it needs your assistance. Do not, therefore, suppose that you don't need to read this section on the grounds that you're going to be using ARC.

Principles of Cocoa Memory Management

The reason why memory must be managed at all is that object references are pointers. As I explained in Chapter 1, the pointers themselves are simple C values (basically they are just integers) and are managed automatically, whereas what an object pointer points to is a hunk of memory that must be explicitly set aside when the object is brought into existence and that must be explicitly freed up when the object goes out of existence. We already know how the memory is set aside — that is what `alloc` does. But how is this memory to be freed up, and when should it happen?

At the very least, an object should certainly go out of existence when no other objects exist that have a pointer to it. An object without a pointer to it is useless; it is occupying memory, but no other object has, or can ever get, a reference to it. This is a *memory leak*. Many computer languages solve this problem through a policy called *garbage collection*. Simply put, the language prevents memory leaks by periodically sweeping through a central list of all objects and destroying those to which no pointer exists. But affixing a form of garbage collection to Objective-C would be an inappropriately expensive strategy on an iOS device, where memory is strictly limited and the processor is relatively slow (and may have only a single core). Thus, memory in iOS must be managed more or less manually.

But manual memory management is no piece of cake, because an object must go out of existence neither too late nor too soon. Suppose we endow the language with the ability for one object to command that another object go out of existence now, this instant. But multiple objects can have a pointer (a reference) to the very same object. If both the object Manny and the object Moe have a pointer to the object Jack, and if Manny tells Jack to go out of existence now, poor old Moe is left with a pointer to nothing (or worse, to garbage). A pointer whose object has been destroyed behind the pointer's back is a *dangling pointer*. If Moe subsequently uses that dangling pointer to send a message to the object that it thinks is there, the app will crash.

To prevent both dangling pointers and memory leakage, Objective-C and Cocoa implement a policy of manual memory management based on a number, maintained by every object, called its *retain count*. Other objects can increment or decrement an object's retain count. As long as an object's retain count is positive, the object will persist. No object has the direct power to tell another object to be destroyed; rather, as soon as an object's retain count is decremented to zero, it is destroyed automatically.

By this policy, every object that needs Jack to persist should increment Jack's retain count, and should decrement it once again when it no longer needs Jack to persist. As long as all objects are well-behaved in accordance with this policy, the problem of manual memory management is effectively solved:

- There cannot be any dangling pointers, because any object that has a pointer to Jack has incremented Jack's retain count, thus ensuring that Jack persists.

- There cannot be any memory leaks, because any object that no longer needs Jack decrements Jack's retain count, thus ensuring that eventually Jack will go out of existence (when the retain count reaches zero, indicating that no object needs Jack any longer).

Obviously, all of this depends upon all objects cooperating in obedience to this memory management policy. Cocoa's objects (objects that are instances of built-in Cocoa classes) are well-behaved in this regard, but *you* must make sure *your* objects are well-behaved. Before ARC, ensuring that your objects were well-behaved was entirely up to you and your explicit code; under ARC, your objects will be well-behaved more or less automatically, provided you understand how to cooperate with ARC's automated behavior.

The Rules of Cocoa Manual Memory Management

An object is well-behaved with respect to memory management as long as it adheres to certain very simple rules in conformity with the basic concepts of memory management outlined in the previous section.

Before I tell you the rules, I remind you (because this is confusing to beginners) that a variable name, including an instance variable, is just a pointer. The variable name pointing to an object is often treated as the object, but it *isn't* the object. The two things are easily confused, so don't fall into the trap of confusing them. When you send a message to a pointer, you are really sending a message *through* that pointer, to the object to which it points. The rules for memory management are rules about objects, not names, references, or pointers. You cannot increment or decrement the retain count of a pointer; there is no such thing. The memory occupied by the pointer is managed automatically (and is tiny). Memory management is concerned with the object to which the pointer points. For this reason, I refer to my example objects by proper names — Manny, Moe, and Jack, or Object A and Object B — and not by variable names. The question of who has retained Jack has nothing to do with the *name* by which any particular object *refers* to Jack.

Here, then, are the rules of Cocoa manual memory management:

- To increment the retain count of any object, send it the `retain` message. This is called *retaining* the object. The object is now guaranteed to persist at least until its retain count is decremented once more. To make this a little more convenient, a `retain` call returns as its value the retained object — that is, [`myObject retain`] returns the object pointed to by `myObject`, but with its retain count incremented.

- When you say `alloc` (or `new`) to a class, the resulting instance comes into the world with its retain count already incremented. You do *not* need to retain an object you've just instantiated by saying `alloc` or `new` (and you should not). Similarly, when you say `copy` to an instance, the resulting new object (the copy) comes into the world

Debugging Memory Management Mistakes

Memory management mistakes are among the most common pitfalls for beginners and even for experienced Cocoa programmers. Though far less likely to occur under ARC, they still *can* occur under ARC, especially because a programmer using ARC is prone to suppose (wrongly) that they can't. What experience really teaches is to use every tool at your disposal to ferret out possible mistakes. Here are some of those tools (and see Chapter 9):

- The memory gauge in the Debug navigator charts memory usage whenever your app runs, allowing you to observe possible memory leakage or other unwarranted heavy memory use.

- The static analyzer (Product → Analyze) knows a lot about memory management and can help call potential memory management mistakes to your attention.

- Instruments (Product → Profile) has excellent tools for noticing leaks and tracking memory management of individual objects.

- Good old caveman debugging can help confirm that your objects are behaving as you want them to. Implement `dealloc` with an `NSLog` call. If it isn't called, your object is not going out of existence. This technique can reveal problems that neither the static analyzer nor Instruments will directly expose.

- Dangling pointers are particularly difficult to track down, but they can often be located by "turning on zombies." This is easy in Instruments with the Zombies template. Alternatively, edit the Run action in your scheme, switch to the Diagnostics tab, and check Enable Zombie Objects. The result is that no object ever goes out of existence; instead, it is replaced by a "zombie" that will report to the console if a message is sent to it ("message sent to deallocated instance"). Be sure to turn zombies back off when you've finished tracking down your dangling pointers. Don't use zombies with the Leaks instrument: zombies *are* leaks.

Even these tools may not help you with every possible memory management issue. For example, some objects, such as a UIView containing a large image, are themselves small (and thus may not cause the memory gauge or Instruments to register large memory use) but require a large backing store nevertheless; maintaining references to too many such objects can cause your app to be summarily killed by the system. This sort of issue is not easy to track down.

with its retain count already incremented. You do *not* need to retain an object you've just instantiated by saying `copy` (and you should not).

- To decrement the retain count of any object, send it the `release` message. This is called *releasing* the object.

- If Object A obtained Object B by saying `alloc` (or `new`) or `copy`, or if Object A has said `retain` to Object B, then Object A should balance this eventually by saying `release` to Object B, *once*. Object A should assume thereafter that Object B no longer exists. This is the *golden rule of memory management* — the rule that makes memory management work coherently and correctly.

A general way of understanding the golden rule of Cocoa memory management is to think in terms of *ownership*. If Manny has said `alloc`, `retain`, or `copy` with regard to Jack, Manny has asserted ownership of Jack. More than one object can own Jack at once, but each such object is responsible only for managing its own ownership of Jack correctly. It is the responsibility of an owner of Jack eventually to release Jack, and a nonowner of Jack must *never* release Jack. As long as all objects that ever take ownership of Jack behave this way, Jack will not leak nor will any pointer to Jack be left dangling.

Now, under ARC, as I shall explain presently in more detail, these rules remain exactly the same, but they are obeyed for you in an automated fashion by the compiler. In an ARC-based app, you *never* say `retain` or `release` — in fact, you're not allowed to. Instead, the compiler says `retain` or `release` for you, using exactly the principles you would have had to use if you *had* said them! Since the compiler is smarter (or at least more ruthlessly tenacious) than you are about this sort of nit-picky rule-based behavior, it won't make any of the mistakes you might have made due to carelessness or confusion.

The moment an object is released, there is a chance it will be destroyed. Before ARC, this fact was a big worry for programmers. In a non-ARC program, you must take care not to send any messages subsequently through any pointer to an object that has been destroyed — including the pointer you just used to release the object. In effect, you've just turned your *own* pointer into a possible dangling pointer! If there is any danger that you might accidentally attempt to use this dangling pointer, a wise policy is to *nilify* the pointer — that is, to set the pointer itself to nil. A message to nil has no effect, so if you do send a message through that pointer, it won't do any good, but at least it won't do any harm (kind of like chicken soup).

In ARC-based code, this policy, too, is strictly followed: ARC will nilify for you any pointer to whose object it has just sent its last balancing `release` message (meaning that the object might now have gone out of existence). Since, as I mentioned in Chapter 3, ARC also sets an instance pointer to nil when you declare it (if you don't initialize it yourself, there and then, to point to an actual instance), there follows as the night the day this delightful corollary: *under ARC, every instance pointer either points to an actual instance or is nil.* (But, alas, as I shall explain, there can still be dangling pointers, because Cocoa itself doesn't use ARC.)

What ARC Is and What It Does

When you create a new Xcode 5 project and choose an application template, ARC is used for that project by default. Here's what that means (among other things):

- The LLVM compiler build setting Objective-C Automatic Reference Counting (CLANG_ENABLE_OBJC_ARC) for your project is set to YES.

- No retain or release statements appear in the project template's *.m* files.

- Any code that Xcode subsequently inserts automatically, such as a property generated by Control-dragging from a nib into code, will conform to ARC conventions.

It is also possible to convert an existing non-ARC project to ARC; choose Edit → Refactor → Convert to Objective-C ARC for assistance with the necessary code changes. You do not have to adopt ARC for an entire project; if you have old non-ARC code, possibly written by someone else, you may wish to incorporate that code into your ARC-based project without substantially altering the non-ARC code. To do so, confine all non-ARC code to its own files, and for each of those files, edit the target, switch to the Build Phases tab, and in the Compile Sources section, double-click the non-ARC file's listing and type -fno-objc-arc in the box (to enter it in the Compiler Flags column).

 ARC is actually a feature of LLVM 3.0 and later, and is one of the main purposes for which the LLVM compiler was developed. For full technical information, see *http://clang.llvm.org/docs/AutomaticReference Counting.html*.

When you compile a *.m* file with ARC, the compiler will treat any explicit retain or release commands as an error, and will instead, behind the scenes, insert its own commands that effectively do the exact same work as retain and release commands. Your code is thus manually memory-managed, in conformity with the principles and golden rule of manual memory management that I've already described, but the author of the manual memory-management code is the compiler (and the memory-management code itself is invisible, unless you feel like reading assembly language).

ARC does its work of inserting retain and release commands in two stages:

1. It behaves very, very conservatively; basically, if in doubt, it retains — and of course it later releases. In effect, ARC retains at every juncture that might have the slightest implications for memory management: it retains when an object is received as an argument, it retains when an object is assigned to a variable, and so forth. It may even insert temporary variables to enable it to refer sufficiently early to an object so that it can retain it. But of course it also releases to match. This means that at the end of the first stage, memory management is technically correct; there may be far

more retains and releases on a single object than you would have put if you were writing those commands yourself, but at least you can be confident that no pointer will dangle and no object will leak.

2. It optimizes, removing as many `retain` and `release` pairs from each object as it possibly can while still ensuring safety with regard to the program's actual behavior. This means that at the end of the second stage, memory management is still technically correct, and it is also efficient.

So, for example, consider the following code:

```
- (void) myMethod {
    NSArray* myArray = [NSArray array];
    NSArray* myOtherArray = myArray;
}
```

Now, in actual fact, no additional memory management code is needed here (for reasons that I'll clarify in the next section). Even if you weren't using ARC, you wouldn't need to add any `retain` or `release` commands to this code. But in its first pass, we may imagine that ARC will behave very, very conservatively: it will ensure that every variable is nil or points to an object, and it will retain every value as it is assigned to a variable, at the same time releasing the value previously pointed to by the variable being assigned to, on the assumption that it previously retained *that* value when assigning it to that variable as well. So we may imagine (though this is unlikely to be exactly correct) a scenario where ARC compiles that code at first into the equivalent of Example 12-1.

Example 12-1. Imaginary scenario: ARC's conservative memory management

```
- (void) myMethod {
    // create all new object pointers as nil
    NSArray* myArray = nil;
    // retain as you assign, release the previous value
    id temp1 = myArray;
    myArray = [NSArray array];
    [myArray retain];
    [temp1 release]; // (no effect, it's nil)
    // create all new object pointers as nil
    NSArray* myOtherArray = nil;
    // retain as you assign, release the previous value
    id temp2 = myOtherArray;
    myOtherArray = myArray;
    [myOtherArray retain];
    [temp2 release]; // (no effect, it's nil)
    // method is ending, balance out retains on local variables
    // nilify when all remaining retains are balanced by release
    [myArray release];
    myArray = nil;
    [myOtherArray release];
    myOtherArray = nil;
}
```

The ARC optimizer will then come along and reduce the amount of work being done here. For example, it may observe that `myArray` and `myOtherArray` turn out to be pointers to the same object, so it may therefore remove some of the intermediate retains and releases. And it may observe that there's no need to send `release` to nil. But retains and releases are so efficient under ARC that it wouldn't much matter if the optimizer didn't remove any of the intermediate retains and releases.

There's more to the manual memory management balancing act than matching `retain` and `release`: in particular, I said earlier that `alloc` and `copy` yielded objects whose retain count had already been incremented, so that they, too, must be balanced by `release`. In order to obey this part of the rules of Cocoa memory management, ARC resorts to *assumptions about how methods are named*.

In particular, when your code receives an object as the returned value of a method call, ARC looks at the opening word (or words) of the camelCased method name. (The term *camelCased* describes a compound word whose individual words are demarcated by internal capitalization, like the words "camel" and "Cased" in the word "camelCased.") If the opening word of the name of that method is `alloc`, `init`, `new`, `copy`, or `mutableCopy`, ARC assumes that the object it returns comes with an incremented retain count that will need to be balanced with a corresponding `release`.

So, in the preceding example, if the array had been received from a call to `[NSArray new]` instead of `[NSArray array]`, ARC would know that an extra `release` will be needed, to balance the incremented retain count of the object returned from a method whose name begins with `new`.

Your own responsibility in this regard, then, is *not* to name any of your methods inappropriately in such a way as to set off that sort of alarm bell in ARC's head. The easiest approach is not to start any of your own method names with `alloc`, `init` (unless you're writing an initializer, of course), `new`, `copy`, or `mutableCopy`. Doing so might not cause any damage, but it is better not to take the risk: obey the ARC naming conventions if you possibly can. (There are ways out of this predicament if you have a wrongly-named method whose name you absolutely can't change, but I'm not going to discuss them here.)

How Cocoa Objects Manage Memory

Built-in Cocoa objects will take ownership of objects you hand them, by retaining them, if it makes sense for them to do so (and will of course then balance that retain with a release later). Indeed, this is so generally true that if a Cocoa object is *not* going to retain an object you hand it, there will be a note to that effect in the documentation. A collection, such as an NSArray or an NSDictionary, is a particularly obvious case in point (see Chapter 10 for a discussion of the common collection classes).

An object can hardly be an element of a collection if that object can go out of existence at any time; so when you add an element to a collection, the collection asserts ownership of the object by retaining it. Thereafter, the collection acts as a well-behaved owner. If this is a mutable collection, then if an element is removed from it, the collection releases that element. If the collection object goes out of existence, it releases all its elements. (And if a former element that has just been released by a collection is not being retained by anything else, the former element itself will then go out of existence.)

Prior to ARC, removing an object from a mutable collection constituted a potential trap. Consider the following:

```
NSString* s = myMutableArray[0];
[myMutableArray removeObjectAtIndex: 0]; // bad idea in non-ARC code!
```

As I just said, when you remove an object from a mutable collection, the collection releases it. So the commented line of code in the previous example involves an implicit release of the object that used to be element 0 of myMutableArray. If this reduces the object's retain count to zero, it will be destroyed. The pointer s will then be a dangling pointer, and a crash may be in our future when we try to use it as if it were a string.

Before ARC, therefore, you had to remember to retain any object extracted from a collection before doing anything that might destroy it (Example 12-2).

Example 12-2. How non-ARC code ensures a collection element's persistence

```
NSString* s = myMutableArray[0];
[s retain]; // this is non-ARC code
[myMutableArray removeObjectAtIndex: 0];
```

Of course, now you have made management of this object your business; you have asserted ownership of it, and must make sure that this retain is eventually balanced by a subsequent release, or the object may leak.

However, the very same code works perfectly under ARC:

```
NSString* s = myMutableArray[0];
[myMutableArray removeObjectAtIndex: 0]; // Just fine under ARC
```

The reason is that, as I mentioned earlier, ARC is insanely conservative at the outset. Just as in Example 12-1, ARC retains on assignment, so we may imagine that ARC will operate according to something like the imaginary scenario shown in Example 12-3.

Example 12-3. Imaginary scenario: ARC ensures a collection element's persistence

```
NSString* s = nil;
// retain as you assign, release the previous value
id temp = s;
s = myMutableArray[0];
[s retain];
[temp release]; // (no effect, it's nil)
// and now this move is safe
```

```
[myMutableArray removeObjectAtIndex: 0];
// ... and later ...
[s release];
s = nil;
```

This turns out to be exactly the right thing to do! By the time the call to removeObject-AtIndex: comes along, the retain count of the object received from the array has been incremented, preserving the object's life, exactly as in our non-ARC Example 12-2.

Autorelease

When you call a method and receive as a result what Chapter 5 calls a ready-made instance, how does memory management work? Consider, for example, this code:

```
NSArray* myArray = [NSArray array];
```

According to the golden rule of memory management, the object now pointed to by myArray doesn't need memory management. You didn't say alloc in order to get it, so you haven't claimed ownership of it and you don't need to release it (and shouldn't do so). But how is this possible? How is the NSArray class able to vend an array that you don't have to release without also leaking that object?

If you don't see why this is mysterious, let's use explicit memory management — that is, we'll use pre-ARC code, so that all the retains and releases become visible — and please pretend that *you* are the NSArray class. How would you implement the array method so as to generate an array that the caller doesn't have to memory-manage? Don't say that you'd just call some *other* NSArray method that vends a ready-made instance; that merely pushes the same problem back one level. You *are* NSArray. Sooner or later, you will have to generate the instance from scratch, and return it:

```
- (NSArray*) array {
    NSArray* arr = [[NSArray alloc] init];
    return arr; // hmmm, not so fast...
}
```

This, it appears, can't work. We generated arr's value by saying alloc. By the golden rule of memory management, this means we must also release the object pointed to by arr. But *when* can we possibly do this? If we do it *before* returning arr, arr will be pointing to garbage and we will be vending garbage. But we cannot do it *after* returning arr, because our method exits when we say return!

Apparently, we need a way to vend this object without decrementing its retain count *now* (so that it stays in existence long enough for the caller to receive and work with it), yet ensure that we *will* decrement its retain count (to balance our alloc call and fulfill our own management of this object's memory). The solution, which is explicit in pre-ARC code, is autorelease:

```
- (NSArray*) array {
    NSArray* arr = [[NSArray alloc] init];
    [arr autorelease];
    return arr;
}
```

Or, because `autorelease` returns the object to which it is sent, we can condense that:

```
- (NSArray*) array {
    NSArray* arr = [[NSArray alloc] init];
    return [arr autorelease];
}
```

Here's how `autorelease` works. Your code runs in the presence of something called an *autorelease pool*. (If you look in *main.m*, you can actually see an autorelease pool being created.) When you send `autorelease` to an object, that object is placed in the autorelease pool, and a number is incremented saying how many times this object has been placed in this autorelease pool. From time to time, when nothing else is going on, the autorelease pool is automatically *drained*. This means that the autorelease pool sends `release` to each of its objects, the same number of times as that object was placed in this autorelease pool, and empties itself of all objects. If that causes an object's retain count to be zero, so be it; the object is destroyed in the usual way. So `autorelease` is just like `release` — effectively, it *is* a form of `release` — but with a proviso, "later, not right this second."

You don't need to know exactly when the current autorelease pool will be drained; indeed, you can't know (unless you force it, as we shall see). The important thing is that in a case like our method `array`, there will be plenty of time for whoever called `array` to continue working with the vended object, and to retain the vended object if desired.

The vended object in a case like our method `array` is called an *autoreleased object*. The object that is doing the vending has in fact completed its memory management of the vended object. The vended object thus potentially has a zero retain count. But it doesn't have a zero retain count just yet. The vended object is not going to vanish right this second, just after your call to [`NSArray array`], because *your code is still running and so the autorelease pool is not going to be drained right this second*. The recipient of such an object needs to bear in mind that this object may be autoreleased. The object won't vanish while the code that called the method that vended the object is running, but if the receiving object wants to be sure that the vended object will persist later on, it should retain it.

That's why you have no memory management responsibilities after receiving a ready-made instance, as with our call to [`NSArray array`]. An instance you receive by means *other* than those listed in the golden rule of memory management isn't under your ownership. Either some other object owns it, or it is autoreleased. If some other object owns it, then this instance won't be destroyed unless the object that owns it is stops owning it (as with the NSMutableArray example in the previous section) or is destroyed;

if you're worried that that might happen, you should take ownership of the object by retaining it (and then it will be up to you to release it later). If the instance is autoreleased, then it will certainly persist long enough for your code to finish (because the autorelease pool won't drain while your code is still running); again, if you need it to persist longer than that, you should take ownership by retaining it.

Under ARC, as you might expect, all the right things happen of their own accord. You don't have to say `autorelease`, and indeed you cannot. Instead, ARC will say it for you. And it says it in accordance with the method naming rule I described earlier. A method called `array`, for example, does not start with a camelCase unit `new`, `init`, `alloc`, `copy`, or `mutableCopy`. Therefore it must return an object whose memory management is balanced, using `autorelease` for the last release. ARC will see to it that this is indeed the case. On the other side of the ledger, the method that called `array` and received an object in return must assume that this object is autoreleased and could go out of existence if we don't retain it. That's exactly what ARC does assume.

Sometimes you may wish to drain the autorelease pool immediately. Consider the following:

```
for (NSString* aWord in myArray) {
    NSString* lowerAndShorter = [[aWord lowercaseString] substringFromIndex:1];
    [myMutableArray addObject: lowerAndShorter];
}
```

Every time through that loop, two objects are added to the autorelease pool: the lowercase version of the string we start with, and the shortened version of that. The first object, the lowercase version of the string, is purely an *intermediate object*: as the current iteration of the loop ends, no one except the autorelease pool has a pointer to it. If this loop had very many repetitions, or if these intermediate objects were themselves very large in size, this could add up to a lot of memory. These intermediate objects will all be released when the autorelease pool drains, so they are not leaking; nevertheless, they are accumulating in memory, and in certain cases there could be a danger that we will run out of memory before the autorelease pool drains. The problem can be even more acute than you think, because you might repeatedly call a built-in Cocoa method that itself, unbeknownst to you, generates a lot of intermediate autoreleased objects.

The solution is to intervene in the autorelease pool mechanism by supplying your own autorelease pool. This works because the autorelease pool used to store an autoreleased object is the most recently created pool. So you can just create an autorelease pool at the top of the loop and drain it at the bottom of the loop, each time through the loop. In modern Objective-C, the notation for doing this is to surround the code that is to run under its own autorelease pool with the directive `@autoreleasepool{}`, like this:

```
for (NSString* aWord in myArray) {
    @autoreleasepool {
        NSString* lowerAndShorter =
            [[aWord lowercaseString] substringFromIndex:1];
        [myMutableArray addObject: lowerAndShorter];
    }
}
```

Many classes provide the programmer with two equivalent ways to obtain an object: either an autoreleased object (ready-made instance) or an object that you create yourself with alloc and some form of init (instantiation from scratch). So, for example, NSMutableArray supplies both the class method array and the instance method init. Which should you use? In general, where you can generate an object with alloc and some form of init, it is probably better to do so. This policy prevents your objects from hanging around in the autorelease pool and keeps your use of memory as low as possible.

Memory Management of Instance Variables (Non-ARC)

Before ARC, the main place for the programmer to make a memory management mistake was with respect to instance variables. Memory management of temporary variables within a single method is pretty easy; you can see the whole method at once, so now just follow the golden rule of memory management, balancing every retain, alloc, or copy with a release (or, if you're returning an object with an incremented retain count, autorelease). But instance variables make things complicated, for many reasons:

Instance variables are persistent
> Your own instance variables will persist when this method is over and your code has stopped running and the autorelease pool has been drained. So if you want an object value pointed to by an instance variable not to vanish in a puff of smoke, leaving you with a dangling pointer, you'd better retain it as you assign it to the instance variable.

Instance variables are managed from different places in your code
> Memory management of an instance variable can be spread out over several different methods, making it difficult to get right and difficult to debug if you get it wrong. For example, if you retained a value assigned to an instance variable, you'll later need to release it, conforming with the golden rule of memory management, to prevent a leak — but in some other method.

Instance variables might not belong to you
> You will often assign to or get a value from an instance variable belonging to another object. You are now sharing access to a value with some other persistent object. If that other object were to go out of existence and release its instance variables, and you have a pointer to the instance variable value coming from that other object and

you haven't asserted your own ownership by retaining that value, you can wind up with a dangling pointer.

Thus, before ARC, the seemingly simple act of assigning an object to an instance variable could be fraught with peril. Consider this code:

```
NSMutableDictionary* d = [NSMutableDictionary dictionary];
// ... code that populates d goes here ...
self->_theData = d; // in non-ARC code this would be a bad idea!
```

Before ARC, that code constituted a serious potential mistake. If our code now comes to a stop, we're left with a persistent pointer to an autoreleased object over which we have never asserted ownership; it might vanish, leaving us with a dangling pointer. The solution, obviously, is to retain this object as we assign it to our instance variable. You could do it like this:

```
[d retain];
self->_theData = d;
```

Or you could do it like this:

```
self->_theData = d;
[self->_theData retain];
```

Or, because `retain` returns the object to which it is sent, you could do it like this:

```
self->_theData = [d retain];
```

But none of those approaches is really satisfactory. Consider what a lot of trouble it will be if you ever want to assign a *different* value to `self->_theData`. You're going to have to remember to release the object already pointed to (to balance the retain you've used here), and you're going to have to remember to retain the next value as well. It would be much better to encapsulate memory management for this instance variable *in an accessor* (a setter). That way, as long as you always pass through the accessor, memory will be managed correctly. A standard template for such an accessor might look like Example 12-4.

Example 12-4. A simple retaining setter

```
- (void) setTheData: (NSMutableArray*) value {
    if (self->_theData != value) {
        [self->_theData release];
        self->_theData = [value retain];
    }
}
```

In Example 12-4, we release the object currently pointed to by our instance variable (and if that object is nil, no harm done) and retain the incoming value before assigning it to our instance variable (and if that value is nil, no harm done either). The test for whether the incoming value is the very same object already pointed to by our instance variable is not just to save a step; it's because if we were to release that object, it could vanish then and there, instantly turning `value` into a dangling pointer — which we would then, horribly, assign to `self->_theData`.

The setter accessor now manages memory correctly for us, provided we always use it to set our instance variable. This is one of the main reasons why accessors are so important! So the assignment to the instance variable in our original code should now look like this:

```
[self setTheData: d];
```

Observe that we can also use this setter subsequently to release the value of the instance variable and nilify the instance variable itself, thus preventing a dangling pointer, all in a single easy step:

```
[self setTheData: nil];
```

So there's yet another benefit of using an accessor to manage memory.

Our memory management for this instance variable is still incomplete, however. We (meaning the object whose instance variable this is) must also remember to release the object pointed to by this instance variable at the last minute before we ourselves go out of existence. Otherwise, if this instance variable points to a retained object, there will be a memory leak. The "last minute" is typically `dealloc`, the NSObject method (Chapter 10) that is called as an object goes out of existence.

In `dealloc`, there is no need to use accessors to refer to an instance variable, and in fact it's not a good idea to do so, because you never know what other side effects an accessor might have. And (under non-ARC code) you must always call `super` last of all. So here's our pre-ARC implementation of this object's `dealloc`:

```
- (void) dealloc {
    [self->_theData release];
    [super dealloc];
}
```

 Never, never call `dealloc` in your code, except to call `super` last of all in your override of `dealloc`. Under ARC, you *can't* call `dealloc` — yet another example of how ARC saves you from yourself.

You can see that, before ARC, memory management for object instance variables could be a lot of work! Not only did you need correctly written setter accessors for your instance variables, but also you had to make sure that *every* object of yours had a `dealloc` that released *every* instance variable whose value had been retained. This, obviously, was one more very good opportunity for you to make a mistake.

But wait, there's more! What about an initializer that sets the value of an instance variable? Memory management is required here too. And you can't use an accessor to help you; just as it's not a good idea to use your own accessors to refer to your own instance variables in `dealloc`, so you should not use your own accessors to refer to your own instance variables in an initializer (see Chapter 5). The reason is in part that the object is not yet fully formed, and in part that an accessor can have other side effects.

To illustrate, I'll rewrite the example initializer from Chapter 5 (Example 5-3). This time I'll allow our object (a Dog) to be initialized with a name. The reason I didn't discuss this possibility in Chapter 5 is that a string is an object whose memory must be managed! So, imagine now that we have an instance variable _name whose value is an NSString, and we want an initializer that allows the caller to pass in a value for this instance variable. It might look like Example 12-5.

Example 12-5. A simple initializer that retains an ivar

```
- (id) initWithName: (NSString*) s {
    self = [super init];
    if (self) {
        self->_name = [s retain];
    }
    return self;
}
```

Actually, it is more likely in the case of an NSString that you would copy it rather than merely retain it. The reason is that NSString has a mutable subclass NSMutableString, so some other object might call `initWithName:` and hand you a mutable string to which it still holds a reference — and then mutate it, thus changing this Dog's name behind your back. So the initializer would look like Example 12-6.

Example 12-6. A simple initializer that copies an ivar

```
- (id) initWithName: (NSString*) s {
    self = [super init];
    if (self) {
        self->_name = [s copy];
    }
    return self;
}
```

In Example 12-6, we don't bother to release the existing value of _name; it is certainly not pointing to any *previous* value (because there is no previous value), so there's no point.

Thus, pre-ARC memory management for an instance variable may take place in as many as *three* places: the initializer, the setter, and `dealloc`. This is a common architecture! It is a lot of work, and a common source of error, having to look in multiple places to check that you are managing memory consistently and correctly, but that's what you must do if you aren't using ARC (though, as I'll point out later in this chapter, at least Objective-C has the ability to write your accessors for you).

Memory Management of Instance Variables (ARC)

If you're using ARC, ARC will manage your instance variable memory for you; you needn't (and, by and large, you can't) do it for yourself. All this means is that ARC will do, literally but invisibly, exactly the things I just described in the preceding section.

Let's start with direct assignment to an instance variable. By default, ARC will treat an instance variable the same way it treats any variable: on assignment to that instance variable, it creates a temporary variable, retains the assigned value in it, releases the current value of the instance variable, and performs the assignment. Thus, you write this code:

```
self->_theData = d;
```

ARC, in effect, in accordance with its rule that it retains on assignment and releases the old value, substitutes something like this scenario:

```
// imaginary scenario: retain on assignment, release the previous value
id temp = self->_theData;
self->_theData = d;
[self->_theData retain];
[temp release];
```

This is exactly the right thing to have happened; in fact, it will not have escaped your attention that it is virtually the same code you would have written for a formal setter such as Example 12-4. So much for worrying about release and retain on assignment!

The same thing is true if we actually write a formal setter. A simple setter is nowhere near as elaborate as a pre-ARC setter; indeed, it might consist of no more than a direct assignment, because ARC is once again doing quite correctly all the attendant manual memory management, in accordance with the scenario I just described:

```
- (void) setTheData: (NSMutableArray*) value {
    self->_theData = value;
}
```

Moreover, when your object goes out of existence, ARC releases its retained instance variable values. So much for worrying about releasing in dealloc! You may still need, under ARC, to implement dealloc for other reasons — for example, it could still be the right place to unregister for a notification (Chapter 11) — but you won't call release on any instance variables there, and you won't call super. (Under ARC, at the time dealloc is called, your instance variables have not yet been released, so it's fine to refer to them in dealloc.)

In the absence of a release call, which is forbidden under ARC, what happens if you want to release an instance variable's value manually? The solution is simple: set the instance variable to nil (possibly by way of the setter). When you nilify a variable, ARC releases its existing value for you by default.

Finally, let's talk about ARC's implications for the way you'll write an initializer that involves setting object instance variable values, as in Example 12-5 and Example 12-6. The code for these initializers will be just the same under ARC as under non-ARC, except that you needn't (and can't) say retain. So Example 12-5 under ARC would look like Example 12-7.

Example 12-7. A simple initializer that retains an ivar under ARC

```
- (id) initWithName: (NSString*) s {
    self = [super init];
    if (self) {
        self->_name = s;
    }
    return self;
}
```

Example 12-6 under ARC will be unchanged, as shown in Example 12-8; you can still say copy under ARC, and ARC understands how to manage the memory of an object returned from a method whose camelCased name starts with (or simply is) copy.

Example 12-8. A simple initializer that copies an ivar under ARC

```
- (id) initWithName: (NSString*) s {
    self = [super init];
    if (self) {
        self->_name = [s copy];
    }
    return self;
}
```

Retain Cycles and Weak References

ARC's behavior is automatic and mindless; it knows nothing of the logic of the relationships between objects in your app. Sometimes, you have to provide ARC with further instructions to prevent it from doing something detrimental. One such detrimental thing is the creation of a retain cycle.

A *retain cycle* is a situation in which Object A and Object B are each retaining one another. Such a situation, if allowed to persist, will result in a leak of both objects, as neither object's retain count can decrement to zero. Another way of looking at it is to say that Object A, by retaining Object B, is also retaining itself, and thus preventing its own destruction.

A retain cycle can arise quite innocently, because relationships in an object graph can run both ways. For example, in a system of orders and items, an order needs to know what its items are and an item might need to know what orders it is a part of, so you might be tempted to let it be the case *both* that an order retains its items *and* that an item retains its orders. That's a retain cycle.

To illustrate the problem, I'll suppose a simple class MyClass with a single ivar _thing and a single public setter setThing:, with logging in dealloc, like this:

```
@implementation MyClass {
    id _thing;
}
- (void) setThing: (id) what {
    self->_thing = what;
}
-(void)dealloc {
    NSLog(@"%@", @"dealloc");
}
@end
```

We now run this code:

```
MyClass* m1 = [MyClass new];
MyClass* m2 = [MyClass new];
m1.thing = m2;
m2.thing = m1;
```

m1 and m2 are now retaining one another, because ARC retains on assignment by default. When the code runs, dealloc is never called for either of our MyClass instances, even after the automatic pointer variables m1 and m2 have gone out of scope and have been destroyed. The two MyClass objects themselves have leaked.

You can prevent an instance variable from retaining the object assigned to it by specifying that the instance variable should be a *weak reference*. You can do this with the __weak qualifier in the instance variable's declaration:

```
@implementation MyClass {
    __weak id _thing;
}
```

Now there is no retain cycle. In our example, there will be no leak; the two MyClass objects will go out of existence after our code finishes running, because ARC sent them each a release message as the automatic variables m1 and m2 went out of scope (to balance the new calls that created them), and no one else is retaining them.

In ARC, a reference not explicitly declared weak is a *strong reference.* Thus, a strong reference is one where ARC retains as it assigns. There is in fact a `__strong` qualifier, but in practice you'll never use it, as it is the default. (There are also two additional but rarely needed qualifiers, `__unsafe_unretained` and `__autoreleasing`.)

In real life, a weak reference is most commonly used to connect an object to its delegate (Chapter 11). A delegate is an independent entity; there is usually no reason why an object needs to claim ownership of its delegate, and indeed an object is usually its delegate's servant, not its owner. Ownership, if there is any, often runs the other way; Object A might create *and retain* Object B, and make itself Object B's delegate. That's potentially a retain cycle. Therefore, most delegates should be declared as weak references.

For example, in a project created from Xcode's Utility Application project template, you'll find this line:

```
@property (weak, nonatomic) id <FlipsideViewControllerDelegate> delegate;
```

The keyword `weak` in the property declaration, as I'll explain more fully later in this chapter, is equivalent to declaring the `_delegate` instance variable as `__weak`.

In non-ARC code, a reference can be prevented from causing a retain cycle merely by not retaining when assigning to that reference in the first place; the reference simply isn't memory-managed at all. You may see this referred to as a weak reference; it is not, however, quite the same thing as an ARC weak reference. A non-ARC weak reference risks turning into a dangling pointer when the instance to which it points is released (by some *other* object that *was* retaining it) and is destroyed. Thus it is possible for the reference to be non-nil and pointing to garbage, so that a message sent to it can have mysteriously disastrous consequences.

Amazingly, however, this cannot happen with an ARC weak reference. When an instance's retain count reaches zero and the instance is about to vanish, any ARC weak reference that was pointing to it is automatically set to nil! (This amazing feat is accomplished by some behind-the-scenes bookkeeping: when an object is assigned to a weak reference, ARC in effect notes this fact on a scratchpad list.) This is yet *another* reason for preferring to use ARC wherever possible. ARC sometimes refers to non-ARC weak references, disdainfully but accurately, as "unsafe." (Non-ARC weak references are in fact the `__unsafe_unretained` references I mentioned a moment ago.)

Unfortunately, *large parts of Cocoa itself don't use ARC.* Cocoa's memory management is carefully written, so that in general its retains and releases are balanced and it shouldn't cause any memory leaks. Nevertheless, properties of built-in Cocoa classes that keep weak references are non-ARC weak references (because they are old and backwards-compatible, whereas ARC is new). Such properties are declared using the keyword `assign`. For example, UINavigationController's `delegate` property is declared like this:

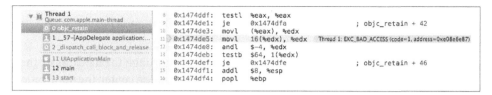

Figure 12-1. A crash from messaging a dangling pointer

```
@property(nonatomic, assign) id<UINavigationControllerDelegate> delegate
```

Thus, even though *your* code is using ARC, the fact that Cocoa's code is *not* using ARC means that memory management mistakes can still occur. A reference such as a UINavigationController's `delegate` can end up as a dangling pointer, pointing at garbage, if the object to which that reference was pointing has gone out of existence. If anyone (you or Cocoa) tries to send a message by way of such a reference, the app will then crash — and, since this typically happens long after the point where the real mistake occurred, figuring out the cause of the crash can be quite difficult. The typical signs of such a crash are that it takes place in Apple's method `objc_retain` and mentions `EXC_BAD_ACCESS` (Figure 12-1). This is the sort of situation in which you might need to turn on zombies in order to debug, as described earlier in this chapter.

Defending against this kind of situation is up to you. If you assign some object to a non-ARC weak reference, such as a UINavigationController's `delegate`, and if that object is about to go out of existence at a time when this reference still exists, you have a duty to assign nil (or some other object) to that reference, thus rendering it harmless.

Unusual Memory Management Situations

NSNotificationCenter presents some curious memory management features. As you are likely to want to use notifications (Chapter 11), you'll need to know about these.

If you registered with the notification center using `addObserver:selector:name:object:`, you handed the notification center a reference to some object (usually `self`) as the first argument; the notification center's reference to this object is a non-ARC weak reference, and there is a danger that after this object goes out of existence the notification center will try to send a notification to whatever is referred to, which will be garbage. That is why you must unregister before that can happen. This is similar to the situation with delegates that I was talking about a moment ago.

If you registered with the notification center using `addObserverForName:object:queue:usingBlock:`, memory management can be quite tricky, under ARC in particular, because:

- The observer token returned from the call to addObserverForName:object:queue:usingBlock: is retained by the notification center until you unregister it.

- The observer token may also be retaining you (self) through the block. If so, then until you unregister the observer token from the notification center, the notification center is retaining you. This means that you will leak until you unregister. But you cannot unregister from the notification center in dealloc, because dealloc isn't going to be called so long as you are registered.

- In addition, if you also retain the observer token, then if the observer token is retaining you, you have a retain cycle on your hands.

Consider, for example, this code, in which we register for a notification and assign the observer token to an instance variable:

```
self->_observer = [[NSNotificationCenter defaultCenter]
    addObserverForName:@"heyho"
    object:nil queue:nil usingBlock:^(NSNotification *n) {
        NSLog(@"%@", self);
    }];
```

Our intention is eventually to unregister the observer; that's why we're keeping a reference to it. It's natural to do this in dealloc:

```
- (void) dealloc {
    [[NSNotificationCenter defaultCenter] removeObserver:self->_observer];
}
```

But that won't work; dealloc is never called, because there's a retain cycle: self is retaining the observer, but because of the block, the observer is also retaining self. Therefore we (self) are leaking and we are never unregistered.

There are two ways to break the retain cycle. One is to release the _observer object as we unregister it. However, dealloc still won't be called until after we've done that, so we need to look for a place other than dealloc where we can unregister the _observer object and release it.

For example, if this is a UIViewController, then one such place might be the view controller's viewDidDisappear:, which is called when the view controller's view is removed from the interface:

```
- (void) viewDidDisappear:(BOOL)animated {
    [super viewDidDisappear:animated];
    [[NSNotificationCenter defaultCenter] removeObserver:self.observer];
    self->_observer = nil; // release the observer
}
```

When the observer is unregistered, it is released by the notification center. When we too release it, no one is retaining it any longer; the observer goes out of existence, and as it does so, it releases self, which is subsequently able to go out of existence in good order — dealloc will be called, and self no longer leaks. Alternatively, if the _observer ivar is marked as __weak, we can omit that last line; when the observer is unregistered, it will be released by the notification center, and since the notification center was the only thing retaining it, the observer is destroyed, releasing self as it goes.

This approach requires some careful management, however, because viewDid-Disappear: can be called more than once over the life of a view controller. We have to register for the notification again in some symmetric location, such as viewWill-Appear:. Plus, if self is *not* a view controller, finding an appropriate place other than dealloc to unregister may not be so easy.

A better solution, in my opinion, is not to allow the observer object to retain self in the first place. That way, there's no retain cycle to begin with. The way to prevent a block from retaining self is not to mention self (or any instance variables of self) within the block. Since there is no retain cycle, dealloc will be called, and we can unregister the observer in dealloc, which is what we wanted to do all along.

So how can you refrain from mentioning self within a block if you need to send a message to self within the block? You use an elegant little technique, commonly called "the weak–strong dance" (Example 12-9). The efficacy of the weak–strong dance lies in the fact that self is never mentioned *directly* in the block. In actual fact, a reference to self does get passed into the block, but at that moment it's a weak reference, which is enough to prevent self from being retained by the block and possibly causing a retain cycle. Once inside the block, this reference is converted to a strong reference, and everything proceeds normally.

Example 12-9. The weak–strong dance prevents a block from retaining self

```
__weak MyClass* wself = self; ❶
self->_observer = [[NSNotificationCenter defaultCenter]
    addObserverForName:@"heyho"
    object:nil queue:nil usingBlock:^(NSNotification *n) {
        MyClass* sself = wself; ❷
        if (sself) {
            // refer to sself freely, but never to self ❸
        }
    }];
```

Here are the steps of the weak–strong dance, as schematized in Example 12-9:

❶   We form a local weak reference to self, outside the block but where the block can see it. It is this weak reference that will pass into the block.

❷ Inside the block, we assign that weak reference to a normal strong reference. Weak references are inherently volatile; there is a chance that a weakly referenced object, even `self`, may vanish out from under us between one line of code and the next. In that case, the weak reference will be nil, but messaging it is expensive, and directly referencing an instance variable of it will be disastrous; moreover, there is no thread-safe way to check whether a weak reference is nil. Assigning to a strong reference solves the problem.

❸ We use the strong reference in place of any references to `self` inside the block. All action involving the strong reference is wrapped in a nil test because, if our weakly referenced object did vanish out from under us, there would be no point continuing.

Another unusual case is NSTimer (Chapter 10). The NSTimer class documentation says that "run loops retain their timers"; it then says of `scheduledTimerWithTimeInterval:target:selector:userInfo:repeats:` that "The target object is retained by the timer and released when the timer is invalidated." This means that as long as a repeating timer has not been invalidated, the target is being retained by the run loop; the only way to stop this is to send the `invalidate` message to the timer. (With a non-repeating timer, the problem doesn't arise, because the timer invalidates itself immediately after firing.)

When you called `scheduledTimerWithTimeInterval:target:selector:userInfo:repeats:`, you probably supplied `self` as the `target:` argument. This means that you (`self`) are being retained, and cannot go out of existence until you invalidate the timer. You can't do this in your `dealloc` implementation, because as long as the timer is repeating and has not been sent the `invalidate` message, `dealloc` won't be called. You therefore need to find another appropriate moment for sending `invalidate` to the timer. There's no good way out of this situation; you simply have to find such a moment, and that's that.

A block-based alternative to a repeating timer is available through GCD. The timer "object" is a `dispatch_source_t`, and must be retained, typically as an instance variable (which ARC will manage for you, even though it's a pseudo-object). The timer will fire repeatedly after you initially "resume" it, and will stop firing when it is released, typically by nilifying the instance variable. But you must *still* take precautions to prevent the timer's block from retaining `self` and causing a retain cycle, just as with notification observers. Here's some typical skeleton code:

```
@implementation MyClass {
    dispatch_source_t _timer; // ARC will manage this pseudo-object
}
- (void)doStart:(id)sender {
    self->_timer = dispatch_source_create(
        DISPATCH_SOURCE_TYPE_TIMER,0,0,dispatch_get_main_queue());
```

```
    dispatch_source_set_timer(
        self->_timer, dispatch_walltime(nil, 0),
        1 * NSEC_PER_SEC, 0.1 * NSEC_PER_SEC
        );
    __weak id wself = self;
    dispatch_source_set_event_handler(self->_timer, ^{
        MyClass* sself = wself;
        if (sself) {
            [sself dummy:nil]; // prevent retain cycle
        }
    });
    dispatch_resume(self->_timer);
}
- (void)doStop:(id)sender {
    self->_timer = nil;
}
- (void) dummy: (id) dummy {
    NSLog(@"timer fired");
}
- (void) dealloc {
    [self doStop:nil];
}
@end
```

Other Cocoa objects with unusual memory management behavior will usually be called out clearly in the documentation. For example, the UIWebView documentation warns: "Before releasing an instance of UIWebView for which you have set a delegate, you must first set its delegate property to nil." And a CAAnimation object *retains its delegate*; this is exceptional and can cause trouble if you're not conscious of it.

There are also situations where the documentation fails to warn of any special memory management considerations, but ARC itself will warn of a possible retain cycle due to the use of self-reference in a block. An example is the completion handler of UIPage-ViewController's `setViewControllers:direction:animated:completion:` instance method; if code in the `completion:` block refers to the same UIPageViewController instance to which the method is sent, the compiler will warn: "Capturing 'pvc' strongly in this block is likely to lead to a retain cycle" (or whatever the name of the page view controller is). Using the weak–strong dance, you capture pvc weakly instead.

Foundation collection classes introduced in iOS 6, NSPointerArray, NSHashTable, and NSMapTable, are similar respectively to NSMutableArray, NSMutableSet, and NSMutableDictionary, but their memory management policy is up to you. An NSHashTable created with the class method `weakObjectsHashTable`, for example, maintains weak references to its elements. Under ARC, these are weak references in the ARC sense: they are replaced by nil if the retain count of the object to which they were pointing has dropped to zero. You may find uses for these classes as a way of avoiding retain cycles.

Nib Loading and Memory Management

On iOS, when a nib loads, the top-level nib objects that it instantiates are autoreleased. So if someone doesn't retain them, they'll soon vanish in a puff of smoke. There are two primary strategies for preventing that from happening:

Retain the top-level objects

When a nib is loaded by calling NSBundle's `loadNibNamed:owner:options:` or UINib's `instantiateWithOwner:options:` (Chapter 7), an NSArray is returned consisting of the top-level objects instantiated by the nib-loading mechanism. So it's sufficient to retain this NSArray, or the objects in it.

For example, when a view controller is automatically instantiated from a storyboard, it is actually loaded from a nib with just one top-level object — the view controller. So the view controller ends up as the sole element of the array returned from `instantiateWithOwner:options:`. The view controller is then retained by the runtime, by assigning it a place in the view controller hierarchy; for instance, in an app with a main storyboard, `UIApplicationMain` instantiates the initial view controller from its nib and assigns it to the window's `rootViewController` property, which retains it.

Object graph

If an object instantiated from a nib is the destination of an outlet, the object at the source of that outlet may retain it — typically through an accessor. Thus a chain of outlets can retain multiple objects (Figure 12-2). For example, when a view controller automatically loads its main view from a nib, its proxy in the nib has a `view` outlet to the top-level UIView in that nib — and UIViewController's `setView:` retains its parameter.

Moreover, a view retains its subviews, so all the subviews of that main view (and their subviews, and so on) are retained as well. (For this reason, an `IBOutlet` instance or property that *you* create in your own view controllers will usually be marked as __weak. It doesn't have to be, but there's usually no need for it to be

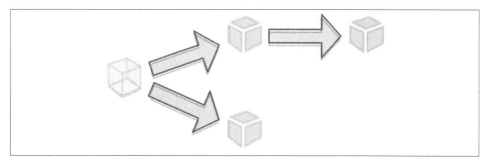

Figure 12-2. An object graph with retain

__strong, because the destination interface object in the nib is already going to be retained through its place in the object graph.)

OS X Programmer Alert

Memory management for nib-loaded instances is different on iOS than on OS X. On OS X, nib-loaded instances are not autoreleased, so they don't have to be retained, and memory management is usually automatic in any case because the file's owner is usually an NSWindowController, which takes care of these things for you. On iOS, top-level nib objects must be memory-managed.

Memory Management of Global Variables

In C, and therefore in Objective-C, it is permitted to declare a variable outside of any method. K&R (Chapter 1) calls this an *external variable* (see K&R 4.3); I call it a *global variable*. It is common practice, though not strictly required, to qualify such a variable's declaration as static; such qualification is a matter of scope and has no effect on the variable's persistence or its global nature.

Global variables are a C variable type, defined at file level; they know nothing of instances. Insofar as they have any relation to object-based programming, they may be defined in a class file so they are effectively class-level variables.

In Objective-C code, a global variable is not uncommonly used as a constant. You can sometimes initialize it as you declare it:

```
NSString* const MYSTRING = @"my string";
```

If the value you want to assign to a global isn't itself a constant, you'll have to assign the value in actual code; the question is then where to put that code. Since a global variable is effectively a class-level variable, it makes sense to initialize it early in the lifetime of the class, namely in initialize (see Chapter 11).

A global variable is a class-level value and thus persists for the lifetime of the program. It has no memory management connected with instances, because it itself is not connected with instances. Thus in some sense it leaks, but deliberately so, in the same innocuous sense that a class object leaks.

If you weren't using ARC, you'd need to manage a global variable like an instance variable: the object being assigned to it must be retained, and if a different object is assigned to it later, the first object should be released. Under ARC, assigning an object to a global variable retains that object, and subsequent assignment manages object memory correctly for you. Typically, an object assigned to a global variable won't be released; it will live as long as the class does, namely for the lifetime of the app itself, and that's fine.

Memory Management of CFTypeRefs

A CFTypeRef (see Chapter 3) is a pointer to a struct; its type name will usually end in "Ref". It is usually obtained through a C function, and there will be C functions for working with it. It is a kind of object, even though it isn't a full-fledged Cocoa Objective-C object, and it must be managed in much the same way as a Cocoa object. ARC, however, will not assist you with this. ARC manages Objective-C objects, not CFTypeRefs. You must manage the memory of CFTypeRefs manually, even if you're using ARC. And when you "cross the bridge" between the CFTypeRef world and the full-fledged Objective-C object world by passing an object from one to the other, you must help ARC to understand its memory management responsibilities.

Just as, in the Objective-C world of objects, certain method names (`alloc`, `copy`, and `retain`) alert you to your memory management responsibilities, so too in the world of CFTypeRefs. The golden rule here is that if you obtained a CFTypeRef object through a function whose name contains the word `Create` or `Copy`, you are responsible for releasing it. By default, you'll release it with the `CFRelease` function; some object creation functions, however, are paired with their own separate object release functions.

As an example, here is some actual code from one of my apps, strongly modeled on Apple's own example code, in which I set up a base pattern color space (for drawing with a pattern):

```
- (void) addPattern: (CGContextRef) context color: (CGColorRef) incolor {
    CGColorSpaceRef baseSpace = CGColorSpaceCreateDeviceRGB();
    CGColorSpaceRef patternSpace = CGColorSpaceCreatePattern(baseSpace);
    CGContextSetFillColorSpace(context, patternSpace);
    CGColorSpaceRelease(patternSpace);
    CGColorSpaceRelease(baseSpace);
    // ...
}
```

Never mind exactly what that code does; the important thing here is that the values for `baseSpace` and `patternSpace` are a CFTypeRef — in particular, a CGColorSpaceRef.

They are obtained through functions with Create in their name, so after we're done using them, we release them with the corresponding release function (here, CGColor-SpaceRelease).

Similarly, you can retain a CFTypeRef object, if you are afraid that it might go out of existence while you still need it, with the CFRetain function, and you are then, once again, responsible for balancing that call with the CFRelease function.

 An Objective-C object can be sent messages even if it is nil. But CFRelease cannot take a nil argument. Be sure that a CFTypeRef variable is not nil before releasing it.

We now come to the business of "crossing the bridge." As I explained in Chapter 3, many Core Foundation object types are toll-free bridged with a corresponding Cocoa object type. (For a list of these, see the "Toll-Free Bridged Types" chapter of Apple's *Core Foundation Design Concepts*.) Now, from a theoretical point of view, memory management is memory management: it makes no difference whether you use Core Foundation memory management or Cocoa memory management. Thus, if you obtain a CFString-Ref through a Create or Copy function and assign it to an NSString variable, sending release to it through the NSString variable is just as good as calling CFRelease on it as a CFStringRef. And before ARC, that was the end of the matter.

ARC, however, is not going to let you hand an object into or out of its memory-management purview without explicit information about how to manage its memory. When an object comes into existence by instantiation under ARC, it is memory-managed by ARC from birth to death, as it were. But when an object is cast from an Objective-C object type to a CFTypeRef, it passes out of the realm of ARC memory management, and ARC will not let it go without more information, because it doesn't understand what its memory management responsibilities should be at this moment. Similarly, when a CFTypeRef is cast to an object type, it passes ready-made into the realm of ARC memory management, and ARC will not accept it without more information. If you try to "cross the bridge" without giving ARC the information it wants, you'll get a compile error: "Implicit conversion … requires a bridged cast."

Providing this information correctly means a little extra thought on your part, but it's a good thing, because it means you can tell ARC to do automatically what you would have done manually. For example, before ARC, you might obtain a CFStringRef through a Create or Copy function, cast it to an NSString, and later send release to it as an NSString. Under ARC, you can't say release, but you can arrange for ARC to do exactly the same thing: as you "cross the bridge", you pass the CFString through the CFBridging-Release function. The result is an id that can be assigned to an NSString variable, and that ARC will eventually release to balance out the incremented retain count generated by the original Create or Copy function.

You have three choices as you cross the toll-free bridge:

__bridge *cast*

You cast explicitly to the across-the-bridge type and qualify the cast with __bridge. This means that memory management responsibilities are independent on either side of the bridge.

Here's an example (from Chapter 9) where we cross from the Objective-C object side of the bridge to the CFTypeRef side:

```
CGImageSourceRef src =
    CGImageSourceCreateWithURL((__bridge CFURLRef)imageSource, nil);
```

imageSource is an NSURL, so it's toll-free bridged with CFURL. But we must tell ARC its memory management responsibilities. Here, it has none: the NSURL object imageSource will continue to live entirely on the Objective-C object side of the bridge, and ARC should continue to manage it normally. We are merely showing imageSource to the CGImageSourceCreateWithURL function momentarily, as it were, so that a CGImageSourceRef can be formed from it. (On the other hand, the CGImageSourceRef object src will live entirely on the CFTypeRef side of the bridge, and we must manage its memory by hand, calling CFRelease on it when we're finished with it.)

CFBridgingRelease *function*

You're crossing the bridge from the CFTypeRef side to the Objective-C object side. You're telling ARC that memory management for this object is incomplete: it has a raised retain count on the CFTypeRef side (probably because you generated it with a Create or Copy function, or called CFRetain on it), and it will be up to ARC to perform, eventually, the corresponding release on the object side. (Alternatively, you can do a __bridge_transfer cast.)

Here's an example (in real life, this code comes right after the preceding example):

```
CFDictionaryRef res1 = CGImageSourceCopyPropertiesAtIndex(src, 0, nil);
NSDictionary* res = CFBridgingRelease(res1);
```

In that example, the CFDictionaryRef object res1 will *never* have CFRelease called on it. It was born on the CFTypeRef side of the bridge, because we needed CGImageSourceCopyPropertiesAtIndex to generate it; and it was born with an elevated retain count (Copy). But it has now crossed the bridge, entirely and permanently. It lives on purely as an Objective-C object, res, and ARC will release it when the time comes.

CFBridgingRetain *function*

This is the exact converse of CFBridgingRelease. Here, you're crossing the bridge from the Objective-C object side to the CFTypeRef side. You're telling ARC that it should leave memory management for this object incomplete: you're aware of the raised retain count on the Objective-C object side, and you intend to call CFRelease on it yourself on the CFTypeRef side. (Alternatively, you can do a __bridge_retained cast.)

A common scenario is that you need to treat an Objective-C object as its toll-free bridged CFTypeRef counterpart in order to work with it using C functions that do things you can't do otherwise. In theory there is no need for memory management on the CFTypeRef side, because the object will persist on the Objective-C object side. But in reality, it might *not* persist on the Objective-C object side: it might be released, in which case your CFTypeRef reference to it will be garbage. To prevent this, call CFBridgingRetain as you cross the bridge, and call CFRelease on it when you're done working on the CFTypeRef side.

Alternatively, it is also perfectly possible to pass an object out of the Objective-C object world with CFBridgingRetain and back into it later with CFBridging-Release.

It is sometimes necessary to assign a CFTypeRef to an id variable or parameter. For example, a CALayer's setContents: method expects an id parameter, but the actual value must be a CGImageRef. This is legal, because (as I mentioned in Chapter 3) any CFTypeRef is toll-free bridged to id; but the compiler will complain unless you typecast to an id, and a __bridge qualifier may also be needed:

```
CGImageRef moi = // something or other
self.v.layer.contents = (__bridge id)moi;
```

However, if the CFTypeRef comes from a built-in method, with no intervening assignment to a variable, the __bridge qualifier may not be needed:

```
self.v.layer.contents = (id)[UIImage imageNamed:@"moi"].CGImage;
```

The reason is that a built-in method such as UIImage's CGImage instance method supplies, itself, the bridging information that satisfies the compiler. You can see this happening in the header:

```
- (CGImageRef)CGImage NS_RETURNS_INNER_POINTER;
```

Memory Management of Pointer-to-Void Context Info

A small number of Cocoa methods take an optional parameter typed as void*, and often called context:. You might think that void*, the universal pointer type, would be the same as id, the universal object type, because a reference to an object is a pointer. But an id is a universal *object* type; void* is just a C pointer. This means that Cocoa won't treat a void* value as an object, and won't manage its memory for you. Thus, making sure that it persists long enough to be useful is up to you.

How long is long enough? Well, the purpose of the context: argument that you pass is that it comes back to you as a context: parameter in a callback, to help identify something or provide supplementary information. For example, if you supply a context: value in your call to beginAnimations:context:, it's because you expect Cocoa to call your animationDidStop:finished:context: implementation with the same context: value. Thus, you need the context: value to persist for as long as the callback, animation-DidStop:finished:context:, might be called.

Sometimes, the context: is just an identifier, where your intention is merely to compare the context: parameter in the callback with the context: argument you passed in originally. It can thus be stored as an external variable in the class that will use it. A commonly recommended pattern is this:

```
static void* const MYCONTEXT = (void*)&MYCONTEXT;
```

Here, the name MYCONTEXT has a value pointing to its own storage, and the context: parameter in the callback can be compared to it directly.

Another commonly recommended identifier context: argument value is self. It certainly has the right persistence — clearly self will exist for as long as it can be sent a callback message.

On the other hand, the context: might be a separate full-fledged object. In that case, you need a place to store it. Here, an instance variable makes the most sense, because an external variable is class-based, and you might need different instances of this class to be working with different context: values.

Under ARC, you can't pass an Objective-C object where a void* value is expected, or *vice versa*, without supplying additional memory management information. This constitutes another case of "crossing the bridge", as discussed in the previous section. Any memory management is already taken care of on the Objective-C side of the bridge, so a simple __bridge cast is sufficient. You'll typecast the value to (__bridge void*) when you pass it as the context: argument, and typecast it back to (__bridge id) when it comes back to you in the callback.

Considerations of this sort do not apply to parameters that are typed as objects. For instance, when you call postNotificationName:object:userInfo:, the userInfo: is typed as an NSDictionary and is retained for you by the notification center (and released after the notification is posted); its memory management behind the scenes is not your concern.

Properties

A *property* (see Chapter 5) is syntactic sugar for calling an accessor by using dot-notation. The following two lines of code, by default, are equivalent ways of calling a setter:

```
[self setTheData: d];
self.theData = d;
```

And these are equivalent ways of calling a getter:

```
d = [self theData];
d = self.theData;
```

The declaration of an accessor method is what permits us to use the corresponding property notation: the declaration of the setter lets us use property notation in an lvalue (to assign to the property), and the declaration of the getter lets us use property notation otherwise (to fetch the property's value).

It is also possible to declare a property explicitly, *instead* of declaring the getter and setter methods. Declaring a property is thus a shorthand for declaring accessors, just as using a property is shorthand for calling an accessor. But declaring a property can do much more for you and your code than that. How much more it can do has increased historically, depending on what system and what version of Xcode you're using; here's a list of the powers of property declaration, roughly in order of increasing power, which is also roughly the order in which those powers were introduced historically:

- A property declaration saves you from having to declare accessor methods. It is simpler to declare one property than to declare two accessor methods.

- A property declaration includes a statement of the setter's *memory management policy*. This lets you, the programmer, know easily, just by glancing at a property declaration, how the incoming value will be treated. You could find this out otherwise only by looking at the setter's code — which, if this setter belongs to a built-in Cocoa class, you cannot do (and even in the case of your own code, it's a pain having to locate and consult the setter directly).

- With a property declaration, you can optionally *omit writing one or both accessors*. The compiler will write them for you! To get the compiler to do this, you include a `@synthesize` directive in your class's implementation section. Such an automatically constructed accessor is called, naturally enough, a *synthesized accessor*.

  Writing accessors is boring and error-prone; any time correct code is written for you automatically, it's a major benefit. Moreover, your class is now key–value coding compliant for the accessor name, with no effort on your part. Furthermore, your setter memory management policy, as specified in the property declaration, is followed by the synthesized setter. Your wish is Cocoa's command!

- With a synthesized accessor, you can optionally *omit declaring the instance variable* that the accessor gets or sets. It is implicitly declared for you! Automatic implicit declaration of instance variables was introduced as part of a major advance in Objective-C: the documentation refers to the earlier period (when you still had to declare instance variables yourself, even with a declared property and a synthesized accessor) as "the legacy runtimes", and the later period (automatic implicit declaration of instance variables) as "the modern runtimes".

  As part of the `@synthesize` directive, you can specify the name of the instance variable that is to be implicitly declared for you.

- The ultimate convenience is the most recent (starting in LLVM compiler version 4.0, Xcode 4.4): you can omit the `@synthesize` directive! The compiler automatically inserts it for you, implicitly. This is called *autosynthesis*.

  The only downside to taking advantage of autosynthesis is that, because the `@synthesize` directive is omitted, you have no place to specify the name of the automatically declared instance variable. That isn't much of a disadvantage; the name is supplied according to a simple rule, and the vast majority of the time you'll be perfectly happy with it.

Thanks to autosynthesis, the mere presence of the property declaration — one line of code — is sufficient to trigger the entire stack of automatic behaviors: it equates to declaration of the accessors, and the accessors are written for you (in accordance with your declared memory management policy), and the instance variable is implicitly declared for you as well.

Property Memory Management Policies

The possible memory management policies for a property correspond directly to what has already been said in this chapter about the ARC reference types and how a setter might behave:

`strong, retain`
: The default. The terms are pure synonyms of one another and can be used in ARC or non-ARC code; `retain` is the term inherited, as it were, from pre-ARC days. Under ARC, the instance variable itself will be a normal (strong) reference, so when a value is assigned to it, by whatever means, ARC will retain the incoming value and release the existing value of the instance variable. Under non-ARC, the setter method will retain the incoming value and release the existing value of the instance variable.

`copy`
: The same as `strong` or `retain`, except that the setter copies the incoming value (by sending `copy` to it) and the copy, which has an increased retain count already, is assigned to the instance variable. This is appropriate particularly when an immut-

able class has a mutable subclass (such as NSString and NSMutableString, or NSArray and NSMutableArray), to prevent the setter's caller from passing in an object of the mutable subclass; it is legal for the setter's caller to do so, because (in accordance with polymorphism, Chapter 5) where an instance of a class is expected, an instance of its subclass can be passed, but the `copy` call creates an instance of the immutable class (Chapter 10), and thus prevents the caller from keeping a reference to the incoming value and later mutating it behind your back.

weak

Under ARC, the instance variable will be a weak reference. ARC will assign the incoming value to it without retaining it. ARC will also magically nilify the instance variable if the instance to which it points goes out of existence. This is useful, as explained earlier in this chapter, for guarding against a potential retain cycle, or to reduce overhead where it is known that no memory management is needed, as with an interface object that is already retained by its superview. The setter method can be synthesized only under ARC; using `weak` in non-ARC code is not strictly impossible but probably makes no sense.

assign

This policy is inherited from pre-ARC days; it is used in the same ways as `weak`. The setter does not manage memory; the incoming value is assigned directly to the instance variable. The instance variable is *not* an ARC weak reference and will *not* be nilified automatically if the instance to which it points goes out of existence; it is a non-ARC weak reference (`__unsafe_unretained`) and can become a dangling pointer.

As I've already said, a property's declared memory management policy is an instruction to the compiler if the setter is synthesized. If the setter is *not* synthesized, the declared memory management policy is "purely conventional" (as the LLVM documentation puts it), meaning that if you write your own setter, you'd better make that setter behave the way you declared you would, but nothing is going to force you to do so.

Property Declaration Syntax

A property may be declared wherever you can declare methods — for example, in a *.h* file's interface section, in a class extension, or in a protocol declaration. Its syntax schema is as follows:

```
@property (attribute, attribute, ...) type name;
```

Here's a real example:

```
@property (nonatomic, strong) NSMutableArray* theData;
```

The *type* and *name* will usually match the type and name of an instance variable, but what you're really indicating here are the name of the property (as used in dot-notation) and the default names of the setter (here, setTheData:) and getter (here, theData), along with the type of value to be passed to the setter and obtained from the getter.

If this property is to be capable of representation by an outlet in a nib, you can say IBOutlet before the *type*. This is a hint to Xcode and has no formal meaning.

The *type* doesn't have to be an object type; it can be a simple type such as BOOL, CGFloat, or CGSize. Of course in that case no memory management is performed (as none is needed), and no memory management policy should be declared; but the advantages of using a property remain — the accessors can be synthesized and the instance variable declared automatically.

The possible *attribute* values are:

A memory management policy
> I listed the names of these in the previous section. You will supply exactly one; under ARC this will usually be strong (which is also the default under ARC if you omit any memory management policy).

nonatomic
> If omitted, the synthesized accessors will use locking to ensure correct operation if your app is multithreaded. This will rarely be a concern, and locking slows down the operation of the accessors, so you'll probably specify nonatomic most of the time. It's a pity that nonatomic isn't the default, but such is life. A build setting, Implicit Atomic Objective-C Properties, can be turned on to cause the compiler to issue a warning in cases where you're accidentally omitting nonatomic.

readwrite *or* readonly
> If omitted, the default is readwrite. If you say readonly, any attempt to call the setter or use the property as a setter will cause a compile error, and if the accessors are to be synthesized, no setter is synthesized.

getter=*gname*, setter=*sname*:
> By default, the property name is used to derive the names of the getter and setter methods that will be called when the property is used. If the property is named myProp, the default getter method name is myProp and the default setter name is setMyProp:. You can use either or both of these attributes to change that. If you say getter=beeblebrox, you're saying that the getter method corresponding to this property is called beeblebrox (and if the accessors are synthesized, the getter will be given this name). Users of the property won't be affected, but calling an accessor method explicitly under a nonexistent name is a compile error.

To *make a property declaration private*, put it in a class extension (Chapter 10). Most commonly, the class extension will be at the top of the implementation (.*m*) file, before the implementation section. As a result, this class can use the property name or call the accessors but other classes cannot (Example 12-10).

Example 12-10. A private property

```
// MyClass.m:
@interface MyClass ()
@property (nonatomic, strong) NSMutableArray* theData; // private
@end

@implementation MyClass
// other code goes here
@end
```

Knowledge of private properties is not inherited by subclasses; the usual solution is to move the class extension interface section off into an isolated *.h* file of its own and import that into the implementation files of both the superclass and the subclass.

Another reason to put a property declaration in a class extension is so as to *redeclare* the property. For example, we might want our property to be `readonly` as far as the rest of the world knows, but `readwrite` for code within our class. To implement this, declare the property `readonly` in the interface section in the header file, which the rest of the world sees, and then redeclare it, *not* as `readonly`, in the class extension in the implementation file, which only this class sees. All other attributes must match between both declarations. The default is `readwrite`, so now this class can call the setter or use the property as an lvalue, and other classes can't.

Property Accessor Synthesis

To request explicitly that the accessors be synthesized for you, use the `@synthesize` directive. It appears anywhere inside the class's implementation section, any number of times, and takes a comma-separated list of property names. The behavior and names of the synthesized accessors will accord with the property declaration attributes I've just talked about. You can state that the synthesized accessors should access an instance variable whose name differs from the property name by using the syntax *property-Name=ivarName* in the `@synthesize` directive's property name list; otherwise, the instance variable will have *the same name as the property*. As I mentioned earlier, you don't have to declare the instance variable; it will be declared for you automatically as part of accessor synthesis.

An instance variable declared automatically through accessor synthesis is strictly private, meaning that it is not inherited by subclasses. This fact will rarely prove troublesome, but if it does, simply declare the instance variable explicitly.

Thus, having declared a property `theData`, to request explicitly that accessors be synthesized, you'd say this in the implementation section:

```
@synthesize theData;
```

The result is that any accessors you don't write (`theData` and `setTheData:`, unless you changed these names in the property declaration) will be written for you behind the scenes, and if you didn't declare an instance variable `theData`, it will be declared for you.

The name of the automatically declared instance variable is likely to be important to you, because you're probably going to need to access the instance variable directly, especially in an initializer (and in `dealloc` if you're not using ARC), as well as in any accessors that you write yourself.

Starting in the Xcode 4.2 application templates, Apple began following a convention where the instance variable was given a name different from that of the property, in that the former was prefixed with an underscore. For example, the AppDelegate class's implementation section contained this line:

```
@synthesize window = _window;
```

The evident value of following this naming convention is that we can refer in our code to the property explicitly as `self.window`, but if we were accidentally to refer to the instance variable directly as `window`, we'd get a compile error, because there is no instance variable `window` (it's called `_window`). The convention thus prevents accidental direct access to the instance variable without passing through the accessors. In addition, it distinguishes clearly in code which names are instance variables — they're the ones prefixed with an underscore. Moreover, this policy frees up the property name (here, `window`) to be used as a local variable in a method, without getting a warning from the compiler that we're overshadowing the name of an instance variable.

Autosynthesis follows the same naming policy. If you *omit* the `@synthesize` directive, the automatically generated name of the automatically declared instance variable is the name of the property *prefixed with an underscore*. For example, a declared property called `theData` will result in an instance variable called `_theData`. If for some reason that isn't what you want, then use the `@synthesize` directive explicitly. (Remember, if you do so, that if you don't specify the instance variable name explicitly, the default instance variable name in that case will be the same as the property name, *without* any underscore.)

To illustrate, Example 12-11 gives the complete implementation for a Dog class with a public `name` property, such as we were positing earlier in this chapter. The property is autosynthesized, so the corresponding ivar, which is also declared automatically, is called `_name`; we must refer to it directly in the initializer.

Example 12-11. Complete example of property autosynthesis

```
// Dog.h:
@interface Dog : NSObject
- (id) initWithName: (NSString*) s;
@property (nonatomic, copy) NSString* name;
@end

// Dog.m:
@implementation Dog
- (id) initWithName: (NSString*) s {
    self = [super init];
    if (self) {
        self->_name = [s copy];
    }
    return self;
}
- (id) init {
    NSAssert(NO, @"Making a nameless dog is forbidden.");
    return nil;
}
@end
```

Regardless of whether you explicitly include a @synthesize directive or you take advantage of autosynthesis, you are permitted to write one or both accessors yourself. Synthesis means that any accessors you *don't* provide will be provided for you. If you use autosynthesis (no @synthesize directive) and you provide *both* accessors, *you won't get any automatically declared instance variable.* This is a very sensible policy: you're taking complete manual control of your accessors, so you're given complete manual control of your instance variable as well.

A useful trick is to take advantage of the @synthesize syntax *propertyName=ivarName* to override the synthesized accessor without losing any of its functionality. What I mean is this. Suppose you want the setter for _myIvar to do more than just set _myIvar. One possibility is to write your own setter; however, writing a setter from scratch is tedious and error-prone, whereas a synthesized setter does the job correctly and writing it is no work at all. The solution is to declare a property myIvar along with a corresponding private property (Example 12-10) — let's call it myIvarAlias — and synthesize the private property myIvarAlias to access the _myIvar instance variable. You must then write the accessors for myIvar by hand, but all they need to do, at a minimum, is use the myIvarAlias properties to set and get the value of _myIvar respectively. The key point is that you can also do *other* stuff in those accessors (Example 12-12); whoever gets or sets the property myIvar will be doing that other stuff.

Example 12-12. Overriding synthesized accessors

```
// In the header file:
@interface MyClass : NSObject
@property (nonatomic, strong) NSNumber* myIvar;
@end

// In the implementation file:
@interface MyClass ()
@property (nonatomic, strong) NSNumber* myIvarAlias;
@end

@implementation MyClass
@synthesize myIvarAlias=_myIvar;
- (void) setMyIvar: (NSNumber*) num {
    // do other stuff here
    self.myIvarAlias = num;
}
- (NSNumber*) myIvar {
    // do other stuff here
    return self.myIvarAlias;
}
@end
```

Dynamic Accessors

Instead of writing your own accessors or providing a @synthesize directive or using autosynthesis, you can accompany a property declaration with a @dynamic directive (in the implementation section). This tells the compiler that even though it doesn't see any implementation of any accessors for this property, it shouldn't provide the accessors for you, and yet it should permit the property declaration anyway, on the grounds that at runtime, when a call to one of the accessors arrives, your code will somehow magically handle it in some way that the compiler can't grasp. Basically, you're suppressing the compiler's warning system; it just gives up and stands aside, and leaves you to hang yourself at runtime.

This is a rare but not unheard-of thing to do. It arises chiefly in two contexts: when defining your own animatable view property, and when using managed object properties in Core Data. In both of those situations, you harness the power of Cocoa to perform the magic handling of the accessor calls; you don't know precisely *how* Cocoa performs this magic, and you don't care.

But what if you wanted to perform this magic yourself? To put it another way, what sort of magic might Cocoa be using in those two situations? The answer lies in the power of Objective-C's dynamic messaging. This is an advanced topic, but it's so cool that I'll show you an example anyway.

I propose to write a class that declares properties name (an NSString) and number (an NSNumber) but that has no accessor methods for name or number and that doesn't use accessor synthesis. Instead, in our implementation section we declare these properties dynamic. Since we're not getting any help from synthesis, we must also declare the instance variables ourselves:

```
// the interface section declares properties "name" and "number"
@implementation MyClass {
    NSString* _name;
    NSNumber* _number;
}
@dynamic name, number;
// ...insert magic here...
@end
```

I can think of a couple of ways to concoct the necessary magic; in this example, I'm going to take advantage of a little-known NSObject class method called resolve-InstanceMethod:.

Sending a message to an object is not the same as calling that method in that object; there are some additional steps, if that method is not found in that object, to resolve the method. One of the first of these steps, the *first* time a given message arrives and is found to have no corresponding method in the object's class, is that the runtime looks for an implementation of resolveInstanceMethod: in that class. If it finds it, it calls it, handing it the selector for the message that is giving us difficulty. resolveInstanceMethod: then returns a BOOL; a YES answer means, "Don't worry, I've got it covered; go ahead and call that method."

How can resolveInstanceMethod: possibly say this? What could it do, if the method doesn't exist, to make it possible to call that method? Well, it could *create that method*. Objective-C is so dynamic that there's a way to do this. And remember, resolve-InstanceMethod: is called just once per method, so once it has created a method and returned YES, the problem is solved forever after for that method.

To create a method in real time, we call the class_addMethod function. This will require importing <objc/runtime.h>, or, if you're using modules, @import ObjectiveC. It takes four parameters:

- The class to which the method is to be added.
- The selector for the method that is being added (basically, this is the name of the method).
- The IMP for the method. What's an IMP? It's the *function that backs this method*. Behind every Objective-C method lies a C function. This function takes the same parameters as the Objective-C method, with the addition of two extra parameters, which come at the start: the object that acts as self within this function, and the selector for the method that this function is backing.

- A C string describing, in a special code, the type of the function's returned value (which is also the type of the method's returned value) and the argument types of the function. When I say "type" I mean little more than C type; every object type is considered the same.

In our example we have four methods to cover (the two accessors for the two dynamic properties) — name, setName:, number, and setNumber:. So in order to call class_add-Method in resolveInstanceMethod:, we will also have to have written C functions to act as the IMP for each of those methods. Now, we could just write four C functions — but that would be pointless! If we were going to do that, why are we going to all the trouble of using a dynamic accessor? Instead, I propose to write just two C functions, one to handle *any* getter that we may care to direct at it, and one to handle *any* setter that we may care to direct at it.

Let's take the getter first, as it is much the simpler case. What must a generalized getter do? It must access the corresponding instance variable. And what's the name of the corresponding instance variable? Well, the way we've set things up, it's the name of the method with an underscore prefixed to it. So, we grab the name of the method (which we can do because it has arrived as the selector, the second parameter to this function), stick an underscore on the front, and return the value of the instance variable whose name we've just derived. To make life simple, I'll obtain the value of that instance variable using key–value coding; the presence of the underscore means that this won't result in any circularity (that is, our function won't end up calling itself in an infinite recursion):

```
id callValueForKey(id self, SEL _cmd) {
    NSString* key = NSStringFromSelector(_cmd);
    key = [@"_" stringByAppendingString:key];
    return [self valueForKey:key];
}
```

Now that we've done that, we can see how to write the setter. It's just a matter of doing a slightly more elaborate manipulation of the selector's name in order to get the name of the instance variable. We must pull the set off the front and the colon off the end, and make sure the first letter is lowercase — and then we prefix the underscore, just as before:

```
void callSetValueForKey(id self, SEL _cmd, id value) {
    NSString* key = NSStringFromSelector(_cmd);
    key = [key substringWithRange:NSMakeRange(3, [key length]-4)];
    NSString* firstCharLower =
        [[key substringWithRange:NSMakeRange(0,1)] lowercaseString];
    key = [key stringByReplacingCharactersInRange:NSMakeRange(0,1)
                                        withString:firstCharLower];
    key = [@"_" stringByAppendingString:key];
    [self setValue:value forKey:key];
}
```

Finally, we're ready to write `resolveInstanceMethod:`. In my implementation, I've used this method as a gatekeeper, explicitly checking that the method to be called is an accessor for one of our dynamic properties:

```
+ (BOOL) resolveInstanceMethod: (SEL) sel {
    // this method will be called
    if (sel == @selector(setName:) || sel == @selector(setNumber:)) {
        class_addMethod([self class], sel, (IMP) callSetValueForKey, "v@:@");
        return YES;
    }
    if (sel == @selector(name) || sel == @selector(number)) {
        class_addMethod([self class], sel, (IMP) callValueForKey, "@@:");
        return YES;
    }
    return [super resolveInstanceMethod:sel];
}
```

(You'll just have to trust me on the encoded C string in the fourth argument to `class_addMethod`; if you don't, read the documentation to see what it means.)

My overall implementation here is simple-minded — in particular, my use of key–value coding is sort of an easy way out, and I've failed to grapple with the need for copy semantics in the NSString setter — but it's quite general, and gives you a peek under the Objective-C hood.

CHAPTER 13

Communication Between Objects

As soon as an app grows to more than a few objects, puzzling questions can arise about how to send a message or communicate data between one object and another. The problem is essentially one of architecture. It may require some planning to construct your code so that all the pieces fit together and information can be shared as needed at the right moment. This chapter presents some organizational considerations that will help you arrange for one object to be able to communicate with another.

The problem of communication often comes down to one object being able to *see* another: the object Manny needs to be able to find the object Jack repeatedly and reliably over the long term so as to be able to send Jack messages.

One obvious solution is an instance variable of Manny whose value *is* Jack. This is appropriate particularly when Manny and Jack share certain responsibilities or supplement one another's functionality. The application object and its delegate, a table view and its data source, a view controller and the view that it controls — these are cases where the former must have an instance variable pointing at the latter.

This does not necessarily imply that Manny needs to assert ownership of Jack (as a matter of memory management policy, Chapter 12). An object does not typically retain its delegate or its data source; similarly, an object that implements the target–action pattern, such as a UIControl, does not retain its target. But then Manny must be prepared for the possibility that its supposed reference to Jack will turn out to be a reference to nil; and care must be taken that this reference doesn't turn into a dangling pointer (luckily, that's less likely to happen under ARC). On the other hand, a view controller is useless without a view to control; once it has a view, it will retain it, releasing it only when it itself goes out of existence. There may be similar situations in which you do want one object to own another.

Objects can also perform two-way communication *without* holding persistent (instance variable) references to one another. For example, Manny might send a message to Jack where one of the parameters is a reference to Manny; this might merely constitute a form of identification, or an invitation to Jack to send a message back to Manny if Jack needs further information while doing whatever this method does. Again, this is a common pattern. The parameter of the delegate message `textFieldShouldBegin-Editing:` is a reference to the UITextField that sent the message. The first parameter of a target–action message is a reference to the sender. Manny thus makes itself, as it were, momentarily visible to Jack; Jack should not wantonly retain Manny (especially since there's an obvious risk of a retain cycle).

But how is Manny to obtain a reference to Jack in the first place? That's a very big question. Much of the art of iOS programming, and of object-oriented programming generally, lies in one object *getting a reference* to some other object. (See also my discussion of this matter in Chapter 5.) Every case is different and must be solved separately, but certain general patterns emerge, and this chapter will outline them.

There are also ways for Manny to send a message that Jack *receives* without having to send it directly *to* Jack, or without knowing or caring who Jack is. Notifications and key-value observing are examples, and I'll discuss them in this chapter as well.

Finally, the chapter ends with a section on the larger question of what kinds of objects *need* to see one another, within the general scope of a typical iOS program.

Visibility by Instantiation

Every instance comes from somewhere and at someone's behest: some object sent a message commanding this instance to come into existence in the first place. The commanding object therefore has a reference to the instance at that moment. When Manny generates Jack, Manny has a reference to Jack.

That simple fact can serve as the starting point for establishment of future communication. If Manny generates Jack and knows that it (Manny) will need a reference to Jack in the future, Manny can keep the reference that it obtained by generating Jack in the first place. Or, it may be that what Manny knows is that Jack will need a reference to Manny in the future; Manny can supply that reference immediately after generating Jack, and Jack will then keep it.

Delegation is a case in point. Manny may create Jack and immediately make itself Jack's delegate. Indeed, if this crucial, you might endow Jack with an initializer so that Manny can create Jack and hand Jack a reference to itself *at the same time*, to help prevent any slip-ups. Compare the approach taken by UIActionSheet and UIAlertView, where the delegate is one of the initializer's parameters, or by UIBarButtonItem, where the target is one of the initializer's parameters.

But delegation is just one example. When Manny creates Jack, it might not be a reference to Manny that Jack needs, but to something that Manny knows or has. You will presumably endow Jack with a method so that Manny can hand that information across; again, it might be reasonable to make that method Jack's initializer, if Jack simply cannot live without the information.

This example, from one of my apps, is from a table view controller. The user has tapped a row of the table. We create a secondary table view controller, a TrackViewController instance, handing it the data it will need, and display the secondary table view. I have deliberately devised TrackViewController to have a designated initializer initWith-MediaItemCollection: to make it virtually obligatory for a TrackViewController to have access, from the moment it comes into existence, to the data it needs:

```
- (void)showItemsForRow: (NSIndexPath*) indexPath {
    // create subtable of tracks and go there
    TrackViewController *t =
        [[TrackViewController alloc] initWithMediaItemCollection:
            (self.albums)[indexPath.row]];
    [self.navigationController pushViewController:t animated:YES];
}
```

In that example, self does not keep a reference to the new TrackViewController instance, nor does the TrackViewController acquire a reference to self. But self does create the TrackViewController instance, and so, for one brief shining moment, it has a reference to it. Therefore self takes advantage of that moment to hand the TrackViewController instance the information it needs. There will be no better moment to do this. Knowing the moment, and taking care not to miss it, is part of the art of data communication.

When a nib loads, the nib's owner is effectively instantiating the objects in the nib. (For a *.xib* file, the owner is the object represented by the File's Owner proxy in the nib; for a storyboard, it is a scene's top-level view controller. See Chapter 7.) By preparing outlets from the nib's owner in the nib, you arrange that the nib's owner will obtain references to the instantiated nib objects at the moment they are instantiated through the nib-loading mechanism.

A slightly different architecture arises when Manny does *not* instantiate Jack; Moe does. But Moe has a reference to Manny, and Moe knows that Manny might have information to share with Jack. Therefore Moe brings Manny and Jack together. That is Manny's moment.

For example, beginners are often puzzled by how two objects are to get a reference to one another if they will be instantiated from *different* nibs — either different *.xib* files or different scenes in a storyboard. It is frustrating that you can't draw a connection between an object in nib A and an object in nib B; it's particularly frustrating when you can see both objects sitting right there in the same storyboard. But as I explained earlier ("Connections Between Nibs" on page 183), such a connection would be meaningless, which is why it's impossible. These are different nibs, and they will load at different times. However, some object (Manny) is going to be the owner when nib A loads, and some object (Jack) is going to be the owner when nib B loads. Perhaps they can then see each other, in which case, given all the necessary outlets, the problem is solved. Or perhaps some third object (Moe) can see both of them and provides a communication path for them.

In a storyboard, that's exactly what does happen. When a segue in a storyboard is triggered, the segue's destination view controller is instantiated, and the segue has a reference to it. At the same time, the segue's source view controller already exists, and the segue has a reference to it as well. So the segue sends the source view controller the `prepareForSegue:sender:` message, containing a reference to itself (the segue). The segue is Moe; it is bringing Manny (the source view controller) and Jack (the destination view controller) together. This is the source view controller's chance (Manny's moment) to obtain a reference to the newly instantiated destination view controller (by asking the segue for it) — and now the source view controller can make itself the destination view controller's delegate, hand it any needed information, and so forth. (If you make a project from the Utility Application template, you can see this very thing happening in the MainViewController code.)

Visibility by Relationship

Objects may acquire the ability to see one another automatically by virtue of their position in a containing structure. Before worrying about how to supply one object with a reference to another, consider whether there may *already* be a chain of references leading from one to the other.

For example, a subview can see its superview, through its `superview` property. A superview can see all its subviews, through its `subviews` property, and can pick out a specific subview through that subview's `tag` property, by calling `viewWithTag:`. A subview in a window can see its window, through its `window` property. Thus, by working up or down the view hierarchy by means of these properties, it may be possible to obtain the desired reference.

In this example from my own code, I have many buttons and many text fields, paired with one another. When a button is tapped, I need to fetch the text of the corresponding text field. Given a particular button, how can I get a reference to the corresponding text field? To make this possible, I've assigned the buttons tags in the nib (101, 102, 103, and so on) and I've given the text fields corresponding tags (1, 2, 3, and so on):

```
UIView* v = sender; // a button
UIView* v2 = [v.superview viewWithTag:(v.tag - 100)];
```

Similarly, a responder (Chapter 11) can see the next responder in the responder chain, through the `nextResponder` method — which also means, because of the structure of the responder chain, that a view controller's main view can see the view controller. In this code, I work my way up from a view to obtain a reference to the view controller that's in charge of this whole scene:

```
UIResponder* r = self; // a UIView in the interface
while (![r isKindOfClass:[UIViewController class]])
    r = r.nextResponder;
```

Similarly, view controllers are themselves part of a containment hierarchy and therefore can see one another. If a view controller is currently presenting a view through a second view controller, the latter is the former's `presentedViewController`, and the former is the latter's `presentingViewController`. If a view controller is contained by a UINavigationController, the latter is its `navigationController`. A UINavigation-Controller's visible view is controlled by its `visibleViewController`. And from any of these, you can reach the view controller's view through its `view` property, and so forth.

All of these relationships are public. So if you can get a reference to just one object within any of these structures or a similar structure, you can effectively navigate the whole structure through a chain of references and lay your hands on any other object within the structure.

Global Visibility

Some objects are globally visible — that is, they are visible to all other objects. Class objects are a trivial example! But classes often have class methods that vend singleton instances. Some of these singletons, in turn, have properties pointing to other objects, making those other objects likewise globally visible.

For example, any object can see the singleton UIApplication instance by calling `[UIApplication sharedApplication]`. So any object can also see the app's primary window, because that is the singleton UIApplication instance's `keyWindow` property, and any object can see the app delegate, because that is its `delegate` property. And the chain continues: any object can see the app's root view controller, because that is the primary window's `rootViewController` — and from there, as I said in the previous section, we can navigate the view controller hierarchy and the view hierarchy.

You, too, can make your own objects globally visible by attaching them to a globally visible object. A public property of the app delegate, which you are free to create, is globally visible by virtue of the app delegate being globally visible (by virtue of the shared application being globally visible).

Another globally visible object is the shared defaults object obtained by calling `[NSUser-Defaults standardUserDefaults]`. This object is the gateway to storage and retrieval of user defaults, which is similar to a dictionary (a collection of values named by keys). The user defaults are automatically saved when your application quits and are automatically available when your application is launched again later, so they are one of the

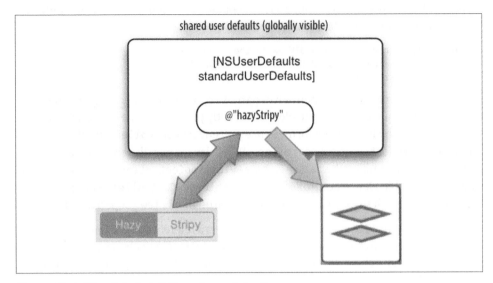

Figure 13-1. The global visibility of user defaults

ways in which your app maintains information between launches. But, being globally visible, they are also a conduit for communicating values within your app.

For example, in one of my apps there's a setting I call @"hazyStripy". This determines whether a certain visible interface object is drawn with a hazy fill or a stripy fill. This is a setting that the user can change, so there is a preferences interface allowing the user to make this change. When the user displays this preferences interface, I examine the @"hazyStripy" setting in the user defaults to configure the interface to reflect it; if the user interacts with the preferences interface to change the @"hazyStripy" setting, I respond by changing the actual @"hazyStripy" setting in the user defaults.

But the preferences interface is not the only object that uses the @"hazyStripy" setting in the user defaults; the drawing code that actually draws the hazy-or-stripy-filled object also uses it, so as to know which way to draw itself. Thus there is no need for the object that draws the hazy-or-stripy-filled object and the object that manages the preferences interface to be able to see one another! They can both see this common object, the @"hazyStripy" user default (Figure 13-1). Indeed, it is not uncommon to "misuse" the user defaults storage to hold information that is *not* used to maintain user preferences, but is placed there just because this is a location globally visible to all objects.

Notifications

Notifications (Chapter 11) can be a way to communicate between objects that are conceptually distant from one another without bothering to provide *any* way for one to see the other. All they really need to have in common is a knowledge of the name of the notification. Every object can see the notification center, so every object can arrange to post or receive a notification.

Using a notification in this way may seem lazy, an evasion of your responsibility to architect your objects sensibly. But sometimes one object doesn't need to know, and indeed shouldn't know, what object (or objects) it is sending a message to.

I gave an example in Chapter 11. Here's another. In one of my apps, the app delegate may detect a need to tear down the interface and build it back up again from scratch. If this is to happen without causing memory leaks (and all sorts of other havoc), every view controller that is currently running a repeating NSTimer needs to invalidate that timer (Chapter 12). Rather than my having to work out what view controllers those might be, and endowing every view controller with a method that can be called, I simply have the app delegate shout "Everybody stop timers!" — by posting a notification. My view controllers that run timers have all registered for this notification, and they know what to do when they receive it.

Key–Value Observing

Key–value observing, or *KVO*, is a mechanism that allows one object to be registered with a second object so as to be notified automatically when a value in the second object changes. In order to perform the act of registration, this requires that at some point the second object must be visible to the first (or that they both be visible to some third object). But thereafter, the second object is able to send messages to the first object without an instance variable referring to the first object and without having any knowledge of the first object's class or publicly declared methods. Architecturally, this is somewhat like the target–action mechanism (Chapter 11), but it works for *any* two objects. (The KVO mechanism is provided through an informal protocol, NSKeyValue-Observing, which is actually a set of categories on NSObject and other classes.) The second object needn't be an instance of your own class; it can be a built-in Cocoa class. The first object, however, must contain your own code, in order to respond when a notification arrives.

 OS X Programmer Alert
OS X bindings don't exist on iOS, but you can sometimes use KVO to achieve similar aims.

KVO can be broken down into three stages:

Registration
> To hear about a change in a value belonging to Object A, Object B must be registered with Object A.

Change

The change takes place in the value belonging to Object A, and it must take place in a special way — a KVO compliant way. Typically, this means using a key–value coding compliant accessor to make the change. (If Object A is of your own class, you can optionally write code that will manually cause other kinds of change to count as KVO compliant.)

Notification

Object B is automatically notified that the value in Object A has changed and can react as desired.

Here's a simple complete example — a rather silly example, but sufficient to demonstrate the KVO mechanism in action. We have a class MyClass1; this will be the class of objectA. We also have a class MyClass2; this will be the class of objectB. Having obtained references to these objects, we register objectB to hear about changes in an instance variable of objectA called value, and then change value. Sure enough, objectB is automatically notified of the change:

```
// MyClass1.h:
@interface MyClass1 : NSObject
@property (nonatomic, copy) NSString* value;
@end

// MyClass2.m:
- (void) observeValueForKeyPath:(NSString *)keyPath
                       ofObject:(id)object
                         change:(NSDictionary *)change
                        context:(void *)context {
    NSLog(@"I heard about the change!");
}

// Somewhere else entirely:
MyClass1* objectA = [MyClass1 new];
MyClass2* objectB = [MyClass2 new];
// register for KVO
[objectA addObserver:objectB forKeyPath:@"value" options:0 context:nil]; ❶
// change the value in a KVO compliant way
objectA.value = @"Hello, world!"; ❷
// result: objectB's observeValueForKeyPath:... is called ❸
```

❶ We call `addObserver:forKeyPath:options:context:` to register `objectB` to hear about changes in `objectA`'s `value`. We didn't use the `options:` or `context:` parameters for anything; I'll talk about the `options:` parameter in a moment. (The `context:` parameter is for handing in a value that will come back as part of the notification; see Chapter 12.)

In real life, it would probably be Object B that would register *itself* to hear about changes in a key path of Object A. I've arranged things in an artificial way just to keep the code as simple as possible.

❷ We change `objectA`'s `value`, and we do it in a KVO compliant way, namely, by passing through the setter (because setting a property is equivalent to passing through the setter). This is another reason why, as I said in Chapter 12, accessors (and properties) are a good thing: they help you guarantee KVO compliance when changing a value.

❸ When we change `objectA`'s `value`, the third stage takes place automatically: a call is made to `objectB`'s `observeValueForKeyPath:....` We have implemented this method in MyClass2 in order to receive the notification. In this simple example, we expect to receive only one notification, so we just log to indicate that we did indeed receive it. In real life, where a single object might be registered to receive more than one KVO notification, you'd use the incoming parameters to distinguish between different notifications and decide what to do.

At the very least, you'll probably want to know, when `observeValueForKeyPath:...` is called, what the new value is. We can find that out easily, because we are handed a reference to the object that changed, along with the key path for the value within that object. Thus we can use KVC to query the changed object in the most general way:

```
- (void) observeValueForKeyPath:(NSString *)keyPath
                       ofObject:(id)object
                         change:(NSDictionary *)change
                        context:(void *)context {
    id newValue = [object valueForKeyPath:keyPath];
    NSLog(@"The key path %@ changed to %@", keyPath, newValue);
}
```

It is also possible to request that the new value be included as part of the notification. This depends upon the `options:` argument passed with the original registration. Here, we'll request that both the old and new values be included with the notification:

```
objectA.value = @"Hello";
[objectA addObserver:objectB forKeyPath:@"value"
    options: NSKeyValueObservingOptionNew | NSKeyValueObservingOptionOld
    context: nil];
objectA.value = @"Goodbye"; // notification is triggered
```

When we receive the notification, we fetch the old and new values out of the change dictionary:

```
- (void) observeValueForKeyPath:(NSString *)keyPath
                         ofObject:(id)object
                           change:(NSDictionary *)change
                          context:(void *)context {
    id newValue = change[NSKeyValueChangeNewKey];
    id oldValue = change[NSKeyValueChangeOldKey];
    NSLog(@"The key path %@ changed from %@ to %@",
          keyPath, oldValue, newValue);
}
```

No memory management happens as part of the registration process, so it is incumbent upon you to unregister Object B before it is destroyed; otherwise, Object A may later attempt to send a notification to a dangling pointer (see Chapter 12). This is done by sending Object A the removeObserver:forKeyPath: message. You must explicitly unregister the observer for every key path for which it is registered; you can't use nil as the second argument to mean "all key paths". In real life, where Object B probably registered itself with Object A, it will also be Object B that will unregister itself with Object A, perhaps in its dealloc implementation. Notice that this requires that Object B have a reference to Object A.

Object B should also unregister itself from Object A if Object A is about to go out of existence! This requirement seems onerous, and I'm unclear on the reason for it; it appears to have something to do with memory management of the internal mechanism that makes KVO work. Fortunately, the runtime will send you a nice warning in the log if an object being observed under KVO goes out of existence. (But you get no warning if an *observer* object goes out of existence; you'll find out about this only when a message is sent through a dangling pointer and your app crashes.)

Beginners are often confused about how to use KVO to observe changes to a mutable array, to be notified when an object is added to, removed from, or replaced within the array. You can't add an observer to an array itself; you have to observe through an object that has a key path to the array (through accessors, for example). The simple-minded solution is then to access the array using mutableArrayValueForKey:, which provides an observable proxy object.

For example, as in Chapter 12, let's posit an object with a property theData which is an array of dictionaries:

```
(
    {
        description = "The one with glasses.";
        name = Manny;
    },
    {
        description = "Looks a little like Governor Dewey.";
```

```
        name = Moe;
    },
    {
        description = "The one without a mustache.";
        name = Jack;
    }
)
```

Suppose this is an NSMutableArray. Then we can register with our object to observe the key path @"theData":

```
[objectA addObserver:objectB forKeyPath:@"theData" options:0 context:nil];
```

Now Object B will be notified of changes to this mutable array, but only if those changes are performed through the mutableArrayValueForKey: proxy object:

```
[[objectA mutableArrayValueForKeyPath:@"theData"] removeObjectAtIndex:0];
// notification is triggered
```

But it seems onerous to require clients to know that they must call mutableArrayValue-ForKey:. The simple solution is for our Object A itself to provide a getter that calls mutableArrayValueForKey:. Here's a possible implementation:

```
// MyClass1.h:
@interface MyClass1 : NSObject
@property (nonatomic, strong, getter=theDataGetter) NSMutableArray* theData;
@end

// MyClass1.m:
- (NSMutableArray*) theDataGetter {
    return [self mutableArrayValueForKey:@"theData"];
}
```

The result is that, as far as any client knows, this object has a key @"theData" and a property theData, and we can register to observe with the key and then access the mutable array through the property:

```
[objectA addObserver:objectB forKeyPath:@"theData"
    options: NSKeyValueObservingOptionNew | NSKeyValueObservingOptionOld
    context:nil];
[objectA.theData removeObjectAtIndex:0]; // notification is triggered
```

If you're going to take this approach, you should really also implement (in MyClass1) the four KVC compliance methods for a mutable array façade (see Chapter 12). Although things will appear to work just fine without them, and although they appear trivial (they are merely delegating to self->_theData the equivalent calls), they will be called by the vended proxy object, which increases its efficiency (and, some would argue, its safety). Without these methods, the proxy object resorts to setting the instance variable directly, replacing the entire mutable array, every time a client changes the mutable array:

```
- (NSUInteger) countOfTheData {
    return [self->_theData count];
}

- (id) objectInTheDataAtIndex: (NSUInteger) ix {
    return self->_theData[ix];
}

- (void) insertObject: (id) val inTheDataAtIndex: (NSUInteger) ix {
    [self->_theData insertObject:val atIndex:ix];
}

- (void) removeObjectFromTheDataAtIndex: (NSUInteger) ix {
    [self->_theData removeObjectAtIndex: ix];
}
```

If what you want to observe are mutations within an individual element of an array, things are more complicated. Suppose our array of dictionaries is an array of mutable dictionaries. To observe changes to the value of the @"description" key of any dictionary in the array, you'd need to register for that key with *each* dictionary in the array, separately. You can do that efficiently with NSArray's instance method addObserver:toObjectsAtIndexes:forKeyPath:options:context:, but if the array *itself* is mutable then you're also going to have to register for that key with any *new* dictionaries that are subsequently added to the array (and unregister when a dictionary is removed from the array). It sounds daunting, and it is.

The properties of Apple's built-in classes are typically KVO compliant. Indeed, so are many classes that don't use properties *per se*; for example, NSUserDefaults is KVO compliant. Unfortunately, Apple warns that undocumented KVO compliance can't necessarily be counted on.

On the other hand, some Cocoa classes explicitly invite the use of KVO; they treat it as a primary notification mechanism, instead of the notification center and NSNotification. For example, the AVPlayer class, which plays media, such as movies, has various properties, such as status and rate, that report whether the media is ready to play and whether it is in fact playing. Apple's *AV Foundation Programming Guide* states that to monitor an AVPlayer's playback, you should use key–value observing on its properties.

Key–value observing is a deep mechanism; consult Apple's *Key-Value Observing Guide* for full information. It does have some unfortunate shortcomings. For one thing, it's a pity that all notifications arrive by calling the same bottleneck method, observeValueForKeyPath:.... And keeping track of who's observing whom, and making sure both observer and observed have appropriate lifetimes and that the observer is unregistered before one of them goes out of existence, can be tricky. But in general, KVO is useful for keeping values coordinated in different objects.

Model–View–Controller

In Apple's documentation and elsewhere, you'll find references to the term *model–view–controller*, or *MVC*. This refers to an architectural goal of maintaining a distinction between three functional aspects of a program that lets the user view and edit information — meaning, in effect, a program with a graphical user interface. The notion goes back to the days of Smalltalk, and much has been written about it since then, but informally, here's what the terms mean:

Model
> The data and its management, often referred to as the program's "business logic," the hard-core stuff that the program is really all about.

View
> What the user sees and interacts with.

Controller
> The mediation between the model and the view.

Consider, for example, a game where the current score is displayed to the user:

- A UILabel that shows the user the current score for the game in progress is *view*; it is effectively nothing but a pixel-maker, and its business is to know how to draw itself. The knowledge of *what* it should draw — the score, and the fact that this *is* a score — lies elsewhere.

  A rookie programmer might try to use the score displayed by the UILabel as the actual score: to increment the score, read the UILabel's string, turn that string into a number, increment the number, turn the number back into a string, and present that string in place of the previous string. That is a gross violation of the MVC philosophy. The view presented to the user should *reflect* the score; it should not *store* the score.

- The score is data being maintained internally; it is *model*. It could be as simple as an instance variable along with a public `increment` method or as complicated as a Score object with a raft of methods.

  The score is numeric, whereas a UILabel displays a string; this alone is enough to show that the view and the model are naturally different.

- Telling the score when to change, and causing the updated score to be reflected in the user interface, is the work of the *controller*. This will be particularly clear if we imagine that the model's numeric score needs to be transformed in some way for presentation to the user.

  For example, suppose the UILabel that presents the score reads: "Your current score is 20". The model is presumably storing and providing the number 20, so what's the source of the phrase "Your current score is…"? Whoever is deciding that this phrase

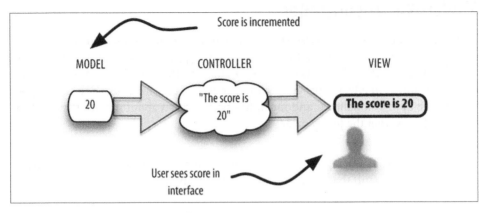

Figure 13-2. Model–view–controller

should precede the score in the presentation of the score to the user, and is making it so, is a controller.

Even this simplistic example (Figure 13-2) illustrates very well the advantages of MVC. By separating powers in this way, we allow the aspects of the program to evolve with a great degree of independence. Do you want a different font and size in the presentation of the score? Change the view; the model and controller need know nothing about it, but will just go on working exactly as they did before. Do you want to change the phrase that precedes the score? Change the controller; the model and view are unchanged.

Adherence to MVC is particularly appropriate in a Cocoa app, because Cocoa itself adheres to it. The very names of Cocoa classes reveal the MVC philosophy that underlies them. A UIView is a view. A UIViewController is a controller; its purpose is to embody the logic that tells the view what to display. In Chapter 11 we saw that a UIPickerView does not hold the data it displays; it gets that data from a data source. So the UIPicker-View is a view; the data source is model.

A further distinction, found in Apple's documentation, is this: true model material and true view material should be quite reusable, in the sense that they can be transferred wholesale into some other app; controller material is generally not reusable, because it is concerned with how *this* app mediates between the model and the view.

In one of my own apps, for example, we download an XML (RSS) news feed and present the article titles to the user as a table. The storage and parsing of the XML are pure model material, and are so reusable that I didn't even write this part of the code (I used some code called FeedParser, by Kevin Ballard). The table is a UITableView, which is obviously reusable, seeing as I obtained it directly from Cocoa. But when the UITableView turns to my code and asks what to display in this cell, and my code turns to the XML and asks for the title of the article corresponding to this row of the table, that's controller code.

MVC helps to provide answers about what objects need to be able to see what other objects in your app. A controller object will usually need to see a model object and a view object. A model object, or a group of model objects, usually won't need to see outside itself. A view object typically doesn't need to see outside itself *specifically*, but structural devices such as delegation, data source, and target–action allow a view object to communicate agnostically with a controller.

Index

A

accessors, 98, 323
accessors and memory management, 342
accessors, dynamic, 368
accessors, naming, 100, 323
accessors, synthesized, 361
Accounts preferences, 204, 231, 238
action connections, 180
action connections, creating, 181
action message, 180
action selector signatures, 314
action target of a control, 312
action, nil-targeted, 316
Ad Hoc distribution, 249, 251
address operator, 24, 67
admin, 231
adopting a protocol, 272
agent, 231
Alfke, Jens, 216
alloc, 86
analyze, 227
angle brackets in import directive, 27
API, 3
app bundle, 139
app delegate instance, how created, 148
app launch process, 147
App Store, 260
App Store distribution, 249
app target, 131

app, name of, 244, 258, 260
app, version number of, 258
AppKiDo, 193, 271
Apple ID, 231
ARC, xiii, 329, 334–360
    (see also memory management)
    dealloc, 345
    GCD pseudo-objects memory management, 352
    initialization to nil, automatic by ARC, 48, 333
    initializer, 346
    memory management of instance variables, 345
    method naming conventions and ARC, 336
    nilifying unsafe references, 349
    nilifying, automatic by ARC, 333
    notifications and retain cycles, 350
    release by nilifying, 346
    timers and retain cycles, 352
    toll-free bridging and ARC, 356
    typecasting and ARC, 358, 360
    unrecognized selector, 61, 64
    unregistering for a notification, 349
    weak references, 347
architecture, 43
archives, 249
argument, 22
arithmetic operators, 15

We'd like to hear your suggestions for improving our indexes. Send email to index@oreilly.com.

delegate, 306
delegation, 306
deleting an outlet, 175
Deployment Target build setting, 200
dereferencing a pointer, 12, 72
description, 215
Design Patterns (book), 43
designated initializer, 89
destinations, 137
Developer folder, 114
development provisioning profile, 235
device, running on, 230
devices in the Organizer window, 238
dictionary, 288
dispatch table, 312
distributing your app, 249
distribution provisioning profile, 250
do loop, 17
dock, 158
Docsets app, 197
document outline, 158
documentation, 187–197
    categories, 270
    delegate methods, 306
    key–value coding method names, 329
    NSObject, 294
    protocols, 276
documentation sets (doc sets), 187
documentation window, 188
dot-notation
    key paths, 327
    properties, 103, 361
    structs, 10
dot-notation called harmful, 105
double vs. single resolution, 145
doxygen, 194
drain, 339
drawing a view, 266
drawing text, 281
dynamic accessor, 368
dynamic directive, 368
dynamic message handling, 368
dynamic message sending, 277

E

edit all in scope, 213
editing the project, 131
editing the target, 131
editing your code, 206

editor, 124
Empty Application template, 149
Empty Window example project, 114, 161, 266, 267
encapsulation, 40
entitlements, 232
entry points, 317
enumerate, 19, 286, 287, 288, 290
enumeration, 7
equality of objects, 285
equality operator, 20
errors
    at-sign, forgetting before NSString literal, 9
    calling dealloc, 343
    calling super, neglecting, 98
    class defined without specifying a base class, 78
    comparing BOOLs to one another, 21
    conflicting signatures, 65
    control event has multiple target–action pairs, 314
    debugging a Release build, 217
    duplicate declaration, 56
    equality operator and assignment operator, confusing, 20
    examining prematurely an NSError set by indirection, 49
    expected identifier, 56
    expression is not assignable, 104
    format specifier and argument mismatch, 215
    garbage pointer, 48
    implicit conversion requires a bridged cast, 357, 360
    initWithFrame, not called for nib-instantiated view, 186
    integer division, 15
    interface type cannot be statically allocated, 47
    method-calling errors, 58
    missing sentinel, 57
    multiple methods found with mismatched result, 65
    nil reference, 60
    nil terminator, forgetting, 57
    no known instance method for selector, 64
    no visible interface declares selector, 60, 62
    Objective-C is C, forgetting, 3
    outlet broken by misused setter name, 327

implementation section, instance variables declared in, 79
import directive, 27
import directive (@import), 154
include directive, 26
increment operator, 15
indirection, 49
Info.plist, 141, 142, 258
  (see also property list settings)
informal protocols, 276
inheritance, 62, 76, 91, 92
init(With...), 87
initialization of C arrays, 13
initialization of instance, 87
initialization of instance variables, 101, 105, 107, 344
initialization of nib-based instances, additional, 184
initialization of structs, 10
initialization of variables, 6, 47
initialization vs. declaration, 47
initialize class method, 299
initializer, 86, 344, 346
initializer, designated, 89
initializer, writing, 105
instance, 36
  assignment of instance, 50
  creating an instance, 85
    (see also instantiation)
  globally visible instances, 377
  initialization of instance, 87
  mutability of instances, 51
  ready-made instance, 85
  reference to an instance, 46, 108
  relationships between instances, built-in, 376
  subclass legal where superclass expected, 91
  vending an instance, 38
  visibility of one instance to another, 373
instance method, 38
instance methods of NSObject, 293
instance references, 46
instance variables, 38, 98
  accessors, 98, 323
  declaring an instance variable, 79
  initialization of instance variables, 101, 105, 107, 344
  key–value coding violates privacy, 325
  memory management of instance variables, 341

nilifying, 333
protected, 99, 323
synthesized instance variable, 365
underscore at beginning of name, 99, 366
instances, an app's first, 147
instancetype, 107
instantiation, 36, 85
instantiation, nib-based, 90, 165
Instruments, 238, 332
Interface Builder, 155
  (see also nib editor)
interface directive, 77
interface section, 77
interface that differs on iPad, 143
International Components for Unicode (see ICU)
internationalization (see localization)
Internet as documentation, 197
introspection, 83, 277, 324
iOS Deployment Target build setting, 200
iOS Developer Program, 231
iPad, code that differs on, 201
iPad, interface that differs on, 143
iPad, property list settings that differ on, 202, 260
iPad, resources that differ on, 202
Issue navigator, 120
iTunes Connect, 260
ivar, 98
  (see also instance variables)

J

jump bar, 124, 210
  Related Files menu, 124
  Tracking menu, 126
jump bar in Debug pane, 220
jump bar in nib editor, 160
jumping to header files, 196

K

K&R, 3
Kay, Alan, 45
Kernighan, Brian, 3
key, 288
key paths, 327
keyboard shortcuts in Xcode, 117
key–value coding, 101, 324–329
key–value coding compliant, 325

N

name of app, 244, 258, 260
namespaces, 84
naming accessors, 323
naming image files, 145, 202
navigating your code, 210
navigation window, 122
Navigator pane, 117
nesting method calls, 55
new, 89
NeXTStep, 45, 155
nib editor, 155
nib files, 90, 143, 155–186
nib objects, 159
nib owner proxy, 169
nib-based instantiation, 90, 165
nib-based instantiation and memory management, 354
nibs, connections between, 183, 375
nil, 20, 48
nil and CFRelease, 357
nil in collections illegal, 291
nil testing, 48
nil, message to, 59
nilifying, 333, 346
nilifying unsafe references, 349
NO, 21
nonatomic, 364
notifications, 300
    registering for a notification, 301
    unregistering for a notification, 303, 349
notifications and retain cycles, 350
notifications matching delegate methods, 308
notifications, when appropriate, 379
NS prefix, 45
NSArray, 286
    literal NSArray, 57, 286
    subscripting, 286
NSArray proxy, key–value coding, 328
NSAttributedString, 281
NSCopying, 273
NSCountedSet, 288
NSData, 284
NSDate, 281
NSDateComponents, 281
NSDateFormatter, 281
NSDictionary, 288
    literal NSDictionary, 289
    subscripting, 289

NSError, 25, 49
NSHashTable, 354
NSIndexSet, 285
NSInteger, 7
NSLinguisticTagger, 280
NSLog, 214
NSMapTable, 354
NSMutableArray, 286
    subscripting, 286
NSMutableData, 284
NSMutableDictionary
    subscripting, 289
NSMutableString, 280
NSNotFound, 278
NSNotification, 300
NSNotificationCenter, 300
NSNull, 291
NSNumber, 282
    literal NSNumber, 102, 283
NSObject, 77, 293–295
NSOrderedSet, 288
    subscripting, 288
NSPointerArray, 354
NSProxy, 78
NSRange, 278
NSRegularExpression, 279
NSScanner, 279
NSSet, 288
NSString, 279
    CFString vs. NSString, 68
    concatenating literal strings, 9
    escaped characters, 9
    literal NSString, 8
    Unicode characters, 9
NSString literal directive, 9
NSTimer, 305
NSTimer, GCD instead of, 352
NSUserDefaults, 377
NSValue, 284
NS_ENUM, 8
NULL, 49

O

object, 33
Object library, 124, 161
object-based programming, 33
object-oriented programming, 97
Objective-C, 3, 45–109, 268–278
Objective-C, history of, 45

optimizing, 238
optional directive, 273
optional methods, 277
Organizer window, 238, 250
Organizer window, archives, 250
Organizer window, devices, 238
orientation of device, 258
orientation of interface at startup, 258
outlet collections, 180
outlet connections, 167, 326
outlet, creating, 172, 176
outlet, deleting, 175
outlets, 167
overloading, 57
overriding, 77, 97
overriding a synthesized accessor, 367

P

parameter, 22, 53
parameter lists, 57
plus sign (class method), 38, 54
pointer to class name, 46
pointer to function, 25, 67
pointer to pointer to NSError, 25, 49
pointer to struct (see CFTypeRef)
pointer-to-void, 12
pointer-to-void, memory management of, 359
pointers, 11
    assignment to a pointer, 13, 50
    creating a pointer, 24
    dangling pointers, 330
    declaring a pointer, 11
    dereferencing a pointer, 12, 72
    garbage pointer, 48
    generic pointer, 12
    indirection, 49
    memory management, 51
    nilifying, 333
    reference to an instance, 24
polymorphism, 91–97
pool, autorelease, 339
Portal, 233
posting a notification, 300
pragma directive, 31, 211
precompiled header, 81, 146
preprocessing, 5
private methods, 272
private properties, 364
product name, 114

profile (see provisioning profile)
profiling, 238
project, 113
project file, 127
project folder, 127, 139
Project navigator, 118, 210
project templates, 114
project window, 116
project, renaming, 138
properties, 361–367
property list settings, 142, 258
property list settings that differ on iPad, 202
property list settings, localized, 244
property lists, 292
protected, 99, 323
protocol directive, 273
protocols, 272
protocols documented separately, 276
provisioning profile, 232
provisioning profile, development, 235
provisioning profile, distribution, 250
proxy objects, 159, 169

Q

qualifiers, 31
Quick Help, 123, 194
Quick Look a variable, 220
quotation marks in import directive, 27

R

random function, 29
readonly, 364
ready-made instance, 85
receiver, 53
Ref suffix, 68
refactoring, 213, 291
Refactoring (book), 43
reference, 45
reference to an instance, 24, 46, 108
reference, getting, 108, 373
reference, keeping, 109
reference, unsafe, 348
reference, weak, 347
region format, 282
registering for a notification, 301
regular expressions, 279
Related Files menu, 124
relational operators, 20

weak-linking a framework, 202
weak-strong dance, 351
while loop, 17
windows, secondary, in Xcode, 125
WWDR Intermediate Certificate, 235

X

Xcode, 113–262
   (see also nib editor)

xib files, 90, 143

Y

YES, 21

Z

zombies, 332

About the Author

Matt Neuburg started programming computers in 1968, when he was 14 years old, as a member of a literally underground high school club, which met once a week to do timesharing on a bank of PDP-10s by way of primitive teletype machines. He also occasionally used Princeton University's IBM-360/67, but gave it up in frustration when one day he dropped his punch cards. He majored in Greek at Swarthmore College, and received his Ph.D. from Cornell University in 1981, writing his doctoral dissertation (about Aeschylus) on a mainframe. He proceeded to teach Classical languages, literature, and culture at many well-known institutions of higher learning, most of which now disavow knowledge of his existence, and to publish numerous scholarly articles unlikely to interest anyone. Meanwhile he obtained an Apple IIc and became hopelessly hooked on computers again, migrating to a Macintosh in 1990. He wrote some educational and utility freeware, became an early regular contributor to the online journal *TidBITS*, and in 1995 left academe to edit *MacTech* magazine. In August 1996 he became a freelancer, which means he has been looking for work ever since. He is the author of *Frontier: The Definitive Guide*, *REALbasic: The Definitive Guide*, and *AppleScript: The Definitive Guide*, as well as *Programming iOS 7* (all for O'Reilly & Associates), and *Take Control of Using Mountain Lion* (TidBITS Publishing).

Colophon

The animal on the cover of *iOS 7 Programming Fundamentals* is a harp seal (*Pagophilus groenlandicus*), a Latin name that translates to "ice-lover from Greenland." These animals are native to the northern Atlantic and Arctic Oceans, and spend most of their time in the water, only going onto ice packs to give birth and molt. As earless ("true") seals, their streamlined bodies and energy-efficient swimming style make them well-equipped for aquatic life. While eared seal species like sea lions are powerful swimmers, they are considered semiaquatic because they mate and rest on land.

The harp seal has silvery-gray fur, with a large black marking on their back that resembles a harp or wishbone. They grow to be 5–6 feet long, and weigh 300–400 pounds as adults. Due to their cold habitat, they have a thick coat of blubber for insulation. A harp seal's diet is very varied, including several species of fish and crustaceans. They can remain underwater for an average of 16 minutes to hunt for food, and are able to dive several hundred feet.

Harp seal pups are born without any protective fat, but are kept warm by their white coat, which absorbs heat from the sun. They are nursed for approximately 12 days, after which they are abandoned (though they will triple their weight in this time due to their mother's high-fat milk) . In the subsequent weeks until they are able to swim off the ice, the pups are very vulnerable to predators and will lose nearly half of their weight. Those that survive reach maturity after 4–8 years (depending on their gender), and have an average lifespan of 35 years.

Harp seals are hunted commercially off the coasts of Canada, Norway, Russia, and Greenland for their meat, oil, and fur. Though some of these governments have regulations and enforce hunting quotas, it is believed that the number of animals killed every year is underreported. Public outcry and efforts by conservationists have resulted in a decline in market demand for seal pelts and other products, however.

The cover image is from Wood's *Animate Creation*. The cover fonts are URW Typewriter and Guardian Sans. The text font is Adobe Minion Pro; the heading font is Adobe Myriad Condensed; and the code font is Dalton Maag's Ubuntu Mono.

Get even more for your money.

Join the O'Reilly Community, and register the O'Reilly books you own. It's free, and you'll get:

- $4.99 ebook upgrade offer
- 40% upgrade offer on O'Reilly print books
- Membership discounts on books and events
- Free lifetime updates to ebooks and videos
- Multiple ebook formats, DRM FREE
- Participation in the O'Reilly community
- Newsletters
- Account management
- 100% Satisfaction Guarantee

Signing up is easy:

1. **Go to: oreilly.com/go/register**
2. **Create an O'Reilly login.**
3. **Provide your address.**
4. **Register your books.**

Note: English-language books only

To order books online:
oreilly.com/store

For questions about products or an order:
orders@oreilly.com

To sign up to get topic-specific email announcements and/or news about upcoming books, conferences, special offers, and new technologies:
elists@oreilly.com

For technical questions about book content:
booktech@oreilly.com

To submit new book proposals to our editors:
proposals@oreilly.com

O'Reilly books are available in multiple DRM-free ebook formats. For more information:
oreilly.com/ebooks

Spreading the knowledge of innovators   oreilly.com

CP can be obtained at www.ICGtesting.com
Pr
LV113
3)0012B/52/P